Methods and Obse
of a Practical Economist

What every executive should know about

Business, Finance, and Economics

Volume One

By

Peter Naylor

Professor of Economics & Finance

Santa Barbara City College

Gate to city of Fes, Morocco

This volume is dedicated to all my teachers and colleagues who helped me in my search for understanding economics. Teachers who love their field, and care about their students, change the world for the better. I give special thanks to Prof. Harvey Botwin of Pitzer College who gave me the opportunity to teach a variety of advanced undergraduate courses in my fields of interest --- Microeconomics, Macroeconomics, International Economics, Public Finance, Psychological Economics, Economic Development, and History of Economic Thought. Harvey's encouragement and enthusiasm were unflagging and contagious. And I thank Irwin Winer who was a devoted tutor to three thousands of our students over ten years at SBCC. Our differences in points of view enriched those students. And I thank Ron McKinnon and Tibor Scitovsky who reignited my passion for economics, when the rigid doctrines of neo-classical economics were frustrating me (and many other graduate students). Both remained curious iconoclasts to the end.

Other terrific teachers who helped me are:

Mike Boskin and Nate Rosenberg, at Stanford University,

Steve Lewis and Bill Gates, at Williams College,

Peter Arnold and John Briggs, at Middlesex School, and

Bill Dunnell and Dave Edgar, at Fenn School.

I also learned a great deal about management from Cmdr. Alan Martin USN, Mike Towbes of the Bank of Montecito, Rob Barrett of AMI Tours and International Travel & Resorts (now, Elite Resorts), and John Noyes, founder of Costa Vida.

Prof. Ron McKinnon   Irwin Winer, tutor   Prof. Harvey Botwin

Stanford University   Santa Barbara City College   Pitzer College, Claremont

Photo by Sunny Scott   photo by Joy Winer   photo by Harriett Botwin

Introduction

Through the years, I have become convinced that the fundamentals of economics, finance, and business can be mastered by anyone of average intelligence, ambition, and diligence. So, as I enter the final phase of my career, I decided to provide a book which would offer the reader the practical knowledge that I wish I'd gained before I became a naval officer, a graduate student, a banker, and a manager.

I believe that these fifty-five lessons can provide the foundation for:

1) the **general business manager** who must juggle many responsibilities and relationships, and who hasn't the time for more formal education. He may choose to use the book as a reference.

2) the **general student** who knows that he must be familiar with business, finance, and economics to be effective in any career, including politics and journalism.

3) the **undergraduate** who wishes to get the most value from his expensive, upper-division specialty courses in business, economics, or finance, and doesn't feel prepared by the typical introductory courses. (Careful reading of this book over the summer before his junior year could make the difference.)

4) the **entering graduate student** who needs to fill gaps in his preparation, or review principles, before tackling a challenging program at a top graduate school.

5) the advanced **graduate student** who needs to review and integrate the basics, before taking his comprehensive examinations.

I have written the book in a conversational style and laced it anecdotes, while minimizing technical requirements, so that readers can connect to the ideas and to their practical use. I wish that such a book had been available to me, while I was at sea for many months in the Navy. I would have read it between watches, and I would have been prepared to take better advantage of the wonderful opportunities that I had at Stanford University, at Bankers' Trust, and at Pitzer College. And I would have been more effective, as a community banker and an executive.

The book has six sections. Each could stand alone as a separate course, and they usually do. However by organizing them into a logical sequence, each section prepares the student for the next, and duplication of material is avoided. Hence, nine lessons are adequate for each subject, and mastery of each subject is possible in ten weeks, instead of fifteen. The sections are:

1. Principles of Business Management (with an international business point of view)
2. Microeconomics (the study of producer and consumer behavior in markets)
3. Finance (financial markets and institutions, and principles of financial management)
4. International Economics (trade, finance, and macroeconomic adjustments)
5. Macroeconomics (production, employment, economic growth, and business cycles)
6. Investing (securities markets, securities analysis, and personal financial planning)

Table of Contents

Preface

A book this long requires some justification. I offer some biographical information, so that you can understand my motivation.

At an early age, I became interested in why some people have terrific opportunities and others do not. A housekeeper would visit us in Wayland to help my mother with fall and spring cleaning. Once, she brought her son, Henry, who was my age. He had never skated, but by the end of the day, he was my equal. I was impressed. Why didn't he have all the opportunities that my family's situation afforded me ?

My father was a commercial pilot, so we could travel freely. I visited my grandmother in Georgia and saw people living in shacks with dirt floors and out-houses. I saw extremes of wealth and poverty in Mexico.

Both great-grandfathers, on my father's side, were industrialists. One founded American Express and was a director of New York Life, and the other was general manager of thirty paper-mills in Western Massachusetts. But my mother's father was a railroad engineer, and there were family stories of hardship during the Great Depression.

My grandfather left $10,000 for education and travel, to each of his grandchildren. The money was invested in a Scudder Balanced Fund. It paid for my private education. After graduate school, $25,000 remained. From this, I learned that capitalism raised many from poverty and premature death, but it raised some more than others.

In preparatory school, I read Samuelson's Principles of Economics. I didn't entirely understand it, but I knew it addressed my interests. At Williams College, many of the economics professors were practicing development economists. I combined Economics with Anthropology (Tom Price) and International Relations (Fred Schumann), and found my passion.

My experience at Williams also taught me that often the very bright and well-connected get superior opportunities. When I applied to graduate schools, only UC Berkeley accepted me. When I told Prof. Steve Lewis, he made one call, after which I was offered a full-scholarship for four years by Stanford University.

I graduated Williams in 1968, the last year of the draft. So, I enlisted in the Navy ahead of induction. Stanford allowed me to defer my acceptance. I was scheduled for Naval Officer Candidate School in November. So, I travelled in Africa for twelve weeks before entering the Navy. I visited eleven countries, where I had acquaintances from Williams. Africa was very open then, and I was able to meet many African civil servants, some of whom even asked me for development advice. I was impressed by the differences of opportunities for, and the similarities of, attitudes toward economic development. In every country there was a civil war, assassination, or political execution, while I was there. Yet, I was treated with every consideration and kindness. I came to love Africans, but acknowledge the deficiencies of their governments.

My three years of active duty in the Navy were very important to my development. My first Captain, Cmdr. Alan F. Martin, set a great example of leadership. I was given First Division with responsibility for the exterior of the ship and all sea-detail duties. I also observed true diversity in the forty men for whom I was responsible. A few were malcontents, but most were good men of varied backgrounds and talents, and shared values of industry and honesty, capable of great sacrifice, if given respect and treated fairly. I'm guessing that my experience was like those of the millions who served in WWII --- I learned that class, race, and ethnicity are irrelevant. And again, enjoying the privileges of an officer, I appreciated that what separates us most are the opportunities that some enjoy and others do not.

In order be discharged a few months early, I arranged to study at the American University in Cairo in the spring of 1972. My purpose was to prepare for graduate school and to familiarize myself with Arab culture and history. I made many friends, and enjoyed the benefits of instruction from Clement Henry Moore in Development Politics and E.H. Valsan in Public Administration. I also encountered a few western scholars who indoctrinated the students with naïve ideas of inevitable progress, while ignoring the genuine obstacles.

At Stanford, I dutifully mastered the "Neo-classical" paradigm, based on Samuelson's Foundations of Economic Analysis, to which we owe at least a half-century of progress in the discipline. However, I felt that this body of knowledge sacrificed realism for the elegance of a unified theory. I completed my course work and exams in six fields, but then suffered a year lost to hepatitis (contracted while interning at Banker's Trust in New York City, not in Africa !).

The summer internship at Bankers' Trust (1975) offered me the opportunity to observe bond trading and asset: liability management with the masters. E.V.P. Charles Sanford had me attend strategy meetings. And Allan Rogers, head trader, was very generous. (When he retired, he became my next door neighbor in Santa Barbara --- quite a surprise for both of us.) So, I learned on Wall St. that many economists would rather guess at how bankers and traders should behave according to their models, rather than observe how they do make the decisions needed to prosper in their profession. (The classic example is the interpretation of the relationship of spot and forward foreign exchange rates. See: Lesson #4.7.) I wanted to learn how bankers and traders really do behave.

Ron McKinnon found me a visiting scholar position at the Brookings Institution in 1976-1977. There, I was treated as an equal by several extraordinary scholars of international economics, including William Cline, Robert Lawrence, and Robert Solomon. I developed my four sector model of Macroeconomics which you will see in Part Five. Also, during that year, I travelled to Paris (OECD), Vienna (OPEC), Istanbul (Bosporus U), Cairo (AUC), Tehran, Kuwait, and Riyadh on a Carnegie grant. All doors were open to the "Brookings scholar." Truly, that year was turning point in my intellectual development.

In Vienna, I had dinner with a family friend who was US Ambassador to the Atomic Energy Commission. I should not have been surprised that I was debriefed by the CIA on my return to Washington. They wanted to hear my theory of OPEC behavior (classic cartel arrangements) and the importance of Saudi Arabia as swing producer and disciplinarian. Why all our talented government economists and diplomats had not figured that out still amazes me.

Upon leaving Brookings, I was recruited to join the faculty of Pitzer College, the newest of the Claremont Colleges. Again, I was very fortunate. Several refugees from the Gerald Ford administration had taken residence at Claremont McKenna College, next door. And Peter

Drucker was still in excellent form at the business school, now the Drucker School of Management. Pitzer was not selective then, but my colleague, Harvey Botwin, and I showed that average students could master difficult topics in economics, if carefully taught. Several of our students went on to doctorates at MIT and the University of Chicago. Meanwhile, I got to teach a wide variety of upper division courses. Preparation required revisiting the classics of each sub-field. Whereas, my teachers at Stanford had introduced me to the literature, teaching at Pitzer permitted me to consolidate my understanding of economics. I also built an elegant twenty-three equation model of the US economy which was surprisingly accurate.

When my wife completed her graduate studies in architecture, I began the next stage of my education. We moved to Santa Barbara, where I became Vice President of a community bank. I asked to do every job in the bank for one week, before taking up my duties. That experience gave me insight into the complexities of bank management and won the support of my staff. I wrote one of the first asset-liability management policies for a community bank in California (according to the state auditors). And I used Yield Curve analysis to predict money market interest movements from which we could price our deposits and loans defensively. I also developed a wide variety of credits, and was given a larger unsecured loan authority than secured loan authority --- most unusual.

After five years, I felt that I'd learned what I could about the behavior of businesses and banks, and accepted a position as the local financial officer for a major resort marketing company with interests in California, New York, and the Caribbean. Working for an aggressive entrepreneur was an education. Most valuable were short-term programs for Tahiti package tours, the acquisition and sale of a local hotel, and the acquisition and development of a major resort in Antigua.

Just as we had decided to consolidate all operations to Miami (the center of Caribbean tourism operations), I was offered a teaching position in Finance at Santa Barbara City College, and the opportunity to sub-divide a fifty acre parcel in the luxury suburb of Montecito. I felt the time was right to return to teaching. I remain concerned about the division between people like myself and my friends who had elite educations and excellent career access, and the mass of my employees in the Navy and at the bank, who have had poor, and few, quality educational and career opportunities. I wanted these students to have the same opportunities and excellent career access that I had during my education. Also teaching allowed me the flexibility to have more time to raise my daughter with my wife.

Over thirty years at SBCC, I have taught Finance, Economics, and International Business to over twelve thousand students. I also spent a year in Namibia teaching Africans both Economics and Finance. The wide variety of my students has convinced me that anyone can learn what they need in the areas of business management, finance, and economics. So, I offer this book as my contribution to expanding opportunity for anyone, anywhere to understand, participate, and benefit from our economic system.

Part One:
Business Management

"Most of what we call management consists of making it difficult for people to work." --- Peter Drucker

"The inherent vice of capitalism is the unequal sharing of blessings; the inherent vice of socialism is the equal sharing of miseries." --- Winston Churchill

Market in Buenos Aires

Lesson #1.1: What is a Business ?

Business is simply a method of organizing resources to meet our material needs. In a market based economy, individuals decide how to participate, as entrepreneurs, managers, employees, and customers. The production of goods and services requires resources, and business organizations compete to bid for the resources that they need. The value of their product is measured by their sales revenue, and the value of the resources which they use is measured by their costs. The difference is called "profit" and represents their net gain as an organization, as well as their increase in financial claims on society's resources (money).

Therefore, profit not only measures the gain to the organization, but also the value added for society. The difference between revenue and costs is a measurement of the increase in value as a result of the activity. ***Profit measures success; loss represents waste.*** Loss occurs when costs exceed revenues, which means the value of the resources used exceeds the value of the product. This is wasteful for society, as well as destructive for the business.

What are the basic strategies of any business ? In order to generate a gain in the form of profit, which justifies the activity as well as rewarding the organizers (entrepreneurs), revenue must exceed total costs. This requires **sales**. For sales to occur, the business must understand its customers and offer them **value**, a combination of the qualities that the customers desire and the price (or sacrifice) which the customer must make to acquire ownership. And the business must control its **costs** by choosing the methods which minimize the payments for the resources needed. In turn, this depends on how much the resources can contribute to production and what must be paid to acquire them, their **opportunity costs**. We describe this process of generating sales as the function of **Marketing** and the process of producing quality at minimum costs as **Operations Management**.

So, the signal of a potential opportunity in business is a difference between the price that customers are willing and able to pay, and the costs of the resources, including processing, that are needed. Prices will be different in different markets, such as different places or times, or differences in quality or quantity of resources available. Having spotted prices differences, then the entrepreneur must ask: Why do these differences exist ? And will those differences persist long enough to reward my efforts ? Prices differ because of differences in Demand or Supply, or because the **transactions costs** (the costs associate with buying in one market and selling in another) preclude arbitrage.

So, to understand the causes and persistence of price differences, we must investigate the local conditions of Demand and Supply. We will learn how to do that in lessons #2.1-2.9 on **microeconomics**. Economics is the study of how societies organize their resources to meet their material needs. Each society must select methods to decide what to produce, how to produce it, how to allocate the available resources that can contribute to production, and how to distribute the products among potential users. This includes balancing resources with uses and maintaining and enhancing potential for future production.

For these activities to occur, the business must acquire a variety of resources. We measure these at financial costs and record them on a balance sheet as investments in assets. **Assets** are simply the resources that we own. Naturally, to acquire these assets, we need **money**, and we record the sources of the money which permits us to purchase the assets, as **Liabilities**. Liabilities include money that has been borrowed (debt) and money provided by the owners (equity).

Hence, the process of organizing a business includes identifying a need that is not being met to the satisfaction of the customers, designing a product that will reduce the dissatisfaction, engineering production that will minimize costs while assuring consistent quality, identifying the assets that will be needed, and acquiring the money to purchase those assets. Equally important is the organization of the people who will participate in the enterprise.

You may already recognize that successful management of a business organization involves a number of critical tasks. The father of modern management, Peter Drucker[1], classified the tasks into six functions:

1) Planning must be thorough and flexible. First, the organization must define its purpose. Sometimes, this is captured in a **mission statement**, which should be brief, direct, and focused. This is what we do, and these are activities that we don't do. The statement reflects a vision of what the business is, and what it shall be. To fulfill this vision, objectives must be stated that will be the criteria for selecting activities. **Objectives** may be sales, market share, profit, team development, and public relations. They must be measureable and timely, in order for progress toward their achievement to be evaluated.

In addition, the organization assesses its **situation**, for example, products, markets, customers, facilities, staff, and reputation. These can be used to identify organizational **strengths** and **weaknesses**. Next, planners address **opportunities** and **threats**. These are often external, such as competition, technical change, government regulations and taxes, civil order, and availability of critical resources.

Integration of this information on opportunities and threats, in comparison to organizational strengths and weaknesses, helps the planners to select activities and establish goals for each. **Goals** must be simple, measureable, accountable, realistic, and timely.

The goals for each activity help us to build **budgets** which identify sources of funding and allocations for the needed assets, based on sales targets and resource requirements.

The final step in planning is continuous **evaluation** of performance against the expectations expressed in the budget. Adjustments are made in a positive manner. Solving problems has priority over assessing blame. That can come much later.

2) Marketing is the second function; it has four elements. First, the business must have the best **product**. That means the best value for the customer. Think of all the qualities that the customer desires and is willing to pay for. The more perfectly these qualities are met, the more valuable the product is to the customer. Now, divide that total by the price. That is "Value." In other words, a product that is twice as good in the perception of the customer can be almost twice as expensive and still garner the sale. So, product development is critical. Naturally, **product engineering** becomes important as we consider the viability of production.

Once, the product has been designed and engineered, we must consider **pricing** strategy. As you will learn in the study of markets, central to the field of economics, a higher price may raise profit per unit, but will reduce sales. So, we consider the price of competitive products, making sure that we offer a bargain ("value"). We may choose a low price to generate rapid growth of sales, or a high price to cream off the "first movers" and establish our brand status. We need to consider customer expectations and any laws limiting our pricing discretion. And we need to consider adequate rewards in the form of mark-ups for our distributors.

Naturally, this leads to our **distribution** strategy. There are two elements: 1) pure distribution which is the design of the chain of organizations that will process the product --- receiving, warehousing, and delivering --- on its way from manufacturer to customer, and 2) logistics, the physical movement in space that must assure the integrity of the product (preventing damage), timeliness and reliability of delivery, and cost.

Only when these three aspects have been resolved (distribution, logistics, and pricing), do we ramp up **promotion**, raising the awareness of customers and distributors for our product, its uses, features, value, and location. Promotion begins with **public relations**, aligning our business activity and our products with the values and priorities of customers, suppliers, employees, and the communities in which we do business. Public relations should begin when we decide to perform serious analysis of the viability of an activity. In that manner, our organizational design can embody those characteristics from the beginning, and no crisis management or manipulation of public opinion will be necessary.

Then, we design **publicity** --- free and credible advertising. We inform the public of the virtues of our organization, our innovations, and our progressive methods. We do this by providing the media with stories which they can place to attract customers for their paid advertisements. For example, we might issue several thirty second "public interest announcements" for radio stations in our market area, and several short "stories" (50; 75; and 100 words) that can be inserted in the print media as fillers. Longer stories with photos and exhibits can also be sent or bartered for inclusion whenever we purchase advertising. The audience of potential customers believes these "spots" are journalism and finds them more credible than paid advertising. The media runs them, if they are interesting to their audience. And these stories save the media the cost of digging out the information for themselves.

Now, we're ready for personal selling, the most important element of promotion. **Personal selling** occurs whenever our representative negotiates directly with the customer. Traditionally, this has been face to face, such as the retail salesperson and the shopper. But personal selling occurs over the telephone, email, fax, or even our web-site, where the customer navigates displays that mimic the interaction with a human salesperson. The salesperson must be disciplined and follow a thoughtful process for the customer to have a satisfactory experience and the sales transaction to be completed. First, the salesperson must have thorough product knowledge, in order to present the product and answer questions. He must assess the customer's desires, display the product, (giving the customer several options from which to choose; each selected on the basis of the customer's expression of preferences), answer questions, and close the sale. The customer must be treated with respect, because all successful relationships are based on respect. However, our sales representative cannot be required to be obsequious, as he will lose motivation and credibility.

Finally, we can think about **advertising**, the most expensive method of promotion. We design it, place it, and pay for it. So, we have control, but customers recognize who is in charge and will be skeptical. For those reasons, advertisements must be placed where our most likely customers will see them, and that must carry a believable message, as well as instructions for action (price, place, time, method of purchase and payment, and how to contact with us). Grabbing the attention of the prospect is important, but it only begins the process. Advertising can be too cute, in which case the message may be lost in the entertainment.

3) The third management task is **Production** ("operations"). We must plan the production process by analyzing (break-down into a sequence) the process, step by step from materials and human resources to customer satisfaction. This process will also lead us to develop a list of all parts and processes, commonly known as a "Bill of Materials". **Lay-out** and **routing** for each stage can be chosen. There are commonly three choices: **fixed** (activity occurs at one location, such as building a house), **process** (where the product is moved to different locations for different activities, such as mining, refining, shaping, assembly), and **assembly line** (where the product moves through a sequence of adjacent stations as it is processed). Ford may have created a proto-type assembly-line at the River Rouge plant, but Disney's variant of moving his audience through a series of sets at Disneyland on various rides is also a good example.

Then, we can choose the location of each activity that suits the lay-out and routing plan. We must consider the quality and availability of resources, as well as reliability and cost. As we organize production, we acquire and install the equipment, build the inventory of parts and equipment *and personnel*. Tracking the availability of the resources is critical to **scheduling**, and today, computer net-work solutions, such as Enterprise Resource Planning programs, pioneered by QAD, provide that link. Orders can be booked by the sales department into an ERP system that identifies the bill of materials and the production process, quickly matching the order to available resources, highlighting bottlenecks, producing a schedule, and dispatching parts and work orders. The final step in production is **follow-up** --- monitoring performance and solving problems. Don't dismiss the importance of follow-up. Success is 10% knowing what to do and 90% being able to do it (execution), as any football coach will tell you.

4) Although we might number the six management tasks, they are all equally important, and poor performance of any damage the entire project. So, recognize that **Personnel** management is critical, too --- and often, it is very badly done. After all, people can be difficult. Skills are important, but motivation is equally so. Managers who see people as a cost, or as tools for their own success, like machinery or equipment, can destroy the effectiveness of their team. As Peter Drucker said, "Management is the achievement of goals through people". So, we must be sensitive, as well as demanding and systematic.

The first step is to assess our personnel needs. We do so by referring to the business plan. How much we wish to produce, and the methods of production chosen (this is what we mean by "technology" --- just method, nothing more), will lead us to identify the tasks that must be done, the skills needed to do those jobs, and the number of employees for each job. Think of a football team of fifty-five players, including eleven different positions on offensive and defensive, as well as specialized skills players, such as punters and field goal kickers.

By comparing the numbers, interests, and abilities of our existing employees, we can locate gaps in our staffing. This leads to **recruiting**. And recruiting is a marketing problem. How do we locate, inform, and motivate the best applicants. It's best to "cast a wide net" --- that is use many methods: ask your existing employees to spread the word, post openings with public and private employment services, communicate with opinion leaders in your area, such as ministers and educators, contact staffing agencies, and advertise selectively in trade journals that prospects actually consult.

Once we have a robust pool of applicants. We screen for their interest in the tasks which they will need to perform (job description), their skills (job specification), and even their psychological make-up (Are they likely to enjoy the work ?). References must be carefully checked, and for critical positions, the help of professional, private detectives is recommended. Character, as well as competence, is important.

Having selected the best recruit, whether within the firm or from outside, orientation and training are important. **Orientation** means the careful introduction of the employee to our firm, its mission, its ways of doing business, and its culture. Orientation is often neglected, leaving the employee confused about what the company does, what are its priorities, and how he fits in. **Training** is task specific, and is usually done, either by the HR department for standard training, or the employee's new department for specialized training. Unfortunately, often the trainer is not motivated, because he is being distracted from the activities which he enjoys and for which he is evaluated. Training must be a central function of every employee and supervisor.

As part of the hiring process, **Compensation** must be determined. Again, too many managers see employees as costs. Good managers know that the best employees can only be motivated by compensation that is fair. There is a saying, "If you pay peanuts, you will hire monkeys." Is that what you want ? So, be aware of the employee's value to the firm (the value of the additional sales that he contributes), his opportunity cost (the mix of compensation which he could gain in alternative activities, including non-market activities), and the compensation being offered to his peers.

Finally, there is employee **Evaluation**. When we fail to evaluate carefully and regularly, we fail to inform ourselves of the talent already available to us, and we signal the employee that he isn't important to us. So, regular evaluation is vital. Whatever the policy is, consider evaluating staff twice as often. Ask the employee to compare his actual work to the job description, and also, to assess the relevance of the job specification. Inaccurate job specifications can exclude some talented applicants and increase costs. When the supervisor and the employee meet, they should compare their views of the tasks being performed, as well as the success of the employee. A good supervisor learns from his employee. In management, as in life, critical skills are the abilities to 1) set your own ego aside, and 2) ask, listen, and evaluate what you hear. Once, any differences of employee and supervisor observations are reconciled, considerations of changes in assignment and compensation can be considered. Finally, be sure to ask about the employee's interest in his job, his career in your organization (What would he like to be doing next ? In two or three years ?), and his life ambitions. Again, this information helps the manager to plan and anticipate. Often, we find talents and interests that we are not using to our advantage. Sometimes, we find that the employee really doesn't like his work. This allows us to consider changes, or separation, without anger or guilt.

5) OK, so we have a plan for products, customers, operations, and staffing. Now, we must bring on the non-human resources. This is the area of **Finance**. The financial manager must assess the needs, in dollars, for the various assets that make operations possible. He does this, as we mentioned above, by comparing plans for sales and associated costs to specific assets classes, such as plant & equipment (in accord with the technologies chosen that associate products with materials and facilities), inventory, cash balances, and sales' credit (accounts receivable). From this assessment, he identifies the funds needed and proceeds to select the combination of liabilities that will bring in the money and an acceptable level of cost and risk. He might borrow short-term from banks or suppliers to support his equally short-term need for inventory, and he might use long-term debt or equity to support long-lived assets such as plant and equipment. Finally, the financial managers allocate the funds to the various activities and monitor performance.

6) This takes us to the **Control** function, usually associated with book-keepers, accountants, and auditors. Monitoring performance continuously ("knowing what's going on") is vital. Only in this way, can we identify and correct problems before they become costly, even fatal, to the business. Accountants design reporting systems and aggregate information into classes that facilitate understanding where we are and where we appear to be going. They help us to understand the outcomes of our past decisions, and to make new, better decisions. We are all familiar with the basic three accounts --- the **balance sheet** (statement of condition) which lists all assets (what we own) and all liabilities (what we owe; where we got the money), as well as the **income statement** which classifies revenue and costs, and thus profit, and finally, the

statement of cash-flows which explains the money that we received and where it went, and thus reconciles the cash that we had at the beginning of the period with the cash that we have at the end. All of these are important, but we need other reports that track activity, such as reservations or orders, shipments, customer acknowledgement of receipts, and equipment usage and failure rates. Many qualitative measures are equally important --- employee turn-over, illness, and absences, public relations, and customer retention. And we must not overlook our ability to conform to the laws and regulations that apply to our activity in our various locations.

Now, that we know what we're looking for, we can consider how to assess the possibilities. This requires understanding the environment in which we will do business. We build up from the foundation. Geography, climate, and demographics help to define the possibilities. They will influence the development of the culture in all of its aspects. **Culture** is simply the behaviors that we learn from our very birth, that help us to achieve our goals where we live. You have probably observed infants smiling. They learn very quickly that smiling brings attention that is pleasant. Whereas, crying may bring food, or a diaper change.

Before we analyze the elements and influences of culture on our business opportunities and risks, you need to be reminded of the foundational importance of geography, climate, demographics, and history. Although I have always been interested in these topics and studied them persistently, I will not claim any particular insights. I urge you to pursue these on your own, as I have.

Maps are one source of confusion in the study of **geography**. They usually take the form of flat projections or round globes. Both can be misleading. The flat projections acquire distortions as the actual shape of the region is flattened onto the paper. In addition, the lack of depth and the colors that code the map can mislead. For example, we see the USA as one color on a map and may conclude that trade within the USA will be easier than trade with the adjacent nation, or nations across the ocean. In fact, trade between California and Mexico, or California and Japan is easier than trade between California and New York, because the proximity and the availability of ocean shipping. In the case of California and New York, several thousand miles, four mountain ranges, miles of plains, and several rivers must be crossed.

Of course, one critical aspect of geography is the distribution of natural resources. If the least costly petroleum is in the Persian Gulf area, then we must go there to produce oil. Mountains of copper at Butte, Montana and Tsumeb, Namibia will lead to mining at those locations. However, the processing may occur elsewhere. The location of activity will depend on all costs, not just the availability of the raw materials.

Rivers are interesting, because they can facilitate trade, as the Mississippi does between north and south, or be obstacles to trade as the same river does between east and west. Similarly, mountains can be obstacles, but they can also have important influences on climate for better or for worse. The conclusion must be that geography can impede, or facilitate commerce, by raising or reducing costs, and so, geography cannot be ignored.

As you study geography, as any area of inquiry, you should practice critical thinking and skepticism. Too many academic geographers and climatologists may be experts in their field, but are ignorant or prejudiced against commerce. Every activity of living things and climate alters our environment. The outcomes that we like are considered benefits, and the outcomes that we don't like, are costs. Every activity has some element of benefits and of costs. And these should be carefully identified, and the values of the net effects estimated. Considering only costs, or only benefits, will lead to faulty conclusions and bad decisions.

Recent debated regarding **Climate Change** provide an excellent example of the confusion that can result in bad policy. A rational approach to the issue would require levels of analysis.

1) Is the climate changing in a systematic way, rather than merely fluctuating ? For example, is our average temperature rising, "global warming" ?

2) What possible explanations (theories) should we consider ? For example, man's economic activity introducing pollutants, or alternatively, changes in solar activity.

3) What are the effects of these changes ? What are the costs and benefits ? And can we measure and value them ?

4) If costs exceed the benefits, what changes in our behavior, would slow the change, or mitigate its effects ? And what are the costs and benefits of those changes ? How do those net costs compare to the costs of doing nothing ?

5) What are the political possibilities for co-operation of individuals, organizations, and communities to implement such policies ? And what are the risks and costs of failure, induced by conflicts that may result from either doing nothing, or trying to change behaviors ?

Only after all these questions have been asked, can we draw the normative conclusion of what action is best, given the desirability of the likely results.

The realities of geography and climate become important in assessing the costs and benefits of our specific business activity, as well. Heat and cold, and humidity and precipitation, influence our way of life. In business, we offer products and services which must appeal to our customers in accordance with their preferences. Hence, we must consider climate, because of its influence on how we live. Saudi Arabia may need air conditioning, but Alaska may not. Thailand must consider drainage and mold, but Mauritania is more concerned with irrigation and desiccation.

Demographics are the characteristics of the people in a region --- not only their numbers, but their age and sex distribution, their education and skills, their culture in all its aspects. Some would argue that demographics are destiny, but that may be an exaggeration. After all, we can change demographics by changes in birth and death rates, by emigration and immigration, and by education and health services. Nevertheless, we are not going to change them on our own. They represent that reality with which we must manage our business.

For more than two centuries, scholars have fretted about population. Malthus and his disciples, Margaret Sanger and Paul Ehrlich to name a few, have warned us about over-population. Others worry about the baby dearth reducing our labor force and thus our ability to produce and to support an aging population. Migration causes anxiety in the countries that experience the loss of the talents of working age adults, and in countries experiencing in-migration with the associated costs of feeding and housing new residents, as well as providing education and health-care. These fears result from a failure to appreciate that *people are both producers and consumers*. They contribute to our ability to produce and they also require investment (health and education) as well as provision of material goods, such as food, clothing, housing, etc. So, the policy issue is how to meet the needs of the population, so that it can contribute to the production that sustains and improves everyone's quality of life.

For those who fear population increase, we can take heart that world-wide, population growth is slowing. And this slowdown in fertility rates is strongly associated with increasing opportunities for women to earn income. So, one value that we share (the importance of equal opportunity for all) supports another value (population growth that coincides with our ability to maintain and enhance the quality of life and our environment). And caution: we should not take too seriously projections of any kind that are way out of our experience. Only two years ago (2012), the UN estimated world population in 2050 to be 9.55 billion. Now (2014), it estimates 9.15 billion. That's 400,000,000 people; quite a difference. Much can happen in the next thirty-five years.

I must note that one region continues to experience rapid population growth. That is Africa. Since the post Second World War independence movements, much of Africa has experienced political and economic instability, even decline. But we must remember that Africa was depopulated over many centuries by slavery, as well as disease. The rapid population growth that we see in Africa currently may be the result of post-independence optimism, as well as improvements in public health, and may represent a return to natural patterns of human settlement and densities. However, the opportunities for advancement in many African nations have not achieved the levels of the first world. On the other hand, the economic tide has turned in a favorable direction during the past decade. Time will tell whether the expected effect on fertility will occur in Africa. Finally, we do have plenty of evidence (from France and Russia encouraging births, and China and India discouraging births) that public policies have little effect on fertility rates, except when particularly they are draconian, such as compulsory sterilization and infanticide.

So, the real issues of population are two-fold:

1) What is the demographic condition and how is it changing ?

2) How do we organize our society to take advantage of these changes by adapting our use of resources to assure that the population changes enhance our ability to provide for each other rather than reduce that capability ?

And then there is **history**. Many have noted that history is written by people (often the victors). The importance of that observation is that people's perception of their history colors their view of themselves and others. The facts of their history may matter less. For example, if you read the history of the development of the petroleum industry in Iran, as reported by the officials of British Petroleum (formerly, Anglo-Iranian) and the same history according to Iranian officials, such as Manuchar Farman Farmanian[2]. You will get very different stories. And you will understand better British attitudes and Iranian attitudes. Remember: you can argue the facts forever, but you might better spend your time understanding the perceptions that other have about those facts. After all, it is their perceptions, whether right or wrong, that will influence their actions and their attitude toward you.

So, wherever we wish to do business, we investigate the **Culture**. We consider **language**, not only for communication, but as a guide to the pattern of thinking associated with the structure of the language. We are interested in the local **religions** as guides to appropriate and inappropriate behaviors, and also as guides to values and priorities. It has been said that all cultures share five common values (avoiding harm, respect for authority, purity, fairness, and community[3]). However, sometimes these values conflict. And different cultures will have different priorities. This can lead to conflict when people believe that they are doing the right thing, while others strongly disagree. (Which is more important: "avoiding harm" or "loyalty to community" ? Buddhists and Judeo-Christians may disagree.)

Customs & manners are the expected social behaviors help us to be comfortable with each other. But these can differ. Offering a guest an alcoholic beverage may be hospitable in the southern states of America, but deeply offensive in Saudi Arabia.

Aesthetics are the sense of beauty. This becomes very important in designing products. Americans like big, and European often prefer small. Chinese like loud colors, such as red or gold. Japanese like subtle design. And these preferences influence **material culture**, the goods that we use and with which we live, such as our houses, appliances, and furniture; our roads, autos, and buses; our clothes, tools, and cosmetics.

Finally, there are the issues of education and social structure. **Education** becomes important when considering the abilities of customers and employees, as well as the relevance of scientific thinking. **Social structure** identifies the roles and relationships that are considered appropriate and comfortable.

You can see that each of these areas provided many opportunities for devastating errors. As always, the best plan is to *ask and listen. Never assume.* In conclusion, we must be aware of the realities of local geography and climate, and of local demographics, including trends. We should be aware of local history, seeking an understanding of events as they happened, and also local interpretations of those same events. Only then can we adapt our strategies to be effective in that environment.

Once we have a foundation of understanding the local variations of geography, climate, demographics, history, and culture. We can consider the influence of culture, political, legal, and economics systems on assessment of business opportunities and risks. Years ago, Michael Porter[4] suggested that we investigate five dimensions of locational advantage:

1) availability of the resources that we need, both with respect to quantity and quality (such as skills and cultural attitudes).

2) demand conditions --- are there plenty of potential customers, and do they have the purchasing power to act ?

3) industrial organization ---is it competitive, monopolistic, or something in between ? We like competition. It keeps us sharp and protects us from arbitrary treatment and favoritism.

4) availability of supporting services --- specialist organizations that can contract to do tasks that we need but would prefer not to do for ourselves. They allow us to focus on the activities that we do best. Examples vary from research universities to janitorial services. As an industry expands in one locale, it attracts talent by the range of employment opportunities, and it expands the possibilities for specialized suppliers.

5) posture of government --- will it assist us or impede us ?
All of this study will help us to identify the best opportunities and avoid dangerous and costly errors. One lesson from these ideas is that *Management Practices should be well-suited to local conditions.*

Some Americans are concerned about "out-sourcing" which takes two forms. One is sub-contracting with specialty suppliers. By locating where there are abundant supporting resources, we can reduce our costs and focus on our competitive advantages. The other form of "out-sourcing" is the relocation of some activities in a foreign country. The motivations are the same --- the reduction of costs and/or the increase in sales revenue. If we would like to gain or retain economic activity in our location, then we should look at the forces that lead to the choices. I think of both the "push" and the "pull." Too often, we obsess on the "pull," usually assumed to be "cheap labor" or possibly government favors. A more complete notion of the attraction of some locations is the presence of the factors listed above. In choosing location, we consider all costs. Labor is often minor. And the quality of resources matters. If the wage of labor in Asia is 1/8 of the American wage, but the American worker is 10x as productive, then the American is less expensive. And yes, some regions will provide tax breaks, cheap credit, infrastructure improvements, and other incentives to attract new business. Usually, we can't do much about that. However, we often forget the "push," the policies that drive business out by raising costs. Most obvious are high taxes and poor public services, but onerous and pointless regulations will discourage business, too. California's labor laws, environment quality laws, land use restrictions, and costly water and energy policies "push" business out. Texas uses the same policies to attract business --- regulations that lower costs rather than raising them. The same could be said of national policies that drive business overseas. These, we can alter by careful review of policies to consider costs and benefits. Don't forget that many laws and regulations reduce costs and improve the efficiency of markets (think of food inspection standards) and the quality of resources (public health and education), and public goods (roads, ports, public safety, enforcement of contracts), but many raise costs and reduce market efficiency.

I recall asking an official from the California Dept. of Labor in 1988 whether an employer attempting to abide by all state labor laws could do so. After a thoughtful pause, the official said, "No, the laws are too complex and contradictory." And that was more than twenty-five years ago ! In contrast, when we were negotiating the purchase of a failing resort in Antigua (West Indies), I asked about local tort laws. "What would be our liability if a guest fell in the bathtub and hurt himself ?" The Minister of Tourism responded, "We put him on a plane and send him home." Our insurance against all risks for our $3,000,000 resort on fifty acres of beachfront property was $30,000 a year. In addition, when I wrote a four page EIR explaining how we would recycle water and dispose of our waste, the government was delighted and approved our application forthwith. How does that compare with permitting in any coastal community in America ? Can you guess what the annual insurance for a hotel in an American community would be ? Also, in Santa Barbara, I spent four years and $600,000 to get permission to build eighteen homes on fifty acres with no deleterious environmental impacts, and with voluntary commitments to build a perimeter bridle path and hiking trail, the remediation of a creek along the property boundary, and other public amenities, and with the full support of my neighbors.

So when we think of location, consider the items that pull us toward that location and the items that push us away. William Easterly has said that the most important conclusion of economics is that people respond to incentives. You should, too.

Review questions and exercises:
What did you learn from this introduction ? Make a list of three central issues addressed in it. What do you think ? Practice critical thinking by listing the major points followed by your personal assessment based on your experience and other evidence.
What is Business ? What are the essential functions of management ?
What is Economics ? What choices must be made in organizing an economy ?

[1] Peter Drucker, <u>Management Tasks, Responsibilities & Practices</u>, Harper & Row 1974
[2] Compare: Manuchar Farman Farmanian, <u>Blood and Oil</u>, Random House 1997 and
            Denis Wright, <u>The English Amongst the Persians</u>, Heinemann 1977
[3] Jonathan Haidt, <u>The Righteous Mind</u>, Allen Lane 2012
[4] Michael Porter, <u>The Competitive Advantage of Nations</u>. *Free Press. 1990*

Lesson #1.2: Culture & Management

In the prior lesson, I introduced business, finance, and economics. We started to develop a discipline for identifying opportunities and managing risks. We skimmed lightly over the responsibilities of management and the characteristics of a desirable business. Finally, we made a few notes regarding geography, climate, demographics, and history, as the initial steps in the process of selecting the best activities. Let us now consider culture.

When we consider culture, we are recognizing that *people behave differently, even when faced with similar situations.* This becomes important, because we have expectations of what constitutes appropriate behavior, and we practice the same in our interactions with others. When others behave in an "inappropriate" way, we may be confused, misinterpret their intentions, and develop distrust. (We may be less aware of how our behavior affects others, but you can see that the same problem arises.) In business, trust is essential to managing risks, and misunderstandings damage trust.

Culture is *the acquired knowledge that people use to interpret experience and generate social behavior.* It is shared by the group, and so there is an assumption that everyone knows how to behave, and a breach of expected behavior shows poor manners, disrespect, and maybe, insanity. Culture is also persistent. The elements of culture are passed from one generation to the next.

Naturally, if these learned behaviors work in the context of our society, we expect them to be effective universally. Hence, we observe **ethnocentrism,** the belief that one's own ways of doing things is superior. When they don't work, we may become frustrated and inflexible. Others may interpret our behavior as disrespectful, arrogant, patronizing, or worse. Less familiar is a concept which I introduced as a graduate student, **ethno-angst**. Many members of societies and cultures which have suffered colonialism, or fallen behind politically or economically, may experience anxiety that their culture is inferior, that their beliefs and methods are inadequate, that their knowledge is not valued, and that new skills are unobtainable without abandoning their most treasured beliefs and values. These people may exhibit fear of failure, lack of confidence, passivity, defensiveness, and resentment. Or they may react by rejecting of their own culture and becoming frustrated with those who would maintain those traditions.

For our business, we must strive to understand the local culture (sometimes cultures) in order to interpret behaviors accurately and to adapt our own behaviors to become successful. Most obviously, we must adapt marketing strategies, and personnel management practices, to fit comfortably into the local environment.

A good place to start is a review of the **elements of culture**: Language, Religion & Values, Customs & Manners, Social Structure, Aesthetics, Material Culture, and Education.

Language structures thinking as well as communication. For example, Chinese has no future or past tense, but Spanish and Portuguese have fifteen, or more, tenses. The former will lack the subtlety of the latter, and so context will be very important in Chinese, but less so in the romance languages. For these reasons, achieving even a small mastery of the local language helps us to understand the way of thinking and associated values. In addition, clichés, idioms, and jargon can be important. Such phrases as "the cheek of the salmon" have no meaning to an American, but are easily understood by the Dutch. Commercial history is replete with costly errors caused by neglect of language. Ford tried to sell a Mercury Comet *Caliente* in Mexico. Sales lagged in a culture in which "Caliente" is slang for hooker. A hair iron marketed under the name "Mist Stick" did poorly in Germany, where "mist" means manure. Other mistakes are more subtle. A visual advertisement that showed soiled clothes on the left, a washing machine in the middle and clean clothes on the right, only confused Arabs who read from right to left.

Distinguishing between high and low context languages may be helpful. High context languages have restricted codes and implicit rules. Communicators are expected to understand unspoken communication --- silence means understanding (not necessarily agreement). The setting, or "context", matters. Information is interpreted according to relationship, roles, and experiences. Japanese and Chinese are languages that exhibit high context characteristics. On the other hand, low context languages are more direct --- the verbal code is primary; the rules of the language are explicit; the communicators speak bluntly. English, German, and Dutch are low context languages. Notice that the communications of a low context culture may appear rude and domineering to the high context communicator, while the high context communication may appear vague and confusing to the low context participant.

In sum, knowledge of local language helps to speed direct communication, improves candor, enhances awareness of nuance and implication, and raises cultural awareness (of thinking patterns and relationships).

The next important elements of culture are **Religion** and **Values**. I link these together, because understanding religion helps us to discern the dominant values of a culture. The study of the local religions provides a guide to good behavior, often with examples, such as the saints. Religion instructs us in the strongly held beliefs and cultural values of its adherents. It may also provide group identity, defining membership in the community and obligations of mutual support. For these reasons, religion influences our behavior and our interpretation of the behavior of others. Religion will prescribe holidays, diets, and social customs, as well as business practices, such as profit, interest, and what are considered legitimate and illegitimate activities.

If we limit ourselves to the comparison of major religions, we will find common principles, such as the Golden Rule, as well as many differences. Protestant Christianity provides many guides to our behavior, but is also silent on many specifics. Islam is believed to be an exhaustive guide to behavior. And much of Islamic scholarship has been elaboration of the Koran to cover more situations. Rather than asking God, or the saints, for help or ascribing outcomes to God's will, Hinduism and Buddhism emphasize that our personal actions have consequences. This is the ultimate statement of individual responsibility. However, Buddhism adds that all beings suffer from ignorance and confusion, which can be remedied by the mindfulness that leads to enlightenment. The main principles of Confucianism are *ren* ("humaneness" or "benevolence"), *li* (ritual norms), *zhong* (loyalty to one's true nature), *shu* (reciprocity), and *xiao* (filial piety). Together these constitute *de* (virtue). Confucianism's focus is on social duty. Taoism (also, Daoism) emphasizes spiritual harmony within the individual complements. Broadly defined, the Tao is the mysterious natural order of the universe. The Tao encompasses all opposite and complementary forces, which are collectively referred to as yin and yang.

I have noted above that all cultures share five core values: avoid harm, respect authority, purity (opposite: pollution), fairness (reciprocal altruism), and community.[2] However, when the requirements of one value conflict with another, cultures may exhibit different priorities. And, because we all believe that we are acting virtuously in our own context, and the other is acting differently (but equally correctly from his point of view), conflict can be irreconcilable.

When we hear of Afghans murdering their daughters for being alone with a man not of their family, we are shocked. To them, "purity" trumps "avoiding harm." For us, the reverse would be true.

Other ways of considering cultural differences are **Value Scales**. This scheme helps us to organize our perception of a culture, and thus, its methods and behaviors. For example, does this culture teach that human nature is good or bad ? If good, there is little need for rules, and relationships of trust come easily. If bad, then we must have many controls to channel behavior onto the correct paths.

Are individual differences good or bad ? If good, then eccentricities may be celebrated. If bad, then conformity is expected.

Do we encourage individualism, or should we act as a team ? (I asked the Japanese father of a friend why the Japanese like baseball. I offered my own explanation that the Japanese like ritual that leads to a "moment of truth." He agreed, but he added that baseball offers the opportunity for the player to sacrifice for his team. Are you happy to sacrifice for your team ?)

Should our behavior be candid, frank, "authentic", or should we conform to expectations, playing our assigned social role, telling others what they wish to hear ? Americans expect candor, but Asians might see that as rude and disruptive.

Should we use our status for personal power and prestige, or for the benefit of the group or organization ? Even in our society the former is common, but we resent it in others. In Africa, the "big man" is expected to benefit from his position, and so will others, when they get their turns.

Can we characterize the society as one of easy trust or rampant distrust ? We "frontier people" are quick to trust, but those of Asia are not. This is a likely result of history. And we should conform. We need to invest in building relationships in Asia. Do not expect immediate trust. On the other hand, once trust is achieved, for example in the Arab world, it becomes a sturdy bond.

Is this a culture in which confrontation is expected, but quickly resolved with no ill-feeling, or is this a culture in which conflict should be avoided, even at the expense of ignoring opportunities to avoid harm ? The Australians are happy to be blunt, but the Arabs would prefer to avoid ill-feeling.

Finally, how do the participants in this culture feel about competition and collaboration ? When I asked my students to form teams to investigate opportunities in different countries, the Americans always chose places that excited their interest. The Japanese always chose Japan. When I asked why, they said that they thought the Americans would need their help to understand Japan. Similarly, we have had trouble with academic cheating by Chinese students. Are they bad people ? I don't think so, but they have been taught to help each other.

I think you can see how differences in religion and values can lead to differences in behavior that are shocking to those from another culture. As usual, don't assume that you understand. Ask, listen, evaluate, before you act.

The study of language and religion leads naturally into the study of **Customs** and **Manners.** These are the appropriate behaviors and established practices, such as greetings, touching, personal space, and privacy. Again, differences can be unsettling. My Egyptian friends who take my hand, draw themselves close to me and talk for what seems to be hours, while I became increasingly uncomfortable. Then, we walk arm in arm, also for hours.

What do we mean by "good manners" ? One useful guide is to recognize that *good manners are the behaviors that make the people comfortable with you,* and bad manners make them uncomfortable. Joking criticism may be acceptable among the Germans and the Dutch, but can lead to violence among Arabs.

There are differences in entertainment, negotiations, and gifts. The Japanese will give expensive and beautiful gifts to signify the importance of the relationship. Be ready to reciprocate. But when bringing a gift to China, don't bring a clock. It would mean, "your time is up " ! In Africa, demonstrate respect for elderly. If you ignore grandma, you are ignorant and disrespectful, and therefore, not trustworthy.

In America, we like to pretend that class differences don't exist. Instead, we substitute racial stereotypes, --- a poor solution. Instead, we should be aware of such **Social Stratification** as exists. We may wish to change it, and we may be able to do so in the small world of our specific firm. But be careful. Class, or caste, imposes a structure of appropriate roles and relationships. Those who understand them may become acutely uncomfortable, when the rules are violated. In India, violation of caste expectations can lead to violence, even murder. So, we must ask, what are the appropriate roles for men and women, adults and children, various ethnic groups or castes ? What about social mobility ? Is society open or closed ? We must remember that class consciousness defines membership and mobility. Violations will lead to tensions and resentments.

I remember the shock with which a Brahmin gentlemen met my suggestion that he contact a Dalit executive at a local hotel. The former was a major landholder with a public stable. The latter was a retired Navy Captain, now working as a concierge. I thought the concierge could direct business to the stable. Oh no ! My friend the landlord would only deal with the hotel's owner, a Brahmin raja. Would the concierge been uncomfortable with my suggestion, too ? Probably. We all know men who are uncomfortable being supervised by women, as well as women who are uncomfortable supervising men. This is changing in many parts of the world, but change is often slow. I am not endorsing racial, class, religious, or gender discrimination. I am asking that we recognize that there are areas of social structure that define appropriate roles, and that these must be acknowledged and approached carefully.

Another important culture element with obvious application to business is **Aesthetics**, our artistic tastes and sense of beauty. Among the Nuer of Sudan, tall and lean is beautiful; among the Waloof of Senegal, obese is attractive. (From personal observation, they are both right.) The Japanese prefer small, elegant, and subtle products and designs. One perfect strawberry is better than a bowl of many average strawberries. For the Chinese (and Americans) bigger, brighter, and louder is better. Give me red and gold.

These tastes influence product design. In China, red is for weddings; white is for death. Don't give your hosts white flowers. you would be wishing them dead. In Brazil, white is for weddings (purity), and red is for hookers (passion). Don't buy your wife, or daughter, a red dress.

Closely related to aesthetics is **Material Culture**. These are the objects that people make and use. They include economic infrastructure, such as transportation, communications, and energy; social infrastructure, such as health service, housing, and education; financial infrastructure, such as banking and insurance; and household goods, such as food, clothing, appliances, and beauty products.

Humans, and their fundamental needs, have not changed during recorded history. We need food, clothing, housing, transportation, education, health care, and entertainment, to name a few. However, the goods and services that we use to satisfy these needs may differ dramatically, as a result of human adaptation to our environment and experiences over many centuries. Therefore, business success requires that we identify the products that are used in our region of interest to meet those fundamental needs. For example, in Asia, men often wear skirts and women wear pants. However, in the West, men wear pants, and until recently, women were expected to wear skirts. In Asia, food may be eaten from common bowls with "chop sticks" but in the West, we use knives and forks.

We ask, what do the people use to meet their needs ? What do they like about these products ? And what disappoints, or frustrates them ? Then, we introduce a new product which is similar in the good ways, but solves the problems. This is the source of most innovation, --- a combination of frustration and curiosity.

Technology influences culture. Access to diverse methods enhances self-confidence and autonomy, and gives businesses greater flexibility. Limits on technology can restrict us, because products and processes must be designed to be useful in local context. As a result, understanding the common methods if living, the material culture, will help us to modify products to meet local needs and conditions.

Our seventh element of culture is **Education**. Each culture must train the new generation in order to replace the skills lost through aging, disability, and death. So, some forms of education are organized. This may include apprenticeships, where we learn from practice with guidance from skilled masters, and formal programs, such as class-room instruction. In business, we are concerned about the skills of our employees and our customers. For example, what is the level of language, mathematics, and scientific literacy ? What are the common attitudes toward cause and effect ? How many people understand and apply the rational thinking central to science (statement of theories of cause and effect, evaluated by repeated reference to evidence) ? How prevalent is scientific and technical training, especially in the skills which we require for our business ? Murray Weidenbaum suggested in The Bamboo Network (1996), that Asia would need one million financial managers during the following decade, as local family owned businesses expanded to become large international corporations.

I recall visiting a village in Palestine in 1972. I was the first outsider, not Arab and non-Israeli, to visit in many years. As a novelty and friend of the first son of a village elder, I was entertained each evening. On one evening, the conversations turned to the recent American landings on the moon. One group believed that we had landed on the moon, because they had seen the videos on their TV. Another group was suspicious that Hollywood may have faked the images. This debate was resolved by my host who stated that Mohammed had visited the moon, proving that man can travel to the moon. Therefore, the Americans had visited the moon. His views were accepted. Note that he was correct in his conclusion, but his logic was not scientific. It was traditional. These non-scientific attitudes persist all over the world, among all cultures. However, their prevalence, and the rigidity with which they are retained, will vary.

We are also concerned about the education of our customers, because it will effect our sales and communications techniques. If our target customers are illiterate, we will not reach them through the print media, but must rely on personal selling, radio, films, and television.

Some analysts find the classification of Geert Hofstede's **cultural dimensions** helpful.[1] He distinguishes 1) Social Orientation: Individualism vs. Collectivism, 2) Power Orientation: Respect vs. Tolerance, 3) Uncertainty Orientation: Acceptance vs. Avoidance, 4) Goal Behavior: Aggressive vs. Passive, and 5) Time Orientation: Long-term vs. Short-term. These can be used to help us understand expectations and conduct. For example, people from cultures which are comfortable with uncertainty will exhibit more confidence and initiative. And people from cultures that exhibit more anxiety about uncertainty will require more training, policy guidance, and supervision.

These differences in culture will influence attitudes toward work. We have often heard of those who live for their work, as opposed to those who work so that they can live. We might think of the Germans or Japanese among the former, and the Africans and Latin Americans among the latter. There is a danger in carrying these stereo-types too far, as cultures do change, albeit slowly. For example, today's Japanese youth are not as committed to work for its own sake, as their parents have been. And we are beginning to see changes in China, where the former attitude of parents ("work harder, save more") is being modified to work hard, save, and enjoy life.

As we consider the influence of culture on attitudes towards work and authority, we think of work ethic and integrity --- will our employees show up every day and meet their obligations, even when doing so is difficult ? There is the story of the Japanese employee who was given a few days off by his American employer, but continued to take the train to the neighborhood of his job, hanging out in pachinko parlors all day, rather than risk the impression among his neighbors that he was not valued by his employer. On the other hand, in Africa, many employees will show up only when they need money, and otherwise, will go about their family and social activities, which are higher priorities for them.

Do workers have a commitment to the success of the organization ? Americans and Japanese lead in commitment and job satisfaction. Our cultures emphasize teamwork. As I search for the best employees, I often look for team sports and military experience, as indicators of exposure to the importance of teamwork. Of course, not everyone gains these experiences.

Fortunately, employees everywhere respond to rewarding work. Although every job requires that some routine, even tedious tasks, be done, sharing the burden and assuring that each employee has some interesting work, will increase job satisfaction and commitment to the organization.

Another important question regards achievement. In this culture, is achievement desired and expected ? High achieving societies value autonomy, challenge, promotion, and earnings; they give less importance to security, benefits, conditions, and time off. Low achieving societies would reverse the priorities. To motivate your employees you must understand their priorities and reward them accordingly.

Attitudes towards time are important. Germans and Americans will be prompt, but Latins are less so, and Africans lackadaisical. (This is not a slap at Africans. It reflects their culture and priorities. On the other hand, I often tell frustrated Europeans, "Don't worry, in Africa, everything works out at the last possible moment." Why ? Because Africans want everyone to be satisfied. They want problems to be solved, and they will be very flexible in finding the solutions, at the last possible moment.) We manage different attitudes towards time by building in flexibility in our scheduling, planning "backstops" in the form of other tasks to be done, while we wait, and most of all, practicing patience. We may also reward efficiency with added compensation, but remember to reward, not punish.

As you can see, the elements and importance of culture are many and complex, and mistakes are potentially costly. Fortunately, the investigation of these is interesting and rewarding. For ourselves and our team members, we should implement **cross-cultural training.** These should include **environmental briefings**, such as those provided by the CIES for Fulbright exchange scholars. Examples are information on climate, geography, schools, housing, healthcare, and other elements of material culture. In this way, our managers will learn what products may be attractive in those markets and what to expect when the family accepts a foreign assignment. Next is **cultural orientation** --- the seven elements of culture with special emphasis on language and values. Language training helps us to "get around" and also shows respect and commitment to our partners. Finally, **workshops** in which business and social situations can be simulated, with the participation of natives, can help us to understand how our behavior will be perceived by others. The workshops may be videotaped and the participants debriefed by the native, who explains the behavior of the participants and how that behavior would be interpreted by the locals. The workshops are a form of "sensitivity training" that develops our awareness of how our actions affect others.

Review questions and exercises:
What did you learn in this lesson ?
Explain each of the six elements of culture.
Explain the ways in which each element is important to business and economics.
    {Give specific applications to marketing and personnel management.}
Explain the differences using Hofstede's cultural dimensions (at least four).
How are these cultural dimensions translated into different attitudes toward work and authority ?
What specific techniques can we use to manage cultural differences ?

[1] Geert Hofstede, Gert Jan Hofstede, and Michael Minkov, <u>Cultures & Organizations: Software of the Mind</u>, 3rd edition, McGraw-Hill 2010
[2] Jonathan Haidt, <u>The Righteous Mind</u>, Allen Lane 2012

Seville Cathedral   Golden Temple, Bangkok

Ismaeli Mosque, Karachi   Jain Temple, Udaipur

Lesson #1.3 Economics, Politics, and Law

Having introduced the foundations of culture, we can discuss the social institutions that have grown out of that culture. In some cases, the political, legal, and economic systems have been imposed through imperialism, such as the French system of law, including property rights, in Cambodia, or imposed by a revolutionary regime, such as Ataturk's reforms in Turkey, or Shah Reza Pahlevi's reforms in Iran. These are doomed. Political and Economic systems will be more successful, if they are consistent with the foundations of local culture. After all, if culture is the learned, effective ways to behave, then a political or economic system that is inconsistent with the local culture will lead to conflict and frustration. This is one reason that I always felt that Communism would fail in China.

So, what is **economics** ? As a discipline, economics is the study of the local methods for deciding the uses of scarce resources. And scarce does not mean small, or finite quantities. *Scarce means, that there is less available than we would like to use.* For example, there is a finite amount of sand in the Sahara, but sand is not scarce, there. On the other hand, there are enormous hydrocarbon resources around the world, in the form of oil, gas, coal, and wood. Yet, hydrocarbons are scarce, because we find them so useful. Accordingly, scarce resources must be rationed among the alternative uses. In other words, choices must be made.

Hence, we say that *Economics is a choice science.* And our methods for analyzing economic systems are founded on the assumption that participants choose among alternatives to achieve their goals. William Easterly has observed that the most important conclusion of Economics is that people respond to incentives, because they weigh benefits against costs, as they choose the best of their alternatives. Some of the economic choices that must be made by any society are 1) What to produce (products and services), 2) How to produce (methods, "technologies"), 3) The allocation of resources to various employments, 4) The distribution of product (who gets to use the products), 5) What do we use now for current satisfaction and what do we commit to maintaining and improving future production ? (consumption vs. investment) and 6) How will these decisions be made ? (coercion, cooperation, or voluntary participation).

We are interested in how these choices are made, in fact, not theory, in the location where we will be conducting business. For example, how do we decide what to produce in America ? We will produce what we can sell profitably. This depends on the costs of production, how many people are willing and able to pay for the product, and how much they will buy. Notice that this does not require that the product be good for the customers, except in the customers' own views. And it does not assure that basic needs are met by all residents. If you do not have the ability to pay, nothing to offer in exchange, you will get nothing through market exchange.

How do we choose our methods of production ? (This is what we mean by "technology.") We choose the method that minimizes our costs. Associated with every technology is a combination of resources. To produce more will require more resources. We must pay for the resources (costs), because they are scarce, and thus we must compete with others for their use. The best technology will be the one that has the combination of resources that produces adequate quality at lowest cost. For example, when I lived in Egypt, I saw children picking bugs off of the cotton plants. Whereas in California, we would use pesticides sprayed from planes to kill the bugs. The same task, ridding the plants of pests, was performed in radically different ways --- labor vs. capital --- based on results (productivity) and cost of resources.

These choices of what to produce and how to produce it, also determine "the allocation of resources", meaning which resources are used where, how, and for what purpose. The resource owner considers the possibilities: what can I gain from various uses of my time and skills, or my capital ? The producers who desire to use the owners' resources bid for them. The owners decide which uses are best. So, Michael Jordan tried baseball, but he returned to basketball, when he realized that he could not match his income playing baseball. And land and buildings get converted from one use to another, as their value changes. I have watched lemon groves be replaced by row crops, and then greenhouses. Each time, the land becomes more valuable, because the new crop fetches more income, or the new method raises production and therefore income. The expanding industry wins the competition for the use of the resource.

Another important decision is "Who gets to enjoy the products ?" Economists call this, **distribution**. There are two elements of distribution: who gets the goods and how do we get the goods to those organizations or individuals. We often call the latter, logistics. In America, by and large, those who are willing and able to pay get the goods. I find it troubling that some very wealthy, elderly couples live in12,000 sq. ft. McMansions, while some poor families live in converted garages, but this is how the system works. And we have already established that we will build the mansions, because there are customers who are willing and able to pay, but we will not build modest housing, if it cannot be done profitably. Notice, for us in business, understanding how the system works, and how to adapt to it, takes precedence over trying to change it.

For any society, deciding what to use for current satisfaction and what to commit to assure future production is important. When we use resources to maintain, or increase, future production, economists call this **investment**. We invest in people in the forms of health, education, and experience. We invest in physical resources by exploration, development, improvements in knowledge (research and development), and by the construction of facilities and equipment. In America, much of our human investment is done politically through public education and health, and much of our physical investment is done privately through households and businesses choosing to commit to their future. Because these investments are often expensive and may take years to pay off, financial markets which encourage saving and lending, are very important for the encouragement of investments and for the growth of our ability to produce.

Finally, we might ask, how are these choices made ? They may be made by voluntary participation, or cooperation with others, or under coercion, such as mandates from the rulers. In general, people prefer to make decisions voluntarily, but they may also realize that some sacrifice to gain the benefits of cooperation may be beneficial, and coercion may be justified from time to time, as for example in the collection of taxes. However, societies for which coercion trumps other methods usually fail, because the costs of assuring compliance mount.

I remember asking myself why the British were able to conquer India with small armies and no particular grand strategy. When I saw the forts of the rajahs and the poverty of the people, I began to realize that the average Indian had no loyalty to his rulers who extracted most of the benefits for themselves. I recall the Amber Fort in Jaipur where the Maharaja had twenty-three wives and three thousand concubines. No wonder he needed a fort, and an army, to protect himself from his own people. After all, if demographics were typical, there must have been three thousand men without wives, but with swords !

In many successful societies, these economic decisions are made by individuals and organizations through voluntary exchange in markets. We exchange one asset (perhaps our time and skills) for another (cash income), and then, we exchange one asset (money) for another (food). For these exchanges to occur, **property rights** must be easily established and transferred. The right to use property motivates us to participate in the market, and we must understand what those rights may be, so we can judge their value to us. Similarly, we need to know with whom we should negotiate to gain their rights in exchange for some of ours.

Understanding these principles help us to see the importance of a **legal system** that records property rights and regulates the process of transfer. And we see that **prices** perform essential functions in facilitating the exchange and the reallocation of resources to those who value them most. *Prices ration the scarce resources.* If a resource is not scarce, there is no need to ration. Everyone can have as much as they can use. But when resources are scarce, those who desire them will compete by bidding, until those who value them less drop out, and only those who value them enough, are able to obtain them. As the price changes in order to ration, the **price signals** given to buyers and sellers change. A high price means great sacrifice for those who would like to use the resource. They must consider whether the property is worth the sacrifice to them. And that same high price encourages producers to consider producing more, if they can, in order to increase their profits (revenue over costs). On the other hand, a low price signals the buyers that the product is abundant in comparison to the quantities that people want, and if they can use it, they should, because there won't be much sacrifice. Similarly, the low price signals producers that this product does not offer opportunity for much profit, and his resources should be used to do something else. So, we say, *prices ration and signal,* and this process determines what we produce and where we employ our resources. Allowing prices to adjust freely to do this job of rationing and signaling is very important, because it assures that both buyers and producers adjust and contribute to bringing into balance what is available with what people are willing and able to purchase.

Resources are also used in the exchange process, and we call these **transactions costs**. For example, we invest in facilities for market exchanges, transportation, and information, and we may pay taxes on exchanges. These activities may be necessary, but they drive a wedge between what the buyer pays and what the sellers receives. Therefore, transactions costs reduce the benefits of exchange and limit markets, because they raise the price to buyers and lower the net proceeds to sellers, thus discouraging exchange. Reducing transactions costs encourages the expansion of markets, as we can see in the rapid growth of international trade, since World War Two. One of the functions of government in the economy is to reduce transactions costs. What happens, if government increases transactions costs with taxes and regulations that are not balanced by benefits to the market participants ?

We all participate in market systems. We participate as buyers and sellers. Most of us sell the services of our resources, such as our labor, and purchase goods and services from others. And so, our **income** (in its purest form, the satisfaction associated with the enjoyment of material goods and services) depends on the resources that we own, their value in the market, how we choose to use them, the prices at which we can purchase the goods and services that we want, and the satisfaction that we derive from those goods. Let us not be confused by income measured in money (dollars) and income measured by satisfaction.

In 1993, I was visiting friends on Wall Street who earned $600,000 per year, while I was earning $100,000 in California. We did a quick comparison of cost of living and realized that the standard of living that I enjoyed on $100,000 would cost $600,000 in New York.

Is the owner of a $72,000 Mercedes automobile three times as well off as the owner of an $24,000 Volkswagen ? Apparently, the MBZ owner thinks so, because he paid three times as much … Would you agree ?

Not all societies rely on market systems. We think of **command economies** where a ruling elite, which may be enforcing traditional activities, or otherwise assigns tasks and distribution. The Soviet Union would be an example. Socialist economies rely heavily on public ownership and control of resources, but may be democratic as well as authoritarian. A **directed economy** is one where the dominant organizations, such as government and industry develop priorities and publicize them. Incentives such as tax, financial and regulatory favors will encourage the national goals, but private property and decision-making remain. This was the policy of France in the post WWII period, and to a lesser extent, Germany. Most economies would be considered **mixed**, using a combination of systems: some market, some government production, and some direction. A particularly common, but problematic structure is **crony capitalism**[1], in which the political and commercial oligarchies support each other and exclude outsiders. This system is usually corrupt, and weakens initiative, competition, and innovation, as well as distorting income distribution and slowing economic growth. An extreme form of crony capitalism is gangster rule (**kleptocracy**) in which criminal gangs rule through terror. We see this in parts of Central and South America, and Africa, but also in Russia and Sicily, today.

So, in business, we must be realistic in our assessment of the local economic system, regardless of what we call the system. How does it truly function ? And can we work with that system to achieve our goals ? Often, we will avoid opportunities, because the risks of a political or economic system that is too weak, arbitrary, or corrupt are just too great. (I remember leaving Shanghai for home after a meeting. Our partner was going to Kazakhstan, a nation of abundant natural resources and economic potential. Later, I asked whether he had found opportunities there. He answered that the level of corruption was simply too great.)

Just exactly what is **politics** ? We'd like to think that it is a system that reconciles conflict, builds consensus, and assures freedom and justice for all. But we cannot afford to confuse an ideal with the reality in which we must work. Looking at history, as well current affairs, I conclude that *politics is usually about acquiring power, keeping it, and using it*. We could use power for the common good, but too often, power is used to benefit the elite and their supporters. Elites seek and maintain power by **pandering** to those whose support is required (perhaps, the security forces, the religious leaders, an ethnic group, or the voters), by providing **patronage** in the forms of positions and income for our supporters (and denying the same to their rivals), and by delivering the **pork** (local projects that provide jobs, profits, and services to their supporters), while rulers enjoy the privileges of power (**perquisites**). I call these the four "Ps" of politics. To organize and manage a business, you must identify how these tools (pandering, patronage, pork, and perquisites) are used in the polity where you will be doing business. To gain and maintain the support of the politicians and bureaucrats, we must acknowledge their need for the four "Ps". We may need to assist them in achieving their goals to avoid being discriminated against, but we definitely cannot be a source of opposition or frustration, if we need their support.

Another useful technique for analyzing any political system is to ask: how are the three functions of government managed in this region ? They are 1) the **legislative** --- how are laws passed and amended ? Who writes and approves laws, and authorizes expenditures ? By what process ? 2) the **executive** --- who enforces laws and implements public programs ? And finally, 3) the **judicial** --- how do they resolve conflicts, determine responsibility, and punish transgressors ? We must understand whether, by whom, and how these functions are performed. And remember, *the formal organization of government may have little to do with the actual performance of these functions.* We might be better off discussing adjustment to regulations with civil servants, or powerful "fixers", than with the legislators. We might better off negotiating services with community organizations, traditional leaders, and voluntary associations, than expecting the government to provide the services. For example, we might do better discussing crime with the traditional village elders than with the local police.

I remember when we decided to purchase, renovate, and operate a failing resort in the West Indies, where our company had been operating for twenty years. Even so, we hired a dissident attorney to represent us, as a way of learning all the details of the local scene. Once we understood the terrain, we gave her a nice separation bonus and hired the right political fixer to represent us in our negotiations with the government. We treated everyone fairly, and we acted with integrity, but we were not foolish enough to think that we understood the realities of local politics, until we had "asked, listened, evaluated," and then, we acted.

As we investigate the political and economic system, we must realize that political actors have different incentives and constraints from those facing businesses. We cannot expect them to behave in the same way. In business, leaders must build a valuable company, they must deliver profit growth, and they must increase the value of ownership. To do so, they must increase sales and control costs. So, they must develop good products and discontinue bad ones. In government, leaders must be popular and trusted. We expect leaders to be like us; we expect them to be sympathetic and helpful; we don't reward them for tough, unpopular decisions. Therefore, you should not be surprised that governments are wasteful. Efficiency is not rewarded, and performance is not measured.

Some of the differences between government (public sector) and business (private sector) include 1) **voting principles** --- in business, consumers vote with their dollars; in politics, citizens get one vote each, regardless of their interest in the decision, 2) **sovereignty** --- governments have rights that common citizens do not; governments can draft citizen soldiers, and jail or execute citizens for criminal behavior, 3) **incentives** --- bonuses and promotions for business; public recognition, job security, and power for politicians, 4) **constraints** --- competition, and profit & loss for businesses, and popularity ("to get along, go along") and agency rivalry for civil servants and elected officials, and 5) **distribution of power** --- consumer sovereignty by voluntary participation for business; coercion by law or regulation for government.

Not surprisingly, governments make different decisions, because of these differences in rights, incentives, and constraints. Governments can break promises (sovereignty). Bureaucracies are unresponsive and self-serving, because they are unchecked by performance measures. (How often does an agency report how much it spent, as an indicator of its success, rather than the results of the spending in achieving its purpose ?)

Governments can grant valuable special favors, or impose costs, through laws, regulations, and taxes. So, **special interests** will organize to influence government either defensively, to avoid harm, or offensively, to obtain advantages. Economists call these unearned benefits, **economic rents**, and the interest groups that lobby for them, **rent seekers**. Politicians compete for election, and find money helpful. ("Money is the mother's milk of politics" --- Jess Unruh). Competition escalates the costs of re-election, and thus, motivates the solicitation of money by the offering favors, or threats of harmful legislation. (Teddy Roosevelt described this in his autobiography. The Clintons are the masters of this technique, and have amassed political power and personal fortunes.)

Another distinction of democracy is the principle that one person gets one vote, as distinguished from the market in which one dollar is one vote. This has two implications for decision-making. We observe that the voters who are best informed and have the most interest in an issue will choose one side or another, but success requires a majority, and the undecided voter is often not well-informed, because he is not very interested in the issue. Yet, these **median voters** determine the majority. We call this result **the voting paradox** (identified by Harold Hotelling) --- those who care the most have the least influence; those who care the least tip the balance.

What can we do about this problem of *expressing the intensity of our preferences* ? Elected bodies have developed the technique of **log-rolling**. Groups that have a strong motivation for one issue and little interest in others, will offer to exchange their support on the unimportant issues for the support of other legislators for their priority issues. The Democrats have done well promising support for **abortion rights** for the support of women voters on many liberal policies. The Republicans have chosen to support **right to life** in exchange for the support of religious conservative voters for tax and spending reductions. In this way, log-rolling creates more support for the issue of passionate interest, and thus, the outcomes can reflect the intensity of the preferences of minorities.

To generate a majority, only a few versions of legislation are permitted by leaders to come to a vote. *Choices are limited, and issues are bundled.* (Extreme examples occurred in the Senate, during the tenure of Harry Reid as majority leader. Many bills passed by the House were never allowed to be voted upon in the Senate, including the annual Federal budgets. The government was funded by "continuing resolutions" during that time.) By limiting the choices, and grouping together a number of issues into one bill, majority coalitions can be constructed. We have seen this in enormous and complex legislation, such as the Affordable Care Act (1,024 pages), Dodd-Frank (financial regulations; 2,300 pages), and Sarbanes-Oxley (another financial reform; 810 pages). And each act authorizes agencies to institute new regulations to implement the intent of the law. (We should not be surprised at the result --- "A camel is a horse designed by a committee.")

In general, we prefer to do business in a political system that exhibits the elements of **democracy.** These elements are 1) limits on power of government, 2) the rule of law, 3) a politically independent judiciary, 4) a non-political state bureaucracy, including police and fire departments, 5) free expression and access to information, and 6) regular elections. Naturally, these are ideals. We must assess the local realities. Especially useful are contacts with dissidents who can inform us of all the problems, from which we can make our own assessments of the issues and risks.

We also consider whether the *several necessary roles of government* in support of a market economy are available in the local system. They are necessary, because government is best situated to perform these tasks. For example, government should provide a legal framework of personal security (public order). It should build and maintain **public goods** (those goods which are neither rivalrous nor exclusive, such as roads, currency, defense, and public safety). Government should regulate market failures, such as monopolies, and external costs and benefits (benefits to others such as vaccines, and harms to others such as pollution). Government should maintain macroeconomic stability through monetary, fiscal, regulatory, and commercial policies.

And finally, government should assure that income distribution is sufficiently fair that all groups acquiesce to the system rather than disrupt it. Let us discuss each in turn.

An important innovation of the West is the **rule of law**. For most of history, the laws have been made and applied by the power elite. Limits on the power of government have evolved through centuries of struggle, in some cases with minimum violence, such as the Magna Carta which resulted from the revolt of the barons against King John of England, or the Glorious Revolution (1688) in which the Stuarts were replaced by William and Mary who accepted limits on their authority in exchange for their new crowns. In some case, revolution was needed, such as the American and French Revolutions, and the Revolutions of 1830 and 1848 in Europe. And some cases, change came as a result of military defeat, colonialism or de-colonialism. The **Rule of Law** is the idea that *the law should be equally applicable to everyone, even the sovereign.* The symbol of "blind justice" represents the principle of treating everyone the same way, regardless of social position. Of course, this is an ideal from which all societies vary. But the closer the ideal, the better we are protected from the costs of favoritism, discrimination, and extortion. If the rules are clear, easily available, and fairly enforced, then we can be confident that we are safe, as long as we conform to the rules. When there is no "rule of law", our business environment is exposed to the caprice of the powerful. You can see this in the relative performance of Argentina before and after the dictatorship of Juan Peron. The fastest growing economy in the world from 1880-1930 became the slowest from 1930-1980. And recently, the Peronist regime of Christina Kirchner destroyed the prosperity of the Argentines by confiscating personal savings, and by arbitrary taxation of agriculture. On other hand, the performance of Mexico since the reforms of Ernesto Zedillo (President from 1994-2000) has been remarkable.

Public Goods are not always provided by government, but they have characteristics which may make public provision desirable. A **public good** is one that, although costly to produce, can be provided to more consumers at no added cost. For that reason, there is no reason to exclude anyone from using it. Once the road or lighthouse is built, there is no reason not to let every driver and navigator use the facilities, until we reach a condition of congestion, at which time, some rationing may be needed. Private goods are exclusive. If you wear the shirt or eat the steak, I can't. The only way to satisfy more consumers of private goods is to make more shirts or grill more steaks. Markets work well for private goods, because we only produce them, if someone is willing to pay for them. But *public goods pose problems for markets*. If your use imposes no added costs on anyone --- your use doesn't interfere with mine, --- then, you should be free to use it. But if everyone is free to use it without any payment, how do we decide how much to produce, and how do we pay for it ? For these reasons, we often rely on a political process to determine the provision of public goods. A region that does so --- good roads, water and sewer systems, ports, defense, police and fire protection, and other forms of infrastructure --- will be a less costly location for our business than one in which we must provide these services for ourselves.

Many economic activities have effects on those not directly involved. We call these **externalities**. For example, if you are inoculated against contagious deceases, you are less likely to contract the illness (private benefit). And I am less likely to catch from you (positive externality). Or the drainage from my farm may pollute the creek with fertilizer run-off. And that reduction in water quality may effect your production downstream. We see this boldly in the use of the Colorado River for irrigation in Arizona and its effect on farms in neighboring Mexico. If the government can implement a system by which the participants, buyers or sellers, must consider these effects, then they will change their behavior. For example, a subsidy of the prices of vaccines will encourage more people to protect themselves, and everyone else. Assignment of the rights to the use of the river, (and with it a requirement that those harmed be compensated), or a tax equal to the damages with the proceeds going to clean up, or compensation, will recognize the true costs of the activity, and as prices adjust, so will the level of production. Notice how this intervention closely reflects our earlier observation that we need government to provide property rights and the rule of law.

We estimate that half of the risks of doing business are general conditions that influence all kinds of activities. We cannot manage these risks, unless perhaps we are both business and government, as for example, the British East India Company. *A government whose policies stabilize the economy reduces our risks* and enhances the appeal of its jurisdiction, as a place for our activities. Germany outpaces Southern Europe, in part because its government, in consultation with business and labor, practices sound policies that lead to low risks to economic activity.

Finally, we are concerned about **income distribution**. This may seem odd, because there is the stereotype of greedy, selfish business leaders. However, once again, the issue is risk management. *Nations with severely unequal income distributions are often unstable.* After all, if I live in a system in which I see others enjoy success for which I am not eligible, I will want to change the system. My alienation may take the form of self-destruction (alcohol, drugs), crime (theft, corruption, or violence), or insurrection. All of these disrupt economic activity and harm everyone. On the other hand, if I believe that the system is fair, and that because of access to opportunities and by making the right decisions, I can succeed like anyone else, I will defend the system. Hence, nations which attend to equality of opportunity, the rule of law, and a social safety net for the truly unfortunate, will be better places for our business.

Let us return to laws and institutions that are so important to us. They clarify appropriate behavior and commercial procedures. They constrain behavior and impose official sanctions for violations. They regulate business transactions and determine redress for grievances. The legal environment reflects ideology and politics that permit and restrict private enterprise. If the legal system does not reflect the culture, there will be conflict. We must understand the system, because it defines the limits of property rights and the procedures for transfer of property. But the performance of the system may be very different from its formal structure. Property rights can be compromised by private action, such as theft, piracy, blackmail, and extortion, and by public action, such as corruption, bribery, taxation, and restrictions on the repatriation of capital or income, or conversion of currency.

An important element of the legal system is **contract law,** which specifies the conditions under which exchange can occur. By stating explicitly the rights and obligations of the parties, a contract clarifies expectations and forms a basis for resolving misunderstandings. Because the law has several sources, such as **common law** --- precedent, tradition and custom, and **civil law** --- legislation and regulatory rules, organized into codes, --- local variations can be substantial.

Valid contracts have six elements upon which we must agree.
1) There must be an **offer** of exchange. The contract specifies the characteristics of what is being given and received by each party.
2) **Acceptance** by both parties must be voluntary. Coercion invalidates a contract. Most obvious is the highwayman's offer, "Your money or your life" --- that's not a contract. (In another context, I remember being pressured to accept a change in terms or face heavy costs. I signed, adding "signed under duress". So, my adversary got my

signature and could not punish me for failing to sign, but he didn't have an enforceable contract.)

3) There must be **consideration**. A contract is not valid unless both parties benefit. Our courts will not judge whether the exchange is "fair", but there must be mutual benefit. This is why you might see on a transfer of property, "for the valuable compensation of one dollar …." (The prior owner of my home gave a strip of land to a neighbor for $8, so that the neighbor could build without violating local zoning. Obviously, the land was worth more than $8, but this satisfied the mutual consideration requirement, making what was truly a gift, a valid transfer.)

4) An often overlooked issue is **competence**. The parties must be authorized to enter into the contract. I have seen businesses enter into contracts, produce and ship goods, only to discover that the representative of the buyer had no authority. Sorting out payment became a nightmare. I always look to the Articles of Incorporation, or a Board of Directors' resolution, that identify the officeholders by title, or name, who can commit the company to a contract. (At other times I have used this to my advantage. I remember receiving a bill {invoice} for a shipment, from Houston to Antigua, of which I was unaware. It had been ordered by the brother-in-law of my boss. He was not an employee, let alone an officer, and he had no authority. I explained to the service provider that I would pay him three months, later. When he objected, I added another month.)

5) Naturally, for a contract to be enforced, the activities described must be **legal** under the appropriate body of law. Perhaps, this is why the illegal drug industry requires so many thugs and experiences so much violence. Contracts for the sale of illegal drugs are not enforced by the police and courts in the usual ways ! What about the sale of alcohol in Saudi Arabia ? What about the "John" who refuses to pay a prostitute ?

6) Finally, the contract must be drawn in **proper form**. This will vary by jurisdiction. Verbal contracts can be enforced in America, but with difficulty, because the parties may present different versions. Written contracts with the appropriate clauses are safer.

Once, I lost out, because I trusted my employer and did not require a contract. I learned from that experience. I had accepted an offer of a $35,000 salary, plus stock options, but once I'd moved my family and bought a house, I was told that I would start at $27,000. And I never saw the stock options. So, for the next two jobs, I required simple, single page contracts. In the first case, my employer claimed poverty, but a short reminder with a copy mailed directly to his attorney brought results. In the second case, I had made sure to have the employer and his wife, who often had title to their properties, sign the contract. When I tired of dunning him for payment, I filed a suit against both of them and filed a notice of pending legal action against all the properties in their names in three counties. After some bluster by my employer, I was paid in full. I suspect the wife told him to pay. *The lesson is "always act with integrity but do not assume others will". When your associates don't need you anymore, they will stop honoring their agreements. So, trust, but always maintain leverage (reasons why they continue to need the relationship). Then, you may have confidence that they will continue to honor their agreements.*

So, I advise you to have contracts, however brief, that specify rights, obligations, and the redress on all important issues. In international business, also agree to the **body of law** that will apply (for example, American, British, French, Saudi) and the **court** which will have jurisdiction (for example, California Federal Court, British Court, Dutch court …), and a very important, detailed dispute resolution agreements, such as **mediation** and **arbitration** procedures. Avoiding litigation can save a lot of time, money, and trouble. There may be a final note in the contract that specifies renegotiation procedures and force majeure exclusions.

In conclusion, the law can be an important support for our activities, but it can also be inconsistent with our experience and expectations. A local attorney, as well as an international commercial attorney, is important. On the other hand, remember that your attorney will focus on protecting you, perhaps so much so that he squelches the deal. Your attorney helps you to manage risks, so it's best to ask him to monitor negotiations and warn us of risks. Then, we choose the level of detail and the terms that balances risk and reward for us.

Review questions and exercises:
Identify the three elements of a political system. ("identify" means name, explain the meaning of the term, and explain its importance.)
Compare and contrast market, command, state-directed, mixed, and crony capitalist economic systems.
What support should the political system give to a market economy ?
What are the elements of a contract and why do they matter ?

[1] An informative study is: Minxin Pei, <u>China's Crony Capitalism</u>, Harvard University Press 2016

The President of Argentina's residence, The Pink Palace, Buenos Aries

Lesson #1.4 Management & Value

How can we identify the best business ? By now, you should be aware of the complexity of managing a business. And more issues are waiting ! Businesses buy and sell. They participate in a variety of markets, so managers must understand how these markets operate. This is one of the reasons why we study economics, which is primarily the scientific analysis of how people behave as buyers and sellers, and how they interact in markets of varied organization, such as competition or monopoly. In addition to our product and labor markets, we must understand financial markets in which we can process payments, save our surplus funds, and borrow to cover deficit spending associated with good opportunities. After all, the deal isn't done, until the check is cashed. So, you will find that this series of lessons covers management, finance, and economics. But before we go there, let's identify for what we are looking.

The Characteristics of a Valuable Company

Success in business has two elements: First, we must identify the best opportunities; second, we must manage the risks associated with undertaking those activities.[1] So, for what should we be looking ?

My friend, successful venture capitalist, Tim Bliss, gave a nice presentation of what he and his partners seek. I have reproduced some key elements here:

1) **Core Values** --- Integrity. The principals must be trusted and trust worthy. They do what they promise, even when it hurts.

2) **Sustainable Differentiation**. The competitive advantages which will continue for many years. They can come from any activity that imparts quality in the perception of the customer, or reduces costs, including errors. They could be the qualities of the product, such as function and reliability, or of the management team, such as people, planning, new product development, or of marketing, such as product design, delivery, after sales service, reputation, or branding. However, we must understand our advantage and plan our activities to enhance and protect it.

3) **Strong Corporate Culture**. Everyone associated with the company understands its values and methods, as well as its goals. Because we have already discussed culture in general, you can easily evaluate the corporate culture of your past and present employers. Learn from them. Clarity and constancy of shared values builds teamwork, loyalty, and motivation. Hypocrisy, or confusion, demoralizes your staff and cause the loss of your best employees and customers. Leadership by cliché is transparent. When a boss says, "My door is always open" or "Excellence is job one," I just want to puke. Lead by example. Skip the talk; do the walk. Everyone will know.

A good set of values puts "Customers First, Employees Second, and Shareholders Third". You may have heard differently, such as "maximize shareholder wealth," "the bottom-line," and "world class." These clichés are meaningless and can be destructive. If we take care of our customers, they will remain our customers. If we take care of our employees (treat them fairly), they will be loyal and motivated. With happy customers and employees, we make money, the company becomes more valuable, and the shareholders are rewarded. (Notice, I did not say,

"Managers and Directors first" --- this is too common, even though such a focus neglects and alienates everyone else.)

I remember an acquaintance who quit Delta Airlines to go to UAL, so his wife could get better free travel benefits. After a few years, he went back to Delta, sacrificing a total of twelve years seniority, because he had to start at the bottom again. He did it, because Delta was a great place to work at that time.

And I remember also a flower grower who sold "babies' breath" all over the West Coast. Although the market price fluctuated between $1.25 in the fall and $2.25 in the spring, he always charged $1.75 and his customers always paid $1.75. Why ? The stable price and quality reduced his risks and theirs. And they all prospered.

4) **A Solid Reputation in Its Industry** --- goes to the public relations issue. People always want to do business with the best. Sometimes, when the best is too busy or expensive, they settle for second best. But when times are hard, and the best is available and discounting their product, customers go to the best and they do not suffer. But the second best loses as part of the general downturn, and loses even more as its customers switch. Reputation matters, because critical methods of risk management are the relationships of trust that we have with customers, suppliers, employees, and local communities.

5) People matter --- a **Strong Management Team** (competent, honest, and committed), and an adequate Board of Directors that can give guidance to the officers. I look for experience in each management area, as well as financial and legal talents for the Board of Directors, and for the management team. Everyone needs oversight and mentoring from time to time, and those who think they don't need an outside view, some constructive criticism, and occasional referrals to specialists, are very foolish, indeed dangerous.

6) The **Right Disciplines**; a **Market Validation Culture**. The managers and directors must constantly check with their customers, actual and potential, to assure that existing needs are being met and future needs anticipated. This issue trumps all others, and this culture can assure that the team maintains its focus, despite naturally human ambitions and tensions. Herb Kelleher, the Chairman of Southwest Airlines during its best years, led by example. He flew economy. He handled reservations and baggage, and he served drinks alongside his employees. He signaled everyone that their job was as important as his. They were a team with different duties, but they were all necessary. (One of my friends gave up a job piloting the Playboy Magazine corporate jet to move to Southwest Airlines. How's that for an endorsement ?)

We have already covered Peter Drucker's typology of management functions, first posed in his book, Management Tasks and Responsibilities. They are Planning, Marketing, Personnel, Production, Finance, and Accounting (Control). Note that many of these tasks require attention to details within the company, such as personnel and operations. But several also require attention to conditions and opportunities outside the company, such as cultivating customers and suppliers, banks, insurance, and securities analysts, monitoring competition, technical developments, and political trends, including the legal and regulatory environment. And then, there are **Public Relations**, assuring that our activities are consistent with the values of our constituents (customers, suppliers, employees, shareholders, political actors, and neighbors).

Management faces two dilemmas in addressing these issues. One is the balance between centralization and decentralization. **Centralization** places all decisions at the top which assures control and co-ordination, "unity" if you will. However, centralization slows the process, because information must flow up to the top and direction must flow down. Much can be lost in translation, or omitted. Egotists along the chain can distort the message for their own purposes. And middle management becomes demoralized as its role is reduced to mere transmitters without the rewards of solving problems and performing tasks. **Decentralization** requires trusting sub-ordinates to make the right decisions, consistent with solving the problems and team goals. However, decentralization requires clear policies, and thorough training in tasks, corporate strategy, and culture. Most of all, it requires trust and confidence. Many managers cannot do this. They won't develop their team; they won't trust their sub-ordinates. Sometimes, they just enjoy the power of making every decision, whether they understand the issues or not. This is sand in the gears of your business. We need communication for control, and responsiveness for results and motivation.

The other dilemma is closely related. We call it, The **Principal-Agent Problem**. Left on their own, most people will pursue their own interests. However, success requires team work. Everyone needs to choose the actions that will lead to team success. All of the employees, from the directors to the maintenance workers, must understand their job and how they contribute to the success of the organization. Rather than each individual being a principal; each is an agent for the organization. Anyone who has played team sports, or served in combat, knows this. I've seen talented teams lose, as everyone tries to carry the team by themselves. And I've seen less talented teams excel, by recognizing their need for each other. (Remember the Japanese father who said that the Japanese like baseball because of the many opportunities to sacrifice for the success of the team.) You can instill these values by example and commitment to integrity (keeping your word) and to fairness. Other solutions include incentive pay, participation in ownership, and supervision (monitoring performance in order solve problems, improve training, and motivate). Setting unrealistic production targets is not planning or supervision.

I remember a friend who managed the second smallest department store in his chain of twenty-two, but it was the second most profitable. So, its profit per square foot was off the charts. A new senior management team dictated a 25% growth in sales goal for every store, regardless of how long they had been open, or their competitive environment. My friend pointed out that a new mall was opening with two department stores that would directly compete with him. He thought a realistic goal was to hold sales steady. Indeed, that would have been a remarkable achievement. His superiors attacked him as a slacker and insisted on their 25% goal. He resigned. Local store sales collapsed, and soon the chain was bought and disappeared.

Now, let's shift gears from an overview of the company to the selection of specific activities. We have already said that too many ideas will come our way, if we are awake and if the public is aware of our abilities. How do we select the best ?

We start by investigating the business environment in the location of the opportunity. We study the geography, climate, demographics, and culture. All of which help us to identify products, customers, and locations which are likely to be attractive. (You may choose to review lesson #1.2). We consider the political/legal system and the local economic institutions. (lesson #1.3). We estimate the financial potential, choose a strategic organization, select method of entry, negotiate entry, organize and commit our resources.

We can use a "check off" list for market assessment, a series of "screens" that will leave only the best projects.

#1 <u>Basic Need & Potential</u>   Who are our potential customers ? What do they want ? We can look at existing pattern of imports, local production, and demographics, including income and lifestyles (material culture and aesthetics). We want to know, can we generate sufficient sales quantities and revenues.

#2 <u>Political & Legal Forces</u>   What are the market entry barriers ? Tariffs, quotas, local content or ownership requirements, investment requirements, and profit and investment remittance restrictions. How reliable is the government ? Stability, laws and regulations, property rights, enforcement of contracts, and corruption issues.

#3 <u>Sociocultural Forces</u> We are looking for a fit with our operations --- languages, work habits, customs, religion and values.

#4 <u>Competitive Environment</u>   Who will be our competitors, and what are their resources ? We may choose to contest markets with competitors in order to put them on the defensive and sharpen our methods and understanding.

#5 <u>Financial & Economic Conditions</u>   Consider market indicators, such as market size (share of world or local market), market intensity (number of local customers and their purchasing power), market growth (annual increase in sales). We eliminate markets that don't meet minimum financial criteria for potential profitability and acceptable risk.

So, we know what we are seeking. We won't make the mistake of choosing a product, or market, with poor possibilities. And we understand the characteristics of a valuable company. But what is a company worth ?

We will learn several methods later in this course. For orientation, we look at the state and trend of the overall economy and of the broad industry group in which the company participates. This serves us to assess **general risk** --- those events which effect all economic activities and are not targeted at us, but will effect our success. Then, we look at the narrow industry group (companies that produce products that compete directly). We identify the customers and check their condition (prosperous customer buy more). We study our competitors and their products to assess our competitive advantage (or theirs !). And then, we look at the quality of management. The analysis of the financial statements and the executives' public statements can tell us whether management has a good strategy, whether they know how to execute their strategy, and whether it generates the anticipated results.

Understanding the nature of the business, we can analyze the financial statements which help us to assess the condition and performance of the company, and thus to formulate modifications of existing activities and the plans for new initiatives. Or, if we are organizing a new activity, we will create "pro-forma" financial statements as a planning tool, to assess needs and project results. The basic financial statements are Income & Expense (operations), The Balance Sheet of Assets & Liabilities (condition), the Statement of Cashflows, and the statement Shareholders' Equity, as well as the Auditor's Opinion.

The basic form of the statements are as follows:

The Income Statement --- a summary of operating results

Revenue all sales income, net of returns and uncollectable accounts. It tells how good we are at selling at strong prices (congratulations to our sales team).

less **Cost of Goods Sold** --- our variable costs, those that occur when we have sales, --- largely inventory. When we sell the product, we book the revenue and reduce our inventory from our balance sheet. Responsibility of our purchasing dept.

equals **Gross Profit** --- this tells us that how good we are at selling product and purchasing materials

less **Gen'l Admin. & Sales Expense** --- fixed costs, overhead; beware of creeping overhead as empire builders in the organization pad their resources. But don't starve the team of R&D, marketing, staff support, or management.

equals **Operating Profit** *(also called "Earnings Before Interest & Taxes")*.
Note that we have accounted for most costs, excepting only income taxes and financing. Operating profit is independent of our chosen financial structure (combination of debt and equity) and our tax planning. It is our best measure of the performance of our line employees.

less **Interest Paid** --- interest on debts. This depends on how much we borrow, and on terms.

less **Taxes** --- taxes on income; tax planning is one of the CFO's duties. It's unfortunate that decisions cannot be based soley on the economics of revenue and costs, but must consider differences in tax treatment. But there you are.

equals **Net Income** --- net profit, the goal !

Net income / shares outstanding = *Earnings per share*

The Balance Sheet, or Statement of Condition, named for the Fundamental

Identity of accounting: **Assets** minus **Liabilities** equals **Net Worth**

We organize the balance sheet by the similarity of purpose and characteristics, such as useful life, risk, and liquidity. The following is a list of Assets and liabilities:

Current Assets (either cash or likely to be used or convert to cash within a year)

Cash & Cash Equivalents (bank deposits and money market instruments)
These are the liquid resources, which ebb and flow as payments are made and received.

Accounts Receivable The payments promised to us for contracts completed.

Inventory The raw materials, goods in process, or finished goods

Pre-paid Expenses   such as rent, insurance, etc.

Long-term Assets (The expected useful life in longer than one year)
Plant & Equipment, less Depreciation

        The process of depreciation is a method of recognizing the cost, as the asset is used, or declines in value. Recognizing that assets have a useful life and must be replaced a some future date.

Investments   The securities of other companies, or miscellaneous assets, which may not be easily liquidated, or which we do not plan to sell.

Intangibles   Goodwill and Patents. These are the result of purchases of assets, or investments in research and development.

Current Liabilities   (debts due in less than one year)
Accounts Payable Credit extended by suppliers to us. We have the goods, but have not yet paid.
Notes Payable   Credit from banks and finance companies.
Accrued Expenses Expenses incurred, but not yet paid, such as salaries.

Long-term Liabilities (Financial Capital)
Long-term Debt   Bonds, mortgages, etc.
Net Worth   Paid in Capital at Par; Paid in Capital in Excess of Par; Retained Earnings
  (note that adjustments to Assets and Liabilities will just offset adjustments to Net Worth)

The Statement of Cashflows   (a Statement of changes in cash position).

Reconciles beginning and ending cash positions. We may choose to start with our initial cash position, then we make adjustments for Operations, adjustments for changes in Assets (Investing), and adjustments for changes in Capital (Financing). We should have a match with our new, current cash position. Let's look in some detail:

The Adjustments for Operations (cashflows resulting from operating activities)

Add Income   profit

Add depreciation   depreciation was deducted as an expense, but cash has already been expended when the asset was acquired, but no cash will be used for this purpose, until the asset is replaced.

Looking now at changes in our Current Assets:

Subtract increases in inventory   (increasing inventory uses cash)

Subtract increases in accounts receivable (we booked the profit, but we don't have the money, yet)
        Extending credit delays the receipt of the cash; sales recorded but not yet paid do not generate cash.

Subtract increases in prepaids (when we paid, we used cash)

Looking now at changes in our Current Liabilities:

Add increases in accounts payable   (supplier credit saves us cash)

Add increases in notes payable   (more borrowing gives us more cash)

Add increases in accrued expenses (delays in payment save us cash)

Now, we have **Operating Cash Flow**. This calculation is hugely important, because it tells us whether in the course of ordinary activities, we generate cash or use it. We need to know this to anticipate needs and opportunities.

Then, we make **adjustments for changes in Investments** in Long-term Assets

Cash is used when assets are bought, and cash is generated when assets are sold.

Finally, we make **adjustments for Financing Activities**

Cash is used when debts and dividends are paid; cash is generated when debts are increased and capital raised. And we must deduct dividends, as use of cash.

Later, in lessons #6.3 - #6.7, we will refine our techniques of valuation. For now, we will introduce four methods for valuing a firm:

We might begin with the **Price: Book Value** Ratio. We compare the current price of a share of common stock (ownership) to the Net Worth per share (Net Worth from the Balance Sheet divided by shares outstanding or fully diluted {all shares that would exist if all options and warrants were exercised}). This seems logical, because we are buying a share of the company, and the value of that share should reflect the value of the company's assets less its debts. Yet, we usually find companies selling at several times their Book Value. Why ? Because value looks to the future (forward), and the balance sheet is a summary of past and present. There are also other issues, such as the accuracy of the valuation of assets, but the main reason is the view of the future. When I offer to buy something, I don't care what it cost you. I only care about what benefits ownership will give me, while I own it, and when I sell it. In other words, I care about the future, not the past or present. So, "Price to Book Value" gives me some feeling for whether I have a bargain (it's worth more than I must pay), or not. In the rare instance, where the company may be liquidated, it may give me some indication of what I might get. But "Price to Book Value" is an unreliable guide to value for me, or for anyone else.

If the value of ownership is closely related to the ability of the company to generate profit, we might look at the ratio of the price of a share to the profit per share. In other words, take the Net Income for the last year (trailing) or estimated for next year (leading) and compare that number to the share Price today. This is called The **Price: Earnings Ratio**. We usually think that a ratio of 15:1 is reasonable. Why ? If I pay $15 for $1 of profit, then, my return is 1/15 = 6.67%. The American economy has averaged 3.3% real growth and 3.3% inflation for the past century. In that case, the earnings of the average company should be growing 6.6% a year and its value increasing accordingly. What if the P:E ratio exceeds 25:1 ? That would suggest a return of 4%. Surely, investors would not take the risks associated with ownership for a return of 4%. When we see a high P:E, we conclude that investors believe that earnings are depressed and will return to normal, or that earnings will grow in the future, at which time the current price will look cheap. We need to ask ourselves, are these expectations realistic ? If the P:E ratio is less than 10:1, the shares look cheap. They appear to offer a 10% return. If that is true, why haven't

43

investors rushed to buy, driving up the price and the ratio ? Perhaps the ratio is depressed because current earnings are inflated and unlikely to be repeated, or investors believe that the company's earnings will deteriorate in the future. Again, understanding the signal, we can reach our own conclusions about the general consensus, right or wrong.

A more sophisticated method of valuation would consider income and capital gains as benefits of ownership. The first of these techniques is called The Gordon Method, after Myron Gordon who presented it in 1956. Gordon posited that the investor is looking for a rate of return that will justify his investment (the price paid). The yield which he experiences depends on a dividend yield (the dividend received divided by the price paid) plus a capital gain which will depend on the growth of the company. Hence, the formula is: **Yield = {Dividend/ Price} plus growth rate.** These terms can be rearranged to read:

Price = Dividend / {required yield – expected growth rate}

This formulation highlights the importance of three elements in determining value, the current dividend (higher is better), the investor's required return (lower is better), and expectations for growth (higher is better).

A variation on the Gordon model, capitalizes Earnings, instead of Dividends. In a world, in which investors are more motivated by expectations for growth of earnings than for dividends (as occurred in US markets in the 1985-1999 era) the formula would be:

Price = Earnings per Share / {required yield – expected growth rate}

Once again, the same variables are important (earnings, required rate, and expected growth) but the required rate of return should be much higher, because we are valuing earnings which may or may not be paid out, and if paid out, taxes will be due, and if not paid out, they may contribute to future growth through the investment of the retained earnings, or not. So, earnings are not cash in hand, and we would compare this investment to other illiquid investments, rather than the money market savings instruments that we compare to dividend paying stocks.

Let's use the formulas. What if a company pays a dividend of $1, the dividend has been growing at 3% per year and we expect that to continue, and we would be happy to earn 6%. Then, the Gordon formula suggests a value of $33.33 (= $1/ {0.06- 0.03}). If we are looking at earnings, and earnings are $2, are expected to grow at 5% but we require a 10% return, then our value would be $40 = $2 / {0.10 - 0.05}. The astute reader has already observed that as our expected growth rate approaches our required rate of return, our estimate of value becomes unstable. And if there are no current earnings, (or actual losses), the formula makes no sense. Finally, the assumption implicit in the formula is that growth will continue at the expected rate indefinitely --- absurd.

So, we have some other methods, such as revaluation of individual assets, and phased growth projections, which we will introduce later (lessons #6.3-6.7). For now, it is important for us to understand that *the value of the firm will depend on our earnings, our dividend, their expected growth rates, and the rate of return required by investors*. The former depend heavily on our management, as well as general economic conditions, as they effect our operations and our customers, but the latter depends heavily on the investors' judgment of the risks associated with our situation and the expected yields of alternative investments. In a low interest environment, our share price may rise simply because the alternatives are not attractive and money flows into our shares. (This has been especially true since the crisis of 2008.) Similarly, we may be doing well, but our share price may suffer, because investors are skeptical of our future, or because opportunities for yield in alternative investments are high (as in the late 1970s).

Although premature, we will close this chapter with some advice for investors. First, note that we use the term carelessly. **Investing** is the act of acquiring resources in order to enhance future production. It's a form of spending. *What we are talking about is actually a form of saving.* We are saving by purchasing an asset which we hope will grow in value and offer some income. Nevertheless, like everyone else, we talk about "investing," when we purchase a security. At least, we're not politicians for whom every kind of spending is sold to the taxpayer as an "investment." Well, education may be an investment, but unemployment insurance is not. It's a form of income support which should stand on its own merits.

So, what should the smart Investor (saver) do ? First, know yourself. What do you need ? Income, liquidity, or capital gain ? What is your overall risk situation, and what is your tolerance for risk ? Are you likely to make mistakes, tripped up by your own fear or greed ? Or do you have realistic expectations, patience, and emotional stability ? We all have strengths and weaknesses. Being honest with ourselves helps us to protect ourselves with disciplines that improve our judgment.

Second, know the characteristics of the instrument. We call financial instruments "securities," because the prudent lender requires that the borrower give a promise that details the rights of the lender and the obligations of the borrower in exchange for the money. Otherwise, the lender may never see his money again. Most certainly, the borrower will repay at his own convenience, unless there is a specific promise. The promise is the lenders' security. So, what is the promise ? One of the most important elements is the promise of future payments. In fact, I often think of a security, as simply the promise of a future cash-flow.

To determine, what I would be willing to pay for that promise, I must identify the promise, evaluate the risk that the actual payments may be different, select a yield which would satisfy me (not too high; that would rule out most investment; or too low, I would jump on the first opportunity and miss some better ones down the road), and then "capitalize" the promise. We did this in the example above for valuing the dividend and earnings of the sample stock.

I will look at a company and build a required return as follows: 1) I need to beat inflation, expected to be 2%, 2) I require a higher yield for accepting higher risks for the entire investment class, I require that my stocks pay 4% more than inflation, 3) I require extra compensation of additional illiquidity and risk within the class (I add 1% for "A" rated NYSE listed stocks and 3% for "B" rated and OTC listed stocks.) So, today, I would look for 7% for "Blue Chips" and 9% for sound but medium sized (>$500m million in sales) companies. (You will note that these are historically low yields in our 2015 exceptionally low interest rate environment.) I will analyze the company's products to estimate growth, and apply the EPS variation of the Gordon model. Of course, I will compare my analysis to others, such as Value Line and Standard & Poor. I would look at their risk and stability ratings, their growth projections and their explanations, while suspicious of inherent biases toward optimism. I would look at returns for my risk class, such statistics as *Beta* and *Alpha* (explained later). Other "investors" will be doing the same, and that will determine our share price and the market value of our company.

Questions for review:

Why would high sales per employee, high sales per total assets, and diverse customers be valuable ? {explain each separately.}

Discuss five other characteristics of a truly valuable company. {identify and give explain importance.}

Explain two of more dilemmas that limit the efficiency of any organization.

Compare and contrast three Valuation techniques:

Price : Earnings ratio, Price : Book Value ratio, The Gordon Model of EPS Capitalization.

[1] My friend and colleague, Ray Bowman, was first to point this out to me.

Tannery in Fes, Morroco

Handloom weaver, Fes, Morocco

Fishing nets in Cochin, India

Lesson #1.5 Marketing

In lesson #1.1, we defined the functions of Marketing. They are often described at the four "P"s, (product, place, price, and promotion), but the essence of marketing is facilitating exchange --- buying and selling. Marketing facilitates exchange by contributing services that enhance satisfaction (in the jargon, "adding utility"). Some of these sources of benefit for the buyers and sellers are transportation and storage (logistics), grading and packaging, providing information on assembly and use, arranging financing, convenience of time and place, after sales service, and managing various risks.

The first step in marketing is **product development**. Having the right product makes every other aspect of business management much easier, and flogging a disappointing product is not only difficult, but demoralizes your entire team, as well as alienating customers. The right product is the one that captures the imagination of your target customers. It serves existing needs better than the other products which may be used for the same purposes, and is sufficiently familiar to be easily adapted and used.

To achieve success, a disciplined strategy of product development must be followed. Otherwise, we might jump impulsively on the first idea, missing minor adjustments and major alternatives which would have greater success. We start generating ideas by consulting top customers (large volume and industry innovation leaders) about their satisfaction and dissatisfaction with existing products, and then about their emerging needs, as they plan future products and services. Suppliers should be quizzed about emerging industry trends among our competitors, as well as products and services which the suppliers are developing for new applications and for our competitors. Our distributors will also be aware of industry developments and customer needs. Our own employees should be encouraged to forward their ideas, and any decision not to implement the employee ideas should be explained to avoid discouragement. Some ideas will be presented by outside sources, eager to use your firm to advance their own.

Important to the assessment of suitability are our product lines and mixes. **Product line** is the variety of products that serve the same needs. Customers like to have choices both for variety and to assure themselves that they have been responsible shoppers. So, a product line may be shoes, sneakers, slippers, and sandals. These have the advantages of appealing to our existing customers and using our existing distribution system. In fact, we may add "related products" which use the same distribution, because our customers are likely to be seeking them at the same venues. For example, complementing our shoes would be socks, stockings, shoe polish, and replacement laces. All together, these constitute our **product mix**.

In the travel business, our product lines were Caribbean resorts of various sizes, locations, and amenities, Caribbean cruise lines, and travel magazines. Together, they constituted our product mix. Can you see the similarities, the mutual support and maintenance of organizational focus ?

When I was an executive at that large resort marketing company, we were offered opportunities to build and operate a resort "on the most beautiful beach in the world", virtually every week. One of the best was on the island of Huahine, (in the Society Islands, also known as Tahiti), including cottages, reception, restaurant, and bar for $50,000. We turned it down. How would you fill a fifty cottage resort on a remote island in competition with 3,000 rooms on the famous islands of Tahiti, and Moorea, nearby ? Worse, at the time, there were only 1,500 air seats a week between the USA and Pape'ete. And after ten hours in the air from the USA, guests would need to travel another 124 miles by ship or small plane to reach Huahine.

Experienced executives know that there are too many ideas, rather than too few, and they must be carefully screened to a reasonable number that merit analysis. The first screen would be asking whether the activity suits our mission, objectives, and capabilities. Loss of focus and exaggeration of abilities will impose heavy costs in distraction and loss of opportunities elsewhere.

Once, our company acquired an oil tool rental company in Taft California, as a favor for a bankrupt friend. Can you see how that would distract an international travel company, leading us to miss many opportunities to build on our existing programs, skills, and relationships ? In fact, our company was started on the recommendation of the famous mobster, Meyer Lansky, who was involved in the Caribbean travel business as a way of "washing" mob revenues. He saw a need for small hotels on Caribbean islands to be represented in the U.S. by an organization that could develop clout with the airlines (AAL & EAL) that served the area, promote a large number of properties, and handle reservations through a central agency. He brought this idea to the attention of a pool-boy who had impressed him. When asked why he didn't do it himself, he responded that he had "bigger fish to fry."

Now, that we have discarded two-thirds of the ideas, leaving a hand-full worthy of analysis. We consider **business analysis**. We are asking not only, is the project viable, but will it be sufficiently rewarding to justify the commitment ? Who are the potential customers? How often do they buy, how much, and what prices ? How are they doing ? For example, Boeing may be a great commercial aircraft manufacturer, but its health depends critically on the prospects of its customers, the world's long and medium distance airlines. The competition in this market must be assessed, and the prospects for a sustainable competitive advantage evaluated. Finally, the number of sales required to break-even must be calculated, and the likelihood of reaching and surpassing the "break-even" number quickly and easily must be determined.

We turned down the Huahine offer, but we considered a failing resort on Antigua worthy of investigation. The property is on an island with a large international airport, one of two in the eastern Caribbean capable of handling jumbo jets. The property has fifty acres, surrounded by national park. It is thirty minutes from the airport, but away from the flight paths. It has two beaches (one could be used for noisy, and one for quiet, activities). There is a nearby village of willing workers. The government was eager to improve tourism, had low levels of corruption, and there was good public safety. Finally, the island has historic ties to wealthy Americans and a reputation as a luxury resort destination. We already represented a dozen resorts on the island and had excellent relations with the serving airlines and the locals. We chose the new concept of an "all-inclusive" to remove the fear of uncontrolled expenses that deter many travelers, and were, for a time, the only "all-inclusive" on the island. To break-even financially, we needed 46 rooms, 90% occupancy at peak season (Dec-Mar) and 75% occupancy in the spring, and 50% occupancy in the summer. As the dominant resort marketing company in the Caribbean, these were reasonable goals, if we could remodel and expand the resort. Our team had managed six resorts in the past, and had the experience to do it again. Can you see the fit and the competitive edge ?

The next stage is **prototype development**. We are asking, can we make it with consistent quality ? Unlike 1945, when US manufacturers faced a world of flattened combatants, inefficient colonials, and backward societies, *international competition requires consistent quality*. Our customers have many choices. And our innovations will be quickly duplicated by others. Proper development will require the coordination of marketing (they should know what the customer wants and values) and engineering (they will design the production process). A balance must be struck between the flexibility that the marketing team would like (and the inclination of engineers to obsess on developing new applications) and the need for scale economies associated with standardization.

Having built the product, or programed the service, we must assure consistent quality through "stress" tests. Even in the resort business, where we would shut down for hurricane season (September) and rehire for the new year, we would have a "soft opening" in October to train and debug operations, before the peak season began at Christmas.

The product must appeal to the target buyers who demonstrate the willingness to pay, and the customer and product must be safe and secure in storage and use. When customers are paying for quality, there can be no disappointments and no excuses.

A local friend developed a major innovation in "traction" devices. In the past, these devices sensed the wheel that was slipping and reduced the transmission to that wheel, in order to reduce spinning and skidding. His new device sensed which wheels had the best traction and directed more power to those wheels. The device was tested on major race tracks by each of the dominant international auto companies for several years, before it was installed in their cars (with distinctive names in each case to tout the innovation).

Having done the analysis, developed and tested the product, we are ready to produce and sell ("commercialization"). We introduce the product in our highest priority markets first. Obviously, these will be the markets with the most potential for profit in terms of differences between selling price and costs, as well as volume. There may be some needs for product modification for local markets, as revealed by our investigation of local culture, especially aesthetics, material culture, and economics. Industrial and commercial products must be compatible with local infrastructure, but otherwise will be sold on the basis of quality and experience.

Consumer products are more likely to require adjustment. Price may be too high or low, depending on income, expectations, and competition. Features may be too complex for local users, or too expensive to provide given local competition and expectations. For example, merchants in areas with unreliable power may prefer mechanical cash registers to electronic ones. Africans require sturdy bicycles with puncture resistant tires for their poor roads.

Cultural Factors, such as customary uses, tastes, and aesthetics, are important. The French buy fresh bread and vegetables daily, and so they prefer small refrigerators. Americans shop less often and prefer large, "double-doors." Southeast Asians prefer exotic fruits for their sodas, such as Tamarind. Tropical regions prefer more sugar in their drinks, than those do in northern climes. Europeans and Americans prefer cosmetics that imitate the glow of a tan, showing both health and leisure. Asians prefer a pale look. For them, tan is associated with the field work of peasants. Convenience and comfort may matter. The Germans prefer firm car seats, and the French prefer soft. Americans want legroom, and fast heaters and air conditioners for their cars.

Products may need to be adapted to accommodate local laws, such as environmental and safety requirements. Provisions must be made for selecting the appropriate languages for the promotional message and for assembly, use, and service instructions. Be very careful to check and recheck translations to avoid confusion and embarrassment. We would have one translator prepare the new message and another check it by translating back in to English. If the return wording made sense, then we were confident in the initial effort.

No product lasts forever. New products are developed that meet the needs of customers better than the existing products, and we must be prepared for this threat. Each product has a "life cycle." We introduce the product with little knowledge of whether the customer will accept the product, what will be the price, or what will be our operating costs. If accepted, we refine both price and costs, as sales grow with customer experience. Once, most potential customers have the product, sales growth slows, and new sales depend on replacements and new markets. Imitations by competitors may be a problem, too. One strategy is to introduce new products, before the existing products fade away. This is particularly important to pharmaceuticals whose most profitable drugs will inevitably "go off patent."

We can extend the life of the product by finding new uses, or new customers. Mazda introduced the Miata as a British style, convertible roadster (small, light, small engine, soft ride), for middle aged American males who wanted some fun, but could not afford a Porsche, or any other high performance sports car. After ten good years, Mazda modified the car to appeal to young, professional women --- pastel colors, automatic transmission, stylish, luxury interior.

As we develop the product, we should also be thinking about **pricing** and **distribution**. Pricing objectives can appear contradictory. As with most decisions, we must remember that we have choices, and what we have done in the past, even in similar situations, may not be best. Net Profit will depend on sales volume as well as price, because volume influences costs, and profit is the difference between total revenue and total costs. Higher prices reduce volume and costs, but revenue may fall even faster. If we are seeking market penetration (market share and sales volume), or if we wish to deter competition, or advance social goals, a low price may be best. However, to promote an image of quality, or exclusivity, as well as a high return on investment, a high price relative to the competition and past customer experience may be best. I have always preferred to price 10-15% under my competition initially to achieve rapid sales growth and customer awareness, after which our price can be adjusted upward.

There are many factors which will influence pricing. Different tastes will lead to different prices. For turkey, Europeans prefer dark meat and Americans light. So, the prices will be reversed. We call these "adjustments for market diversity." Perceived quality will influence the willingness to pay premium prices. Mercedes Benz in Japan would surprise no one, but what about Woolworth's in Eastern Europe, where they remember a luxury department store from the inter-war years ! Attitudes toward consumer debt financing may be important. When customers are willing to pay in installments, they will be able to pay more for the goods that they prefer. Government controls, such as price ceilings and floors may be influential. Sometimes, you may benefit, if price ceilings for your parts and materials reduce your costs. Other times, you suffer, as when price floors raise your costs. (For example, dairy and sugar price supports in the United States hammered ice cream and candy manufacturers.) Of course, those same arrangements can destroy your profitability as Argentine soy farmers discovered, when their government limited prices, propped up the Peso foreign exchange rate, and imposed new export and profit taxes.

A special area of concern and risk occurs, when the foreign exchange value of your currency fluctuates. When your currency declines, you may be able to increase the profitability of your foreign sales, as well as your market share. It's a good time to reduce your local price, and build customer and distributor loyalty. Then, when your currency rises and foreign sales are no longer as profitable, the inevitable need to raise your foreign price may not be as damaging.

Another influence on price is the **distribution chain**. Each party that handles your product needs a mark-up. And each mark-up raises the price for the final consumer, without raising revenue for you. Make sure that the mark-up for each chain member reflects their contribution to value. Shorten the chain, where you can efficiently consolidate functions. And try to position your firm as the **channel leader**, meaning the one upon whom everyone else depends. Systems analysis of the production and distribution process from raw materials to customer satisfaction will help you to identify the critical steps. The channel leader has leverage on everyone else and can dictate terms. Finally, local sourcing may reduce costs and protect you from currency fluctuations.

We must consider cost, volume, and pricing to determine the quantity that must be sold in order to break-even. We balance high prices against low sales, and low prices against high sales, to determine the best strategy. Quantity of sales requirements must be realistic. As you develop your pricing strategy, clear understanding of **Break-even Revenues** and **Quantities** is vital. Divide your costs into "fixed" (overhead) and "variable" (changing with volume). Because breakeven occurs, where revenue equals total costs,

Price times Quantity = Fixed Costs plus {Variable Cost per unit times Quantity}
So, the formula for **the Operating Breakeven Point is:**

Break-even Quantity equals Fixed Costs / (Price - Variable Costs per unit)
Thus, high fixed costs will require more sales to break-even. So will a low price or high variable costs. All three must be weighed in our decision of price and operating leverage strategy. An example may help:

Years ago, we had a great opportunity to match surplus air space and resort rooms into an affordable travel package for one week in Tahiti. American Hawaii Cruises offered us space on their Boeing 747 air charters at $400 per person round-trip but with a required guarantee of 100 passengers a week ($40,000) after thirty days to ramp up. We arranged for rooms at resorts at three levels ($10 p/p/d budget; $20 p/p/d moderate; $30 p/p/d luxury). Additional variable costs included $10 p/p for a greeter in Pape'ete, and FedEx posting of tickets $4.50. So, our variable costs per passenger for the seven day/night budget package were initially **$484.50.**

Our fixed costs (overhead) included direct mail to travel agents once every six weeks, cost $6,000; newspaper advertisements on Thursday and Sunday at $600 each; office occupancy and incoming telephone service $1,100 per month; and reservations operators (@$10 hour) $4,800 per month; and a supervisor $2,500 per month. So, Fixed Costs per month were **$17,200.**

Our problem was to decide what price to charge. We considered pricing objectives: fast sales growth (market penetration), customer expectations, customer incomes, market density (potential volumes), competitors' prices, cash-flow, and profitability.

We needed to encourage early sales to gain the confidence of travelers and travel agents, so we could achieve 100 passengers per week within thirty days. Southern California has a large population that would love to go to Tahiti, but had been discouraged by high prices. Our competition was charging $1,399 for roundtrip air alone, and retail hotel rooms are ($100, $200, & $300) per night. So, we had a great opportunity to offer huge savings and gain rapid support from travel agents. We chose prices of $589 (budget), $689 (moderate), and $789 (luxury). Applying our formula:

Fixed Costs / (Price – variable cost per unit) = break-even Quantity

$17,200 / ($589 - $484.50) = 165 passengers for the first month

What happens in thirty days when we must pay a minimum of $40,000 per WEEK ?

Fixed Costs $173,333 for the air guarantee plus $17,200 per month.

Gross Profit Margin (for first 100 passengers) is $504.50

Break-even Quantity = FC/ GPM = $190, 533 / 504.50 = 378 passengers per month.

Or (378 x 12) /52 = eighty-seven per week.

Can we hit 87 passengers a week within a month ? If not, we may need a higher price, but risk slower acceleration of sales. You will be glad to know that

1) We sent our first passenger three days after signing the contract.

2) We sent exactly 100 passengers in the first week after 30 days.

3) Soon, we were sending 200 passengers a week and we raised our prices in stages to $888 Budget, $1088 Moderate, and $1288 luxury.

4) We continued to send more than 200 passengers a week through the summer and fall, making more than $80,000 profit each week.

5) We ended the program when our competitors (UTA, Air France, and Continental Airlines) lowered their prices and eroded our profit margins.

The important lesson to learn is that we have some flexibility in designing our operations to choose between fixed and variable costs. Initially, we like to keep our breakeven low, and so we choose low overhead. Later, when we are confident of our likely sales volume, we can bring in more activities, substituting more fixed for less variable costs. Select a price which is yields a realistic break-even sales quantity, so you can reduce the time and volume of money that is "burned" before the project becomes self-sustaining. A restaurant with large sunk costs for facilities, and large overhead of rent and staff, must charge high prices and generate substantial volume to break-even. Is that realistic ? We see so many Mexican restaurants, because their food costs are typically < 17% of their ticket price. This leaves 83% to cover overhead, which is also low, because diners do not expect fancy facilities, and qualified staff are abundant. 3-5 star French cuisine is at the opposite end of the organizational spectrum.

Distribution has two elements. First, we must consider who will handle the product and what tasks will they perform to add value. Second, we must move the product physically from processing location to the place where the final consumer expects to obtain it. This is the **logistics** issue.

A typical distribution system may involve manufacturing inside the country near suppliers. Then, the product is delivered to wholesalers &/or retailers, or sold directly to customer via Internet, or direct mail solicitation. If we manufacture outside the country, then initial contact with an import agent, or broker may be desirable. The agent (or broker) represents us and takes orders which we fulfill. The wholesaler receives shipments, and delivers them to retailers who display and sell to final customers. General line retailers will carry a variety related products. Department stores and home improvement stores would be examples. Specialty retailers are focused more narrowly and require a dense market of potential customers and sales. A toy store, or designer salon, would be examples. Critical factors in the selection of a distribution system include: 1) market density --- the number of customers and potential sales volume within reach of your location. Low density suggests use agents and wholesalers; high density suggests use specialty retailers and company owned stores, and 2) decisions regarding how we will provide necessary customer services, such as credit financing, warehousing and show room facilities, training, processing returns, and after sales service.

Often, the first distributor to seek to carry your product is not the best. He may need you more than you need him, and he may not be able to deliver on his promises. We begin by locating possible distributors through industry contacts, trade associations, such as chambers of commerce, often with the assistance of commercial attaches from the embassies, or through large service firms, such as international banks, insurance, and accounting firms. We compare the possible partners. First, they must be financially strong, to be sure that they can meet their obligations and participate in seizing opportunities. We find out from bank references and public reports. Second, we inquire as to the marketing services that the distributor is capable of performing --- packaging and repackaging, warehousing and shipping, training the local sales force, preparing information on assembly and use, and providing convenience to customers. Preparation service before the sale, and maintenance service after the sale, may be important. Finally, local knowledge and connections fill a gap in our knowledge, and lower risks and delays. In all areas, promises are easily made, but ability to execute must be confirmed. If all of these criteria are met, then we consider how strong is the distributor's need for our product and therefore, how much effort will he make to promote our product and what performance commitments will he guarantee ? If he has complementary lines, but no competing lines, he may need us a lot. For example, he sells shoes but has no sneakers, or he has small trucks, but no vans, then our sneakers or vans complete his product mix, and he will want our business and push our sales. If he has other sneakers or vans, he may sit on our distribution, while he pushes his existing lines.

You must consider the importance of developing a strong service organization. Determine the product/service balance, meaning providing the right amount of service. Is service, before, during, or after the sale an important selling point ? Is the customer willing to pay for it ? In your distribution chain, who will accept responsibility for the service component, and can they deliver ? Remember materials handling and storage !

Having entered into an agreement with a distributor, we want to support and encourage him to move our product. We may contribute market research and sales forecasts, and prepare and share the costs of co-operative promotions. Taking responsibility for returns can be important in reducing the risks of the distributor and thus winning his commitment to us. Sales incentives should be tied to results rather than preceding performance. And exclusive marketing arrangements in geographic territories should be avoided, unless tied to specific sales targets and subject to cancellation. Promises of expanding territories, after goals have been reached, may be good incentives.

Having preliminary agreements for distribution, we must plan **transportation**. Again, careful enumeration of the process must be made. How does the product move from raw materials → to storage → to manufacturing plant → to warehouse → to retailer → to customer. There are three important qualities to any method of logistics. They cluster in 1) "time to door" --- scheduling dependability, shipping frequency, and speed, 2) "predictability" --- accessibility, ease of handling, and security, and 3) cost and regulations vs. needs and perishability. Without the other two, cost is irrelevant --- it will be too high ! We like containers that are secure (sealed), and shift-able between transport modes such as trucks and trains, and trackable.

There are many transport modes. We like water, such as ocean, river, and canal shipping. It's flexible and cheap. We can use containers, roll-on-roll-off, and LASH barges. It's traditional, for large strong products (autos), but the availability of port services matters. We must check the compatibility of piers, cranes, and warehouses. Air shipping is flexible, but expensive. If we use air, it's best to negotiate "space available" terms to trim costs. Pipelines are dependable and frequent, but have limited reach and may have handling problems. We are all familiar with roads (highways). They are versatile and accessible, but may be undependable and costly, because of small capacities and poor security. Trucks also require loading and unloading, adding to our risks of damage or theft. In many areas, railroads are accessible and offer good handling, but they may be unreliable, and usually are slow. Careful planning and scheduling can reduce transportation costs enormously.

As we plan transportation, we must consider **materials handling**. **Packaging** is an important element of product planning. Packaging protects the product and may improve display, but it adds to bulk and weight. Poor packaging can raise costs through damage and waste. Intermodal containers can reduce such losses. We have mentioned the compatibility of **handling equipment**, such as pumps, pipelines, cranes, barges, and trucks.

I remember a friend who was selling polyethylene feeder stocks to China. In most markets, this would be shipped by pipeline and bulk tanker, but China was still using 55 gallon drums and pallets --- what a nightmare !

We need to be concerned about **storage** facilities. What is the availability, configuration, and security of the warehouses at each stage of the product's journey ? These are necessary for for temporary storage, including breakdown, or consolidation (assembly), and for processing --- value added, before sale or shipment. **Foreign trade zones** can be helpful in this regard, offering a convenient location for storage or processing, close to the final destination, and in some cases, they give us "made in" status.

I remember a friend who was mining gold in remote Guinea. When civil war in Liberia spilled over and threatened his operations, he withdrew his equipment to the capital (Conakry,

Guinea) to wait out the problem. When he returned a year later, all of his equipment had been stolen and sold to a competing company. Don't take the security of your facilities for granted !

After all that planning of product, distribution, and logistics, we are finally ready for **promotion**. Premature promotion can be disastrous, destroying any hope of trust with distributors or customers. But once, we are confident that we can deliver the product as promised, we must stimulate demand by raising awareness and persuasion.

Public relations are the foundation of any promotion program. Our activities must be designed to align with the values of all "stakeholders" (those who can influence our success, or who will be impacted by our activities).Thus, PR must begin in the first phase of project evaluation and continue through every subsequent strategic consideration. A common definition (which I learned from my friend, Jam'y Brown) is *Public Relations identifies, establishes, and maintains mutually beneficial relationships between the organization and the various publics on whom its success or failure depends.* So, the public relations function requires *anticipating, analyzing, and interpreting public opinion, attitudes and issues which might impact the organization and counselling management with regard to policy decisions, considering their public ramifications and the organization's social responsibilities.* Finally, PR requires identifying and evaluating the programs of action that will 1) understand "stakeholder" goals and values, 2) associate our activities with those goals and values, and thus, 3) create a positive image and association for our firm and its programs. To do so, we must develop and maintain respectful relationships with all constituencies, even those which we are not disposed to like. They include governments and non-governmental agencies, labor unions, educational institutions, charities, community and neighborhood associations, and even social clubs.

In 2008, Tata Motors made a terrible blunder in planning an auto plant in Bengal, exclusively through the local and regional governments. Tata assumed that the locals whom it planned to hire for good jobs, would back the plant and only the onerous task of obtaining official permits (hard enough in India) was needed. Tata persuaded the local government to seize land for the plant by eminent domain. The farmers revolted out of fear of losing their land and their livelihood. They were unaware of the opportunities that they might enjoy. Tata pulled out, and everyone lost.

The second element of promotion is **publicity**. The media needs stories that will appeal its target audiences, and journalism is expensive. When you distribute a stream of press releases that will meet the media's need for stories, you will receive free and credible advertising. We would issue stories of 50/75/100 words about our company, our products, and our public service, every week. In addition, when we placed paid advertising, we would negotiate a few articles about some program that we wanted to tout, and we would provide both the written copy and the photos. Readers assume that these articles are written by disinterested journalists and give them more attention and credence than the paid advertisements, nearby.

The next two elements of promotion are **personal selling** and **advertising**. These are expensive and must be very carefully considered. Media representatives hound us to advertise with them, but can they reach our target customers with the right message that leads to sales ? So, we must select our message and our media very carefully.

We ask who is our most likely customer and what value is that customer seeking ? We review all the ways that we add value (in the jargon, "the value package"). Knowing in what ways the customer is dissatisfied by his current product and buying experience, is valuable. For example, the customer may be influenced by atmospherics, image, brand name, service, price, package, or speed of delivery. Other factors are the buyer's past experience, the reputation of producer, and the warrantees or guarantees. We need to consider the aspects of distribution that add value (the "distribution utilities") such as form (size and package), information (on assembly, use, and service), location of acquisition (delivery method), possession method (cash, credit, title transfer), and time (when is the product available ?). When we understand what is important to our customer and where we have an advantage, those become our selling points to be emphasized in our promotional materials, whether advertising or personal selling.

We may be able to use the same approach in many markets, for example when selling products with standard uses of commercial and industrial products where performance is the dominant issue. However, when the product is used in a variety of ways, it may need to be modified or the sales message modified. Do customers prefer top-loading or front-loading washing machines ? Firm or soft car seats ? Large or small refrigerators ?

Personal selling is the most important promotional technique. In many businesses, personal selling consumes 50% of the promotional budget, --- as much as than PR, publicity, and advertising combined. Personal selling is the direct contact of customer with sales representative. It occurs in stores, by telephone, and over the internet. Your staff must understand the selling process, including those who do not participate directly. First, everyone must understand your product, its specifications, its features, its functions, its advantages and disadvantages, and the variety available to your customer. Similar knowledge of the competing products is very helpful, too. So, train your staff !

The first step in selling is "prospecting." Who is likely to buy my product and how do I contact them ? I need to know *who makes the decision to buy ?* In the resort business, we know that the wife decides where the family will vacation. We need to reach and persuade her. Once, we are prepared with product and prospect knowledge, we choose our method of approach. If we are using telemarketing, do my prospects have telephones ? If the we use the internet, how do my customer use their IT devices ? As in so many other areas of life, the best approach to the prospect is to indicate the intent to help them. Asking what they are seeking is a good beginning. Then, we select several products to demonstrate. Customers need three from which to choose in order to feel that they are responsible shoppers. Describe the product and its features. Do not state the obvious (this car is red and has cup holders). Share the "inside knowledge" that makes the customer feel special. Also, do not assume that what you recently learned in training is new knowledge to the customer. Some effort to learn about the customer's prior experience and product knowledge will pay dividends in creating a trusting relationship. The customer will have some questions and even objections; candid answers will be rewarded. Don't let your staff mislead the customer or devalue his issues. Consider them fairly and help the customer weight costs and benefits. One solution is to bring out more choices, with special attention to removing the objections to the first group. As the customer demonstrates satisfaction with a particular product, the salesman must "close the deal." A positive attitude (Great, shall I wrap it up ? Where would you like it delivered ? How would you like to pay ?) will help prompt the purchase. And don't forget to follow up. We like to believe that we make wise decisions. We are prone to become attached to what we possess. So, a card, email, or phone call to acknowledge the customer and offer further assistance helps to consolidate the relationship and generate referrals and repeat business. I prefer the post-card or an email. They are unobtrusive, but demonstrate continued interest in the customer.

I am not an enthusiast for **advertising**. It's a non-personal and expensive approach. So, we must plan advertising with great care. First, advertising must be aimed at a target. Who is our likely customer ? If a business, family, or group will purchase the product, who makes the decision ? How is the product used ? If we understand these issues, we can consider which media and what message will be most effective.

As we consider the message, effective advertising must 1) target the likely buyer, 2) grab their attention, 3) inform them of the need that the product satisfies, 4) explain how the product meets those needs, and 5) tell them how to take action: price, place, and possession.

Having worked as a financial manager for a large marketing company, I have observed a number of ghastly mistakes. My favorite story is about the "Secret" deodorant campaign in Japan that used a cartoon image of an octopus applying deodorant under one of its eight arms. Too late, the advertising team learned that in the Japanese language, Octopus have eight legs, not eight arms. Can you see why that would be a problem ? In another case, a colleague of mine wanted to produce a TV ad for Tahiti travel that shows beautiful people, especially Polynesian girls, enjoying a cocktail party with a babble of French chatter and Polynesian music. What American woman would find that scene inviting ? Instead, we produced an ad showing a romantic couple walking away on an isolated beach, a nice buffet, and a lovely cottage (twin beds). The message was: put yourself in this picture --- peace, romance, no cooking, and restful private accommodations.

Don't forget to associate your product with the need and inform the customer of the required action. Several times, I had to fire an associate who omitted the price of the product, or the address of our location, or the telephone number by which we could be reached. I also fired salesmen who failed to answer the phone. That's equivalent to the customer announcing, (as I have done !) "I'm here, I have money, I want to buy, will anyone help me ?" only to be ignored by the sales staff.

Choosing the best media is also important. Just as the message doesn't need to be "creative," just successful in generating sales, the media should not be chosen for being "cool" or "leading edge." It should be effective. Radio is great for creating awareness, and for reminder advertising. It's cheap and your message can be repeated often. Of course, you must be sure that your target will be listening. Newspapers have limited life and sweep. Who reads this newspaper and how many will see each copy ? Magazines have the advantage that they can be chosen to target to only those buyers with specific interests, and they have a longer life. We published convention guides and magazines for airlines, and for professional offices, such as doctors, dentists, and attorneys. These magazines have long lives and multiple readers, who are almost captives, as they wait for their appointment or flight. I'm not keen on television. It gives too broad a sweep. It is expensive, because we pay to reach many people who will have no interest in our product. Fortunately, the variety of cable specialties improves our ability to choose the shows and stations that appeal to our most likely customer. I do like Billboards. They provide visibility in high traffic areas and are especially effective for promotion of local products or vendors. Of course, today, everyone is excited to exploit the Internet. It is important to recognize that this is just another tool. Remember that the principles remain the same, even though the tools may change. For the Internet, we must ask: How do we get our customers to our site ? How do we communicate with them ? This is a form of personal selling, but the usual tasks of the salesman are being performed by computer programs. Because this puts so much burden on the shopper, internet selling must be "user friendly" (Idiot proof ?).The best strategy is to integrate all promotional activity, so that PR, publicity, personal selling, and advertising present uniform messages, and direct the customer to the easiest method of acquiring information and completing the transaction. Have you ever given up on an intended purchase, because the salesman was inconsiderate, or the web-site difficult to navigate ? These are unforgiveable blunders by the company.

Questions for reflection, review, and tests:
Explain the essential characteristics of each of the four methods of promotion: public relations, publicity, personal selling, and advertising.
Explain the importance of product development and engineering.
What factors influence the need to modify products for new markets ?
Identify three factors that must be considered in pricing domestic and international sales.
Identify the five criteria for selecting a local distributor, and five methods of support for your local distributor.
Explain the issues of materials management, with special attention to transportation.

Restaurante Sobrino de Botin, Madrid, Spain. founded in 1725

Lecture #1.6 Production Management and Strategic Alliances

Production is the creation of finished goods and services using resources (sometimes called "factors of production") --- natural resources such as land, and their improvements (physical capital), and human resources (labor, entrepreneurship, & information). The production process transforms the resources, adding value.

Efficiency is achieving greater value from similar, less valuable, or fewer resources. The Industrial Revolution (1750-1860) improved efficiency by increasing the use of inanimate sources of energy, such as water, wind, steam, and electric power, to replace human and animal power. Major early contributors were mechanization and standardization, pioneered in manufacturing by Eli Whitney's cotton gin and Colt's firearms, in transportation by Fulton's steamboat and Trevithick's steam locomotive, and in mass production by Ford's automobile assembly-line. The second production revolution was the application of these principles to the organization of labor (1900-1960), such as Frederick Taylor's scientific management (1911). Taylor applied scientific method (theory and observation) to management. This led to "time/motion" studies and later to automation, the organization of production with minimum human intervention. Workers think, plan, organize, and adjust the machines. The third phase, identified and named by Peter Drucker "The Knowledge Revolution", dates from the space race (1960), and continues today. The major differences are that during the industrial revolution work was centralized near to the sources of cheap power. Factories ceased to be mere warehouses and became the sites of processing. During the scientific management revolution, processes were "fine-tuned" to reduce waste and increase the speed of activities. However, in both cases, the design of new processes was achieved by using new ways of employing existing resources, to improve the quality of products, the speed of completion, and the reduction in costs. The Knowledge Revolution starts with the question "What would be the characteristics of the ideal product and the ideal materials ?" Then, the new materials are engineered that have these qualities, although they may not exist in a state of nature.

The production process starts with combination of method (production technology) which defines the design of the process. We talk of "systems analysis" which is just identifying the end result (customer satisfaction) and the beginning (raw materials), and the steps from the beginning to the end. So, we ask: "What is required?" Three results:

1) build and deliver products, in response to the customer, at a scheduled delivery time
2) provide an acceptable quality level
3) provide everything at lowest cost

As we consider the manufacturing processes, we realize that each transformation is either "synthetic" which change or combine materials, such as an assembly process which puts together components, or "analytic" which breaks down materials, such as petroleum refining. We may further distinguish processes that are "continuous" (the assembly line) or "intermittent" such as real estate construction.

In any case, production control has five elements. 1) **Planning** requires a "bill of materials" which identifies all the resources required to manufacture the product, including parts and materials, equipment, and workers. This bill of materials must be checked against inventory, and the missing materials ordered and received to be available as, when, and where they are needed, so that production will not be interrupted. 2) **Routing** lays out the sequence of operations and the path of progress. 3) Then, we identify the **Lay-out** for each stage. We think of three lay-out variations, any or all of which may be used at the various stages of production.

The **process lay-out** places production tasks at discrete locations containing specialized equipment. For example, repainting your car would involve removing old paint (often by sandblasting) at one location, filling and sanding at another, and priming and painting in a "clean room". By separating the activities, we avoid dust that would spoil the smooth final coats that are so important. The second method is the **assembly-line** lay-out. In this case, the flow of work proceeds along a line of stations, sub-assemblies feed in, and the flow is continuous. The product moves through the various stations, until it emerges complete. Think of the automobile beginning as a frame to which are added wheels, engine, transmission, floor, interior, and exterior. The third method is the **fixed position** lay-out, in which the product stays in one place, and the work is brought to it. This would be most common in hard to move products. Ships are assembled in dry-docks, and homes are built on prepared sites. The sequence of homebuilding would be grading, "off-sites" (trenching for utilities), foundation, frame, roof and exterior walls (for protection from the elements), plumbing and electrical, interior walls and ceilings, floors, painting, and finally landscaping.

Walt Disney's innovation in entertainment at Disneyland was to take an activity which usually involves fixed position, (the audience sits and the entertainers come and go on stage), and replace it with an assembly-line (the audience moves from stage to stage, by boat, train, spaceship, or other variant, while the entertainers {often "animatronics"} stay in the same location repeating their "set pieces" for each group, as they pass by).

The next step of production management is **Scheduling**. During the analysis of the sequence of tasks that need to be done that led to the development of our bill of materials, routing, and lay-out, we will also estimate the time needed to do each task and identify the critical path, (the sequence which may not be violated, such as the foundation precedes the framing of a house, or installation of the engine precedes the attachment of fenders and hood). A GANTT chart is a bar chart showing the sequence of activities, the time required for each, and therefore, the dates at which each phase of production should occur. The **Critical Path** focuses on sequence of most difficult processes, taking the longest times, and upon whose completion the next step must wait. Other activities are planned around them. For example, we have already remarked on the stages of home construction. Less critical activities might be the construction of perimeter walls, or ancillary buildings. Because they can be done anytime without disrupting the most important activities, workers and materials can be shunted to and from them, as they are available, to avoid the cost of idle resources.

There are a number of new refinements to these techniques, with common acronyms. We have already described GANTT, or Critical Path scheduling. A variation is PERT (program evaluation and review technique) which uses statistical probabilities drawn from experience to refine the time requirements of each step. For small samples and businesses, PERT would not be useful, because the statistics would be scarce and expensive to measure. Finally, we usually add a few "slack" days along the way, so that the inevitable disruptions can be accommodated without destroying the entire schedule.

Further refinements are MRP systems. This acronym stands for Materials Requirement Planning. It uses computer based spreadsheets to integrate the sales forecasts and inventory data to re-order parts, assure timely delivery, schedule operations, and shipping. MRP2 is Manufacturing Resource Planning, an advanced version of MRP that includes personnel, plant capacity, and distribution constraints. The next phase is ERP, or Enterprise Resource Planning, which connects multiple firms into one integrated production unit. The ERP system monitors progress at all linked firms simultaneously.

To understand how these systems work, consider first the delivery date for the customer. Then, work back from that date to identify when each stage must be completed, and therefore, when that stage must be begun. As the schedule of production is being laid out, so is the need for materials, various skilled laborers, and the availability of the equipment for each activity. A nicely designed computer spreadsheet can quickly translate an order for our product into a schedule of activities, check of inventory available against the bill of materials, place orders for missing materials with suppliers, including required delivery dates, and finally, identify bottlenecks when materials, labor, or equipment will not be available as needed.

Once all these interdependent elements are resolved, **work orders** can be dispatched and distributed to supervisors for final checks and action.

The fifth and final stage of production is **follow-up and control**. The importance of anticipating and handling delays cannot be exaggerated. To assure quality, parts, sub-assemblies, and final products must be tested at each stage to avoid the costs of trouble-shooting at the very end which would require much more difficult and expensive deconstruction.

We use a check list to assure that we can meet our goals, so that 1) Our sales forecast gives us an estimate of the capacity required, from which we can check 2) our raw materials inventory, against the bill of materials for our expected sales, and 3) our installed equipment against the needs for our production volume, and 4) similarly, our manpower (numbers, skills, and availability), and finally, 5) our quality standards and testing results.

There are a variety of techniques which we use to reduce "time to market" --- from concept to product to production and delivery.

1) **Computer-Aided Design and Manufacturing** uses the creation and storage of designs on a computer system which makes modifications of existing designs fast and easy. The design to suit customers is matched to the production process which must make it. Production managers prefer simple and standard, while salesmen like offer exactly what the customer desires (mass customization). These preferences need to be reconciled.

2) **Simultaneous engineering** means designing the product and engineering the process to make it. This speeds accommodation of both needs.

3) **Flexible manufacturing** uses programmable machines (robots) to do several tasks, so they can produce a variety of similar products, further facilitating the integration of design and production.

4) **Lean manufacturing** means production using fewer resources (parts and materials, machinery and equipment, space and time, management supervision, and labor). This can be achieved through continuous modification or re-design of product and/or process. Robots can be used for repetitive and standard procedures. Labor can be trained for a variety of tasks.

5) **Just-In-Time inventory** control contributes to lean manufacturing and reduces inventory costs. The concept is for suppliers deliver parts to the assembly location only as needed. This is accomplished by 1) the manufacturer sets a production schedule 2) the supplier is linked to the manufacturer with an MRP or ERP system, and so immediately knows the order and required delivery date and time for his parts. So, the supplier can schedule his production and delivery, and 3) quality requirements are specified in the contracts with suppliers, including incentives and penalties. When manufacturers are able to accept many deliveries daily, they can maintain small inventories. Package delivery companies, such as FedEx and UPS, have reinvented their mission from "delivery" to "logistics" and "supply

chain management." Sometimes, they will even contract to provide after sales service, such as repairs, to add value.

6) The concept of **Total Quality** is applied to production management. The goal is to provide the customer with satisfaction at the instant that he becomes aware of a need. Quality control uses measuring products against standards. Total quality is achieved by attention to each component and step. First, we identify what is important to the customer. Then, we set standards and incorporate them into contracts with suppliers and even our own operating groups with incentives. Third, we test at each level in order to spot and correct problems, quickly and inexpensively.

7) A review of **Edwards Deming**'s principles is worthwhile. As Drucker is the father of modern management, Deming is the father of quality control. Although his system was developed in war-time production and relies heavily on statistical evaluation, many of his principles are about the importance of leadership: 1) Maintain constancy of purpose. Hewlett-Packard was an enviable company, while the principals lived and the company's culture emphasized quality engineering. Its descent was rapid when Carly Fiorina changed direction to focus on sales growth. 2) Adopt a new philosophy --- leadership. Your job is to make your team members effective. 3) Cease dependence on inspection to achieve quality. Quality comes from the commitment and attention to detail of your people. 4) Minimize total cost through supplier relationships. 5) Improve constantly to reduce costs. Small incremental savings build up; so does progressive degradation. 6) Institute training on the job; implement education and self-improvement programs. 7) Drive out fear. Intimidation alienates and demoralizes. 8) Break down barriers between departments. Teach and reward teamwork. 9) Eliminate slogans and targets. They create adversaries. 10) Eliminate work standards and "management by objective". Substitute leadership. 11) Eliminate barriers to pride in work. Emphasize quality over quantity.

8) Deming also lists obstacles to quality. Among them are: 1) Emphasis on short-term profits and shifting priorities. 2) Mobility of management who move on before their results are apparent. 3) Relying on visible figures only, while ignoring qualitative measures such as employee development, stability, and morale, public relations, and supplier relationships. 4) Neglecting long-range planning. 5) Relying on technology to solve problems. 6) Seeking examples to follow rather than developing solutions. And my favorite, 7) Making excuses.

9) There seems to be popular confusion about the choice of production locations. The central motivation is to keep costs low. But wages and benefits are only one set of costs, and may not be the most important. Other considerations include available skills of workers, local labor market organization, quality of life for key employees, the availability and quality of suppliers (including R&D), proximity to customers and/or materials, cost of land, laws and regulations (including land use regulation and environmental reviews), taxes, government support or resistance. Fortunately, information technology permits greater dispersion of activities, and costing a group or portfolio of products together can help.

An important decision is: which processes to do yourself and which to "outsource" to suppliers or distributors. Being able to focus on the most profitable activities, the activities that take advantage of our abilities, and those that are critical to the supply chain, and therefore give us control are great. However, we can't rely on weak partners.

We weigh the advantages of doing it ourselves (*Make*) --- sometimes lower costs if we achieve large volume, protection of proprietary technology, justification for specialized investments, and improved scheduling, vs. the advantages of outsourcing (*Buy*) --- strategic flexibility to switch suppliers and vary costs, focus, international offsets (local content requirements). ERP (Enterprise Resource Planning) systems reduce the advantages of "Make" over "Buy." Later in this lesson, we go over the important qualifications for selecting an alliance partner.

We are most interested in a triad, --- quality, reliability, & costs, --- in that order. To achieve all three may involve ownership, or equity stake, in suppliers. This can speed development and adaptation of the supplier's products to our changing needs. Our equity stake gives some say in product development, but must not lead us to compromise on our quality standards, a problem for some conglomerates. Often, independent sources are preferred for cost, reliability, and quality. They can be encouraged to seek additional customers who will share development costs, and raise production volume, thus lowering costs to us. This is common among the OEMs (original equipment manufacturers) of the international automobile industry. The supplier with other customers may increase innovation, and awareness of new methods and opportunities.

The best strategy is to diversify among reliable suppliers. Form a strong alliance with the best supplier in the area, but reserve 10-20% for back-up suppliers, to maintain leverage. Develop trust and respect with your suppliers, but monitor them closely, not only by testing parts on delivery, but also maintaining personal ties with key personnel. Communicate early, and often, with suppliers --- treat them as partners, while maintaining trade secrets.

If we choose strategic alliances, (co-operative agreements between potential and actual competitors, or suppliers), we can co-plan product development. We see this in the automobile and commercial aircraft industries, as well as computer hardware. However, these alliances come with strategic risk. We need to protect our proprietary technologies, especially if they are the primary source of our competitive advantage. So, we manage our dependence on key suppliers by encouraging our partners to make large, long-term investments. We may also choose to take equity positions in our partners, or form joint-ventures for specific programs. If our alliance is with a customer, then we develop products to match their anticipated needs. Various inventory and scheduling programs, such as JIT, ERP, CAD-CAM systems will facilitate co-ordination and lower costs for the group.

Among the advantages of alliances is access to technologies, including management expertise and market knowledge. By integrating our inventory systems, we can speed products to market ("time to market accelerators") and stabilize our sales, market share, and cash-flow. Alliances with local firms can facilitate our entry into new markets. We can share risks, match complementary skills and assets, and establish industry standards. Recall how Microsoft and IBM partnered to overtake Apple in the early years of PCs. Apple rejected alliances and declined rapidly, despite having superior products.

The major disadvantages of alliances are the risk of giving away technology, thus creating a competitor, and "hollowing out" production, when many tasks evolve to your ally and your own activities dwindle. One third to one-half of alliances fail. So, careful attention must be paid to making alliances work. There are three critical skills: alliance selection, structure, and management.

1) Partner Selection. The partner must have capabilities which the firm lacks. (Boeing will partner with Rolls Royce, or Pratt & Whitney, for engines.) Often, we divide

responsibilities for the key management functions: we may be good at R&D, finance, planning, and production; our partner, because of local knowledge, is good at personnel, marketing, and production.

2) The partner must share the vision of the alliance's purposes. (A friend's plan to build simple taxis in China using innovative, inexpensive methods failed, because his money partner kept insisting on making limousines for which the chassis would be inadequate. The plant manager was caught in the middle.)

3) To minimize the likelihood that the partner will exploit the alliance for its own ends, multiple relations and reputation can help. That is why so many companies choose the same ally for a number of projects, for example, petroleum concessions, exploration, and production.

We will often be approached by potential partners who have good ideas but may not be the best at execution. So, we must assess a partner's suitability. We collect information on potential allies by surveying third parties for their experience with candidates, and investing in getting to know potential partners in advance. Remember that they are trying to impress, so be thorough. Look for capabilities and results, not promises.

Having selected a capable partner with shared vision and complementary abilities, we structure the alliance to build a lasting relationship and protect our critical advantages. Unfortunately, in business, as in many personal relationships, we only are assured of our partner's attention, as long as they need us to achieve their own objectives. So, we elicit substantial resource commitments (so they can't walk away). We specify, in advance, performance expectations. We build in contractual safeguards, for example exclusion from traditional markets. And we "wall off" sensitive technologies, such as critical steps in R&D, production (supplier network), or marketing (customer lists, distribution, and promotion).

Once established, we must manage the alliance for continued value. We must build trust, personally and between organizations. And we should learn from our partners, and apply the lessons to our firm.

Ford and Mazda had a partnership for many years, in which Ford learned Mazda's product development and quality methods, and Mazda learned about global marketing. When Toyota recognized that it would need to manufacture in the U.S. to by-pass Voluntary Export Restrictions, Toyota choose a joint venture with General Motors in Fremont, California, called "NUMMI." When they had learned enough, Toyota went off on its own by opening a plant in Kentucky. (Tesla now owns the Fremont plant.)

Questions for review and tests:
List and explain the five steps in the production control process
        {Be sure to explain the appropriate management techniques at each stage.}
What are the advantages and disadvantages of out-sourcing ? {buying rather than making.}
What are time to market accelerators ? {Give and explain techniques}
What are the advantages and disadvantages of strategic alliances ?
How do you select a partner ?
How do you structure the alliance (initial agreements) ?
How to you manage the alliance (on-going activities) ?

Lumber mill in Oregon   Copper mine in Tsumeb, Namibia

 Ltjg Peter Naylor, USNR, on the USS McCaffery (DD860)
where I served twice with Cmdr Alan Martin who led by example.
He taught me the importance of preparation, attention to detail, and
respect for every member of the team.

Mike Towbes, Owner and Chairman of the Bank of Montecito, a very
disciplined and focused executive. Shown here with me, and with our
wives, Susette Naylor and Anne Towbes.

Lesson #1.7: Human Resource Management and Leadership

One of the most important, but often carelessly executed, management functions is Human Resources (personnel). Management is "the achievement of goals through people", as Peter Drucker stated. Drucker quoted an exchange with the executive who built General Motors, Alfred Sloan. When Drucker informed Sloan, "You know Mr. Sloan, you spend 65% of your time on personnel matters," Sloan pondered before responding, "You're right, Drucker. It's not enough." Thus, HR may be the most important task. But people are complex and difficult, so managers often avoid giving it the attention that it deserves and requires. What is involved ?

Organizational design is the structuring of workers to accomplish goals. We must balance needs for information, direction, coordination, and control, with needs for motivation, initiative, responsiveness, and flexibility. **Bureaucracy** is the structure for gathering information, setting policies, and monitoring performance. Key elements are 1) a chain of command --- each employee takes direction from a senior; each supervisor directs his subordinates, 2) policies, rules and regulations guide employees who understand that they must conform to their intent of the policies, 3) organization by management function, and 4) communication both vertical and horizontal (lack of information creates confusion and gives rise to rumors).

For most of us, the concept of bureaucracy connotes unresponsiveness. To improve performance, the French sociologist, **Henri Fayol**, suggested several principles of organization:

1) **Order**: Everything in its place. This will prevent ambiguity and confusion.
2) **Authority**: Managers can give orders and expect them to be carried out.
3) **Hierarchy of Authority**: Each reports to next level. Often, this is called "the chain of command." We are familiar with the unhappy employee who resists direction from his immediate supervisor and insists on bringing his issue to the supervisor's boss, or someone even further up the chain. While listening to the grievance can provide information, the boss who overrules his subordinate managers, undermines their authority, and rewards the complainant's insubordination. (While in the Navy and in private industry, I insisted that my peers and superiors never talk to my employees, except to greet them. All requests must come through me, so I could weigh priorities and avoid distractions to my staff. You might consider what passive-aggressive strategies you would use, when others disrupt your team.)
4) **Unity of command**: Each worker reports to one boss. Often, supervisors believe that they may issue directives to any and all employees, whether or not, they have direct reporting authority. I first saw this in this Navy, where senior officers would direct enlisted men to do a task without considering what those sailors were doing at the time. This interference demoralizes the employees who feel pulled in several directions and unable to complete one task before being giving another. The practice also undermines the authority of the direct supervisor, and disrupts to the priorities of the organization.
5) Closely related to these principles of unity and hierarchy is the requirement for clear **channels of communication**. Information and direction must flow quickly and accurately. The team must understand not only what to do, but why. Often the "why" is neglected, and this contributes to difficulty in the sub-ordination of individual interests to organizational goals.
6) **Equity**: When employees are not treated fairly, their motivation suffers. Neglect of employee relationships and worse, favoritism, is very destructive. Favoritism may take the form of special benefits for those that we like, or failure to reprimand poor performance. Weakness can be as destructive as arrogance. (I remember a manager with

drug and alcohol problems was paid 20% more than the best manager at his level {Vice President}, and he had much shorter service. Not surprisingly, the better Vice President moved on.) Employees are acutely aware of fairness; managers must be, too.

7) **Morale**: Pride and loyalty for organization is directly related to the coincidence of corporate culture and personal values, as well as the correlation of corporate success with the advancement of personal goals. Do not over-look the fact that your employees, however humble, share many of your person aspirations and should have opportunities to find fulfillment in their work.

Max Weber is famous for characterizing the layers of authority: senior executives who are decision and policy makers; middle managers who develop and implement rules & procedures for supporting the programs and policies; workers and their supervisors who carry out specific tasks. In the military, these would be the generals and admirals, the "line" officers, and the enlisted men, including non-coms.

Weber also highlighted the importance of **job descriptions** which state the responsibilities and expectations of each assignment. They are useful for recruitment and for planning (identifying the tasks to be done and the staffing levels required). Similarly, he pointed out the value of written rules, policy guidelines, detailed records, and consistent procedures and policies.

However, I believe that Weber's greatest contribution was the principle *that staffing and promotion should be solely based on qualifications and performance* (**merit**). This assures fairness, as well as achievement. Of course, in some cultures, social structure may challenge our desire to base assignments on ability. For example, in India supervision of a Brahmin by a Dalit would be unacceptable, and in Korea, supervision of men by a woman would be very difficult.

With these guidelines, we can consider the design of our organization. One issue is the **span of control** --- the breadth of responsibility of each manager. This assignment will depend on the capabilities of manager, the capabilities of sub-ordinates, the complexity of the jobs, the need for coordination and planning, and the geographic proximity. Current management information systems permit constant reporting of activities and regular generation of performance measuring reports. These facilitate broader spans of control, and therefore, flatter organizations.

There are a variety of organizational models from which to choose. The most traditional is the **Line** organization in which the employees who perform the tasks are supervised directly, and their supervisors report to managers who report to top executives. Each has the direct authority and responsibility to perform tasks or direct those who do. **Line and Staff** organizations include supporting activities such as Human Resources, Legal, Finance, and Accounting which, while critical to success, do not direct the activity of production or distribution. The military is organized in this way.

A newer form is **matrix** organization in which staff is assigned to two core responsibilities, such as pairings of department structure, regional group, product group, and/or a management function. This assures team representation in two hierarchies, as well as depth of skills. This should improve planning and coordination. However, it can violate the principle of unity and create conflicting loyalties and rivalries.

Departments exist to divide tasks into homogeneous groups. When department structures are well-designed, the firm benefits from centralization of resources (scale economies), the development of specialized expertise, and ease of direction and control. However, there are risks of employee identification with their department rather than the whole organization, lack of communication with other departments, and narrowing of skills. Departments may also become resistant to change.

Departments may be organized by product (e.g. autos; family sedan), function (e.g. marketing; finance), customer group (e.g. rental car companies), geography (e.g. regions), or process (e.g. assembly, painting, shipping). The best choice will depend on the importance of unity in performing the task. An important customer does not want to be contacted by a variety of your employees, and would prefer to have one contact at your company who can solve all his problems. A specialized manufacturing process should be unified for coordination and control. Similar customers can be approached in similar ways, but radically diverse customers will require different attention. And we must assure that each management function receives the attention that it requires and makes its contribution to the success of the group at every stage.

Having considered all variations of organizational design and selecting a structure which integrates each into a coordinated but responsive whole, we can address the tasks of **Human Resource Management**. The first step is to *assess our needs* from our strategic business plan. Knowing what we want for the future of the organization and the specific activities which we will undertake, as well as the goals for each, permits us to identify the jobs that must be done, the skills that are required, and the number of employees for each of the tasks.

For example, if we envision a soccer team, we know that we will need eleven to thirteen players, including one goalie, two defenders, five mid-fielders, three attack forwards, and two substitutes. Logically, this analysis leads to the design of **Job Descriptions** (the list of tasks which the employee in that position is expected to perform) and **Job Specifications** (the education, training, and experience which is required for the employee to succeed in those tasks). The descriptions must be accurate and can be refined by asking current occupants to explain exactly what they do. (A good time to ask is during their employee evaluation.) And the specifications must be accurate to balance the need for the skills that lead to success with inclusive recruitment and employee growth and satisfaction.

We compare our needs to our **human resource inventory**. The inventory is a list of employees by talents, experience, and interests. Many organizations fail to maintain an inventory and will hire to fill an opening with the best from a shallow pool, or worse with anybody available, in a panic to put a body on the job. Even worse, they may hire "the Lone Ranger," the applicant who persuades them that he can magically solve all their problems with his "silver bullet." A better strategy is to use regular evaluations to uncover talents and ambitions among your employees, and carefully file these for reference. Better still, when the employee expresses interest in a position, or reveals talents not yet used in his present assignment, we design a training and internship program that assures that he will be ready when that coveted opening occurs. The opportunity can be conditional upon continued excellence in his current assignment, and he may be given responsibility to identify and train his replacement.

As we compare our HR Inventory to our needs as revealed in our strategic plan, we develop a **depth chart**. As in team sports, we know who will replace the employee, when he moves on, or moves up. Deficiencies in depth can be corrected by developing existing talent, or by recruitment.

Having identified the gaps between our available talent and our needs, according to our business plan, we organize **recruitment**. Our goal should be to cast a wide net, bringing in a large number of well-qualified applicants who would be happy undertaking the assignments that we have in mind. This means the wide dissemination of job announcements, with both job descriptions and job specifications. We will inform our employees by postings in work spaces and by announcements in newsletters and emails. But we should post with private and public job placement firms, and encourage employees to alert their network of professional contacts.

Years ago, I attended a meeting of HR directors whose objective was to improve minority recruitment, but they had not considered Spanish language newspapers or radio, nor African-American churches. Clearly, they had not identified traditional methods of "spreading the word." In another search, irrelevant criteria were inserted --- a master's degree in education, for an outside sales position. This could have led to an affirmative action lawsuit.

The pool of applicants may include host country nationals, ex-patriots, and third party nationals. The locals should have local knowledge, connections, and a lower cost of living. Our own (American) ex-patriots should be familiar with our management culture and local conditions, but often they exaggerate their connections and local reputation. Third party nationals need to be very independent, and sometimes are patronizing towards us and the locals. Each group has strengths and weaknesses.

So, we must have well-considered **screening criteria**, which guide our review of evaluations, resumes, and references for desired characteristics. Age, experience, and education are a beginning. The young should have current education and be open to training and to new experiences. Veterans of the industry should bring problem solving experience and contacts. I look for evidence of logical thinking and broad perspective. A solid foundation of liberal education, including communication, quantitative skills, and culture, as well as the engineering or business degree, is valuable. Evidence of motivation, leadership, and self-reliance can be found in special project experience, hobbies, and avocations. Adaptability may be demonstrated by foreign experience, fluency in several languages, team experience (including sports and military), and problem solving experience. The physical and emotional health, and family status, can be important in coping with the stress of new responsibilities. However, we must be cautious not to violate local privacy and discrimination regulations.

When we have our pool of applicants, we must first screen, and then hire. If the initial pool is inadequate, you must assess your recruitment methods and try again. I have seen Boards of Directors narrow a pool to four candidates of which two are qualified but not interested (just attempting to "test the waters" and put pressure on their current employers) and two were totally unqualified by skills and temperament. The worst was chosen in the hope that "she might surprise us." It was an expensive fiasco. Rethink your approach to getting the right person for the position, and try again.

From the pool, we first *check the resumes and references* for their fit with the job specifications. We will find both strengths and weaknesses, and must consider the importance of each. (No wishful thinking is permitted.) Careful consideration of references, including personal conversations with the referee, is essential. For important or sensitive positions, a basic background search by a qualified investigator is necessary. Ask the reference, "yes or no" questions can avoid evasive answers. Remember, the referee doesn't want blowback from the applicant. One of the best questions is the last one: "If you had an opening, would you hire Miss X again ?" And the best response, "If I could, I'd hire her in a heart-beat !"

When satisfied by the references and resume (I've seen estimates of false statements on resumes as high as 30%), we should *test for skills and for attitude*. We want to make sure the employee can perform the tasks at the level expected of new hires, and we want to know that the employee is suited to the job and likely to enjoy the work. Salesmen are different from accountants, and the person who would be happy doing either, or both tasks, is exceptional.

Finally, we can interview, but we must be careful not to exaggerate our ability to assess an individual on the basis of a twenty minute interview. I've yet to meet anyone that clever, and I have made some bad hires from an inflated view of my discernment. In one case, an applicant for a management job swept into the room, like Miss America. Her appearance was even more impressive, because she followed an extremely shy mouse in the sequence of interviews. Once hired, she alienated all of her workmates by her patronizing attitude, even as she asked them to do her work. Her classic line, relayed to me just before we fired her, was "There are elephants and ants, I work well with elephants, but you are an ant." First impressions are often wrong. So, treat the interview as a final check on a careful process in which no step has been short-changed.

To make a considered judgment which weighs all of these matters, extensive interviews with several potential associates is necessary. We can start with the interview by a personnel officer, followed by personality tests and task competency assessments. Then, interviews with the immediate supervisor and the team leader can be followed by debriefing of the candidate and those managers who will be working with him. We must reach a consensus on the choice. The responsibility for the hire must be shared. No one should be pressured to "go along" by accepting someone else's testimony as an excuse from their duty of due diligence. People are just too important, and mistakes are too expensive.

I remember an executive search in which the CEO position was offered to an experienced executive who had just suffered a vote of "no confidence" from 93% of his employees. No one had thought to visit his existing firm, or even contact friends working at that firm, for their observations. Fortunately, some of our own employees, upon learning of the offer, contacted their friends, learned about the vote and informed our Board --- how embarrassing and potentially expensive.

Having selected the employee and agreed to terms, we must **orient** him to our organization, its mission and its culture. In addition, specific training must be implemented to assure that the new employee can function effectively and with well-grounded confidence. Our mission and values provide the guides for his discretion, when policies are not appropriate. The **specific training** integrates the new employee into our methods of performance. Training should alter the employee's behavior and attitudes to increase the likelihood of success. We may use a combination of standardized training programs and tailor-made training. I have found that community colleges often offer standardized training at convenient times and low cost. Sharing the burden with the employee shows a matching commitment. For example, I like classes taught at 4 p.m. The employee uses some of our time and some of his for his development. Successful course, or certificate, completion leads to full reimbursement. Then, we offer training through our own staff, or under contract, classes and workshops for specific needs and methods, including our policies and procedures. In the case of foreign assignments, we should offer training for the family, as well.

I have often hired a less experienced, but highly motivated candidate with solid foundation of general skills and an understanding of our mission and overall operating strategy. Too much experience with a specific set of responsibilities with another firm may render the candidate unteachable. If he was so good at these duties, why is he leaving the other firm ? If he was unhappy there, he may be unhappy with us. The source of discontent may be the mismatch of job description and his personal attitudes and ambitions. Working for us may trap the candidate in an unhappy career. The novice brings no such baggage.

After a period of **probation**, during which the employer and the employee become better acquainted and make a joint decision whether to continue the relationship, **compensation** must be settled. The objective must be to assure that employee is treated fairly and not disadvantaged by his assignment. We consider the base salary for class and grade. Then, we adjust for unfavorable conditions. Benefits must be comparable, wherever the employee is assigned. Similarly, adjustments can be made for differences in cost of living, and special allowances for hardships, such as may be encountered in remote, or foreign, environments. Finally, compensation may be adjusted for tax equalization or protection, so that net income after tax is similar to his peers. Although many employers insist that their employees not compare salaries, in a foolish attempt to save money through discrimination, employees will learn the truth and resent any differences, unless they are obviously justified. Too many employers see their staff as a source of expense, rather than a wealth of talent. They neglect the effective use and motivation of the talent, and focus on minimizing labor costs. They will lose their best people and demoralize the rest.

Frequent and careful **evaluation** of employees should be among the highest priorities of our organization. The process clarifies expectations, elicits useful information, and improves employee morale. If your policy requires annual evaluations, do it twice a year. If the policy is semi-annual evaluation, do it quarterly. While in the Navy, I interviewed each of the forty men who reported to me, every quarter, and for a minimum of twenty minutes. I gave them job descriptions to review, asked them to self-assess and report their conclusions. I shared my view of their performance. I asked what other duties were required of them and did they feel those duties appropriate. I had in front of me the assessments of their immediate supervisors, but I had also been observing them personally, (mainly to assure that their supervisors were treating them fairly and setting their own examples of good work habits). Then, I asked about their personal ambitions, including their life goals, and offered to consider any personal issues which they cared to share. (Many employees have no one with whom to discuss serious personal issues. Certainly, my sailors were happy to lean on me. However, we must not pry. Sometimes, referral to professional counselors is appropriate.) Once, I understood the employee's view of his present assignment, and his ambitions for his future, we would work out a plan to make his work more interesting, and to prepare him for his next assignment. This interview not only gave me valuable information in developing my "depth chart," but also drove my annual training plan and gave a huge boost to employee morale and loyalty.

On the other hand, I remember accepting a job and moving my family, only to be informed that my beginning salary would be 75% of the earlier agreed amount. After a full year, I had not been evaluated at all, and I was denied a vacation after a year of service, because I began on May 1st. I'm please to say that of the dozen corporate officers at that time, only two of us remained three years later. The owners cleaned house, and, by improving personnel management, developed a strong and highly profitable company.

Another important responsibility of Human Resources is attention to career planning and reassignment facilitation. For the employee, a new assignment (unless it is a promotion to a job which the employee has been closely associated) may be frustrating, even disorienting. He may be giving up the autonomy, authority, responsibility, and recognition that came with his last assignment. He may find his new team unwelcoming. He feels that his experience is not valued, his career has been side-tracked, and changes in technology, policies, and even local or corporate culture challenge his abilities. For all of these reasons, the employees should have a mentor in his area and a personal contact in the HR department. The next assignment that would follow from success in the current assignment should be agreed, including performance expectations. The idea is to clarify expectations and timelines, and maintain communication.

A note on leadership

"Management is the achievement of goals through people." Yet, we spend very little time developing leadership. *Leadership is ability to build a team for the achievement of common goals.* To be a leader, you must understand that everyone in your team has the same personal goals of security and achievement that you have. And everyone has sensitivities and cognitive biases that obstruct communication and lead to misunderstandings. Hence, the effective leader must control his ego, but understand that most others cannot.

Poor leaders treat their subordinates like tools who exist only to advance the manager's goals. As my friend, John Reid, once remarked, *"Peter, you must understand that to most people you are merely a 'prop' on the stage set of their life."* On the other hand, a good leader recognizes that the employee is giving us a substantial portion of their life for which wages and benefits are a minor consolation. We should make sure that our teammates find their work satisfying, and that requires that we understand their motivations, as well as their abilities, and that we tailor their assignments to help them to achieve their personal goals, as far as possible. And we must share the load of undesirable but necessary tasks.

A sound understanding of human nature is valuable to the leader. Many people will focus exclusively on their own goals, and select actions in terms of their effect on their own advancement. They may compromise the success of the organization. We call this issue, the **Principal-Agent problem**. (We introduced this issue in lesson #1.4.) We would like all members of the team to act to advance the organization; they are agents of the organization that employs them. Instead, too many employees will act as principals, because what matters to them is their own success. (I call them, *the disrupters*.)

There is another group of co-workers who know what should be done, but won't speak up, because they see no personal reward for criticizing their colleagues, and because they fear retribution from those who would be frustrated and offended. I call this latter group, the *followers*. They will respond to leadership. They will join the leader who is willing to speak up. Finally, there are the genuine *team players* who become demoralized, when the disrupters are allowed their own ways at the expense of group success.

There are several ways to address this principal-agent problem. Usually, the alignment of incentives is emphasized --- bonuses for achieving company goals would be an example. However, I suggest four steps: 1) Be sure to **understand** each employee for whom you are responsible. The evaluation process is an opportunity to identify their goals and motivations. 2) **Involve** all employees in the planning process *for their area*, and familiarize all employees with the business plan, so they understand how they can contribute. 3) In strategy sessions, **don't allow the few to dominate**. They usually have agendas of their own. Follow the six steps of creativity (see below) to define the problem and to share the development of the course of action. Before leaving a topic, ask everyone in the meeting to comment in turn. This will deny avoidance to those who would hide (the followers), and expose to the disrupters that they are in the minority. 4) When meeting the selfish employee one-on-one, **listen carefully** to their proposals to remove any feeling that they have been ignored, **explain** group priorities and the roles of team members, and **clarify** how this employee will benefit from group success. If he continues to be a problem, undermining team success by pursuing personal goals, then separation may be required. *I believe this "principal-agent" problem to be the most destructive issue of personnel management.* Many people will try to use the organization to achieve their own goals, and do not care about the mission. Those employees who do care must be supported, and to do so, the leader must make tough choices with respect to those who would just use the others.

I have already written about the importance of regular evaluations, especially to clarify our understanding of expectations and performance. Evaluations also offer the opportunity to help your teammates formulate their personal goals, and for you to design a program to develop the needed skills and experience through their job assignments, as well as by training programs.

Team sports and team projects are excellent preparation for leadership, particularly if coaches and more experienced players model the best practices. Anyone who has played team sports has learned the importance of sharing the ball, fulfilling one's own responsibilities, and trusting others to do theirs. Even participation on losing teams can teach us the sources of dysfunction.

In high school, our class (1964) was not particularly gifted. The class above us ('63) and the class that followed ('65) had better athletes. Ours was to be a "building year." Yet, we won league championships in football and ice hockey. When playing for the football championship, the game was tied at the half and we were down 8-0 at the end of the third quarter. However, we won 29-8. We were prepared and conditioned by our coaches, we trusted each other, and we were relentless. In hockey, we only lost one game. My left wing had been in an accident over the weekend, and we had to move the right wing to left and promote a new right wing. I realized later that my efforts to cover for the new right wing led me to neglect my own duties and cost us the game. In baseball, we were less successful (9-6), but we enjoyed ourselves every day and never blamed others for our mistakes.

The leader can use his position to improve planning and team commitment. For many years, I have been asking "creative" people how they do what they do. The answer is always the same. I share it with you, for problem solving and team building. **Six steps to creativity**:

Step One: **define the problem**. Too often we walk into a meeting with a solution, or even worse, without even sharing the agenda. Naturally, there are many conflicting solutions, because we do not share the same idea of the problem to be solved. Initiate the discussion by asking, "What are we trying to accomplish ?" Once a consensus is reached, everyone understands what information is needed.

Step Two: **gather information**. Among your team, there are likely to be many different talents that can be tapped to gather information about the problem and the various approaches which could be used to solve it. These need to be discussed and vetted.

Step Three: **identify** the possible solutions and evaluate them. When everyone understands the problem and our objectives, when everyone has had a chance to share information, and propose and discuss the various solutions, the best solution will be obvious. Be sure to ask everyone on the team to comment at every stage, so one or a few cannot dominate and we are sure of the views of the entire team.

Step Four: **implement** the highest ranked solution by assigning responsibility and matching authority, and committing the resources needed. Establish SMART goals.

Step Five, **monitor** performance by measuring activity and comparing it to our benchmarks. Conditions will change, and outcomes will not be exactly what we anticipated. Uncover the discrepancies and identify the problems.

Step Six: **modify** to improve performance, or replace the failed method with an alternative. Remember that your job as a supervisor is to make your teammates effective. Don't criticize, pitch in to help.

I have used this six step approach to creativity for years. The results are impressive. People feel respected, they understand what we are doing and why, they understand their role and the roles of others, and they understand that they can take risks without fear, as long as their intention is to achieve the common goal.

Much has been written about *the importance of setting an example*. When I was a Naval Officer, I was sure to perform all of my duties, never cutting corners. I would stand my watches on the quarterdeck, in port, even in the biting cold. Other officers would leave the enlisted men on deck, while they hid in the warm wardroom. I didn't realize it then, but the enlisted men knew and passed judgment on their officers. I informed my division that my job was always to completion the mission and bring them back healthy, and that they could always ask me why we were doing something. I would never ask them to do something that I wouldn't do. This was very important in two instances. In the first, a radar at the top of the mast had broken loose and was in danger of falling. The Electronics Technicians refused to secure it, so I was told to have one of my men do it. We were in very rough seas and the ship was pitching and rolling severely. I knew this was dangerous. So, I told my Chief Petty Officer that I would climb the mast and secure the radar, and he would tend a rope tied to my life-vest, in case I would fall. We secured the radar. The second occasion was similar. In this case, a light standard was loose and was banging against the bulkhead, disturbing the XO's sleep. The light was on the forecastle and we were in a storm, "taking green water over the bridge". Again, I viewed this as too dangerous for my men, so I secured the lamp between waves with the CPO tending my lifeline. I didn't think about how the men would interpret this at the time. I was just making a judgment that I couldn't ask them to do it, so I had to do it myself. However, I found later that all the sailors in the squadron knew about it and were very loyal to and protective of me.

After a year, I was transferred from my first ship (DD860) to my second (DD739). Again, I was given 1st Division and assigned responsibility for Planned Program Maintenance. On my second day, inspectors arrived from CINCLANTFLEET, and we failed their inspection. Because of my assignment, the blame fell on me, and not the Annapolis graduate whom I had replaced only days before. The next day, I met with the Chief Petty Officers and asked them what we should do. I pointed out that failing the next test would not just reflect on the Captain and the Executive Officer, but on us as leaders and professionals. Three weeks later, we were re-tested and we received the unprecedented score of 100%. CINCLANTFLEET was sure that we had cheated, or bribed someone, so another team was sent and we scored 100% again. How could this happen ? People will rise to the challenge, when they believe in what they are doing, when they trust their leaders, and when they know that they will receive the credit for what they have done. You can appeal to their pride, when they trust you and believe in the tasks assigned.

The night before we deployed, I went on deck to get some air at midnight and found my sailors busy swabbing, sweeping, and generally cleaning up. We were leaving in the morning, and many of the sailors were married, and others had friends and family whom they would not see for six months. I instructed the men to go home and come back at seven a.m. The Chief and I would finish up. He may not have handled a mop in ten years, but when I grabbed one and started swabbing, he did, too. We never had a morale problem after that.

Another important aspect of leadership is *establishing priorities*. Many commanders will dress up their ship to look good leaving port, or returning, in order to impress their superiors. My first Captain, Cmdr. Allen Martin, reported to the McCaffery (DD860) a month before I did and took command three days, after I had arrived. I was given 1st Division with responsibility for the exterior of the ship. We were leaving for a NATO cruise the next day. Capt. Martin ordered me to have my men scrape, prime and paint the bilges, the lowest and dirtiest part of the ship, invisible to anyone. I had expected to be asked to clean up the exterior. I asked him why he wanted bilges cleaned. His answer was the importance of working from the inside out, and signaling the ship that he wasn't about impressing outsiders, he was about making sure that the ship was sound, and all systems were reliable. Once a month, the entire ship would be inspected with the department officers, each inspecting an area outside of their own responsibility. The captain would dawn his overalls and crawl through the most obscure parts of the ship. Six months later, when we left the NATO squadron of six ships from six nations, we received a signal from the Dutch Commodore, "McCaffery is the finest ship with which I have ever served in my thirty years at sea." Capt. Martin's leadership had taken us from the joke of the Atlantic fleet to the best, in less than one year. He had no choice of staff or equipment. He made the best of the resources at his disposal by treating everyone with respect and setting an example.

A good leader understands and implements Fayol's principles: **order, authority, unity, equity, morale,** and **communication**. Plans, work orders, and progress reports help us monitor programs and solve problems, before they become disasters. Authority must match responsibility. Employees must report to one supervisor and be allowed to complete one task before being assigned another. An important task of the supervisor may be to protect his team from the interference of other managers. Regular and honest communication instills confidence and preempts the distractions of rumors. Equity and morale are closely related. A disaffected employee is often one who feels unfairly treated. Monitoring and counseling your team must be a priority to assure that they understand how and why decisions are made, and to assure we are acting fairly. Give everyone chances to excel.

Each time that I joined a ship, I found the problem of interference. Sailors were demoralized by conflicting instructions. (Some "leaders" think that leading is just giving orders and then blaming the recipient {passing the buck}.) I ruthlessly enforced the principle of "chain of command" and protected my people from interference. Even the Captain was not allowed to ask my men to perform tasks. He would need to ask me, or in an emergency, my Chief Petty Officer. Actually, all of the captains obliged, but some of the Executive Officers (XOs) resented this limit on their power. (Perhaps, that's why several never got their own commands.) Once, while we were in dry dock, a time when 1st Division is especially busy, working fourteen hour days including weekends, I discovered that none of my men were at their assigned tasks. I learned that they had been pulled by the Operations Officer (his people had nothing to do in dry dock) for "look-out" training. I couldn't overrule a superior officer, so I directed the Chief to give the men the rest of the day off. (They hadn't had a day off in a month.) The next morning, the Captain asked why I had given them the day off, and I reported that if we had time for look-out training, then we had time to give them their first day off in a month. I didn't criticize the Ops officer, but he was passed over for promotion, soon thereafter.)

At the bank where I worked, we had a CEO who also owned 33% of the bank. He was not a banker and was constantly interfering and distracting the staff, not just officers, but tellers and clerks, too. This caused chaos and anxiety. Finally, he was asked to move his office from the downtown headquarters to my branch, the original home office. To preempt problems, I welcomed him with the instruction that he could talk to me anytime, but he could only greet my staff, but never communicate any direction of any kind. In the year and one-half that he was in my office, we had no problems and no misunderstandings. My staff became comfortable with his presence.

Once in the travel business, we hit a cash-flow crisis. The chairman warned me that we wouldn't be able to pay the staff in December. I told him that would not work, and designed a plan to meet all of our obligations, which required some changes in assignments. We called a meeting. I led off by saying that because of all the initiatives underway, we needed to make some changes, but no one would lose their job, no one would take a pay cut, and no one would be asked to work longer hours. Then, I introduced my boss who explained what we would do. As we left after a good meeting, my boss demanded to know why I had mentioned jobs, wages, and hours. I explained that everyone sensed that changes were coming, and they were only worried about their job, their income, and work hours. Until those questions were answered, they wouldn't hear anything else that we said. Communication and trust are vital to morale.

Finally, the good leader is humble. He never assumes that he has all the answers, or that he is smarter than other people. I ask my students to recite the mantra, **"Ask, Listen, Evaluate, and Act"**. When I was working at the bank, the owner commissioned an appraisal of a piece of property that lay between two other properties that he owned. I asked, "Why are you paying $10,000 for an appraisal, when you know more about the value of that land than anyone else ?" He answered that someday an appraiser would find something that he didn't know and save him from a big mistake. He never assumed that he was the smartest guy in the room, even though he probably was. In addition to avoiding blunders, this approach of never assuming, and always asking/ listening/ evaluating/ acting motivates your team to be informed and offer their best advice, as well as assuring that you are using to your best advantage the talents that you have available. Why do so few managers exhibit these behaviors ? EGO --- their insecurity is evident in their unwillingness to admit their limitations.

The smart and humble leader makes sure that those who deserve credit, receive it. Every employee fears that their contribution is not recognized or appreciated. Investing the time to know who is doing what, who is responsible, and who needs help, is vital. Why would anyone make extraordinary effort, only to be rebuffed, or ignored ? Or to see someone else receive the credit ? Ironically, many poor leaders act as if they believe that their employees only exist to make them look good. These employees will not care about "the boss's" project. On the other hand, if the leaders sees his job as making his team effective, then everyone will succeed, and he will look good !

When I started at the bank, my branch was a mess with high turn-over and low morale. I realized that everyone had simply been plugged into some job that needed to be done regardless of ability or motivation. No effort was made to help them understand the bank, or their place in it. So, I implemented a training program. Every Thursday from 4:30-5:30, after the staff had balanced their cash drawers, I taught my twelve employees the business of banking, including the products, how they were priced and why, as well as the various jobs and how they contributed to the bank's goals. Instead of tellers or new accounts clerks, they became bankers. They gained confidence in their interactions with our customers and the other bank employees. We became the training branch for the bank. Thirty years later, my first hire was recognized by the bank (she had risen to be controller). For the first time, the bank gave a recognition reception honoring an employee for service. She asked that I be invited, saying that she had fashioned her management style after me. (I had not seen her in many years, and was touched to be remembered in that way.)

On the other hand, I recall a competing bank which had a campaign to increase deposits. Staff were encouraged to "cross sell" existing customers. One of the ladies was particularly successful by taking long lunches with wealthy, senior male customers. All the other women in the office knew what was going on. Can you imagine how they felt when there regional Vice President showed up for a meeting to acknowledge her with a nice bonus and a plaque ?

My last president at the bank expressed his insecurity by threats. He had a steady series of resignations by his best managers. Although my team with 12% of the staff contributed 50% of the bank's profits, I was the lowest paid Vice President and received a $500 bonus at the end of my last year. Immediately, I started looking for another position. Two years later, that president approached me and stated that he had misjudged me and that I was a very effective banker. I thanked him for the acknowledgement, but will always wonder whether he understood his failings as a leader.

What kind of leader will you be ?

Review and test questions:
What are Fayol's principals of organization ? Which you do consider important and why ? (2)
What is a Human Resource Inventory and how is it constructed ? (2)
How do corporations screen and select the best talent ? (2)
What are the critical issues of compensation ? (2)
What are the key elements of effective leadership ? (2)

Appendix : Notes from Robert Gates' recent book,
A Passion for Leadership, Techniques for Implementing Change

1) Get people from different parts of the organization working together.
2) Demand and demonstrate transparency and information about implementation. Candor is critical.
3) Be wary of consensus. Look at any recommendation --- does it advance the agenda ?
4) Analysis must not lead to paralysis. Deadlines are important.
5) Master information, make decisions, assign responsibility, require regular reports, and hold people accountable. "Micro-knowledge is necessary; micro-management is not."
6) People need to know that their work is considered important. Treat people with respect and dignity while getting rid of deadwood.
7) Empower subordinates. Give credit to others. Give excellent employees opportunities for advancement.

Students at the University of Namibia. 1995

Lesson #1.8 Strategic Planning and Entry Methods

Later, we will develop techniques for valuing and ranking projects (lessons #3.6-3.9). I will conclude this initial cluster of lessons that describe the functions of management with strategic planning, entry selection, and entry negotiation.

The beginning of planning is the design of the strategic planning process. Who will be involved, in what ways, with which decisions ? This requires an understanding of communication within the organization. There will be informal communication, sometimes called "the grapevine" or "the rumor mill." People need information and will fill any void with rumors. Once a rumor spreads, it is very hard to correct. So, formal methods, such as meetings, emails, and internal newsletters are very important. Your stakeholders --- customers, suppliers, and especially employees, --- need to know what is going on, and what is planned for the company and their team. Equally important is the briefing of managers with the requirement that they share information with their team. This may fight the tendency of poor managers to hoard information in the hope of gaining and retaining power. That attitude will undermine trust and morale. Identifying and briefing opinion leaders is important, too --- even if you have identified them as the sources of the rumors. They will be talking, and they will be believed, so make sure they have the facts, even if they annoy you.

Next, consider balancing the need for centralized decision-making to assure coordination and control, with the need for decentralized decision-making for responsiveness, enhanced morale, and leadership development. A good rule is to move the decision to the level that includes everyone who will be impacted by the decision. They should be consulted, and their insights evaluated and reconciled. By participating in the process, they will become committed to its success. Finally, the exposure of the company to risk must be considered. The greater the risk, the higher in the organization must be the final decision. However, having final authority does not mean "micro-managing" or "second guessing" the recommendations of the working group that evaluated the project and designed the strategy. Instead, review their work and their reasoning, adding information of which they may be unaware, asking pointed questions, and demanding thoughtful answers. When the final plan is agreed, you have done your job by empowering the team to make the best decision for the organization, and giving them confidence as well as developing their competence. Your respect for their work gains their trust and commitment.

Next, we must monitor performance, continuously. This is the **control** function. We often refer to the bookkeeping and accounting reports as controls, and they are important, if used. Too many businesses generate accounting reports, but fail to use them. (An astounding number of directors of major corporations can't interpret financial statements !) The numbers are important, if they are organized in helpful ways. This is the skill of accounting professionals. They know how to design reporting systems that give us reports that tell us the results of our past actions. Bookkeepers know how to make the entries that generate the reports. Do not use the expensive accountants to make bookkeeping entries; that would be a needless cost. Equally importantly, make sure that the accountants train the bookkeepers and audit their work to assure that it is accurate. Then, take the reports and analyze them. These reports tell us a story. We must "torture the numbers until they confess." We must understand the reports sufficiently to tease out the story that will help us to understand what happened and make new and better decisions. (See lessons #3.5 and #6.5.)

But the standard accounting statements are not enough. We need a variety of reports that organize our understanding of the past (balance sheet, income statement, cash-flow statement), and reports that monitor the present (receiving, production, shipping, staffing), and the likely future (reservations, orders, leads, aging of receivables, schedules {production, equipment, and personnel}). Fortunately, our computer network with the support of our IT department can integrate the information of all groups into current reports on any and all of the above issues. As managers, we review each and ask the reporting manager to explain discrepancies, so that we can help solve problems before they arise. Do not "nit pic," and do not harass. Just note the discrepancy, ask for an explanation, insist on a direct and complete answer ---such as: what happened ? what we are doing about it ? and why ? Do not accept incomplete or evasive answers, but make clear your desire to help solve the problem. (Later you can worry about accountability.)

Often, we are comparing performance against goals. In a few paragraphs, we will discuss criteria for good goals. For now, it's enough to acknowledge (as in Deming's principles in lesson #1.6) that we need both quantitative goals, as embodied in budgets, and qualitative goals, such as leadership, employee development, staff stability, public relations, relations with other working groups, etc. And these latter are not about office politics; they are about professionalism.

Having considered the issues of communication and centralization/decentralization, we can design our strategic planning process. Our plan gives us a unified sense of direction and specific guidance with respect to activities and resources. The plan is subject to regular revision, but it cannot be neglected. Peter Drucker said, "The business that fails to plan, is planning to fail." We also know that the plans of generals usually last only until the battle is engaged. Then, they must be revised in the course of the battle. So too, with the business plan. Without a plan, anything can happen. With a plan, we can adjust tactically, but still achieve our strategic objectives.

The first step is to develop a clear understanding of what we want our organization to be. We define ourselves. The more focused this **vision**, the more likely that we can work together and succeed. So, we ask, "What do we do ? What won't we do ? What will we look like in five years ? In ten years ?" That is: 1) What activities will be doing ? 2) What resources will we command ? 3) Who will be our customers ? And our suppliers? 4) How will we operate ? (What are our values ?) The temptation to avoid tough decisions and promise to do everything for everyone, or at least everything that anyone on the team would like to do, is very strong. It is also deadly. We can't be all things to all people; we must focus on what we do best (our competitive advantage) in those areas that provide the best combination of opportunities and synergies. Often, the vision will be defined in a simple statement which all employees can understand and guides them in their work. A good mission for a bank might be: "We offer the responsible people of central California risk management in the forms of deposit, payments, and loan services." This defines the cluster of services, the target customers, and the region to be served.

In order to implement this vision, we need basic criteria upon which to select activities. These are described as **objectives**, or minimum criteria. For example, Jack Welsh had a market share objective for GE's groups: they must be first or second in their product or industry. DuPont had an objective in the 1950s: projects must generate a minimum 20% rate of return on investment. These will serve as the first "cut" in evaluating proposals.

Armed with these criteria, we review our **situation**. Where are we ? What do we do ? Who are our customers ? What resources do we have available, --- physical, human, and relationships ? Obviously, our financial reports and human resource inventories are essential to this analysis.

This work prepares us for our **environmental assessment**. We use the situation analysis to identify our strengths and weaknesses (internal). We add the assessment of external threats and opportunities. The threats may come from changing customer needs, competition, technology, or politics. All opportunities should considered, but those that do not fit our mission, or our resources, should be discarded. The best opportunities, and the actions required to manage risks, will be subject to systems analysis and evaluation (see lesson #3.8). When activities are ranked highly, goals and timetables for each will be developed.

Once we have decided to undertake an activity, we must establish **goals**. They must be **SMART** (simple, measureable, accountable, realistic, and timely). They should include quantitative goals such as sales, market share, and profit, and qualitative goals, such as community relations, staff development, and quality standards. The acronym SMART reminds us that for goals to be useful, they must be easily understood (simple: sell cars), measurable (sell 100 cars), accountable (Bob, the sales manager is responsible), realistic (there are more than 1000 families in our region planning to purchase cars, and we will give Bob the resources that he needs), and timely, (sell 100 cars by March 31st). If the goals are not realistic, there will be no commitment by the team members and failure is assured. If there is no accountability, no one will take charge, and no one will speak up, as the project drifts onto the rocks. And if the goals are not time specific, the project may drag on, inconclusively, forever.

Now, we are ready for **implementation**. This requires the commitment of resources, both human and physical. The latter can be planned by the construction of a pro-forma budget. The budget lists the assets to be available to the operation and the sources of funding. Expected sales, costs, and profit are estimated in a pro forma income statement. The flow of financial resources through operations is given in the cash budget, which adjusts sales for receipt of settlement and costs for time of payment. These financial plans must be negotiated carefully with the managers of the various operations. Naturally, they will want generous allocations of resources that assure success. Similarly, senior management would always like the operating groups to achieve more with less. We cannot starve operations of resources, but we don't wish to "gold plate" them either. In the end, the accountable parties, the key management team, must agree that, with the resources promised, they can meet our goals. Do not ram these allocations down their throats. They won't be committed; they will be demoralized; and we won't succeed. Only when they accept the plan sincerely, can we be sure of their commitment and able to hold them accountable.

There is a tradition in the Navy that a ship's captain, or task force commander, is required to refuse to take his ships to sea, if he believes that they lack the resources to achieve their mission. This would be a good principle for us to follow in business, too. (Do you remember my story about a friend who managed the only local department store in my town ? It benefitted from a local monopoly. One year, senior management dictated to all stores a goal of 25% sale growth. My friend pointed out that a new mall was nearing completion and he would face two new local competitors. He felt a realistic goal was to hold sales and profit constant. His objections were rejected; he quit; and the company was soon in such bad shape that it had to be sold.)

The final and most vital stage of strategic planning is the **continuous monitoring of performance**. With grace and charm, we monitor each project, noting discrepancies and offering assistance in solving problems. We call this process, evaluation and modification. Years ago, Hollis Chenery did a study of the first twenty years of the World Bank, in order to identify the reasons for project success and failure. His conclusion was that all projects have problems. The successes only differed from the failures, to the extent that the successful teams were committed to solving every problem that arose.

If we like what we discover above, we move on to **strategy formulation**. We need to identify our edge --- the source of our sustainable competitive advantage. We perform an *external* environmental assessment. We gather information from experts (economists, futurists, and marketers) and analyze the trends that they report. We consult managers and survey customers and suppliers. We review our internal situation. (We can use our strategic plan.) What physical and human resources are available ? We analyze the value chain associated with the project of activity: they are **inbound logistics**: receiving, storing, materials handling, warehousing; **operations**: machining, assembly, testing, packaging; **outbound logistics:** distribution and transport. We may add value through our skills --- **marketing and sales**, including **after sales service** (such as repair, product adjustment, training, and parts supply). Or our strength may be in **management skills**, or **research and development**. An honest assessment of our strengths and weaknesses helps us to focus on those activities that offer us the best chance of success.

We can now use this information to assess the bargaining power of our customers (Can we keep them ?), the bargaining power of our suppliers (Do they need us ? Can we trust them ?), and the risks of potential new entry (Defend by cultivating our customers, and use our friends in government to limit competition). Now, we are ready to consider those SMART goals that we discussed above.

Having identified some great opportunities through a rational process that vets ideas for value and fit, we need to select the method of entry into the target market. As we have seen so many times before, we have choices.

1) Exporting involves production in one or more countries, with delivery to customers in other countries. We often begin to enter a new market by exporting, in response to leads from existing customers who operate there, or inquiries from distributors there. Exporting allows us to gain experience with minimum resource commitments and exposure to risks. On the other hand, we will not learn as much about the market and its potential, when we cede control of sales and distribution to our local partner. While exporting may save fixed costs, it may involve high operating costs, including logistics management, and customs duties and procedures.

2) Licensing involves an agreement with a local producer to manufacture and sell our product in a foreign market, in exchange for fees based on sales or profit. These fees are called **royalties**. We help the licensee set up production, and may supply equipment and/or parts and materials. We are granting the licensee local rights to our methods and brand name, our intellectual property. Licensing earns us a stream of income from a new market without the development costs, financial commitments, and risks of learning from experience. Of course, our methods may not be well-suited to local conditions, in which case, we are dependent on the local licensee to adapt our technology without compromising our reputation. We lose control of local production and marketing. We miss some benefits of experience and of location economies, and we fail to integrate this market into a coherent global strategy. Most critically, we risk creating a competitor who learns our methods (technologies) from us and then abandons the relationship to poach our customers.

I remember a friend who introduced a Texas oil equipment maker to a Chinese oil production company which was interested in obtaining a license to make some drilling equipment. The Texas company negotiated a licensing agreement which gave the Chinese the technology, but restricted its use to the PRC. Within a year, the Chinese were selling the drilling equipment all over South East Asia, in violation of the agreement. My friend was shocked to be sued for more than $100,000,000 by the Texas company. (Because he had not profited from the introduction, the suit was dismissed, but how would you feel to be served with a law suit of that size ?)

We can protect ourselves, while licensing qualified producers in small markets by using cross-licensing and joint-ventures with equity stakes. When companies have multiple relationships, they are less likely to violate one agreement, to the peril of others. Similarly, companies with substantial financial commitments to joint-ventures are less likely to undermine their success.

An example of a successful licensing agreement is the arrangement between Holsten beer and Namibian Breweries (NB) that gives NB the capability to brew and sell a very high quality German beer, with an international reputation, in a large market (SADC), and gives Holsten a nice revenue stream without the headache of operations in Southern Africa. Under the agreement, NB must not only use exactly the same process as Holsten, but even source the same raw materials, hops and malt, from Germany and the Czech Republic. NB was acquired by Carlsburg in 2004 and now produces, under license, Heineken and Amstel.

4) Franchising is a specialized form of licensing, involving much greater commitment by both parties, including transfer of technology, training, and continued support in the forms of marketing, operations, and supplies. To assure quality consistent with the other operations, both company-owned and franchised, and to protect the reputation of the brand, strict controls of business methods are imposed and monitored. The franchisor penetrates new markets and obtains revenue as a share of the franchisee's gross sales and from ongoing sales of services and supplies, while the franchisee gains a complete package of management strategies, tools, supplies and equipment, and continuing support. However, the need for uniformity requires constant surveillance, restricts responsiveness to local tastes and practices.

When Manpower, the temporary help agency, expanded globally, they found labor laws and practices varied a great deal. The Swedes believed that temporary employees replace permanent workers, rather than temporary employment serving as a gateway to full-time jobs. Many years later, the Swedes invited Manpower to help write the labor laws that would enable temporary employment. In Brazil, Manpower franchised several local employment agencies, only to find that the Manpower methods failed there. Manpower had to buy back the franchises, and set up and operate company-owned offices in several cities, in order to adapt Manpower methods to local conditions. After several years of learning, Manpower was able to franchise again, but they kept the company owned offices to stay abreast of local conditions to better understand and support their franchisees.

5) Turnkey Projects involve setting up an operation and turning it over to the contracting company, after a shake-down period. The contractor handles all aspects of project, including training. This is a nice way to earn high returns on core competencies, it avoids many risks of doing business in a foreign location, and it can accommodate the goals of local companies and regions. However, the purchaser may have no interest in long-term relationship, and indeed, may become a competitor.

6) Joint-Ventures involve the establishment of a new firm that is owned by two, or more, companies. Often, the parties have complementary skills, but a shared vision. For example, an Asian partner may have manufacturing facilities, local contacts, and even financial resources, but he may lack the marketing and research capabilities, and operating technologies that his European, or American, partner has.

The joint-venture has the obvious advantages of access to local knowledge, sharing of political risks, and also sharing of share development costs and risks. On the other hand, there is the danger of giving away technology to your partner and creating in him, a competitor. Furthermore, conflict over strategy, goals, and objectives is common. And the joint venture may not give us adequate control to gain experience, or globalize to reduce costs and contain expenses.

I recall an auto project in China which was conceived for sales of fleets to businesses and local governments, before the Chinese people were permitted to purchase private cars. The design and engineering partner developed a terrific taxi, well-suited to local conditions, inexpensive and 100% recyclable. However, the Chinese "money partner," whose role was to open doors, kept interfering with production. He wanted to build limousines, totally unsuited to the manufacturing technology. Meanwhile the marketing issues of distribution and service were completely neglected, until the window of opportunity had closed. Which leads us to …

7) Wholly-owned Subsidiaries are controlled by the parent. A new company may be established, or an existing company may be purchased. The control facilitates protection of our technologic advantages, including trade secrets and management methods. We can also schedule operations and protect our quality and reputation. Finally, we can integrate the local company into our global strategy. However, the commitment of resources makes subsidiaries the most expensive method of entry, and the risks of learning and adapting to local conditions are highest. Finally, the acquisition strategy may lead to clashes of corporate cultures, as we have seen recently in the failed merger of Chrysler and Daimler-Benz.

We select our method of entry by considering our core competencies. We choose the method that best uses our capabilities. For example, if our technology is our source of competitive advantage, we protect it through a subsidiary. If we have developed a great management system or a strong brand, then, licensing or franchising may be the best solution. If we produce a "commodity", meaning a standard product, facing competitive pressures for cost reduction, then global integration involving shifting production to a low cost location, followed by exporting may be best.

Review questions and exercises:
Explain the six steps of strategic planning.
Compare and contrast entry methods:
{Identify each, and explain the advantages and disadvantages associated with each.}
1) exporting
2) turn-key projects
3) licensing
4) franchising
5) joint ventures
6) subsidiaries.
What criteria would you use to select the best of these six alternatives for your venture ?

Lesson #1.9 Political Risk and Negotiation

Having developed our strategic plan, chosen our allies, and our method of entry, we are ready to negotiate with stake holders. Business consists of two tasks, identifying the best opportunities and managing the risks associated with undertaking those opportunities, (as observed by my friend, Ray Bowman). It's important to recognize that **risk** is the possibility of any outcome other than what we expect. Therefore, risks can be both positive and negative. We prepare for the risks that we should anticipate, so that the unanticipated risks don't bury us, when they occur. As an example of managing risks through negotiations, I will present **political risk**, but the principles are the same, with whomever we need to negotiate. They could be anyone, or any group that can contribute to our success or failure.

Political risk includes all political forces that can facilitate or impede the attainment of objectives. It's helpful to distinguish **macro risk**, those nation-wide forces that effect many activities, and **micro risk**, those forces that target our specific industry or company. The risks can be present in the political environment (legal, administrative, legislative), the economic environment (inflation, currency convertibility, insecurity of property and person), and the external environment (third party activities, such as social movements, insurgencies, crime, neighborhood associations, other non-governmental organizations, and labor movements). We must carefully consider the social forces that are present, the participants, and the possible outcomes. As you may guess, public relations is vital. We must identify and approach each stakeholder from the very beginning, in order to assess their interests, and to preempt rumors and misunderstandings. This is the first of four steps in negotiation.

First, we **identify the issues**. Before we become too emotionally attached to the project, we must rationally weigh the benefits against the costs of doing this business. Then, we can consider how to increase the benefits and reduce the costs, and identify the best terms of entry that we can imagine and the worst terms that we would accept (that would still leave the project viable).

Second, we **evaluate the positions** of the participants. Although our negotiations are usually sequential, one party at a time, we know that the party across the table may be influenced by absent players, and that whatever agreements we can reach must be compatible with necessary commitments to other parties. So, we make four lists:

1) What are our strengths ? What can we offer the other party ?
2) What are our needs ? What do we want from the other party ?
3) What are their needs ? What do they want from us ?
4) What are their strengths ? What can they offer us ?

Each list is ordered from most important to least important (for needs) and from least costly to most costly (for concessions). For example, as a multinational enterprise, we need permission to operate (a charter), access to public goods such as water, power, roads and ports, a qualified labor pool, and protection of our property rights through enforcement of contracts, and personal and property security. The host government wants jobs, export earnings, transfer of technology and capital, and tax revenue. Of course, these four lists are kept "close to our vests" and will be revised during negotiations, as the other party's needs and concerns become clearer. The same preparation must be done, in advance, for all stakeholders --- local partners, suppliers, distributors, labor contractors, and community groups. Remember, they will be trying to influence our negotiations with every party, as well as negotiating directly with us.

As we list and rank the needs and offers, we locate **acceptance zones**, those areas within which we are willing to negotiate. What are the worst terms of agreement that would be acceptable and what are the best that we could ever obtain ? What are their limits (best and worst) ? For example, we would identify three prices: the initial offer, the expected price, and the maximum price beyond which there is no deal. The acceptance zones of the parties in negotiations must intersect for agreement to be attainable, although multiple areas of negotiation mean multiple zones and possible trade-offs. We identify the limits by considering the best alternatives available to us and to them. Then, because we have listed and ranked our needs, their needs, and what we can offer, as well as what we can reasonably expect them to offer, we are ready for step three:

Third, we assess the **behavioral characteristics** of the participants, and prepare our own behavioral strategy. In short, how can we expect them to behave, and how should we behave, to achieve our goals ? For example, there are cultural differences in offer strategies. Some cultural groups will begin with extreme offers and expect to make large concessions (Arabs, Indians, and Africans), and some will make "fair" offers and be surprised to be rejected (Japanese and Germans). Some negotiators will be very emotional sensitive and others are strictly rational in appealing to their self-interest. Everyone responds well to respect, but some cultures expect flattery (Arabs), some are very serious (Germans), and others enjoy banter (Africans). For Americans, and many western cultures results matter most, but for some, honor, dignity, and face-saving are vital. It's good to remember that everyone prefers all of these virtues; I am highlighting differences of priority and degree. In other words, don't embarrass anyone, and everyone likes good results. But the "faux-pas" may not derail the negotiations in Europe, as it would in Asia.

I strongly recommend that our team agree on objectives and strategy for the overall negotiations and for the specific meeting that day. The leader is the spokesman and the rest of the members of the team are resources, with specific knowledge. They will also monitor the responses of the members of the other team to every exchange. (Of course, we must be aware that our responses are being monitored, too. Calm, but attentive, is always a good demeanor.) If the leader wants a contribution from another team member during the meeting, he should ask for it. And each member should be briefed in advance of the leader's expectations for participation and for behavior. Americans tend to talk too much and give away too much. I can remember warning a colleague, "Today, you must be Polynesian," meaning "warm and friendly". But on another day, I asked the same colleague to "Be German, today; we need to show that we are tough."

Another important difference is the expectation of the agreement. Are contracts detailed, or do we leave minor, or unlikely complications for ad hoc problem solving later ? The Japanese will expect to negotiate the "big picture" --- sketching out rights and responsibilities. We, Americans, like to work out the details, spelling out the handling of many possible turns of events. Our attorneys are trying to protect us, as well as making expectations very clear. However, the Japanese understand that all relationships are based in trust, contracts will not compensate for failures of trust. They wonder if the American who insists on all these details is hiding something. Maybe, he doesn't trust us; perhaps, he is not trustworthy.

Years ago, a Japanese mining company approached a friend of mine to purchase his concession in Guinea. They settled on one million dollars for a 50% interest in the concession. The Japanese who had only known my friend for a few days wrote a check on the spot, before the contract had been drafted and reviewed. Needless to say, he didn't cash the check, until the formalities had been concluded.

Can we expect the other party to be spontaneous, reacting quickly and decisively to our proposals, or will they be methodical, taking time (perhaps several days) to respond and develop a new position ? The Japanese will be methodical, because they will need to confer with their superiors as well as the operations groups who will be participating in the project, before modifying their position. We, Americans, will too often over-react to new information, rushing to blurt out our new counter-proposals. This may throw the other party off-balance, but worse, they may conclude that they gave too much and undervalued their concession. They will be more difficult later.

I mentioned above, extreme offers. What can we expect their initial posture to be ? Extreme or fair ? Is the party across the table tough, but expecting bargaining and willing to make concessions, or is this initial offer, their best offer, and they don't expect to make any concessions ? This will condition our response. In a culture that presents extreme offers, a light-hearted response may be an "ice-breaker," but as with the Japanese, who present what they believe is a fair offer, a joking response would be insulting. They would need to be convinced that a modification of their offer would be best for both of us. This reminds me that we should always check to be sure that our negotiating partners have the technology to evaluate benefits and costs of concessions. My brother-in-law would always carry a spare lap-top computer loaded with spread sheets. He would lend the spare to the other team, so that they could enter changes and see the implications, quickly. This reassured them that he wasn't trying to "pull a fast one" and sped the negotiations to successful conclusions.

I also mentioned emotional sensitivity. This plays out in the negotiators commitment to process or task. We like to get to the deal as fast as possible. We are task oriented. But business relationships must be cultivated, nurtured, and protected. So, we must understand the process that the other party expects, and we should honor that process. Agreement will be much easier to achieve. I remember some Egyptian friends who were offended by Japanese who would not alter their position at every meeting. And an African who completed an agreement with me by saying, "You're OK for a white guy. I really resent those 'African Americans'." I asked him, "Why ?" His answer was that they paid his "first price," they refused to negotiate, and therefore, they felt superior to him. The Americans were mostly likely trying to be fair to their African brothers, but they overlooked the social process of negotiation which builds relationships.

Must relationship development precede negotiation ? In cultures which have evolved high levels of trust, the relationship develops during the process of doing business. We start with a few small transactions and get to know each other. The relationship grows with experience. In cultures that have high levels of distrust (many of these have experienced repeated invasions through the millennia, as well as predatory governments and other insecurities), an investment in personal relationships must precede negotiations.

Years ago, I was in Kuwait and visited a friend who was the President of the local industrial bank. A French salesman who was peddling large desalination plants offered to take us to lunch. My Kuwaiti friend included most of his staff. We enjoyed the best food in Kuwait (the lunch buffet at the Intercontinental). Mohammed and I spoke of Arab history and culture throughout the lunch, and then we got up to leave. As we thanked our host, he was clearly confused. "We didn't discuss the desalinization plants at all" he blurted. Mohammed, "Yes, well, thank-you, but that is the point". In other words, he had invited me in order to signal to the Frenchman, "If you want to do business with us, you must take a genuine interest in us. You must invest in getting to know us." By the way, once a relationship is formed, it is very strong. Arabs are extremely loyal to those who have earned their trust.

In Italy, you can expect to be invited to stay with the family of your opposite number. It's a way of establishing a personal bond, but also an opportunity to observe your social behavior and assess your trustworthiness. How would they feel that we do not reciprocate, in the same way, here in America ?

Now, that we understand how they will behave and how they will interpret our behavior, we can consider the fourth step: **understanding their decision process**. Can negotiators across the table make concessions or must they refer to others ? Is the party who appears to be leading their team actually in charge, or is it the old man in the corner, or today, the mature lady who appears to be his secretary but is, in fact, one of the principals ? I have conducted negotiations in which I was given clear instructions, but did not have the final word. Often, this can avoid any emotional investment in the project that would cloud our judgment, but it can also be a ploy to extract greater concessions. We reach a provisional agreement at the table, but when the other party returns, he explains with great, feigned embarrassment, or even anger, that he requires more concessions to placate his bosses.

As we proceed with negotiations, exchanging and explaining offers and counter-offers, making demands and offering concessions, we must remember our opponent's susceptibility to outside influences. We may believe that our offer meets our needs and theirs, at little cost to either of us, but we are over-looking the costs to others that they must consider. It's best if our proposals can also give our opponent ways to please those other forces and build his creditability with them.

By offering bargain air-travel for Tahitians to the USA within our larger program of budget packages for Americans to Tahiti, we helped the local government gain support from their people. When our French competition tried to shut us down, they found that the local government would not help them. In the West Indies, we offered to donate 5% of our profits to support local charities, as selected by the local politicians. In exchange, they agreed to prevent any government employees from expecting bribes for permits. This arrangement was tested only once, and worked perfectly. So, by anticipating the mobilization of the French government by our rivals at Air France and UTA, we prevented interference. And in the Caribbean, we used the needs of politicians to prevent the predations of the bureaucracy.

Finally, consider the issue of language and communication. Do we understand each other ? Especially, if all parties share a common language, such as English, the possibilities of misunderstanding are great. Some of us may be translating our thinking from our native language to the shared language. In addition, usage, jargon, and syntax will vary. We think that we understand, but we don't. Or we take offense at the tone that is not intended. So, having translators allows everyone to hear the message twice and also buys us time to consider the message and formulate our response. And remember, the other parties may understand your language as well as you do, but they are hiding their knowledge behind their translator. When you make an aside to a colleague, very likely your opponent understands every word.

I point out all of these considerations, because I firmly believe that in negotiations, the better prepared party will gain most of the shared benefits. Often, I've discovered during negotiations that I understand the other party's needs and capabilities better than they do. Then, I must lead them to the mutually acceptable outcome, without appearing to do so. And we will obtain everything that we need at minimal sacrifice.

As for our own behavior, I urge you to build relationships. Multiple contacts will allow both parties to become acquainted in varied situations. Many people react badly to pressure. Demonstrate an interest in learning what is important and what concerns the other party. Be patient. Even at the formal negotiating session, wait for the party to bring up business. Don't be frivolous. (I have seen some fools prattle on with inane jokes and asides, or cell phone interruptions.) Show interest in the other party, but let them make the first presentation. This may save you from making the wrong, or expensive, concessions in search of objectives which they are already willing to concede.

Your response to their presentation should always be one of serious consideration and probing questions for clarification. This shows that you are paying attention and giving respect. It also avoids subsequent confusion. (Do you remember: ask, hear, evaluate, and then act ?) You need to know whether your opponent expects compromise, or is he inflexible ? If inflexible, you will need to be patient and repeatedly demonstrate how the change in terms will benefit both of you. If reciprocity is expected, do so, but avoid appearing too eager. An overreaction may lead your opponent to fear that he has given away too much. Once you are certain that you understand the offer, acknowledge the offer, perhaps by restating it. Then, ask for time to consider it, and to fashion an appropriate response than honors his generosity. This might take a few minutes in the hall with your colleagues, or several days in which to confer with your supervisors. You should have a plan which identifies the possible concessions that they may offer and links each to a concession of similar importance to them, for us to offer. Often, what is most important to them is not costly, and may even be desirable, for us. Naturally, we like to make concessions that are important to them but nearly to costless to us.

Be aware of **time limits**. Knowing your opponents time constraints gives you leverage. Just as buying car on the last day of the month, or negotiating the purchase of property at the end of the quarter, can get us the best price, the same principles of putting the time pressure on your opponent can be an advantage in negotiations. You are serious, professional, and focused but also polite, relaxed, and never rushed or pressed. And never discuss pending plans which will give away your time line, such as another meeting in another location in the near future.

I remember when we negotiated to purchase a failing resort in Antigua. We knew that the current owners were losing $5,000 a month through the peak winter season and more as spring and summer arrived. We knew that the current management was more suited to a rest home than a tropical resort. Hence, although we needed to occupy the resort by July in order to ready it for the next winter season, the owners were bleeding, and we knew that it could only get worse. So, while we raised the money to purchase the property through a limited partnership, I went to complete the negotiations with the owner in Britain. We had offered $2,000,000. The controlling owner was expecting full payment in cash at closing, but we knew that he was anxious to get out soon. We had tea, while I presented our plan: two partnership interests ($200,000), plus $300,000 cash on closing, and six subsequent payments of $250,000, each quarter for six quarters. I left him to reflect upon our offer and arranged a second meeting at the Castle at Thornbury, then owned by friends. We met the next day and he accepted our offer, after which we had dinner with my friends. (By the way, the value of his two shares generously rewarded him for all his time, trouble, and money wasted.)

I like to travel with an open return ticket. After initial meetings, I will excuse myself to explore the cultural resources of the locale. This shows sincere interest in the culture and a willingness to invest in local knowledge, and it gives the other party a chance to consider my overtures. When we meet again, we exchange pleasantries and then I ask for their proposal by using non-verbal behaviors. I wait in silence, making eye contact, as if to say, "Well, what are you proposing ?" People hate silence in a pressure situation, and often will fill it with indiscretions.

As the negotiations proceed, continue to ask for clarification of their presentations and ask for questions from them about your offers. Do not try to impress them by telling them how great this proposal is for them. That would insult their intelligence. The same objective can be achieved by answering their questions.

As we trade concessions, don't bet on promises for future consideration in exchange for current obligations. Those promises will soon be forgotten. Instead, match concessions in value and timing, and be prepared to reciprocate. Having made commitments, keep them. The other party will know whether they are painful, and will accept your need to balance the scale later.

Two final observations that should be obvious: 1) Avoid self-disclosure. Prudence requires that we listen more than we talk. The more the opponent knows of your situation, the greater his ability to work negotiations to his advantage, and 2) Never make threats. They are a sign of weakness. If you feel that you must break off negotiations, or "to get even," just do it. Don't talk about it. And when you do it, be gracious, even as you turn the screws. I love the saying attributed to E. B. White, "He was a real gentleman. He never offended anyone, except intentionally."

Once we are operating, we must adjust our management techniques to limit our exposure to political risks. We use three strategies that appear contradictory, but are not. The first are **integrative techniques** which help us to be less noticeable as a foreign firm. Public relations are central to this effort. (You may wish to refer to lesson #1.5.) Choose a local name. Develop relationships with local suppliers and local producers.

We named our resort in Antigua, The Pineapple Beach Club. The Antiguans are proud of their local black pineapple, so the name appealed to them. "Beach" was for our customers who want beach-front location. And "Club" was to present an image of selectivity and privilege for our guests and our employees. We also designed the resort to resemble a Caribbean village, and added other local touches, such as local foods on the menu, and Thursday evening lectures on local culture and history.

The second technique is the use of joint-ventures and partnerships. We find local partners who share our vision and bring resources that we lack. We are seeking compatibility in terms of their firm specific advantages and our strategic objectives. In addition, their local knowledge can protect us from pressures for unethical behavior.

Finally, we use **Protective/ Defensive** techniques. These are strategies to discourage interference in our activities. Our best assurance that our associates will honor their commitments is their continued need for our services and cooperation. Hence, the protective/ defensive methods may be non-integrative. We keep key knowledge and control with ex-patriot staff. For example, at the resort, our marketing relationships, reservations, and financial records were the exclusive domain of our three American managers. In China, an English engineer supervises quality control and shipping, and all products are delivered to us in the U.S., before being repackaged and delivered to our customers. Otherwise, our Chinese partner would try to by-pass us and sell directly to our customers. Another important protective/defensive method is to locate research and development elsewhere and limit local access to key technologies. We share as needed, but do the essential work at home. A third technique is to borrow money locally, so that assets and liabilities are balanced in local currency. This may also prevent interference, which would exposes local investors and lenders to risk. As a result, we gain their support. As a final protection, we diversify production and suppliers to reduce the leverage of our associates. In Tahiti, we knew that American Hawaii Cruises could pullout anytime, leaving us with several hundred passengers expecting a holiday vacation that we couldn't deliver. Accordingly, we obtained allocations from another airline, and directed 10% of our travelers to it. When AHC cancelled, we shifted our passengers and didn't miss a beat. (We also claimed damages from AHC and quickly settled for what we owed them for past travel, saving us $100,000.)

Before we conclude the topic of risk and negotiation, we must note that all agreements expire, or must be altered in response to changing circumstances. As we head toward expiration, new agreements must be reached. So, we should include in our initial agreements, provisions specifying triggers for renegotiation. And we should remember that in dealing with governments, sovereigns have rights that we do not. Hence, we should be planning for the eventual expiration of agreements, including beginning early to repeat the steps described above, so that the new agreements are reached before there is unfavorable time pressure.

Review questions and exercises:
Define Political Risk, and explain its significance.
Contrast Macro and Micro political risk.
Identify the three major areas of risk which must be examined to assess the degree of political risk.
In the area of negotiation, explain the issues of evaluating positions, participant behavior, and negotiating tactics.
What three strategies are used to manage political risk ?

Bibliography for Part One: International Business
Raymond Bowman, International Business Basics, {self-published}, 2002, Santa Barbara
Dowling, Welch, & Schuler, International Human Resources Management, SouthWest 1999
Peter Drucker, Management Tasks, Responsibilities & Practices, Harper & Row 1974
        and Adventures of a Bystander, Harper Collins 1979
Manuchar Farman Farmanian, Blood and Oil, Random House 1997
Robert Gates, A Passion for Leadership, Knopf 2016
Lawrence Harrison & Samuel Huntington, eds. Culture Matters Basic Books 2000
Geert Hofstede, Gert Jan Hofstede, and Michael Minkov, Cultures & Organizations: Software of the Mind, 3rd edition, McGraw-Hill 2010
John Micklethwait & AdrianWoolridge, A Future Perfect, Crown, 2000
Michael Porter, The Competitive Advantage of Nations. *Free Press, 1990*
Ludwig Von Mises, Bureaucracy, Yale Press, 1944
Murray Weidenbaum, The Bamboo Network, Free Press, 1996
Denis Wright, The English Amongst the Persians, Heinemann, 1977

I have also benefited from using a variety of texts over the quarter century of teaching International Business. Among the best which have influenced my thinking, presentation, and teaching methods are:
Alan Rugman & Richard Hodgetts, International Business McGraw-Hill 1994
Ricky Griffin & Michael Pustay, International Business, 7th edition, Pearson Education 2012

Part Two
Microeconomics, the Study of Markets

"The function of education is to teach one to think intensively and to think critically. Intelligence plus character, that is the goal of true education."
--- Martin Luther King, Jr.

Open market in Portland, Ore.

Lesson #2.1 Why Economics ?

In the first segment of this course, we introduced business and described methods for managing our business. Because businesses participate in markets, as do individuals, families, and other forms of social organization, we need to understand how people behave in markets and how markets function. These are the central issues of microeconomics. The foundation of economic analysis is the issue of *scarcity,* the concept of an imbalance between our desire to use resources in a variety of ways and the resources available. Therefore, economics is the study of how scarce resources are allocated among alternative uses. Microeconomics is about analyzing the methods of decision-making choices and explaining the outcomes of those choices. *How do societies organize people (labor) and other resources to make the choices which must be made because of scarcity ?*

From this definition of the domain of economics derive two vital conclusions:

1) There is abundant evidence that people respond to incentives; therefore, ignoring the effect of a policy on incentives is dangerously misleading.

2) When resources are scarce, every chosen use precludes some other valuable use. The value of that next best use of the resources is the sacrifice associated with the choice. We call that sacrifice the **opportunity cost**.

Economists are proud of their tradition of applying scientific method to the study of economic behavior. In fact, Paul Samuelson reoriented the profession for half a century by deriving many useful results from five simple assumptions of choice behavior. (See his doctoral thesis, later published as Foundations of Economic Analysis.) This was also the basis for his transformative text book. He formalized the two techniques of economic analysis: 1) decision-makers will strive for the best choice of those available (maximizing some function) and 2) markets will tend towards a stable equilibrium (a balance of the forces of supply and demand).

Milton Friedman[1] elaborated on the application of scientific method to economics in his paper, "The Methodology of Positive Economics". Following John Neville Keynes, Friedman distinguished positive science ("a body of systematized knowledge concerning what is"), normative science ("a body of systematized knowledge discussing the criteria of what ought to be"), and art ("a system of rules for attainment of a given end"). **Positive analysis** measures cause and effect, and is independent of any particular ethical judgments. Its performance should be judged by validity of its predictions. Our willingness to investigate possibilities of cause and effect should not be limited by normative values. **Normative analysis** considers the desirability of various possible actions in terms of their outcomes. However, this is not the same as opinion. Normative analysis requires comparing the outcomes of various actions, and considering the choices which will lead to those outcomes. Therefore, it cannot be independent of positive science. Our values will influence our assessment of the desirability of the outcomes, the associated costs (sacrifices) and benefits (gains). However, the careful statement of the logic of cause and effect (the theory) and the estimation of outcomes from observation will help us to make the best choice to improve our welfare. In other words, normative judgment should not be based on feelings and opinion.

To clarify these concepts, let's consider the issue of Global Warming, now called "Climate Change." There are a number of issues which should be carefully investigated, before we introduce public policies, or even voluntarily change our individual behaviors. Some of these issues fall in the domains of natural science, politics, economics, or ethics. I will list six:

1) Is the earth getting warmer ? (a scientific question), 2) If so, what are the causes ? (also, a scientific question), 3) If so, what are the costs & benefits ? (both scientific and economic questions), 4) Given 1-3, can we do anything about it ? (scientific and political questions) 5) If #1-4, is political action likely to be effective ? (a political question) and 6) Should we do anything about it ? (a normative question). Notice that much of our public discourse jumps from #1 straight to #6 without considering the other issues. This may advance the interests of one group, or another, but it is likely to lead to flawed choices and poor policies.

Finally, we must keep in mind that all science requires the development and testing of theories of cause and effect. A theory should be accepted, if it explains and predicts the phenomena of interest. All action is based in some theory. However, while we use of theories all the time, we must be open to revising, or replacing, our theories, when they do not provide enough accuracy, or when a new theory proves to be more accurate. Unfortunately, we tend to become committed to specific theories and reluctant to consider new, or different, ones. We may also make the mistake of using a theory where it does not apply (outside of its scope).

Scientific theories are often presented in the form of **models** which are formal statements of the specific theory of cause and effect. The model begins with a statement of assumptions which defines the conditions under which we expect the theory to apply (explain and predict). From the assumptions, we state structural relationships between the causes (independent variables) and the effects (the outcomes, the dependent variables). Then, we logically deduce conclusions from the assumptions and structure of the model. Finally, we test the model against observations (data). The tests permit us to assess the limits to the validity of the theory. The model helps us to be specific about the applicability of the model, and to maintain logical rigor. Most importantly, the model permits others to understand exactly what we are trying to explain, where the theory may be useful (scope), and how we reached our conclusions. Therefore, others can check our work and our evidence, and can perform their own tests of our theory.

For us to apply economic method, I suggest a three step process:

1) *Is this an economic issue, therefore economic methods will apply ?*
Economic issues involve choices in the use of scarce resources. Hence, working in the garden vs. painting the house is an economic issue. However, who to date on Saturday night is not.

2) *If it is an economic issue, is it a choice issue or a market equilibrium issue ?* For example, "which job I will take" is a choice issue, but the level of employment and wages is a market issue. In the first case, we use the tools of "optimization" We identify the choices and constraints and identify the best attainable. This becomes the predicted choice. If we have a market issue, we identify the schedule of planned purchases (Demand) and the schedule of planned offers for sale (Supply). Then, using the two as simultaneous equations, we look for the outcome that matches Demand to Supply, predicting the "equilibrium" price and quantity.

3) *Apply the correct technique to the problem and evaluate the results.*

Every society must organize its resources. To understand the economy of any community, we ask how does this community perform five tasks: a) fixing standards: How do they measure the resources sacrificed and the products gained ? Among other techniques, our standard accounting practices serve this purpose. b) organizing production: How is the allocation of resources determined and coordinated ? In a market economy, we compete for resources which flow to the purchaser who is willing to pay the most for them. c) distribution: How do we decide who gets the products ? In a market economy, the goods will go to those who are willing and able to pay the most. d) maintenance & improvement: What portion of our product will be used to maintain and enhance our ability to produce in the future ? This is the issue of investment.

People, machinery and equipment, research and development of new knowledge and new methods (technologies), changes in the environment, and social and political institutions, all have issues of investment. And society must sacrifice some current satisfaction to use resources for maintenance and growth. For us, financial markets facilitate the decisions of saving (abstinence, sacrifice) and investing (using resources to maintain or increase our ability to produce in the future).e) All societies must find ways to balance the use of resources (absorption) with the resources available (production). In our case, we use markets to ration.

We notice that the societies that are able to provide the most material goods and services for their people, have the greatest degree of specialization and the most opportunities for exchange. Specialization permits us to use our natural talents, develop specific skills and knowledge, focus on a few tasks out of many, take advantage of local differences in natural resources, employ highly specific machinery and equipment that would not be practical if it were rarely used, and make minor improvements through experience.

On the other hand, specialization requires trust and co-ordination. We become interdependent. So, now we need to organize activities, and that requires resources, too. We discussed these issues in a different context in the first nine lessons of this book. The conflict between the gains in efficiency through specialization and the increases in costs of greater management, helps to explain why some organizations are large and others are small. In the former, there is more room for expansion, before the costs of management outweigh the benefits of further specialization.

Focusing on economic organization through markets, we can identify five important aspects: the choices, prices, property rights, transactions costs, and market systems.

Because participation in markets is voluntary, we perceive that the participants are making choices. Again, there are five: 1) **What to produce ?** What will be the volume and combination of products ? We might call this, **the product mix**. For example, how many homes and how many tanks and ships ? The Soviet Union's commitment of one-third of its economy to defense caused neglect of consumer welfare, and contributed ultimately to its collapse. We decide what to produce based on what people are willing and able to purchase. The closer we can approximate what the customer desires, the more he is willing purchase and the more he is willing to pay. This system is not guarantee to provide the best possible outcome, but does provide incentives to meet people's desires. 2) **How shall we produce ?** That is, what methods (**technology**) shall we use ? In many cases, the methods are the same that have always been used, and the results tend to remain the same, too. In our society, we strive to find the methods that produce adequate quality at lowest cost. Notice in both of these issues, what to produce and how to produce, the incentive is the search for profit. 3) **Who gets the products ?** This is the issue of **distribution**. In our market economy, those who have more wealth, (the ownership of valuable assets), or income, (the recurrent payment for the services of their assets), are able to bid for more of the products, and hence, enjoy more of the products. In other words, who gets the goods ? Whoever is willing and able to pay for them. 4) **What portion of current production will be enjoyed now and what portion will be used to maintain and increase future production ?** This is the split between **consumption and investment**. And finally, 5) **Who, and how, will the choices be made ?** In our society, we use a variety of methods, purely voluntary participation, co-operation with others, such as families and associations, and coercion, whether by law, custom, or contract. In other societies, the choices, including the distribution of product may be decided by tradition, or by some elite. In the last case, the elite often selects the products that it values most, the methods that use the resources owned by the elite, and then, extracts more and more of the product for itself, reducing the rewards and incentives for the rest of the society. Needless to say, this tends to lead to stagnation and alienates the unrewarded. The Communist party in the Soviet Union is one example, and the Mughal Empire in India would be another. The Soviet Union collapsed, and a small British force chipped away at the Indian Rajahs, until Britain ruled all of India. In both cases, I believe the collapse occurred, because most of the population had no stake in the existing system.

We choose to organize as much as two-thirds of our economic activity through markets. Other institutions are also important: governments, families, social associations, and not-for-profit organizations. Here, we wish to understand markets. Markets provide an arrangement for buyers and sellers to exchange. Markets provide information, and they provide choices. Competition in markets prevents exploitation, provides incentives for innovation and cost reduction, and results in greater gains for consumers, and in the real sense, higher income.

There are three essential elements for the success of markets. First, there must be clear rights to the ownership and transfer of property. Ownership means the exclusive privilege to decide the use of a scarce resource. The motivation for participation in market exchange is the acquisition of those rights. For example, we offer the services of our assets (labor, time and skills; and capital, physical property) in exchange for income. We are paid income which we exchange for other resources which we prefer. And the renter or purchaser obtains the temporary, or permanent, use of the resource. The respect for **property rights** must evolve as markets develop, and the registration of rights, and their protection through public safety and the enforcement of contracts is vital. There are interesting studies of this transformation of Western societies from traditional to contractual in books by Gertrude Himmelfarb and Karl Polanyi.

Second, **prices** have vital roles in the development and functioning of markets. Prices signal the owners of resources and producers of products, the sacrifice that others are willing to make to obtain those resources and products, and thus the opportunity costs of using the resources as they do, now. A high price signals an opportunity to gain from production and sale, and a low price signals that there may be better uses for our resources and better products to provde. A low price is a signal to discontinue production and shift resources to something more valuable. From the point of view of the prospective buyer, the price signals the sacrifice that is required to obtain the product or resource. A high price suggests only buying, if the product is especially valuable to the consumer, considering substitutes and other activities. A low price encourages the consumer to enjoy more, and even find more uses for this abundant good or service.

When prices change, the signals change and both buyers and sellers adjust their behavior. Prices change in order to **ration**. After all, if there is enough of the resource or product to meet all needs, there is no need for exclusive property rights, or rationing. There is no scarcity. However, if more is desired than is available, it must be rationed, and pricing is the method of markets. The price will adjust up, or down, until the quantity that is offered equals the quantity that buyers are willing to purchase. Notice, that if a product is abundant, it's price will fall. Buyers will choose to buy more and sellers will choose to provide less. If a product is scarce, the price will rise, until sellers are willing to provide more and buyers are willing to settle for less. As production changes, so does the allocation of resources, from one activity to another. Hence, the ability of prices to adjust freely to first ration, and then to signal, leads to the flexibility of production, and resource employment, that helps us to produce the desired mix of products and minimize the waste of resources.

The third element of markets is **transactions cost**. Just as the coordination of all the specialization in production requires the costs of management, markets also have organizational costs. We use resources in the process of exchange. Most obviously, we have the supply chain of distributors who move the goods to the customer. We should also consider costs to the consumer of finding and acquiring the product, even allowing for the possibility that many of us enjoy shopping. There is the opportunity cost associated with this use of our time. In the market transaction, the seller considers his net proceeds from the exchange and the buyer considers his total costs. A transaction cost drives a wedge between the two. That is why we often see a product selling for a higher price in Africa than in Europe --- the transaction costs are high: transportation, security, breakage, corruption, crime, taxes. The seller compares "net" in each market. Why sell in Cameroon for $3 and net $2, when I can sell in the USA for $2.50 and net $2.25 ? The lower the transactions costs, the less the buyer must pay and the more the seller keeps. Hence, *lower transactions costs are an incentive to engage in exchange*, increase the desirability of establishing property rights, and as a result, influence whether a market will develop, and whether the market will allocate resources efficiently.

Today, we can see vividly how rapidly markets develop when property rights are secure, prices are free to adjust, and transactions costs are low, in countries such as China, Mexico, South Korea, and Botswana. And we can see the decline where these three are absent (Russia, Cuba, and North Korea) and where they wax and wane in unpredictable ways (Argentina, Bolivia, and Venezuela).

Now that we understand the foundations of markets, we can build a model of market interaction. What happens in markets ? Buyers and sellers exchange offers and negotiate a transfer of property rights. So, our analysis requires three parts: 1) characterizing the buyers behavior (Demand) 2) characterizing the seller's behavior (Supply), and 3) considering the likely outcome of their interaction. We will start with basic **Supply and Demand Analysis** in free and competitive markets.

To do so, clear understanding of **value** is essential. Confusion on value bedeviled the classical economists, such as Smith, Malthus, and Ricardo, as well Karl Marx and his successors. An important insight that we gained in the last century is that *value is determined by expectations for the future and not the past*. Value depends on the net benefits that will accrue over the time that we have use of the product or resource. What it cost to produce, what prior owners paid, how many resources were used, are irrelevant to the buyer. He considers: what is the value that I will gain from acquiring this, and what must I sacrifice ? What you paid for that painting has nothing to do with what I'd be willing to pay.

Another source of confusion about value has been the common coincidence of price and cost. This is the result of producers expanding production as long as their added revenue (price) exceeds their added costs, and stopping as they approach equality. However, this is cost following value in exchange, not value being determined by cost. When two numbers are equal, confusing the direction of cause and effect is an easy mistake to make.

We should distinguish "value in use" from "value in exchange". Value in use is a psychological, or financial measure, of usefulness, for example the joy of an ice cream cone, or the value added by a new machine. This is most important in measuring the success of an economic system, but of course, the measurement of psychological value is beyond our abilities, so far. Value in exchange is what I'd be willing to accept in a sale, or pay in a purchase. What am I willing to sacrifice ? These two values should be the same at the limit --- the most that I would pay is equal to the satisfaction added by the gain in exchange. However, we know from the research in Behavioral Economics that these values may differ. What I'd be willing to pay for acquire a good is often much less than the minimum that I would accept to trade it away. We call this the *possession bias*.

The concept of cost must be confirmed. **Costs** are the value of the sacrifices that must be made to acquire the product. Often distinguishing between one-time costs such as the purchase of a car (sunk costs), continuing costs that are independent of the level of production or sales such as regular maintenance and insurance for your car (commonly called over-head or fixed costs), and those costs which change with production or sales, such as the gas, oil, and tires whose replacement depends on the use of the car (variable costs). Once paid, sunk costs may or may not be recovered, but will not recur, when we are more active. For example, if I purchase a ticket to a show, I have paid that cost. Whether I stay for the show depends on costs and benefits of attending. I might fail to go or leave early, because a better opportunity appeared, or I hate the show and staying makes me worse off. Does this explain why fans will leave the game before it ends to avoid traffic, even though they paid for the tickets ?

All of these are different from the price which represents the agreed exchange. We expect the price to be just high enough to sell the last unit to the last buyer, although where participants can discriminate between buyers (or sellers), there may be many deals at many prices. Where competition and full information occur, we can expect the market to settle on one price. There is no reason for anyone to pay more, or to accept less. Another source of confusion is the common expression, "The price is XYZ", what is your price ? In this case, the word "price" is being used for "offer". Some offers are clearly ridiculous in the sense that no one would accept them. However, using the word "price" confers some credibility to the number which may "anchor" a participant's perception as he considers subsequent offers. *Price is the value in exchange which balances the Demand for the last unit exchanged with the willingness to sell that last unit, Supply.* Price is meaningful, only if an exchange actually occurs.

As we consider the motivations and likely choices of buyers and sellers, we make a behavioral assumption --- each participant will assess his opportunities and make the decision which gives him his greatest net benefit, the difference between gains and sacrifices of an action. To make the best choice, the decision-maker must be able to identify the best opportunities and measure benefits and costs associated with each. So, complete information is an important, associated assumption.

We recognize the importance of incremental decisions. Much of the time, our choice is to do little more or a little less. Only occasionally is the choice all or nothing. This means that usually we are comparing the benefits of a little more to the costs of a little more. We call these the incremental or "marginal" benefits and costs. Given our optimization assumption, we can deduce that the rational decision-maker will undertake an activity, if he expects the total benefits to exceed the total costs, and he will do more of the activity, until the added benefits no longer exceed the added costs.

Let us characterize the buyers. As usual in economics, primarily we are interested in the quantities. The **Theory of Demand** has been formulated to explain the quantity that buyers intend to purchase under expected conditions. There are five causes of this intention. First, the product must be useful. If it is not useful, then I wouldn't bother to shop for it, and I wouldn't sacrifice to obtain it. Economists use the code-word "tastes" to capture all the dimensions of usefulness. Experimental social psychologists and behavioral economists investigate the nature of tastes, their origins, their stability, and their variety. Often, when we investigate one market at one time, we assume that tastes are what they are and change slowly over time. This is obviously more likely for less emotionally loaded products than for fads and fashions. The important point is that the more useful a product is to more people, the larger the quantity that people will intend to purchase. Second, the buyers need the ability to purchase. They need income, or wealth. The two are closely related. Income is what we receive for the services of our assets, such as the salary for our labor. Wealth is the price which we could receive if we sold our assets. The connection is the interest rate. We talk about capitalizing income. For example, if I can earn $1,000 per month renting out my apartment, that would be net income of $8,000 per year after expenses. A reasonable saver might be willing to buy the apartment for $100,000, because he would be satisfied to earn 8% on his purchase. Either way, if you want to purchase or rent something, you need to be prepared to offer something in exchange. *Tastes give us the motivation, income gives us the ability, to participate in the market.* Third, we consider the offers in the market: the offering price, the offering prices of substitutes, and of complements (products used jointly with the one that we are considering). If the prices of substitutes fall, we will be less willing to buy the quantities of the original product. If the prices of complements fall, the combined cost has fallen, and we will be willing to buy more. Fourth, the size of the market matters. This can be estimated by reference to demographics, identifying the numbers within the market area who can be expected to have a taste for the product and the income to act upon it. Finally, expectations can influence the quantity demanded. If we expect a greater need or expect the price to rise, we may purchase more now. If we expect more limited use or a lower price in the future, we may buy less now. We might use some symbols from mathematics:

The Quantity Demanded is a function of Tastes, Income, Price, Prices of substitutes, Prices of complements, Demographics, and Expectations. We would choose a functional form, and using data from several similar markets, or the same market at different times, estimate the importance of each causal relationship. (Scientists, unlike adolescent males, are always looking for meaningful relationships.) An example would be:

$$Q = P^a \ P_{sub}^b \ P_{comp}^c \ D^d \ E^e$$ where the capitals stand for the variables and the small letters are exponents which will be estimated as coefficients. We can transform the function into logarithms, $$Ln \ (Q) = a \ Ln \ (P) + b \ Ln \ (P_{sub}) + c \ Ln \ (P_{comp}) + d \ Ln \ (D) + e \ Ln \ (E)$$ You may notice that there is no variable "T" for "tastes" in these equations. The excuse is that we can't measure tastes directly. Instead, we conclude that any residual variance in the Quantity Demanded, that is not explained by variance in the other causes, must be the result of a change in tastes. This is a bit of sleight of hand. What if the residual is the result of some other left-out variable, or a fundamental flaw in our theory ? The reason that I present these equations here is to remind you that in science, we must state formally, the relationships including the structure of our theory, and then subject the resulting model to empirical tests. Using mathematics also helps us to avoid errors in logic, and helps others to understand our theories, check our thinking and our results, and pursue their own tests.

Often, we focus on the relationship between the price of the good and the quantity demanded, this is only one dimension of Demand, but if the others change slowly over time, and there is an imbalance between the quantity demanded and the quantity supplied, it is this relation between price and quantity that will see the biggest and fastest adjustments to ration, and thus change the signal for the participants, leading to adjustments in their choices.

One of the results of the focus on how the buyer responds to changing prices has been observed so consistently that we call it **The Law of Demand** (like the Law of Gravity). It is a theory of cause and effect. If the price falls, the quantity demanded will increase, and if the price rises, the quantity demanded will fall. The Law of Demand is consistent with the assumption of rational consumer behavior. If buyers are rational, they will buy less when a price rises, for two reasons; their budget does not permit them to buy as much, and at the new price, the product is less attractive in comparison to the alternatives. We call these the income and the substitution effects.

A Demand Schedule is a table showing the Quantities Demanded at various prices, and a Demand Curve is a graphic representation of the Demand Schedule, usually using Cartesian coordinates with quantity on the x-axis and price on the y-axis. (I know this is strange, but it is an accident of history, when 19th century economists were focusing on the quantities demanded and supplied determining the equilibrium price.)

In the early 1990s, we had a drought in Santa Barbara. The politicians wanted to decrease water use by one-third to stretch existing supplies from two to three years, buying time to obtain access to state water and to construct a desalination plant. But the officials were worried about revenue, so along with a media campaign for conservation, they raised the price of water by one-third. Actual use fell by 50%. The politicians under-estimated the incentive effect of higher prices. An 18% increase in price would have brought the desired 30% conservation response. Their mistake put the politicians in the awkward position of encouraging citizens to use more water during the water emergency. Policy makers often ignore incentive effects. One of the central conclusions of economics is that people do respond to incentives.

The other side of the market is the offer to sell. It will depend on the opportunity for profit. So, the price of the good (value in exchange) is essential, because **revenue** is just the quantity sold times the price. The calculation of costs is more complicated. **Costs** will depend on the technology available. Technology is a fancy word for method, and associated with each method is a combination of resources. As we consider the resource requirements of each technology, we also consider the costs of those resources. We must compete for the resources. Our offer must be the best one received by the resource owners. Therefore, the prices of other products which use the same resources and their productivity in those processes, will influence what we must pay (their opportunity costs), and thus our choice of method. Finally, the number of sellers, the flexibility of their production facilities, and their expectations for prices and costs will influence how much they plan to bring to market.

Because a greater difference between price and costs offers more profit, we have a theory that the higher the price of a good, the greater will be the Supply. We call it, **The Law of Supply**. It's just as reliable as the Law of Demand. Of course, if any of the factors determining costs change, that will impact the willingness to Supply, as well.

We have been discussing the plans of buyers and sellers. We use our first technique of analysis to predict outcomes. We assume that the actors (buyers and sellers) are rational. They will choose a combination of products and activities that maximize their satisfaction (buyers) or their profit (sellers). We call this technique **optimization**, and naturally we use the tools of calculus, specifying functions including constraints, and then, finding the maximum, or minimum, of the function. This is the first technique of economic analysis.

To recapitulate, we assume the decision-maker is rational (goal-directed). Then, the decision-maker will 1) assess opportunities for achieving his goals, 2) consider his tastes (his assessment of the usefulness of the outcome) and 3) choose the action which takes him as close to his goals as possible. We call this process of making the best decision from those attainable, optimization.

Now, let's consider the interaction of buyers and sellers. We want to estimate the likely outcome. We suspect that if Demand and Supply are different, prices and behavior will change. For example, if sellers plan to sell more than the buyers want, we expect price to fall. Sellers will plan to sell less next time, and buyers will purchase more at the lower price. When the Quantity Demanded equals the Quantity Supplied, there is no need for prices, or behavior, to change. The market is balanced. In systems analysis terms, the market is in equilibrium.

So, we try to determine this equilibrium. When will the quantity demanded equal the quantity supplied? Fortunately, if the laws of demand and supply hold --- people buy less as price rises and suppliers offer more, therefore the shortage is reduced --- then, the system will be stable. We can estimate the two functions and solve them together for the price and quantity that represent balance. We can be confident that the system will tend to that conclusion. This method of **Equilibrium Analysis** is the second technique of economists. (Aren't you glad that there are only two ?)

In fact, we have just described one of the key marvels of the market system. When there is an imbalance between plans to purchase (Demand) and plans to sell (Supply), the price adjusts and both sides of the market adjust their behavior. This brings the system into balance much faster, and with fewer traumas, than any other rationing system that I can identify. And the larger the market, the easier the adjustment becomes. In a free trade environment, if price rises or falls by enough to cover any additional transactions costs, a surge of exports (the surplus situation of falling price) or a surge of imports (the shortage and rising price situation) will bring the market into balance quickly and with minimal income redistribution.

Notice also that through voluntary participation in markets, both buyers and sellers gain. If we buy as long as the value to us exceeds the sacrifice (the price we pay), we have a net gain, which economists call **consumer surplus**. Similarly, if the seller produces and sells as long as his sacrifice (his marginal costs) are less than his reward (the selling price), he too has a gain. We call his gain **producer surplus**. Now, buyers and sellers may be aware of the other party's net gain and try to appropriate it. Why do I charge you less than the maximum that you would be willing to pay ? One answer is that competition that gives you choices. Another answer is that finding out that maximum may be difficult, or costly. Finally, I can only charge different customers different prices for the same product, if I can prevent resale. This process of charging different customers different prices is called **price discrimination**. We will revisit it, later.

Questions for review:
Define the subject of Economics.
What is scientific method ?
Explain the roles of prices in solving the economic problems of production, technology, and income distribution. {Be specific about each.}
Demonstrate a simple model of cause and effect using a function (formula) and two dimensional graph or diagram. {Be sure to label all axes & functions.}
Identify five or more determinants of *Demand* in a market.
Identify the determinants of *Supply*
What is *Consumer Surplus* ? What is *Producer Surplus* ?
How they relate to Price Discrimination ? {Hint: a diagram may help.}

[1] Friedman, Milton <u>The Methodology of Positive Economics</u> 1953

Lesson #2.2 Consumer Behavior

In this lesson, we develop more detailed theories of buyer behavior. There is little that economists say about the origin and modification of "tastes." Fortunately, Experimental Social Psychologists and Behavioral Economists continue to investigate this topic. Although we need more complete and consistent understanding of tastes, there are some important conclusions that we can reach from some modest and plausible assumptions.

Let's assume that consumer Demand depends on 1) expected usefulness (tastes or satisfaction) and 2) that as we consume more, at some point, even more has decreasing value to us. Gains in satisfaction would still be positive; the gains would just be smaller. Possibly, more of the good might make us worse off, but we don't expect anyone to continue to consume more at that point even if the good is free. If the good was free, they would consumer, until more would provide no more gains. Assumption 3) consumers will make the best choice available to them. They have goals for satisfaction, a budget that limits their choices, and prices which signal sacrifices. They will choose the combination of goods and services that offers them the most satisfaction attainable with their limited budget.

For example, if we are thirsty, a drink of water would be very important to us. If we have already had three glasses of water, a fourth is unlikely to be as important to us as that first glass, and a tenth glass might be considered "water torture." So, the willingness to spend suggests expected gains in satisfaction, but as we gain more of a good, we expect that our willingness to sacrifice diminishes. Of course, the point at which additions to satisfaction begin to decline will depend on the individual's tastes. After all, Imelda Marcos had three thousand pairs of shoes. I stopped at thirty-seven. How about you ?

Economists call this **the principle of diminishing marginal utility**. The expression is an example of scientific jargon which Axel Leijonhufvud mocked so beautifully in his essay, "Life Among the Econ" 1973 WEJ. The concept is that at some stage, the additions (marginal) to satisfaction (John Stuart Mill's utility) associated with more consumption, while still positive, become smaller (diminish).

With these three assumptions, we can build a powerful model of consumer behavior. The consumer has tastes that exhibit diminishing marginal utility; he also has a budget. The combination of his budget and the prices of the goods which he desires, limit the attainable combinations of goods that he can acquire. In fact, the prices of the various goods signal trade-offs in choices. For example, a bottle of red wine at $20 costs the same as two bottles of white wine at $10 each. The trade-off is one red or two white. Recalling our third assumption, "maximizing behavior," the consumer will only purchase more of one good, such as red wine, if it adds more to his satisfaction than the alternatives would do. For example, he will only buy the red wine if he feels it is at least twice as satisfying as the white, or four times as satisfying as the $5 hamburger. We could go further and speculate that the consumer will continue to purchase the red wine until the next bottle would not be worth two bottles of white. So, even if the consumer has a passion for red, as he purchases more, the additional satisfaction of another bottle declines, and at some point he stops purchasing more. We theorize that the consumer makes choices based on his personal assessment of incremental (marginal) benefits and costs, and he stops before marginal costs exceed marginal benefits.

We conclude with a **choice rule**, reasoning that consumers observe market their opportunities, as signaled by **relative prices,** and consider their expected satisfaction. They then choose the combination of quantities which balance their **willingness to substitute** (a psychological satisfaction trade-off) with the **market opportunity to substitute** (the relative prices). Example: red wine is worth twice as much as white to me, and the price ratio is $20:$10, also twice as much.

Consider a different choice. What if I purchased a bottle of red for $20 instead of two bottles of white, and at that point, the bottle of red was less satisfying than two bottles of white ? Wouldn't I be worse off than if I'd chosen the two whites ? All of this sounds like a long explanation of the obvious. A lot of scientific theories are … once you work them out and state them, carefully.

What happens if an important price changes ? There will be two effects. If an important price, such as rent, increases, the same budget will not cover the same pattern of expenditures. To buy the same goods would require more money. (The same should be true of small changes in minor budget items, but the effects may be smaller and more difficult to observe.) The increase in price is similar to having less income. In fact, economists would say, the consumer has less **real income**, meaning less purchasing power. The consumer must adjust his consumption. Having less purchasing power, he will buy a little less of everything, until the satisfaction of the last dollar spent on each good is similar. We call this the **income effect**. In the same way, a lower price relaxes the budget constraint, more goods become attainable, and because we want more of all goods, we will purchase more, again until the added satisfaction of one more dollar spent is equal across goods.

If we recall that relative prices matter, the change in one price also effects the comparison of relative prices. In order to achieve maximum satisfaction, we will buy less of what is now relatively more expensive, and more of what is now relatively less expensive. For example, we were willing to buy the red wine as long as it was twice as good, even though it was twice as expensive. If the red wine price goes to $30, it will need to be at least three times as good as the $10 white wine, or we won't buy it. Our preferences haven't changed, but our opportunities have. We will substitute the good whose relative price fell for the good whose relative price increased. We call this the **substitution effect**.

Our new pattern of purchases will depend on the strength of both the income and the substitution effects. Because an increase in price discourages consumption for both reasons, (we can't afford as much and it's relatively more expensive), we have a nice theoretic explanation of **The Law of Demand** --- why people will buy less as the price increases.

Back in the 1970s, a number economists ran experiments to test choice theory using laboratory rats. The rats were given a choice between Tom Collins Mix and Root Beer. To receive drinks, the rats had to push a different lever for each drink. Each drink had its price, the number of pushes required. Each rat was given income, a total number of lever pushes, after which the device would lock up. Prices were changed, but budgets adjusted so that prior consumption could be maintained. For example, if Tom Collins cost 10 pushes and Root Beer cost 5 pushes, and the rat used his budget of 100 pushes to "purchase" five TC and 10 RBs, but we change the price of RB to 10 pushes, the rat would need a budget of 150 pushes to continue to consume the same 15 drinks. By the changing the budget, the income effect of the price change was neutralized. The result was that all of the rats shifted to more of the *relatively less* expensive drink, in this case Tom Collins. Thus, the substitution effect was observed and the theory confirmed.[1] Many other studies have confirmed the income and substitution effects.

The implication for public policy is profound. For example, if we are concerned that rising energy prices will harm poor people. We might try to limit prices. If we do, we remove the signal to produce more energy and to conserve what we have, and we subsidize the rich consumers who purchase more energy. A better policy would be to let price do its job (ration and signal) and then offer a targeted subsidy to poor people equal to the additional cost of their traditional consumption pattern. Then, they could choose to consume as before, or they could substitute other goods. They might wear sweaters and use the savings to buy food or insulation. They would be responding to the price signal using the substitution effect. We would achieve the desired result of protecting the poor from harm, while encouraging conservation and increased supply. We could do the same for a housing shortage. Of course, this does involve discrimination against all those who receive no subsidy. Those without subsidy would be competing with everyone, including those with subsidies, and they would suffer the full income effect of the higher price. It could mean that the price increase would be greater, as the subsidized are not rationed out quite as quickly. Finally, who would pay the subsidy ?

Before we leave the model of rational consumer behavior, let's try the application of income and substitution effects to the **saving** decision. In this case, the choice is between consumption now or later. We can separate the timing of income from the timing of spending by borrowing and saving. The **interest rate** is the bridge that allows us to transform purchasing power. If we save, we sacrifice current satisfaction for future satisfaction, including the gain of interest. If we borrow, we gain current satisfaction, but lose future satisfaction, including the payment of interest.

As an example, consider income of $50,000. If we can borrow or lend at 10%, then, each dollar of this year's consumption costs us the $1.10 of consumption that we could have next year. A rational consumer would weigh the satisfaction obtainable for an extra dollar now vs. an extra $1.10 next year. Different preferences would lead to different choices by different people, even if they have the same income or wealth.

Now, consider what would happen if the interest rate changed. The opportunity would change and the decision maker would need to recalculate. For example, if the interest rate went to 15%, each dollar spent today would cost us $1.15 in lost consumption next year. Current consumption would become more expensive. The substitution effect suggests that we should save more (future satisfaction is relatively cheaper, now). But something else is happening; the reward for saving increased. I earn an extra $0.05 for every dollar that I save. It's as if my income increased. Why not enjoy some of that extra income now, as well as later ? The income effect suggests that we won't save as much as before, because we can reach our savings goals without savings quite as much. Unlike the earlier discussion of changing prices, in which the income and substitution effects work in same direction, in the case of interest rate changes and saving & borrowing behavior, they work in the opposite directions. Higher interest rates encourage savings (substitution effect) and also discourage it (income effect). This may explain why individuals may change their behavior, but overall we see little change in the national saving rate, when interest rates change. Savings is more strongly influenced by income and expectations.

A final note on **wealth effects**: Economists have always been interested in the effect of wealth on spending. If wealth is merely capitalized cash-flow, (wealth = income / interest rate), then there will be a statistical bias in models that include both wealth and income as variables. And when we look at measures of wealth, such as home values or stock market values, we see some inconsistencies. Changes in real estate values appear to influence spending, but changes in stock market values are less reliable. This is one of those anomalies of consumer behavior that appear irrational. Until we understand it better, I'll rely on average income, as the best predictor of consumer spending.

Although there are many confirmations of this simple consumer theory of rational, fully-informed actors making predictable decisions to buy less when price rise, we still find many exceptions that should make us uncomfortable. For some economists their economic model becomes their reality, and they will complain when consumers fail to act rationally, that is fail to conform to the predictions of their model. This is not science. When reality fails to conform to our model, we should revise, or replace our model, not vice versa.

Fred Hirsch (Social Limits to Growth, 1976) pointed out that some of the goods that we seek are strictly limited in supply --- there will only be one President of the USA, and only a limited number of beachfront homes in Santa Barbara. If many strive to obtain these goods, they will only drive up the price as needed to ration these scarce **"positional" goods**. We see this happening in desirable locations around the world, as the fortunate few impose land use restrictions against new construction, "to protect the environment." Prices rise for the benefit of existing owners, but prospective buyers may feel frustrated, even cheated. These scarce goods may become status markers, and even more desired. Prices go higher still, and more people are disappointed.

This result may have occurred as a perverse outcome of well-intended social change that increased economic opportunities for women to earn income over the past fifty years. Consider two families with one earner and one stay-at-home adult. Their income is $50,000 and they can afford house payments of $25,000 per year, including property taxes and insurance, and a mortgage rate of 6%, they might consider a thirty year mortgage of $275,000, and offer $325,000 for the house, including a $50,000 down payment. If both adults work, their income might go to $90,000, and their ability to support house payments goes to $45,000. They now feel comfortable with a thirty year 6% mortgage of $550,000 and make an offer of $600,000. If this is a broad trend in family income, in a normal market, the bidding among dual income households would lead to a construction boom, increase in the supply of homes and moderate price increases, but what if land use regulations prevent new construction ? The prices of the existing homes will rise as needed to ration the limited inventory, and the buyers will be no better off for choosing two jobs. Their increase in income is "mortgaged" for that home that they purchase at the price inflated by competition with similar households. The sellers and their realtors will appropriate some of the benefit from the rise in two income families. This is also a nice example of "the fallacy of composition" (or as the British call it, "The fallacy of the heap") --- what is good for the individual, more income, is not good for the group --- it only raises prices. And this helps to explain why some many people say that they must have two incomes in order to have the house that they want. They do, because others are making the same choices. I am not arguing against two income families, I am merely pointing out the implications and one explanation of the housing inflation of the 1970-1990 period.

In the 1970s, Tibor Scitovsky in The Joyless Economy and George Katona in Psychological Economics, began integrating consumer behavior and social psychology. Acknowledging the complexity of human motivations and the limits of cognition, they helped us to understand the limits of rational choice, and thus, the limits of economic analysis that depends on the assumption of rational actors.

Nearing his own retirement and dissatisfied with the dominant theory, Tibor borrowed a psychological theory of the time and applied it to consumer choice. One of the interesting ideas (he liked the word, "notions") was that we seek an optimal level of psychological stimulation, not too much and not too little, a psychological equilibrium. If we find our environment not sufficiently stimulating, we will seek to raise our level of stimulation by our actions and activities. This might explain why the passengers in the car want to listen to the radio, and why teenagers prefer action movies and violent video games. Perhaps, it is the reason the bored housewife shops, until she drops. If we find our environment overwhelming, we will seek to lower our level of stimulation. This would explain why the driver of the car wants the radio off, and the tired homemaker or worker chooses to read a book, or meditates. In this view, the extrovert is someone trying to raise his level of stimulation, and the introvert is someone trying to lower theirs. Both are seeking a comfort zone of stimulation.

Another important insight is the notion that we get used to a level of consumption. If we maintain that level of consumption, we are satisfied, but not thrilled. If we do not maintain that level of satisfaction, we are unhappy and feel deprived. On the other hand, increases beyond that to which we have become accustomed raise our level of pleasure. You may be familiar with this idea from addiction theory. The implication is that maintaining levels of consumption bring no joy. Rather we are on a treadmill of work and consumption. (Hence, Tibor's title, The Joyless Economy.)

In his book, Predictably Irrational, Dan Ariely gives many examples of consumer behavior that violate the assumptions of conventional theory, but have their own logic, nonetheless. For example, there are **social influences**. We like to belong, so celebrity endorsements and peer opinions matter. We may choose to purchase what is popular. (When my wife and I were planning our wedding, we found that a sales lady at Bloomingdale's kept recommending popular patterns of china and silver. I asked why. She responded that most shoppers want what their friends have.)

Paul David developed the concept of "network externalities." His point is that we may choose a product, because it gives us greater access to a large network. For example, my computer needs to be compatible with the programs that we all use at work, because I need to communicate with my peers. And having chosen one technology, I may be reluctant to change, if there are substantial switching costs. Apple needed many years to realize that its incompatibility with Microsoft limited its appeal to PC users, even though the Apple products and software were demonstrably superior. How does Hewlett-Packard use this quirk to its advantage in selling computer printers ? (We buy the printer for a song, but pay regularly for expensive printer cartridges.)

Many experiments have demonstrated that people like to be treated fairly and will attempt to treat others fairly, even when there is no penalty for taking advantage of others. An obvious example is that we leave reasonable tips for waiters, even when we never intend to return. The implication is that businesses will be reluctant to change prices or quality, if to do so would risk their reputation, even if scarcity or rising costs justify those price increases. So, businesses may raise prices when costs increase, but only slowly.

A particularly troubling behavior is the failure of decision makers to ignore non-monetary opportunity costs. This is what Krueger calls "the endowment effect." On several occasions, I tried watching a Will Farrell movie, --- after all he is very popular and his films do very well. When I buy my ticket for $10, it is a sunk cost, meaning that there is no refund if decide to leave early. I discovered that I hate his films. Sitting there for another hour is too painful to contemplate. A rational decision-maker would weigh the pleasure and the pain, and decide to leave. The ticket price is no longer relevant; nothing is going to change that $10 expense, already paid. I would leave, but many people would be stubborn --- I paid for it and I'm going to stay --- even though staying makes them worse off. This is irrational, but common.

An interesting variation occurs, when we compare what we would be willing to pay to acquire something to what we would be willing to receive to give it up. Have you ever been reluctant to buy something for $50 but having bought it, refused to sell it for $100 ? We appear to value what we have over what we don't yet have. We called this **the endowment effect**.

Dan Ariely has demonstrated that **arbitrary coherence** distorts our purchase decisions. I have a friend who sells oriental carpets. Each carpet is unique, and most people rarely buy a carpet, so the consumer has little information about what he should pay. Of course, no consumer will pay more than it is worth to him. The problem is in negotiating. My friend has a bright yellow tag with red writing on each piece. There is a price, such as $5,000 and then a slash, 50% offer, price $2,500. Even though initial price is arbitrary, it fixes in our mind and influences our perception of what the price should be. This strategy also plays to our desire for bargains.

Ariely also reports that people participating in economic activities also subscribe to various **social norms**. After a particularly sumptuous Thanks-giving dinner, he offered his mother-in-law $400 in payment. He violated a social norm. She had fixed the feast out of love for her family; the offer of payment insulted her. (I am often insulted by friends who will not permit me to act as host, by both inviting them to dinner and paying for it. I am particularly annoyed when they finally agree to let me pay, with the parting comment, "We'll pay next time." This may make them feel less like mooches, but it denies me the pleasure of being generous.) In another case, Ariely advised a daycare center to charge parents who pick up their children late. The problem became worse, not better, because the parents now felt justified to be late, --- they were paying for the privilege.

Psychologist Daniel Gilbert has offered some relevant insights in his recent book, Stumbling on Happiness. He believes that humans are the only animals that think about the future and can imagine abstractions. He believes that humans add what they know about the past to what they perceive currently, in order to predict the future. Therefore, we should be able to imagine our future tastes and preferences, but instead, we make mistakes which are both regular and systematic. Some of the explanation is physiological. The frontal lobe allows us to imagine the future, and the frontal lobe is the last to mature, and first to deteriorate with old age. We notice what captures our attention. We file it away. We recall it by association. Even information acquired after the event can color our memory of the event. Accordingly, because they are selective, memories of experiences are unreliable. Gilbert quotes Immanuel Kant to the effect that our perceptions are the result of our psychological process that combines what our senses detect with what we already think, feel, know, want, and believe. So, we imagine an event based on selective memory and association, and then, under the illusion of control, we overestimate the likelihood of the event occurring as we imagine it. When we make predictions, we overlook the fact that our brains have performed this recall and integration activity.

Other problems include 1) The inability to think about absent stimuli (We treat future events that we don't imagine, as if they are not going to happen.) 2) Presentism (Current experience to influences our view of the past and the future.) 3) Habituation (Feelings about experiences decline with repetition.) and 4) Resilience (We find positive ways to view things.). Gilbert calls this last mental trick, "a psychological immune system." So, we select favorable facts from memory and perception.

In 2002, Daniel Kahneman received the Nobel Prize in Economics for work in Cognitive Psychology. Many of his ideas are included in his book, Thinking Fast and Slow. I will summarize a few:

1) Our reactions to stimuli follow two processes: **System One** is associative memory. It constructs a coherent interpretation of what is going on. It operates automatically and quickly, with little or no effort, and no sense of voluntary control. System one constructs the best possible story that incorporates ideas currently available, but it does not allow for information it does not have. It jumps to conclusions.
    System Two allocates attention to the effortful mental activities that demand it, including complex calculations. It has the ability to change the way System One works, but it is lazy.
2) **Heuristics and Biases**
    a) Collections of random events appear to behave in a highly regular fashion.
    b) We are prone to exaggerate the consistency and coherence of what we see.
    c) Our judgment is influenced by uninformative numbers, the anchoring effect. An example would be college tuition. A "scholarship" of $15,000 seems great when our thinking is "anchored" in tuition of costs of $45,000. But we are still paying $30,000. This isn't a bargain; it is price discrimination (charging different customers different prices for the same product).
    d) The sins of representativeness:
        a. excessive willingness to predict the occurrence of unlikely events (ignoring base rates).
        b. insensitivity to the quality of evidence ("What you see is all there is" bias).
    e) We substitute plausible for probable. The most coherent stories are not necessarily the most probable, but they are plausible.
3) **Overconfidence and the narrative fallacy**
    a) The halo effect keeps narratives simple and coherent.
    b) We ignore what we don't know.
    c) We filter information and construct memories to support our egos.
    d) We are also subject to hindsight and outcome biases.
    e) The possibility that luck plays a role in outcomes is largely ignored.
4) **Choices:** People are neither fully rational nor completely selfish. And their tastes are not stable.
5) Kahneman distinguishes two selves: one that experiences and another that remembers. Because tastes and decisions are shaped by memories, and memories can be distorted, choices can be wrong.

As a result of his work, Kahneman replaces the rational actor model with **prospect theory**. When responding to choices, he believes that there are two steps: editing and evaluation. First, we select what we consider relevant information. We choose a reference point, (the anchor), to which possible outcomes are compared. We weigh gains and losses of the choices as deviations from that point. We are **loss averse**, meaning that we value gains less than losses, when we evaluate opportunities. This last insight helps us to understand **the endowment effect**. Once we acquire something, we shift our reference point. And being selective in our recall and organization of relevant information, we are guided by the immediate emotional impact of gains and losses, not by long-term prospects. We don't have the global view of all possible choices, but instead, we focus on a few alternatives that come to mind.

Kahneman's **prospect theory** posits that decision-makers are "frame bound" rather than "reality bound." We are narrow framers, grouping choices narrowly rather than employing the comprehensive strategy assumed of rational actors. This help to explain susceptibility to the sunk cost fallacy. (Remember the money spent for the movie ticket to the Will Farrell movie that was torture for me ?)

Many examples of the failure to ignore sunk costs come from business. Many years ago, my friend, Brooks Firestone, returned from Europe to alert the Board of Firestone Tire and Rubber that Michelin was introducing a superior tire, the radial. If Firestone didn't bring out a radial tire, Michelin would wipe Firestone out. The old men in charge demurred --- they had just invested heavily in modernizing their plants, and they wanted to recover their investment before trying something new. As predicted, Michelin grabbed the market, and Firestone never quite recovered.

In another example, COMPAC overtook IBM in the PC market, when IBM waited to introduce a new Intel processor until their inventory was sold, while COMPAC adapted the chip right away.

All of this means that our thinking is inevitably distorted and helps to explain the variety of memories of participants in the same events. The implications for economics are clearly that there are limits to our ability to make the best decisions. Understanding the processes that lead to systematic errors can help us to design better decision methods. In the meantime, some humility in the application of rational actor models is important.

Questions
How does a **price increase** alter consumption choices ?
(Distinguish income and substitution effects.)
Why do we expect all demand curves to slope down {negative slopes} ?
How does ignoring "non-monetary opportunity costs" and "sunk costs" lead to less satisfactory decisions ?

*Kagel, Grenn, Battalio, Bassman, & Klemm "Experimental Studies of Consumer Demand Behavior Using Laboratory Animals" Economic Inquiry March 1975

Appendix: Elasticity

Knowing the Laws of Demand and Supply is helpful, but knowing the amount of the price change needed to balance Demand and Supply would be even better. And if we expect a price or income change, we'd like to know not just the direction of the consumer's response, but the amount, as well. This is why we have a measure called, **The Price Elasticity of Demand**.

We might use the slope of the Demand function, but the slope depends on units of measure. If we use Dollars or Euros, we get a different slope. If we use Liters or Quarts, we get different measures. But if we compare percentages changes in quantity to percentage changes in price, the units of measure don't matter.

Consider two observations: 1) at a price of $10, we sell 20 shirts, and 2) at a price of $8, we sell 30 shirts. We could describe the function as

$$\textbf{Quantity}_{shirts} = \textbf{70 - \{5 x Price}_{shirts\}}$$

The slope **dQ/ dP is -5.** The percentage change would be **{dQ/Q / dP/P} or {dQ/dP x P/Q}**

Unfortunately, depending on whether we begin at 1) {$10,20} or at 2) {$8,30}, our calculations will change:

Elasticity₁ = -2.5   Elasticity₂ = -1.33

To avoid this problem, when we have large movements, we compare use the average price and average quantity in calculating our percentages.

Price Elasticity of Demand = -5 x 9/25 = -1.8

So, our measure of price sensitivity is **The Price Elasticity of Demand**. It is measured as *the percentage change in quantity demanded for a percentage change in price.* When there are large changes in price or quantity, we use the average of the beginning and ending observations in order to get consistent measure that is independent of the units of measure chosen. We expect it to be negative (A price increase implies less purchases). Price Elasticity of Demand is useful in predicting quantities of sales and revenue. As an example, we estimate the price elasticity of demand for Gasoline to be -0.40 in the short-run (< one year) and -1.5 in the long-run (>3 years). So, if gasoline price increased 20%, sale should fall 5% soon, and 30% after three years.

    The Income Elasticity of Demand is similar. It measures consumers' response to changes in income. As you can imagine, we calculate the Income Elasticity of Demand as the *percentage change in the Quantity Demanded for a percentage change in Income.* We expect this relationship to be positive. (More income implies more purchases) For example, we estimate the Income Elasticity of Demand for owner occupied housing to be 0.07 short-run and 2.45 long-run. Can you explain this ? (Remodeling our home, or buying a new one, requires time and planning.)

    We can also measure the response of Supply to changes in price. We call that measure, **The Price Elasticity of Supply**. Even though we are using the same data points of price and quantity, the functions that we use are different. The Demand function includes income, the prices of substitutes, and demographics. The Supply function includes Costs. So, if we specify the functions correctly, we will get two different measures.

    Finally, we can estimate the effects of the prices of substitutes and complements on sales of the product which interests us. We called this measure, **The Cross-Price Elasticity**. The formula is dQx/Qx divided by dPy/Py If the result is positive, goodsd X & Y are substitutes. If the measure is negative, then they are complements (used together). Can you explain why ?

    We can use elasticities to predict price or quantity adjustments to imbalances between Demand and Supply. Here are two examples:

Calculating Price & Quantity Adjustments #1
Consider the following conditions:
Current Price = $5.00
Quantity Demanded = 110
Quantity Supplied = 90
Shortage = 20
Price Elasticity of Demand = 1.5
Price Elasticity of Supply   = 2.0
What is the price increase necessary to balance Demand and Supply ?

Calculation:

The total elasticity is $\{dQ/Q\} / \{dP/P\} = 3.5$

We need a 20% change in Quantity   **20% = 3.5 {dP/P} --> necessary price increase = 5.7%**

Calculating Price & Quantity Adjustments #2

Current Price = $10.00

Quantity Demanded = 110

Quantity Supplied = 90

Expected Price Increase = $0.50 {5%}

Price Elasticity of Demand = 0.7

Price Elasticity of Domestic Supply = 2.0

Effect on Demand ?   {-0.7} 5% = -3.5% = - 3.85

Effect on Domestic Production ?   2 x 5% = 10% = + 9

If the shortage had been filled by Imports, and now the price changes, what would be the effect on Imports ?

-12.85

Leather shop in Montevideo, Uruguay

Lesson #2.3 Costs and Production

Having looked at consumer behavior, which we describe as **Demand**, the quantities that consumers intend to purchase under various conditions of tastes, income, and prices, we turn our attention to **Supply**, the quantities that firms intend to offer for sale under various conditions of product prices and costs. Consider that the producer who sells the product that you prefer, that you believe will make you better off, doesn't get to enjoy the product that he provides you. You get to enjoy that product. So, what is the producer's motivation ? Firms are organized to earn profit, the difference between what you pay them (revenue) and the costs associated with making that product available to you. Doesn't the producer deserve a reward ? That reward is **Profit**, and the anticipation of that reward is the incentive that leads him to produce it for you. There may be additional incentives and rewards, such as the pleasure of helping others and the satisfaction of creating a product or service. However, without profit, the producer will soon need to turn his attention to other activities. So, we start with the assumption that production is organized to make profit, and the producer's decisions will be made to maximize their profit. This pursuit of profit contributes to solving the economic issues of what to produce and how to produce.

Profit is the difference between revenue and cost. To understand profit requires the analysis of both. Revenue is the result of the quantity sold and the prices at which they are sold. Naturally, the producer would like to charge each consumer the maximum that they are willing to pay for each sale, but there are some practical problems that make that difficult. For example, how do I determine the highest price that each customer would be willing to pay ? And if I offer one price to one customer and a difference price to another customer, how do I prevent the one who enjoys the low price from reselling to the one facing the high price ? We will return to these issues. For now, let's remember that revenue depends on the selling prices and quantities.

Cost is what we pay for the resources that we need to make and deliver the product. We must pay for these, because we must bid against other producers and resource owners. Scarce resources have **opportunity costs**. If we fail to make the best offer, the resource owners will use their resources in some other way, and we won't be able to produce. For that reason, producers have an interest in limiting the opportunities of resource owners to find rewarding employment for their resources. Does this explain slavery, various forms of irrelevant discrimination (such as racial or ethnic), and vagrancy laws (that prevent people from moving around to look for work) ? Because we need scarce resources to produce, we must compete (bid) for them, and we have costs.

Classifying costs becomes helpful in evaluating opportunities. **Cost Accounting** is an important branch of the Accounting profession. We distinguish **Fixed Costs** which are *on-going costs independent of production volumes*. Examples would be rent, insurance, lease payments, some utilities, and salaries. In business, we call fixed costs, **overhead**, or in business slang, "the nut we have to crack every month," meaning a cost that we must cover from our gross profit, if we are to survive. **Variable Costs** change with level of output. Without production or sales, there would still be fixed costs, but there would be no variable costs. An important class of variable costs is inventory. Every time I sell, I reduce my inventory, and I deduct those costs. Other variable costs may be sales' commissions, shipping to the customer, excise and sales taxes, and some utilities. In many cases, management can choose to acquire the resource as a fixed cost, such as your regular monthly salary, or a variable cost, such as your hourly wage, or sales commission. There are also **Sunk Costs**. They are costs that we pay only once, such as the purchase of land, machinery, office, or factory. If we rent a machine or building, it is a fixed cost for the term of the lease, if we choose to own the building there is the one time purchase price (a sunk cost) plus the fixed costs of maintenance, insurance, and taxes. The one time purchase reduces our rental expense; this one-time cost replaces the largest of the fixed costs associated with renting.

Total costs are then sunk costs, fixed costs, and variable costs, but the only costs that continue regularly, as we operate our business are the fixed and variable costs. The sunk costs are important, when we organize our business and select ownership or rental, but once those one-time costs are paid, they do not recur (although there may be some associated fixed or variable costs, as noted above). This is important, because as we choose a level of production, we must consider all the future revenues and future costs that will result. Just as the consumer really doesn't care what it cost to produce the product, or what you paid for it, he only cares about what he must sacrifice (pay) vs. the future benefits of ownership which he will attain, *the producer considers what are the future costs (fixed and variable) and benefits (revenue) which he can obtain by producing more for you.*

This leads to another important concept. We have talked about the incremental, or additional, satisfaction from another unit of consumption. We called this, marginal utility. (Should I have another hamburger ? Gee, that first one was great, but will the next one be worth the price ?) Now, we are talking about the additional cost of producing and selling one more unit of product. What will the additional costs be for producing one more burger, and what additional revenue will it bring ? We call these **marginal cost** and **marginal revenue**. Marginal costs arc *the addition to Total Costs of a change in the level of production.*

The payments for resources that we call "costs" have a variety of names, depending on the resources. We call the payments to labor, wages and salaries. Wages are often hourly and may be considered variable costs traditionally, but today, many wages are paid weekly or monthly. Salaries are almost always fixed costs paid regularly, without regard to production. Employers will often pay wages, until they know the worker, have confidence in his ability and dedication, and demand long hours. At forty hours a week, a wage may be cheap, but the same worker expected to work sixty hours as a "committed" manager, may be cheaper on salary. From our point of view, the importance is either as a fixed cost or a variable cost. We refer to the costs associated with obtaining the services of capital as **rent**. We rent a machine or a building. This would be a fixed cost. Of course, we could purchase the machine, or building, and reduce our fixed cost by incurring a large, one time, sunk cost. Naturally, we would compare the two costs, in which case the interest rate measures the opportunity cost of our funds and provides a bridge that allows us to compare the rental choice to the purchase choice. Natural resources are an important form of capital. They are called "natural" because they exist in a state of nature, before any intervention by man. We pay for them only because someone owns them (the property owner) and we won't get to use them, unless we make the best offer available. Even if we own the natural resource, or any other form of capital, ourselves, we should consider the opportunity cost of using it versus renting or selling it. So, the same comparison of value is equally important. We call the payments for natural resources, **pure rents**. They are pure in the sense that we pay to use them even though there was no cost in creating them, despite the fact that there were costs in discovering them, establishing property rights, and preparing them for extraction. Those associated costs would be capital, labor, and entrepreneurship.

Entrepreneurship is a special type of labor that envisions opportunities, acquires and organizes resources, and accepts the risks of production. The payments to entrepreneurs are called, **profits**. So now we have come full circle, returning to the concept of profit. There is an illusion that all entrepreneurs reap large profits. That may because the successes are very visible and celebrated (or vilified). The hope for these large rewards motivates people to become entrepreneurs, but many fail, or realize that their rewards fail to meet their personal opportunity costs, or their profit is enough to keep going, but not enough to make them rich. We need entrepreneurs to take initiative, innovate, and organize resources, including providing employment to most of us. And so, we need honestly earned profits.

Two important questions are: 1) How does the business select its level of production ? and 2) How does it choose its production methods (technology) ? You will not be surprised to find that the opportunity for profit and the comparison of costs will influence those decisions.

To understand how costs influence production, we need theories to describe technologies. **Technology** is a commonly abused concept. It merely means a method of production. Associated with every technology is a combination of resources that can be transformed into products. It is best to think of technology as knowledge, what we formerly called, "know how." How sad that we don't seem to value "know how" as much as our predecessors, and fail to give it the attention that we give to positive and normative theories. Every technology requires specific skills of labor, specific equipment, and natural resources. The knowledge is useless, unless the appropriate capital and labor are available. We talk about technology being "embodied" in specialized labor and capital.

These ideas have led to economists' theories of the relation of resources in to product out, or "inputs" to "outputs." Simon Kuznets, among others, pioneered measuring these relations during World War Two. As we try to specify the relationship between the use of more resources and the changes in resulting product, a few key concepts emerge. If we start with a factory, but no workers, there is unlikely to be any production. If we add workers, we will have rapid increases in production, as we increase the employment of the existing equipment and enjoy the benefits of specialization among our workers. In fact, initial increases in production may be more than proportionate to the increase in labor. Think of a pizza parlor with only one worker who must take and deliver order, prepare the pizza pie, and cook it. He won't get much done. Three workers who divide the tasks are likely to produce many more than three times the number pizzas produced by the solo worker. We call this phase, *increasing returns to the addition of one resource*. Now, if we can increase production faster than we increase the resources, our additional (marginal) costs will be low, and our average costs will be falling. As we expand employment without increasing the size of our facility or adding to our equipment (ovens, preparation tables, delivery vehicles), the contribution of the new workers may be proportionate for a while (*constant returns*), but at some stage the contribution of even more workers will be small, for lack of equipment. When that happens, and new workers can't produce much, the costs of additional production increase, and we call that, *diminishing returns*. We may still be gaining more production, but not much more. Production isn't yet falling; it is just not increasing as rapidly as before. (I have friends with a Sushi bar. They were so successful that the dining room was always packed. They kept adding Sushi makers, until they were fighting for space. Those last few sushi chefs didn't add much to production.)

I visited Pakistan and saw locals repairing an irrigation canal. (They call it a barrage, a low earth dam.) There were three men sharing a shovel. Now, a shovel without a man produces nothing. Give a man a shovel and he can increase his production. Put two men on one shovel (one on each side) and you may have doubled labor, but you won't double production. Add a third man with a rope attached to the shovel to help pull it out of the dirt bank, and you might get a little more production, but surely not a 50% gain. These are diminishing returns to additional labor inputs. Can you see why if you want to increase production, but you don't get proportionate increases in production from added labor, you need to add a lot of labor and your marginal costs will rise ? What do you think causes these diminishing returns, and rising marginal costs (that increase your average costs, too) ? Perhaps if we added more of the other resources, more shovels or more pizza ovens, we could avoid diminishing returns and rising costs per unit.

When we add all resources in same proportion as existing production, we talk about changing **the scale of production**. We might replicate our existing facility, doubling all the resources: facilities, inventory, staff, and equipment, even managers. If this doubles our product, as we anticipate, we say that we are enjoying **constant returns to scale**. Sometimes, if we can avoid doubling some inputs, such as management overhead, but we double everything else, we may enjoy doubling production without doubling costs, and we say that we are enjoying **economies of scale**. But this isn't quite true, as we haven't increased all resource inputs, proportionately. The more interesting cases are when we do, and our production increases more than proportionately, so our average costs fall. Two examples come to mind.

If you double all the dimensions of a bulk carrier ship (height, width, and length), you will increase capacity eight times (2x2x2). However the resistance through the water depends mostly on the height and depth, so the costs of driving the ship through the water may only increase by four times (2x2), and we are unlikely to need eight times the staff or other equipment. Hence, we obtain much more production (capacity) than our increase in resources used and their associated costs.

Thomas Edison's assistant, Samuel Insull, recognized economies of scale in the generation of electricity. If you can double the size of your generator, you can more than double production. He concluded that the limit on the size of your generator, and your ability to lower average costs, was the size of your market. He did everything that he could to increase demand for electricity in Chicago, including the elevated railroad, so that he could build bigger generating plants and lower his costs. He passed much of this benefit to his customers in the form of lower charges for power.

You might ask, "Is there no limit to the size of the bulk carriers or to the electrical generator plants ?" There are limits. For ships, the limit is the strength and structural integrity of the large ship, as it pushes through the ocean, flexing along in all dimensions. Too large a ship will break up. For the electricity industry, generation is part of the issue, and distribution is the remainder. Resistance reduces the power, as it is distributed. Distribution over long distances, or in small amounts, will waste power and increase costs.

These two insights into the relation of resources to production, decreasing returns to adding more of one resource without adding the others, and decreasing returns to scale (adding all resources proportionally but no longer achieving proportional increases in product), offer two explanations for increasing marginal and average costs as production increases. We might think of the management choosing an initial scale for production, based on expected sales. Facilities are found, equipment is installed, and labor is hired and trained. As we increase production average costs fall; we are beginning to use all this installed capacity. We gain productivity through specialization and full employment of our capacity. However, if we continue to push production, because of heavy demand, we reach the limits of our capacity. Additional resources fail to yield proportionate gains. To get the desired product, we must add more than proportional resources, and so, our costs per unit rise.

To understand fully the importance of the changing shape of production function, the relationship of resources "in" to product "out," the concepts of "marginal cost" and "average cost" are important. **Marginal Costs** are *the addition to Total Costs of a change in the level of production.* **Average Costs** are *Total Costs divided by quantity produced.* We can consider Average Fixed Costs, Average Variable Costs, and Average Total Costs. In each case, we take the measure of costs that interest us, and divide by the quantity produced. The principles of the production function described above suggest that Average Costs will fall initially, as we add resources and production grows more than proportionately, because we are using our capacity (fixed costs are spread over larger quantities) and enjoying specialization. There may be a range of stable average costs; we enjoy constant returns --- gains in production proportionate to the increased resources employed. And then, we expect rising costs, as the gains of spreading fixed costs over larger quantities are exhausted, and marginal costs rise, because of diminishing returns. In this final phase, we apply ever more resources to get a boost in production, but the rewards are small. These rising costs are important, because they explain why businesses will not increase production indefinitely, but will reach a point at which rising costs outweigh any further increase in revenue from additional sales.

Another important contribution of cost analysis is the explanation of **choice of technology**. There are usually several, or even many, ways to produce the product that we intend to sell. As we consider the opportunity for sales, we ask, "How can I produce this product in sufficient quantity with consistent quality ?" We identify the alternatives available, and analyze the resource requirements of each method.

For example, if we are planning to grow cotton, we need land, water, seeds, and fertilizer. We also need to prepare the land, plant, irrigate, remove pests, and harvest the crop. Egypt and America both produce quality cotton, but Egypt often uses manual labor for the same tasks that Americans use machines. Why ? The producer who wishes to make a profit will also wish to minimize costs. When we understand the resources required to produce the target quantity of product, we can also scan the market to discover what we must pay to obtain those resources. (Do you remember what determines those prices ? The opportunity costs of those resources. If I wish to hire you, or rent some land, I must make you your best offer, and the make the land owner also the best offer that he can obtain.) The quantity of resources associated with each technology (method) and the prices of those resources (wages, rents, etc.) will determine the costs of production for that technology. Finally, I compare the costs associated with each technology, and choose the least cost method.

The way in which economists describe (model) these choices is similar to the technique of consumer analysis. The producer has opportunities to hire resources. Their prices will determine how much he can hire for a given budget. And the producer has several technologies available, each requiring a difference combination of resources. Hence, by choosing one method rather than another to achieve the same production goal, he is, in a sense, substituting one combination of resources for another. Now, why would he choose one method rather than another ? Because, it is cheaper.

If we are American farmers adjusting to rising labor costs, we would ask, "Can I substitute some capital equipment for some labor and reduce my costs ?" My ability to substitute depends on the availability of a different, more **capital intensive** method. My opportunity to substitute depends on the costs of capital in comparison to the cost of labor. Consider a situation in which a machine can do the work of three men. If the weekly rent of the machine is less than the weekly wage of the three men, then we choose the machine. A more interesting case occurs when we consider a machine which can do the work of eight men, but cost seven times their wage. What should we do ? Using the machine will save money; the product will cost 7/8th of the labor intensive alternative.

Another interesting case occurs when we choose different types of labor. When Korea first started exporting autos to the USA, American producers complained that they couldn't compete with cheap Korean labor. Korean auto workers were paid 1/8th of the hourly cost of employing an American in the USA. What was overlooked is that Detroit's methods required 1/8th the number of labor hours to make the car. In other words, there was no cost advantage.

When I was in Washington during the Carter years, American shoe companies were complaining about cheap Korean shoes. My friend, Bill Cline, was asked to investigate. He surveyed American shoes retailers, and discovered no cost advantage. The American retailers were buying Korean shoes, because their customers liked their styles better. Tell me, what excuse do the American manufacturers have for not understanding their customers as well as the Koreans do ?

To return to the cotton example, if we visit the Central Valley of California, we will see helicopters spraying insecticides on the cotton plants. In Egypt, we see children being herded through the fields, removing the bugs by hand. Both methods work to remove the pests. Why don't the Egyptians use helicopters to spray ? What will happen in Egypt, as the nation develops better opportunities for children to receive education and workers to get more productive jobs ?

The answer is captured in *The Principle of Substitution* --- a change in relative resource prices will lead to a change in technology choice and resource employment. In the most prosperous regions of the world, this has been occurring for several centuries. The Luddites were wrong. They thought that machinery put people out work. More often the scarcity of labor raises wages, and the proliferation of capital through investment reduces rents. Sooner or later, the producer switches methods to substitute the now cheaper capital for the more expensive labor. Remember that "cheap" or "expensive" is the result of a comparison of 1) what must I pay with 2) what is the value of the product that the resource produces for me.

Years ago, my wife and her partner were working very hard, but barely breaking even financially. They are architects, and his wife is a management consultant, and of course, I am an economist. Our spouses had been hiring young, inexperienced draftsmen and recent architecture graduates. By paying $15 an hour, they thought that they would save money. In fact, the principals spent a lot of time directing their staff, supervising them, and correcting their mistakes. Lois and I kept saying: "Hire licensed architects and experienced draftsmen. You will pay them 50% more but they will be twice as productive". After several years, (after we stopped bugging them about it), they tried hiring more productive employees and paying them accordingly. The firm started making money.

Back in the 1970s, the Japanese recognized that they were investing $100,000 per citizen to raise them to working age. To use this talent in low wage assembly work (not to mention as elevator operators) was wasteful. The government encouraged industry to move the simple assembly work to poorer parts of Asia where those jobs would be welcome, and develop robots to raise the productivity of Japanese labor. Only in that way could Japanese wages continue to rise --- productivity increases would exceed or match wage increases.

Now, we have the parts that can be assembled to understand why each firm produces the quantities that they do. They consider the change in revenue associated with additional production; we call that **marginal revenue**. It's a combination of the additional quantity and the additional price. With a competitive commodity, the producer can sell more or less of the standard product without moving the market price, so marginal revenue is the price of the next sale, and it doesn't change. The producer compares this gain in revenue to the additional costs of production, the **marginal cost**. If he can add more to his revenue than he adds to his cost, he will do it. If he finds that he is adding more to his costs than his revenue, he shouldn't do it. In the first case, the net proceeds are available to cover fixed costs, if they are not yet covered, or to add to his profit. In the second case, more production and sales will reduce his total profit (or increase his loss). So, *the basic condition of profit maximization is to increase production as long as the additional sales increase revenue more than costs.* However, this alone does not assure a profit. We know that we don't want to miss any opportunity to raise our revenue more than our costs, and we don't want to pursue sales that add more to our costs than to our revenue. But we need one final check: at that level of production does *Total Revenue exceed Total Costs* ? Recall that when revenue exceeds variable costs, those sales are attractive, but they say nothing about our ability to cover fixed costs. We need to cover both, to be profitable.

When I was a financial officer for a company that promoted resorts in the Caribbean. My boss had operated several resorts and had turned around six losers. We saw an opportunity to purchase a terrific property that was losing a lot of money. We spent $3,000,000 to buy it and renovate it (sunk costs). When we opened six months later, I budgeted $1,000,000 for fixed costs (over-head; mostly marketing). We operated The Pineapple Beach Club as an all-inclusive resort, a new concept at the time. We calculated that each guest imposed variable costs of $58 per day (food, beverages, room, and activities). In the winter, we could charge $150 per person per day, in the spring we could charge $125 per person per day, and in the summer we could charge $75 per person per day. Should we stay open in the summer ? Yes, if we charge $75 and have added costs of $58, we profit $17 per customer per day, not as profitable as the winter trade, but valuable nonetheless.

Now, consider whether this pricing and operating strategy would be profitable. We had forty-six rooms, so we could accommodate 92 guests. Each season had one hundred days. In the winter, we could run 90% occupancy, so expected profit would be {($150-58) x100 days x 90% x 92 = $761,760). In the spring, occupancy would be 75% {($125-58) x 100 x 75% x 96 = $323,080}. Notice that if we hit our targets for winter and spring, we could cover our fixed costs and make a small profit ($761,760 + $323,080 = $1,084,840 > $1,000,000). However, by staying open in the summer, even with 50% occupancy, we added {($75-58) x 100 x 505 x 96 =$81,600} almost doubling our profit in the first year. So, keep producing as long as you can add more to your revenue than you add to your costs. Then, check to make sure that your total revenue exceeds your total costs.

You might ask, would such an undertaking be worthwhile, if you can only make a profit of $166,440 on an investment of $3,000,000, a yield of 5.5% ? Well, that depends on your opportunity costs, and your feelings about the other rewards of this type of work. In our case, we demonstrated our ability; we finished the year within $3,000 of every item of my budget. That allowed us to borrow the money to expand, at very low interest rates. And the expansion raised our revenue, with very little addition to our fixed costs. Consider doubling our net revenue with only a 70% increase in fixed costs, including interest payments, {Net Revenue = $2,332,880 minus Fixed Costs = $1,700,000}. Profit becomes $632,880, a 21% return on our investment of $3,000,000. And that was not the end. For what could you sell a business that earns $632,880 a year and has the potential to grow further ? Would a buyer accept an initial yield of 12% ? If so, he would pay $5,274,000. In 2 ½ years, we have a gain of 75% on our investment, as well as two years profits, in total almost doubling our money.

So, now we understand the decision to produce. As the price for our product varies, we adjust production, until the new price equals the marginal cost at the new level of production. If all producers are making similar calculations, the market price will reflect the marginal costs of production for all producers, and the consumers will received the correct signal --- this price represents what it costs to provide you with the last unit that we sell. Fortunately, earlier quantities cost enough less to cover our fixed costs, and perhaps, return a profit.

One of the many reasons that business hate to be subject to competition in the product market is their inability to prevent the expansion of competitors, as well as the entry of new firms. If the costs of organizing a new business are small, such as low initial sunk costs, and there is the ability to stop production without great closing costs, such as continuing fixed costs in the form of rent and lease contracts, then other producers will be attracted by our unusual profits. Often, our new competitors are people familiar with our business model, perhaps former employees, customers, or suppliers, maybe even bankers, accountants, or consultants who have observed our success. These new producers will add to the capacity of the industry and producing at price equals their marginal cost will add to the supply in the market. But for the market to absorb more total supply, prices must decline. Thus, our success breeds additional supply which erodes prices and profits for all of us. This is particularly frustrating, if the new competitors have misread the market and their capabilities. They may cause all of us to lose money. Then, who will survive ?

As the market price declines, we will all reduce production, until price equal marginal cost again, and we will check total revenue against total costs. We hope that we are still profitable, but often we are not. What do we do, when we are losing money ? Obviously, we'd like to raise our price, but competition prevents that. And we would like to lower our costs, but if we could do that, why did we wait until we're losing money ? We may struggle to cut costs and contain our losses, until some competitors drop out and the market corrects. In the meantime, do we stay open, or go on holiday ? *Firms must compare losses of continued operation to losses of shutting-down.* If remaining open generates more revenue than variable costs, then we have some net revenue to put against our fixed costs, and thus, reduce our losses. In that case, we will produce at price equals marginal cost, and try to negotiate cost reductions and unload some overhead, reducing fixed costs by sub-letting leases and reducing salaried staff, while we stay open.

If operating at price equals marginal cost doesn't bring in enough revenue to cover our variable costs, then we are just making a bad situation worse by continuing to produce. In that case, our losses will be minimized by shutting down.

These principles explain why we see businesses continuing to operate even though they appear to have few customers and must be losing money. They are bringing in enough to cover variable costs and some fixed costs. They are suffering, but they are following a strategy that minimizes their losses. I watched a restaurant in my home town lose money for several years, while doing very well at another location. They stayed open, until the owner could sell his lease and escape. That day came after two years and was a great relief for him.

Let us make one final observation about costs. Have you ever wondered why businesses come in many sizes ? Why do we have large department stores and small boutiques ? Why huge super markets and small greengrocers ? Could it be costs ? When we organize a small business, we rely on many associated businesses, suppliers and customers. We co-ordinate with them through market transactions. When we organize a large company, we do more for ourselves. We rely more heavily on internal management. Both strategies involve costs. Firms which find that they can outsource using market transactions to reduce their costs will do so; firms that find those transaction costs high, but management costs low, will grow larger and internalize more operations. And these differences in costs are not uniform for each industry. Some locations are dense with supporting industries and can support many small companies that outsource. Other locations offer few opportunities to outsource, and more work must be done "in-house." Even management styles matter. We may like the idea of a small research house, where everyone is deeply committed to the team, but the small shop can't bring the resources of a large company. On the other hand, only exceptional management can motivate the members of a huge company. And so, we see companies of various sizes competing within the same industry. Small banks compete with large ones, by cultivating small customers. They leave the large customers, that they couldn't handle, to the big banks. And those big banks know that they can't offer the attention to small customers that those customers require.

Have you had enough of costs ? In our next lesson, we will put together the actions of consumers (Demand) and producers (Supply) and see what we can say about the efficiency of competitive markets.

Questions for review and examination:
Compare and contrast: Fixed Costs, Variable Costs, Sunk Costs, and Marginal Costs. Contrast The Law of Diminishing Returns and Diseconomies of Scale.
Why should a producer expand production until Marginal Costs equal the selling Price of the product ?
When should a business continue, even though it is suffering losses ?
Explain why the resources, Capital and Labor, are considered both complements and substitutes in production.

A small business in Buenos Aires. A dog walker. How many dogs can he manage before he needs to hire and assistant ?

119

Lesson #2.4 Efficiency, Competition, and Price Controls

Economists have long theorized that competitive markets would generate efficiency. These views have also been repeatedly challenged by those who distrust the outcomes of many millions of people and organizations making choices of how to use their resources, how to employ the resources of others, how to organize production, and how to buy and sell, all without any guidance from a coordinating agency. Both views deserve attention. We count on government to provide the **Rule of Law** which defines and protects property rights, specifies the commercial code of conduct by which we make exchanges, and finally, enforces contracts. A rule maker is very valuable, because well-known rules reduce transactions costs, and thus, encourage exchange. In addition, a government which provides a means of payment of stable value (**money**) that facilities exchange, saving, and credit, all of which encourage economic growth and improve income distribution. We ask government to **regulate inefficient markets**, such as monopolies and markets with large third party costs. Finally, every economist, that I know, shares a belief that some attention to **income redistribution** from the most successful to the least successful is desirable, as compassion, and from the practical acknowledgement that the disadvantaged may disrupt the system to everyone's loss. So, we're not talking about the absence of any role for government. We are talking about the possibilities for efficiency in truly competitive markets.

We participate in a variety of markets. We may use our time, talents, and other resources, ourselves, but we often make them available to others, in exchange for payments which we call **income**. Then, after receiving revenue from the sale of our products, or income from the rent of our services, we purchase the goods and services that we desire but choose not to produce for ourselves. This is how we take advantage of specialization and exchange, to increase our material welfare. Notice that the value of our resources in the market, and our choice of how to employ them (which offers to accept) determine the payments and income that we receive, and the prices that we pay for what we want to buy determine what we get to enjoy. To an economist, the term **income** refers to the psychological satisfaction that we obtain from the use of our resources. It *will depend on the resources that we own, their value in alternative uses, how we choose to use them, and what we can purchase.* Thus, the resources that we have, and the prices that we receive and pay, are essential. That is why we are likely to agree that a world in which everyone can reach their potential, and have opportunities to acquire resources, such as skills, through education and experience, as well as open access, without any discrimination except competence and character, to all opportunities for employment and exchange, are such appealing values. Do competitive markets contribute to these efficiencies ?

The Italian Economist, Wilfred Pareto, is considered the father of the field of **Welfare Economics**. He attempted to be very rigorous in his application of logic and mathematics to our field. He found that defining a satisfactory notion of efficiency that would be irrefutable was difficult. He settled for a definition which appears very mild*: A situation is already efficient if a change to improve anyone, results in loss for someone else. (*Or you might say, *a situation is already efficient, if we can't make anyone better off, except by making someone else worse off.)* Consider the alternative. If we have a situation in which someone could be made better off without anyone losing, that situation cannot be efficient. After all, why not let someone benefit, if no one else is harmed ? On the other hand, there are many efficient situations, such as one in which Imelda Marcos has all the shoes in the world and the rest of us have none. (She was known to have 3,000 pairs of shoes.) Who is to say that she would not be harmed to have a pair taken away to be given to someone else ? And here's the real rub ---- how can we prove that the receiver's gain exceeds the loser's harm ? Our emotions tell us that it must be true, but we can't prove it. After all, the loser actually sacrificed to get the good which is being taken, and the beneficiary of the transfer didn't make the choice to buy it. So, shouldn't the presumption be that the good is worth more to the former than to the latter ? A corollary is that for every inefficient situation, there must be a superior efficient situation --- of course, it's the one in which we do make someone better without harming anyone else. OK, so now we have a definition of **efficiency**, even if we aren't thrilled with it, and many issues appear to be unresolved. The idea that "anytime you can make someone better off without harming anyone else, you should do it" could be restated as **"Don't Waste Resources !"** Pareto identified three form of efficiency and we will take them in order: Exchange Efficiency, Production Efficiency, and Product Mix Efficiency.

    Exchange Efficiency would be achieved if all improvements in welfare from voluntary trade have been achieved. How would that work ? Buyers and Sellers consider their tastes and opportunities, as we described in lessons #2.2 and #2.3. Tastes are psychological expectations of satisfaction, and consumer opportunities depend on their income and the prices that they must pay. We will buy and sell as long as the value received exceeds the value sacrificed. Notice that exchange requires that buyers and sellers have different preferences for the goods to be exchanged. We stop exchanging more goods, when our willingness to substitute the goods equals the market opportunity to do so, the price ratio. At that point, there are no gains from further exchange. For example, I will buy more soda costing $1, until the next soda would no longer be worth $1 to me. And so does every other participant in the soda market. That means that if we all face the same prices, we will all choose combinations of goods which reflect the same willingness to exchange, because we are reacting to the same opportunities, the price ratios. (Notice that this is why we feel that price discrimination, charging different customer different prices for the same good, is wrong --- it would be inefficient.) If we do face the same prices, could we improve on the efficiency of these voluntary choices ? No, any reallocation would reduce one person's satisfaction more than it would raise another's. How do we know ? To repeat the argument made in the last paragraph: *The person from whom we would be taking, voluntarily paid the price. The good must have been worth the price or more. The person to whom we would give the property values it less. He had the opportunity to buy it by paying the price, but he chose not to buy it. It must be worth less to him.*

    What about the consumer with no income, or money ? How do we know what the product is worth to him ? We don't. But if he has the opportunity to earn the money and chooses not to, then isn't that confirmation ? *You can see the recurrent theme of the importance of equality of opportunity in our theories of efficiency.*

    Production Efficiency would be production at lowest resource cost. In the pursuit of profit, we try to minimize costs. So, we compare the methods of production which will provide adequate quality, the resources required by each method (technology), and the prices of those resources. We choose the method that allows us to substitute one resource for another, as long as its relative productivity exceeds its relative cost. In that way, scarce and productive resources commanding high prices will be rationed, and abundant and inexpensive resources will be selected, whenever the combination of their productivity and their price makes this possible. In that manner, resources will flow to the uses of highest value and productivity. What if we were to arbitrarily reassign some resources from one employment to another ? If we are in a situation in which all producers face the same resource prices, and they have chosen their methods and their resources accordingly, then the transfer of resources from one use to another would raise costs in the one case more than it would reduce them in the other, and this would reduce efficiency.

During the Gulf War, some Congressmen, concerned about the costs of the war, opened discussion of renewing **conscription**. By drafting young men and paying them a token salary, the government could reduce expenses. Would this be efficient ? Would it reduce the costs of the war ? We would not be paying our soldiers their opportunity costs. We would lose the value of their production elsewhere, and they would lose the income which they should earn. We would be transferring some of the costs of the war from the taxpayers to the draftees. Economists believe that we should weigh all costs against all benefits. The government budget might look better, but the economy would not. (And we might consider conscription unfair to the draftees.)

Product Mix Efficiency is achieved when we produce the combination of goods that consumers value most. Producers decide what to produce by comparing opportunities for profit. If consumers choose based on relative product prices, and if producers choose to produce until Price equals Marginal Cost, (also checking to assure that Total Revenue exceeds Total Cost), then, the consumers' willingness to pay equals the opportunity cost to society of providing the good or service. And so, we only use expensive resources, if the product is highly valued by the consumer. We obtain the best product mix.

For example, a friend in the wine business must decide how much of several wines to produce. Some wines can use lower quality grapes and simpler production methods to produce at lower costs. Others require much more careful sorting of grapes, and longer aging. If consumers value the former at $15 per bottle, and the latter at $45 per bottle, he is willing to produce the latter up to the point of marginal cost $45. In other words, he is willing to bear three times the cost, only if the wine is worth three times as much to the consumer.

We can begin to discern how competitive markets determine income distribution. Income distribution in a perfectly competitive economy would be **Pareto Efficient**. Bidding for our resources by employers assures that they are employed where they are most valued, and that is in the production of what consumers value most, and those who offer the most valuable resources enjoy the most income and most products. This is the power of the incentive system of free and competitive markets.

But what about the people who own no valuable resources, no capital and no labor skills ? They will earn no income and obtain no goods. How do you feel about that ? Wouldn't a redistribution from those who fairly earned it to those who contributed nothing (or nearly nothing) be inefficient ? In this ideal world of perfect competition, such a redistribution would be inefficient. However, *efficiency is only one of our social values, not our only value.* We might (and do) choose to sacrifice some efficiency, for some other gain, such as compassion, generosity, peace of mind, or avoiding conflict. A healthy debate could occur weighing the costs of the inefficiency caused by the redistributive distortions against the gains just mentioned. Unfortunately, this debate rarely occurs as one side rails against the extortion of taxes, and the other dreams up more entitlements and rights to the property of others. The essential point from the economic view is that taxes and subsidies alter price signals, and reduce efficiency. To tax the income of some reduces their incentive to contribute, and to subsidize the income of others reduces their incentive to contribute, too. Could the same be said for redistribution of wealth ? Would that reduce the incentive to accumulate wealth ?

These notions of efficient markets have been extended to financial markets by economists such as Eugene Fama[1] and Burton Malkiel.[2] Their idea is that, in markets of broad participation and numerous trades (breadth and depth), prices reflect judgments of value by buyers and sellers.

Therefore, differences in prices reflect different perceptions of value. If two products, or securities, were truly the same, buyers would purchase the cheaper and sell the dearer, until their prices are equal. (Sometimes, we call this **The Law of One Price** --- there can only be one price for the identical product in the same market.) So, if a product sells for twice the price of its substitute, buyers must believe that it is twice as useful to them, twice as valuable. Of course, for this arbitrage to occur, and thus for prices to reflect relative value, there must be information. We distinguish three levels of market efficiency based on information: 1) **weak**: prices show no trend; they merely adjust to current conditions, 2) **semi-strong**: new public information is quickly assimilated and prices adjust according, and 3) **strong**: all public and private (insider) information is known and acted upon by enough participants to generate efficient pricing.

Behavioral economists have challenged these ideas. And I have always believed that profits can be made by those who have information and act upon it. They profit, and their actions correct the errors in prices. Even my brief time on Wall Street persuaded me that important information leaks out and influences positions and prices very quickly to the benefit of the well-informed.

So, prices convey some information. Prices signal to the producer the marginal value of the good to the consumer. Prices signal to the consumer the marginal cost of producing the good. But buyers and sellers also need information about the qualities of the product and the terms of the transaction. When we participate rarely in a market, when the market is shallow or narrow --- few transactions and few participants --- value may be hard to determine. Think about the difference between buying coffee every day, and buying a new car, once every five years. You have a clear idea of what you are getting and what you expect to pay when you buy coffee, but what about the car ? And the seller has a similar problem. What is the value in the market of that unique house on the hill ?

Often, the prices, which are available, surprise and please us, as when we find a bargain, or receive a generous offer, but we also find disappointment, when we are offered a low price, or wage, for something we value, such as our time and skills. As often, we encounter a price which seems very high and we are resentful. We forget that prices adjust to ration scarce resources among those who wish to have them, and, as they adjust, the signals to buyers and sellers change. The high price signals that a lot of the good or service is desired, and we should only use it, if it is worth that much, or more, to us. And the high price signals that we might profit from producing more of the good. Similarly, the low price signals that this resource is abundant, and that we should consider using more of it. If we are producers, the low price signals that we should consider using our resources in other ways that might be more valuable to our customers and more profitable for us. Thinking that we should be paid more, because we need the money, or that we should pay less to buy something, because we'd like more of the good, is just childish.

Yet, we are often blind to the needs of others and resent the outcome of competitive market pricing. Then, we propose an alternative method for signaling resource priorities and rationing the results. Can you think of a better system than competitive markets ?

What about a **lottery** ? A lottery may give everyone an equal chance, but does everyone value the outcome equally ? And can we prevent resale by the winners to losers with strong preferences ? Doesn't a lottery simply provide a wind-fall to the winners, while excluding the losers ? The market system allows each participant to express the intensity of their preferences by bidding. Does the purchase of multiple lottery tickets do the same ? It would increase the probability of a win, but still does not relate willingness to sacrifice to social costs. When our government introduced a **Draft Lottery** to reduce opposition to the Vietnam War among young men, our cohort was split between winners who went on with their lives uninterrupted, and losers who sacrificed several years of their lives at sub-standard pay (and risked injury and death). Was this fair ? Or did one group bear disproportionate costs ?

What about **queuing**, a fancy word for "first come, first serve" ? Does this assure that those who value the scarce resource get it ? No, those who have the information about the pending offer, and the time to wait in line, will get the goods, and they may not value them more than anyone else does. We used to joke that the shortages of goods in the USSR made grandmothers valuable. They could wait in line on behalf of the family, whose adults were off at work. In addition, the time in line is a valuable resource wasted. If resale is permitted (we call it "scalping"), then the market reasserts itself. Those who are willing to wait in line can profit, but now we're just creating a new and wasteful form of employment, not an improvement on market transactions.

Discrimination on the basis of irrelevant characteristics was once common. Nat "King" Cole was denied the right to purchase a home on Balboa Island, because of racial exclusion covenants on the land deeds. As a college student, I worked the mid-night shift at the Postal Distribution Center in Jacksonville, Florida. Most of my co-workers were black. One had a M.S. degree in Chemical Engineering. Sorting mail was not fair to him and his family, and was wasteful for society. Historically, women were excluded from many educational programs and careers. The jobs were rationed to white males first. Is this fair ? Is it efficient ?

If we focus on the discrimination which is based on the personal characteristics of the buyers, such as race, will the product go to whoever values it the most ? Years ago, women paid more for the same autos than men paid. Why ? Dealers discovered that women knew less about the qualities of the cars, and less about their pricing choices. If the man buys a car at $21,000 and the woman who would have paid $22,000, doesn't buy because the best offer which she receives is $23,000, then is the car going to the buyer who values it most ?

In the old Soviet Union, scarce consumer goods were rationed by **coupons**. Families received ration coupon books, as well as rubles, for work. They needed both to buy. The Party decided the entitlement of ration coupons for each family. Can you see how this would lead to corruption and favoritism ? Jimmy Carter attempted to introduce ration coupons for gasoline during the shortages of the late 1970s (caused by price controls). The government spent millions of dollars to print up coupons, but never used them. There was no agreement on how to decide who gets the coupons (rights to purchase) or how many.

When we try any of these alternatives, the differences in preferences and willingness to pay remain. Those who receive goods which they value less will be willing to exchange with others who value the goods more. The fortunate owners of property rights negotiate with the frustrated buyers. Unsanctioned markets will develop and confidence in the fairness of the system erodes.

What about **price controls** ? Let's consider the impact of a price ceiling, for example **rent controls**. Governments will introduce rent controls when Demand is increasing faster than Supply, and rents are increasing. The relocations caused by World War Two disrupted residential apartment markets, such as New York City's. Unfortunately, limiting prices or rents to a maximum reduces the profitability of building and maintaining rental properties, never an easy activity, as any landlord will attest. *Rent control transfers a property right from the owner to the lucky tenant.* This creates conflict between tenants and landlords. I have a relative who sublets his NY apartment to friends at close to market rates when he is away, while paying his usual controlled rent. He pockets the difference. When tenants need repairs, the landlord is reluctant to respond. Why pay for repairs that we cannot recover through rents ? In Cairo, I never saw an elevator that worked in rent controlled apartment building. Landlords could not afford maintenance, while collecting 1950s rents and facing 1970s expenses.

And the continuing low rent encourages demand for the controlled apartments. Why settle for a one-bedroom apartment for $1,500/month, when you might get a three bedroom controlled apartment for $300/month ? And why vacate a large apartment that we no longer need, when the kids are grown and gone, if the new, smaller one would cost more ? Better to keep the apartment and take in boarders.

In the absence of price as a rationing device, how will the scarce apartments be rationed ? Do you think that young families, unusual ethnic families, or students will be favored ? The apartments need to be rationed. I would choose quiet, elderly tenants with regular income. They'll be less trouble and easier on the property. But are they the ones who would value the apartment the most ?

New York City introduced rent control during World War Two. Although the properties subject to "rent stabilization" have declined, many distortions remain. Between 1965 & 1987 114,000 rental units were withdrawn from the market. In 1987, NYC landlords refused to rent another 90,000 apartments. They were waiting until 15% of the apartments in a building were vacant, at which time the owners would be permitted convert the apartments to condominiums. The owners would even offer the tenants a discount to buy. And the tenant could flip the property to another at the market price, a clear measure of the property right distortion of the rent control.

Of the many examples of corruption resulting from rent controls, my favorite involves Congressman Charles Rangel who was censured in 2007 for having four rent controlled apartments in New York City. He combined three into a 2,500 sq. ft. home, and the fourth was used as a campaign office. He paid $3,894 per month for all four. Single, market rate (uncontrolled) apartments in the same building rent for as much as $8,125 per month. Can you calculate the subsidy which he was receiving ? I have known many middle and upper income residents of New York who enjoy rent controlled apartments. Some enjoy rent control in New York City, while also owning summer homes in the Hamptons.

Consider the opposite problem, the impact of a **price floor**. If the floor is high enough, it will signal producers to expand production. It will also discourage Demand. As a result, price floors tend to create surpluses. Since the Great Depression, the Federal Government has distorted many agricultural markets. Among the strangest were acreage limits for tobacco farming to reduce over production. The permits were not tied to specific parcels of land. So, heirs with no connection to tobacco farming, could rent their allocations to farmers who needed them. Also, for many years, our government set price floors for milk to support dairymen. The higher milk prices harmed consumers. They encouraged consumers, including creameries to substitute less expensive ingredients. A friend in the ice cream business, who was proud to produce all natural product, was incessantly approached by salesmen offering him artificial fillers and sweeteners (sugar prices are also kept high by import tariffs and quotas), as ways to reduce his costs. (How much of that ice cream sandwich that you just enjoyed is plastic ?) Meanwhile, dairymen would expand their herds with high volume cows such as Holsteins, rather than high quality cows, such as Guernseys, Jerseys, or Brown Swiss. To keep the price up, the government had to buy any surplus and was spending $400 million/yr. in 1990. When the program ended in 1992, Vermont switched from Republican to Democrat, and dairies were sold to become retirement and summer homes for city folks. A similar transition occurred, when the woolen mills of New England declined gradually in the prior sixty years. Farmers reduced their herds of sheep. Wouldn't an earlier transition been a better use of resources for the dairymen, too ?

Several concepts keep popping up as we analyze markets. One is the concept of multiple and sometimes contradictory consequences. For example, when we purchase a product, we exchange money for the product. We can look at this as the Demand for the product or the Supply of money offered. We can also look at it from the other point of view: the seller demands money and supplies the product ! The interactions in the market depend on the demand for both items to be exchanged, as well as the supply offered of each. In this view, *money is no different from any other commodity* --- it is desired because it is useful, and it is valuable in exchange, because it is scarce.

Another concept that reappears is the **fallacy of composition** (sometimes called "the fallacy of the heap"). It is the mistaken assumption that what is true for the individual is also true for the group. For example, consider two possibilities: 1) you have more money or 2) everyone has more money. In the first case, you are better off, because you can afford more goods. In the second case, no one is better off, because everyone is trying to buy scarce goods. The competition for those goods merely increases their prices.

In the 1970s and 1980s, the fallacy of heap caused problems, but never as badly as in the 2000-2008 period. (Let me assure you that I am a feminist. I believe in equal opportunity for everyone. The success of civil rights over the past fifty years is a great achievement. And I believe people should be free to marry whomever they please.) Nevertheless, consider the effect of more women obtaining educational and employment opportunities that raised their incomes and contributed to national growth. As Richard Herrnstein and Charles Murray[3] pointed out, well-educated, high-income ($100k) men meet and marry well-educated, high-income ($100k) women. And low-income ($50k)men and ($50k) women also meet and marry. This attenuates the income distribution by family (the former pair have income of $200,000; the latter have income of $100,000; even though both couples work). Now, they bid for their first home, dream home, or retirement home. They are bidding against similar couples. Whereas, before the wife worked, the high-income family could only bid $400,000 for the house. Now, their income has doubled, and they can bid $800,000. They think that they must earn more to afford the house. They don't realize that the price of housing is rising, because so many couples have increased their incomes through dual careers. So, who benefits from the wife's higher income ? Their parents' generation that are cashing out at inflated prices. Adding insult to injury, this bidding for scarce housing is worsened by the proliferation of land use policies which limit construction and raise costs. So, the usual Supply response to rising prices is choked off in the name of protecting the environment or the neighborhood, to the extraordinary benefit of existing property owners. (If you think that you have read this before. You are correct. See lesson #2.2 wealth effects. The analysis is so unconventional that it bears repeating.)

I often observe that those who oppose building homes, or businesses, complain about the high-cost of housing and the shortage of jobs. The idea that building affordable housing is good, but market rate housing is bad is particularly mistaken. Whenever we build a house, we add to the supply of residences. If we build a condominium for the elderly, they move out of their house. The next family moves up to that house, and out of their current abode. The chain continues. Any new housing adds to the housing stock and benefits low income families along with others. When we do build "affordable" housing, I find that is often goes to "insiders," those with early knowledge of the opportunity, such as the employees of the public agency, contractor, or bank involved in the project. And when local governments refuse to allow businesses to expand, workers are deprived of opportunities. Existing employers are protected from the competition for workers that should prevail. And local incomes are lower than they should be.

In the late 1990s, there was a political consensus that we should increase home ownership from the persistent 65% of families. Public policy in the form of "community reinvestment" guidelines and commitments by government agencies (Fannie Mae and Freddie Mac) to purchase "sub-prime" and "no doc" mortgages increased the ability of hitherto unqualified buyers to compete in the market for homeownership. Without limits to how much they could borrow, naïve homebuyers bid prices and contracted for mortgages that they could not afford. Home prices took off, but homeownership only increased by 1%. When house prices stopped rising and overextended buyers defaulted, a financial and economic crisis resulted. Few people reflect on the millions who bought home for inflated prices, because of the competition of others and continue to service debts and sacrifice. And they are expected to pay taxes to bail out the ones who caused them to pay so much in the first place. Who benefited from this bubble ? Sellers, realtors, contractors, and lenders --- as long as they passed their "hot potatoes," before the crash.

As these examples attest, the efficiency of free markets with secure property rights, free movement of prices, and low transactions costs is very powerful. I have mentioned a few examples of interference with markets and the waste and corruption that results. Now, we must turn in our next lesson to the many circumstances when markets don't work nearly as well as we'd like.

Questions for Review and examination:
Explain the three types of Economic efficiency.
How does a competitive economy achieve the three forms of economic efficiency ?
Explain how price controls distort economic decisions and create inefficiencies.

[1]*Fama, Eugene F. (September–October 1965). "Random Walks In Stock Market Prices". Financial Analysts Journal 21 (5): 55–59.*
[2]Burton Malkiel A Random Walk Down Wall Street W W Norton 1973
[3]Richard Hernstein and Charles Murray, The Bell Curve, Free Press 1994 chapter four

Lesson #2.5 Market Failures, Taxation, and Information

As we learned in lesson #2.1, prices have crucial roles in determining the use of scarce resources by rationing among competing users, and by signaling opportunities and sacrifices. In the last lesson, we discussed the role of prices in generating efficiency. Now, we should consider conditions under which prices will give the wrong signals, and the decisions that result will not be the best. Let's begin by considering the effect of taxation.

Taxes are necessary as the primary method by which we finance the activities of government. There are at least four necessary roles for government, even in the most libertarian of societies: 1) establishing and maintaining the rule of law, including regulating property rights and public safety, 2) regulating market failures, such as external effects and public goods (lesson #2.6), 3) stabilizing the economy, including regulating the financial system and the value of money (Part five: Macroeconomics), and 4) adjusting income distribution to provide for the most needy, and to avoid the alienation which can lead to disruption by the disenfranchised. Of course, government is likely to try to provide whatever goods and services or redistributions that are demanded by those in power, whether those activities are necessary, or even constitutional. And all of these activities require resources. The resources can be mobilized by government through coercion, or by purchase. And if purchased, government needs money, which can only come from taxation or from borrowing.

What are the characteristics of a good tax system ? As we will soon learn, *taxes discourage activity*. Accordingly, taxes are often used to alter prices and incentives, and subsequently behavior. For example, part of our motivation for taxing tobacco and alcohol is to discourage consumption of these products which we believe are unhealthy. However, if we take the view that individuals should be allowed to make their own decisions, based on opportunity costs, then, we would say that *taxes should raise revenue with the minimum distortion of those choices and therefore of economic activity*. Going after the easy money by taxing those who have the most is tempting. But, if we believe that the individual's income is related to their contribution to production, then taxes shouldn't punish success. Any tax system requires compliance and thus transactions costs for the payer and the recipient. So, a good tax system would be administratively easy, and the costs of compliance and collection should be minimal. How do you think our tax systems scores in these criteria ?

A trickier criterion to establish is fairness. It requires normative judgments --- judging the desirability of an action by its effects. Economists distinguish two concepts of fairness. **Horizontal equity** is the notion of taxing equal incomes equally. For example, the doctor who earns $200,000/yr. should pay the same as the landlord who earns $200,000/yr. Perhaps, we can agree that this would be fair. Unfortunately, politicians love to do favors for supporters and punish opponents, so our tax system has many areas of special treatment, depending on the source of income. The second concept is **vertical equity**, the notion of treating unequals unequally. Can we agree that people with more income should pay more ? There is evidence to support the idea that consumption of public services is proportionate to income. (Differences in the types of public services consumed are important, such as police and fire protection vs. public parks or public education.) Selecting the best design to assure that those with higher incomes pay more than those with lower incomes is difficult, as the following table shows:

Tax Rate:	Low income: $ 40,000		High Income: $200,000	
proportional at 20%	tax	$ 8,000	tax 20%	$ 40,000
progressive at 20%	tax	$ 8,000	tax 40%	$ 80,000

        regressive at   20%   tax $ 8,000   tax   15% $ 30,000

As you can see, all three systems result in the high income earner paying substantially more, although the percentage of income paid varies a lot. So, which is fair ? I don't know. I like the idea of measuring the benefits of public services consumed. (Economists call this *expenditure incidence*.) If this were done, we'd probably choose a proportional tax system. But the truth is that governments will generally operate under the principal that "we need the service and they should pay for it." As a result, we have a highly complex and distortionary jungle of taxes and fees, as well as many taxing authorities.

The Federal Tax Code scores badly by any criteria of fairness or efficiency. (The National Football League is classified as a not-for profit entity.) The Code is now 9,000 pages long, and there were 4,600 changes in the Tax Code from 2001-2012. America has the highest corporate tax rate among developed nations, leading to US businesses to stash $2.1 trillion of earnings overseas. Compliance requires 6.1 billion man-hours each year (equivalent to 3 million full-time workers).[1]

Our Federal government relies primarily on personal income taxes (45% of revenue) and payroll taxes (37%). State and local governments use sales taxes (21%), property taxes (18%), income taxes (12%), federal grants (16%) and all other taxes (33%).

The consequence of a tax is to drive a wedge between the price paid by buyers and the revenue received by the sellers. The increase in the price paid by buyers discourages Demand, and the decrease in the price received by sellers discourages Supply. The economic activity and exchange that is taxed, is discouraged. Our government gives us some useful examples, such as the luxury tax on yachts, autos, and private planes costing more than $30,000 in the 1989 Tax Act, a budget compromise that may have cost President George H.W. Bush reelection. Congress expected to raise $1,000,000,000 in revenue from this luxury tax. How did market participants react ? Luxury auto makers, such as BMW and MBZ, developed new models that could be sold for less than $30,000. Sales of expensive, new boats and planes stopped. The prices and sales of used boats and planes, the substitutes, increased. Hardly any revenue was raised. Boat and plane manufacturers cut way back of production, or went out of business. Once Congress faced the reality of its policy, the tax was repealed.

So, we see that taxes reduce the incentives to produce and consume. On the other hand, we expect that **transfers** (subsidies) will increase the incentives to produce and consume. We see some of this in the subsidies for alternative ("green") energy. These changes in incentives will alter the mix and level of economic activity. Because we have learned that economic growth increases income equality, as well as opportunities for earning income and enjoying material goods, we should be sensitive to these incentive effects.

As long as we are studying the effect of taxes, we might contrast government decision-making with private sector management decisions, recognizing that human nature and incentives influence both processes.[2] In markets, we are able to express the intensity of our preferences by what we are offering to pay. Under a system of one man = one vote, acting on strong preferences becomes a problem. **The Voting Paradox** derives from the observation that the **median voter** determines the majority, and the median voter is the least informed voter. By **log-rolling** (I'll support your issue, if you support mine), we achieve more influence in what matters to us, but this is not efficient. In addition, because governments can grant, or withhold, valuable special favors, interest groups will seek to influence policy and to extract rents through special treatment. The extreme form is **Crony Capitalism**. Because of the importance of government favors, competition for influence escalates the costs of election, and elected officials become captives, trading favors for campaign contributions. Other issues are 1) Sovereignty (governments have powers that civilians do not, such as the power to tax, conscript soldiers, and execute offenders). Governments can break promises and contracts, and 2) Bureaucracy (public employees are more concerned with getting along than generating results).

Let's compare and contrast the incentives, constraints, and behaviors of politicians, bureaucrats, and businessmen.

Politicians enjoy the illusions of power that derive from the ability to reward supporters with favors and the award of contracts, and to punish opponents with discriminatory laws, taxes, regulations, and denials of contracts. Politicians enjoy the fawning attention of favor seekers, the privileges of office (perquisites), and the fame (publicity and honors). But they are constrained by the need to gather campaign contributions and to maintain popularity. They also suffer the loss of privacy. So, they must 1) provide patronage jobs, 2) deliver projects for supporters ("pork"), and 3) pander to supporters' needs and prejudices. They cannot afford to make unpopular decisions. And they must offer symbolic gratification to voters and donors. (These involve validating prejudices and granting recognition.)

Civil servants (bureaucrats) enjoy security and regular promotions, generous and stable salaries, benefits, and pensions. They gain status from their civil service ranks, and they are protected by lack of accountability for their actions, as long as they don't violate the law, or the codes of civil service behavior (a cultural element). They must avoid taking any action which could lead to criticism. Better to take no action than the wrong action. They must cultivate the support of peers, and please their patrons by total loyalty. They must spend all budgeted funds before year end, or lose in the next round of budgeting. As long as budget is spent, results don't matter. So, civil servants play it safe, delay decisions, monitor superiors, and cater to their needs.

Business executives enjoy salaries, and bonuses, including options . They may obtain status and wealth, including perquisites. Their ability to grant or cancel contracts, hire, promote, and fire employees gives them some power, and subordinates will defer to and flatter them. On the other hand, business managers must meet their budgets for revenue, costs, and profit. And they must grow company revenue and profit, in order to increase the value of the owners' investments (the share price). Finally, they must please customers, directors, and shareholders. All of these elements of measureable performance lead to accountability that is absent in government. Business executives seek opportunities to innovate in order to meet customer needs, minimize costs, maximize profits, and stifle competition. Of course, they will also lobby government for favors and to prevent harmful government actions.

We can conclude that, because individuals make choices in which they consider benefits as well as costs, incentives matter. When incentives and constraints differ, we should expect different decisions and different results. Public policy makers should consider benefits and costs, but often lack the incentives to do so. Some of the important costs are monitoring, compliance, and administration. Results should matter, too.

In our study of market behavior, we have assumed that both buyers and sellers have all necessary **information** to make good decisions. They know the characteristics of the products, the costs of production, the potential for satisfaction and for profit. They agree on a price. But what happens if one, or both, parties don't have this information ?

Sometimes, we judge quality by price. We assume that the higher priced good is better, because other customers won't pay more, unless there is a proportionate benefit. This is a fundamental principle of arbitrage and efficient markets. We seek value which we calculate as the ratio of quality to price. For example, we would judge a wine that is twice as good, as a real bargain, if its price is less than twice as high as the alternative. If others do the same, then this decision to judge quality by price, may be helpful for those products that sell in large volumes to numerous well-informed customers --- what we call broad and deep markets. But what about those products that are highly differentiated, even unique, and rarely purchased ? What if most customers are as poorly informed, as we are ? The price we pay may be the result of emotional decisions, as described in our section on Behavioral Economics. (See lesson #2.2.)

Two of my teachers at Stanford, Joe Stiglitz and Mike Spence, investigated the information problem and shared the Nobel Prize in Economics for 2001. They postulated that markets will develop for valuable, but scarce information. That is: people will be willing to pay for information that helps them to make better choices. However, there will be some problems in purchasing information. How does the customer estimate the value of information to be purchased before he has it ? And how credible is the source of the information being offered ?

An example would be the market for used cars. The dealer knows the history and condition of the auto, but the customer does not. As a result, the dealer has an expectation of a price that reflects value, but the buyer does not. The buyer will protect himself by making a low offer, in case the quality is poor and repairs become necessary. In order to get a better price, the seller will try to signal quality. A direct method would be offering a guarantee or a warrantee. (You may be familiar with the now common 50,000 mile warrantee for a new car to assure customers of quality and reduce maintenance costs.) An indirect, and less reliable, signal is the construction of fancy facilities, as a sign of success and stability.

At the center of the search problem is the issue of costs and benefits. What is the cost of spending more time and resources gathering information vs. the benefits of obtaining a better product and a better price ? If gathering information is costly, sellers may take advantage of the buyer's reluctance to invest in gathering more information.

A traditional solution to the information problem is to hire someone who is knowledgeable and active in the market for this product. Hence, we hire professional agents, often called "brokers." Of course, when we list retail brokers, such as real estate brokers, travel agents, or stock brokers, we immediately recognize the credibility problem. (And the potential for conflict of interest) Is the real estate agent truly knowledgeable, or just an amateur ? Real estate transactions can be very complex with many risks. Is the travel agent familiar with our particular travel preferences ? How can she know about all the transportation and hospitality options ? Is the stock broker working for us, or is he under pressure from his firm to generate commissions ? Rarely is the stock broker a qualified securities analysis or portfolio manager. So, what value does the broker provide for us ?

An alternative is the use of consumer services which test and report on various products. An independent firm, such as *Consumer Reports*, tests household goods, autos, and electronic equipment. They sell their results inexpensively through their magazine and web-site. AAA offers evaluations of autos, and auto insurance companies provide information on auto prices and costs. The Internet is a major source of comparison pricing, as well as consumer opinions. Of course, the reliability of these offers and opinions is a problem, again.

What then is the reason for the existence of retailers ? Department stores, groceries, and other retailers may be considered **information intermediaries**. In addition to providing convenient locations and times for us to purchase goods, they shop for us. The first job of a new retail executive is as a buyer. They search for products which will appeal to their customers. Why would I pay $800 for an Italian suit which Nordstrom's can buy for $400 ? The answer is the transactions costs of searching for myself (gathering information). I would need to travel to Italy and visit a number of manufacturers to find this suit. How does Nordstrom's profit ? They enjoy economies of scale by shopping and buying large volumes.

For many years, economists couldn't explain the importance of **advertising**. They believed that advertising was a zero sum game, just shifting purchases from one producer to another. This silly conclusion reflected their conviction that buyers are rational and fully informed. Once, we recognize the information problem, the role of advertising becomes obvious, as do other forms of sales promotion. *Advertising conveys information.* It grabs the attention of the prospect, alerts him of an opportunity, or reminds him of a need. It associates the product with his needs, and informs the customer of how to obtain the product. Advertising should be targeted towards the best prospects, those most likely to buy the product, and this will dictate the placement of the advertisement --- lingerie in *Vogue* magazine and beer in *Sports Illustrated*. Advertising persuades by associating the product with the customer's needs, and informs the prospect of how he can obtain the product --- price, place, financing options, and time.

We'll address one final issue before leaving the information problem. If customers are only vaguely familiar with their choices, at best partial informed, do producers have incentives to provide **quality** ? The existence of private property provides a strong incentive. If I own it, I will want to maintain and improve it in order to enjoy it, and later obtain the best price for it. I will also be confident that I will receive all the value in exchange. In the absence of private property, I will not bother with these costs, because someone else may take it or sell it, and I get little or no benefit.

Contracts provide another solution. When we sell under a contract that specifies the rights and obligations of both parties, we have more confidence in making the exchange. To be entitled to the best price, the seller agrees to quality standards and will invest in meeting them to avoid the repercussions associated with violating the contract. And he will receive full compensation, or redress from the buyer. Contracts often include contingency clauses, escapes, and penalties, so both parties understand the benefits and costs of the exchange. Finally, where repeat business is important, businesses will bear the costs of maintaining consistent quality in order to build a reputation which encourages more sales and allows them to charge the higher prices associated with better quality. We call that higher price a **reputation rent**. It's no accident that when repeat customers are not expected, quality suffers.

Questions for Review and Examination:
How does a tax influence prices and quantities exchanged ?
What are the features of a good tax system ?
In what ways do governments face different constraints and incentives from private enterprises ?
What is the likely outcome of inadequate or asymmetric information ?
Explain the ways in which buyers try to improve their information to make better choices ?
How do sellers try to influence the buyers' perceptions of quality and value ?
What institutions exist to reduce the transactions costs associated with inadequate information and how do they provide value ?

[1]Robert W. Wood "Twenty Really Stupid Things about the US Tax Code" *Forbes* Dec.16,2014
[2] Harvey Leibenstein, <u>Beyond Economic Man</u>, 1976, Harvard U. Press
    Prof. Leibenstein tackles the issue of "X-inefficiency" in management, where protection from competition leads to suboptimal outcomes.

Lesson #2.6 More Market Failures: Public Goods and Externalities

In the last two lessons, we discussed the efficiency of perfectly competitive markets, and then some of the distortions caused by taxation and problems of inadequate or asymmetric (unbalanced) information. Here, we will discuss problems intrinsic to the goods themselves, before moving forward into failures for lack of competition, in the next lesson.

Typically, we are thinking of private goods. Much of what we consume is private, in the sense that each good has only one consumer, (or at least one consumer at a time). If I am wearing my shoes, you can't wear them. And if I'm not wearing them, you may not want to wear them after me ! So, we say, that private goods are exclusive. My use precludes your use. When that is true, we are rivals for the scarce good. We bid against each other in the market, and whoever values the goods the most, will get them. Those who value them less will choose to drop out. For the same reason, the exclusiveness quality, we can only satisfy more consumers by producing more goods. If more people want shoes, and are willing to pay for them, we must make more shoes to satisfy them. And the production of more shoes requires more resources. The price equal to marginal cost production criterion will lead to the right level of production. The price that equals the marginal cost of production is the right price.

However, there are goods which, by their very nature, are not private. We call products that are not exclusive and therefore not rivalrous, **public goods**. This does not mean that they are, or must be, produced by the government. That is the wrong idea. The public good requires resources to produce and therefore has costs of production, (provision), but once produced and available, one consumer's use of the good does not exclude others from using it. Consider the lighthouse which, once constructed, can serve many ships as a navigational aid, with no additional resource cost. And there are many other examples: roads, beaches, police protection, national defense, and national parks. Once constructed, (and overlooking maintenance and congestion issues for the moment), there are no additional costs to letting more consumers use the road or the beach, or to be protected by police, or national defense. In other words, satisfying more consumers doesn't require more production. In fact, the unnecessary effort to exclude consumers reduces total satisfaction for no reason, and thus, is undesirable. If the *marginal cost* of satisfying more consumers is zero, then the correct price to charge the consumer also would be zero. In effect, no rationing is needed. If we charge for access to the public good, we discourage consumption for no reason, and reduce total satisfaction.

Why is this a problem ? Public goods must be produced. They require resources. Someone must pay. How will we pay for the initial provision ? How will we assure that we produce the right amount, neither too little, nor too much ? We just stated that, if the marginal cost of making the good available to another user is zero, then the appropriate price is zero. If we charge the consumer any price above zero, they will buy too little, but if we don't charge, where will we get the money to provide it at all ? One additional complication is that consumers often recognize that a good is "public", and that their use imposes no additional costs on anyone. They will feel justified to use the public good without paying for it. Economists call this the **Free Rider Problem.**

When I was a child, some neighbors, the Hendersons, had a nice tennis court across the road from their house. They realized that they had built a public good. They informed us kids that we could play on the court anytime we wished, unless there were Hendersons who wanted to play. Then, we would vacate the court and wait for them to finish. As a result, the court was well-used, and we were all happy. However, notice that the Hendersons only were willing to build one court. That's all they needed, although the neighborhood could have used more. When another family built a second court, they sold shares entitling the contributors to certain days and times. We kids were not contributors, so we didn't get to play on this court. It was empty half the week --- wasted capacity.

There was a golf course down by the river. We kids realized that our use of the golf course didn't impose any costs on anyone, as long as we didn't tear it up, or interfere with other players. We would sneak on the course, from the river, in a canoe. If caught, we'd escape onto the river. The golf course was underused, and resources were wasted trying to exclude us. Hopefully, these examples will clarify for you the problem of inefficiencies associated with goods that have this "public" characteristic.

What is the public good worth ? Let's reason carefully and compare the result to the demand for private goods. In the case of private goods, we must produce more to enjoy more. Each individual who would like to use of the public good has a Demand. If we could measure that Demand, we can take advantage of the fact that we don't need to produce more of the public good to satisfy the demand of each individual to produce the right quantity. One way to think about this issue to contrast the private and public demand functions:

    a) For **private** (exclusive, rivalrous) goods, we must produce more goods to satisfy more
    individuals, and so (on a Cartesian graph of price vs. quantity) the total demand is the
    horizontal sum of the individual demands.
    b) For **public** goods, *we don't need to produce more to allow more people to use the*
    public good, so, we can add up the willingness of each participant to pay to get the total
    value to consumers (each consumer paying for the same good). On Cartesian graph, the
    total demand is the vertical sum of the individual demands.

Thus, we can create a total demand function that represents how much each quantity of public goods is worth to the consumers. If we could collect these payments, we could produce the efficient quantity of the public good. Here comes the problem: How do we get the individuals to reveal what the public good is worth to them ? They know that their use imposes no additional production costs, and therefore, they shouldn't pay to use the good. And so, they will understate their true willingness to pay in order to reduce their dollar assessment (the free rider problem). This is truly a dilemma. There is no perfect solution.

In fact, we do produce and provide public goods in three different ways, each of which has efficiency problems. Like any other good, we must answer four questions: How much should we produce ? Who pays for the production of the public good ? How will we produce it (technology) ? And who gets to consume public good ?

Many public goods are privately provided. Consider the privately owned golf course. The owner must charge high greens fees to cover his operating costs and yield a return on his investment, whether it was the sunk cost of construction or the purchase price. Fees will be high, and use will be low. In my town, Sandpiper is such a course with fees of $100 per round. It is half-empty most of time. Many more golfers could be accommodated but are excluded in order to collect the high fees from the few.

Another solution is the public golf course provided by local government. In this case, the tax payers are assessed for the construction of the course, and the fees only cover operating costs. More people are able to play, but many tax payers never play, even though they support the course through their taxes.

An intermediate solution is a private club. A group of golfers organize a club. They pay an initial membership fee for the construction of the course. They pay a monthly fee to cover fixed operating costs. Then, they pay a small use fee (the greens fee) to cover the wear and tear of their play (the variable costs of their use). The small greens fee encourages use. Non-golfers don't join the club and never pay at all. Even so, the course is underused, and often resources are wasted keeping non-members out. Can you see that none of these solutions is ideal ?

As a side-light, many economists view **fiscal federalism** as similar to the country club solution to the public goods problem. If we have a large number of communities from which to choose, we can elect to reside in the community with the level and mix of public goods that we prefer and are willing to pay for. Buying a home, or paying the rent that offers the owner a return on his investment is similar to the membership fee that gives us access to the services. Then, our taxes pay for the operating costs, and user fees may be associated with non-zero marginal costs. Of course, even here there are free riders --- those who believe that they should live in Beverly Hills without buying in.

Another important area of public goods is **technology**. Basic research is a public good. When we create new knowledge, there is no additional cost to allowing others to use it. In fact, we would like for the useful knowledge to be widely used, whenever, and wherever anyone can benefit. However, if the new methods are immediately diffused, what incentive remains to make the original investment in research and development which is inherently costly and risky ? Our founding fathers recognized the importance of innovation and incentives. For that reason, the **Patent Office** was authorized under Article 1, section 8, of the US Constitution. Successful patents grant the holder exclusive use for a period of time. The right can be sold, or leased in exchange for royalties.

Because the external benefits of knowledge (research, development, innovation, and diffusion are the four stages) may be substantial to other firms, to consumers, and to society, there is another dilemma: how broad and how long should the exclusive property right be ? The longer and broader patent provides a greater incentive, but also slows the diffusion to other users. This may explains heavy government subsidies for research, either directly through government research institutions, such as the National Institute of Health, or through grants to private institutions, such as by the National Science Foundation, or by tax concessions, such as tax credit, tariffs, or import quotas. Anti-trust regulations may be relaxed as well. In these last three cases, consumers will bear the burden of paying for the subsidy, in the form of higher product prices.

Another area of pricing problems is products with **externalities**. These products have effects on outsiders, people other than the buyers and the sellers. Sometimes, we call these out-siders, "third parties." The buyers and sellers are the first and second parties. If the sellers and buyers are weighing costs and benefits, when deciding how much to produce or consume, and what price to accept or pay, they may over-look the benefits to others, or the costs imposed on others, by their activity. As a result, all the costs and benefits are not captured in the market price.

We distinguish **positive externalities**, benefits of the activity, not enjoyed by the buyers or sellers, and **negative externalities**, costs of the activity, not borne by the buyers or the sellers. When I fix up my house and landscape my yard, my neighbors enjoy the improvements, as they walk by. When, my family gets vaccinations to protect ourselves from illness, our neighbors are less likely to catch disease from us. When we consider these activities, we weigh the costs that we pay against the prices that we must pay. We don't consider the external benefit to our neighbors. If we did, we would be willing to pay more and would buy more. Hence, we say, consumer pays **too much** for a good which has **positive externalities**, and will buy **too little.**

When we first moved into our home, it had been neglected by the widow who had lived there for fifty-five years. We cleaned it up. One day, I found a note in my mailbox, "We love what you have done to the house; we enjoy your garden everyday as we walk our dog." I left a basket with a note, "Thank-you for your kind note, leave money, so I can do more."

On the other hand, sometimes, we indulge in activities which are unpleasant, or even harmful to others, without even being aware of these costs which we are imposing on them. And what is a positive externality for some can be a negative externality for others. (I enjoy smelling the smoke from a good cigar, even if someone else smokes it, but others may find the same smell offensive and worry about harm to their health.) Pollution is the classic case of a negative externality with which we are all familiar. A producer saves costs by putting his waste into the atmosphere or local water, but the damage to the air or water harms people, flora, or fauna down-wind, or down-stream. In this case, competition among producers drives down the product price. The producer argues that he can't reduce pollution, because the costs of clean up would drive him out of business. And the consumer enjoys a low price, ignorant of the costs to the outsiders. The consumer pays **too little** for a good which has **negative externalities**, and so, responds by buying **too much.**

My great-grandfather managed thirty paper mills in New England, mainly around Holyoke, Mass. He retired in 1923, and the companies migrated south and west. His old locations slowly were abandoned, finally closing in 1973. Only thirty years later did the state government agree to hold new industries in the same location harmless from the pollution left by their predecessors, the paper-mills. I imagine that none of the paper consumers understood that their fine writing paper was only cheap, because the true costs were not assessed, because the waste chemicals were disposed by polluting the ground around the factories.

What should we do, and what do we do, about externalities ? In the case of positive externalities, we'd like to assess the external beneficiaries in proportion to their gains, thus reducing the costs to the first party consumer and increasing the reward to the second party producer. This may be difficult to do, so we often use government subsidies to encourage production and use. For example, we subsidize the provision of vaccines, to encourage vaccinations to protect us all. And we subsidize education. Because elementary education provides large external benefits to the community, enabling our residents can support themselves, we grant large subsidies in the form of free public education. The subsidies are reduced for higher education, because we recognize that most of the benefit of college and graduate school educations accrues to the graduate in the form of higher income, and the difference to the rest of us is small.

On the other hand, we tax cigarettes and alcohol sales, in part to discourage their use, and in part to raise revenue to support public health. We believe that these products not only impose health risks for the consumers, which they may consider when choosing to use them, but also impose costs to the rest of us, in second-hand smoke irritation, alcohol related sociopathic behaviors, and publicly funded health care costs.

These are examples of the **Tax and Subsidy Response.** The idea is to change incentives, and as a result, to change choices. We would tax production that generate negative externalities, and subsidize those with positive externalities. Ideally, the tax or subsidy would reflect the cost of the negative externality, or the benefit of the positive externality. The tax would be paid by the consumer, and the subsidy received by the consumer, or the producer. The tax revenue would to go to those harmed, and the subsidy be paid by the external beneficiaries. As you can imagine, these conditions are difficult to meet, and generally, the tax revenue is diverted to any purpose that the revenue agency prefers, and the subsidy comes from general tax revenues. Nevertheless, there may be improvement in the market price signals and changes in behavior in the desired direction. Has smoking declined because of changes in social attitudes, because of large increases in tobacco taxes, or some combination of both ?

We also use the **coercion** solution, when we require youth to attend school, or residents to get vaccinations.

In the case of negative externalities, such as pollution, our first instinct is the **Regulatory Response,** or "command and control." We, Americans, love to pass laws, thinking that new laws will lead to immediate and substantial changes in behavior. We neglect the costs of compliance and the likelihood of evasion. How does the regulatory response work ? The agency establishes limits for the undesirable activity. It monitors performance, issues cease and desist orders, and punishes violators with fines. The problem with this method is that it doesn't weigh costs against benefits. The alternative to the undesirable activity may be costly, too. The paper mill that puts waste in the river produces a valuable product. What is the value of the damage to the watershed ? What would be the resource cost of alternative disposal ? In other words, how important is this form of waste disposal ? Changing the example, what if we limit everyone to driving 100 miles a week, as a way of reducing air pollution ? Would we all be impacted in the same way ? Is driving as important to the retiree, as to the commuting worker ? Should we require campers in Alaska to haul out their bodily waste, when there are no other humans for hundreds of miles in any direction ? Should the ranchers in Wyoming have the same auto emission standards, as the residents of Los Angeles, or New York City ?

I remember a few years ago, a hot dispute over logging in the Pacific Northwest. The logging industry enjoyed heavily subsidized access to government lands and wanted to continue. The environmentalists wanted to limit access to those lands. Their chosen issue was the **Northern Spotted Owl**. The claim was that the Northern Spotted Owl was endangered, and only nested in virgin forests. Hence, harvesting in those forests should be prohibited. They lobbied for three million acres of forest to be set aside. The industry argued that the Northern Spotted Owl was not a unique species, just a variation, and did not deserve protection. A compromise was reached. Within months, a pair of Northern Spotted Owls was observed nesting in a telephone pole beside a strip mall in Oregon. Years later, biologists realized that the threat to the Northern Spotted Owl wasn't logging, but the invasion of its territory by a larger, more aggressive owl. In the meantime, mills shut down, and towns lost their reason for existing and slowly depopulated.

We might conclude that the regulatory solution is likely to degenerate into a political struggle in which one side sees only benefits and the other side sees only costs, and whoever wins, the outcome is likely to lead to a sub-optimal use of the scarce resource.

Years ago, Ron Coase made the profound observation, (pioneered by A. C. Pigou), that *externalities may be a property rights problem*. Because neither the buyer nor the seller has the right to the externality, the right to enjoy the benefit or the responsibility to bear the cost, the external effect is ignored by the parties to the transaction. If the right could be assigned to one party, or the other, then someone would be considering that cost, or benefit, in their calculation, and the price would adjust to give the correct signal. Hence, he concluded that the correct resource allocation can occur, if the property rights to all effects of the activity are assigned and marketable.

Sometimes, private action resolves externality issues. In Oregon and California, orchard farmers can benefit from apiaries installed in their orchards by bee-keepers. They get more fruit. And the bee-keepers benefit from being able to put their bee hives in the orchards. Their bees produce more honey. In one region, the orchard farmers pay the bee-keepers to bring their bees into the orchards. In the other region, the bee-keepers pay the orchards to allow them to install their hives. Can you explain these opposite approaches to external benefits ?

I observed a successful application of Coase's principle in game management in Southern Africa. To the African farmer, the wild game is a pest. The baboons, or the elephants, arrive just as his harvest is ready, and destroy it. Perhaps, they destroy his huts, as well. Not surprisingly, he will find a poacher who will rid him of these vermin and reward him with some of the meat, or perhaps a radio. The governments of Namibia, South Africa, Botswana, and elsewhere recognized the problem. They issue hunting permits for big game – lion, elephant, rhino, water buffalo. The fees from the permits fund the Nature Conservancy. And the hunters provide services by culling the large animals, which are old and infirm, allowing the younger ones to breed. Next, the government offers to remove offending animals, which are relocated or sold at auction to farmers and game lodges that want them. The farmers are compensated for any damage from the wild animals. Finally, the farmers who are neighbors to the game reserves share in tourism revenues. The result is that the game becomes a valuable resource to the farmers who now protect them. The nations that follow these policies have healthy populations of wild animals. Some have even gone so far as ranching indigenous antelope for quality protein, further increasing their value and their populations.

On the other hand, what happens when governments prohibit hunting of elephant or rhinoceros and burn confiscated tusks ? The price of scarce tusks rises, poaching is encouraged and traders who can protect their inventory (often via corruption) are enriched. And of course, the destroyed tusks are completely wasted.

Let us consider the rights to a river. If the paper mill has the right to use the river, then it will weigh the costs of polluting the river against other forms of waste disposal. If the people down river suffer from the pollution, they can organize and offer to rent, or purchase, the right to use the river. Then, the mill owners must consider either using the river or collecting the side-payment and using some other disposal method for their waste. Choosing the least costly method assures the best use of the river. Alternatively, if the people down river have the rights, the mill will offer them a payment to let the mill use the river. The offer will be less than the cost of the next best waste disposal method. The people down river must decide to use the river for themselves, or to take the payment and suffer the costs. Again, the assignment of the right leads to the best use of the river. The ownership of the property right determines who compensates whom, but does not alter the efficient solution.

This may seem to be a shocking result, but remember, we want to use scarce resources efficiently. If a small amount of pollution does little or no damage, and clean up would require other, more expensive resources, then we should pollute. Perhaps, we learned from the ill-considered subsidies and mandates for ethanol use in fuel, that producing four gallons of corn based fuel which requires three gallons of oil consumption during the growing of the corn, and pollutes rivers and erodes soil, is not an efficient, or environmentally friendly policy, though the subsidized farmers may like it. And some remote and ignorant environmentalists may feel good about it.

The Coase Theorem have given rise to policies such as **Cap & Trade**. The idea is that rather than influencing prices through tax and subsidy, changing incentives and leading to new quantity choices, we could *issue permits for the desired quantity of activity and allow trading of permits*. The price of the permits would reflect their scarcity and the costs of the alternatives. This approach has been used with some success locally and regionally. In Santa Barbara, we limited commercial real estate square footage in three classes: industrial, commercial, and tourism (hotel rooms). Once the limit had been built, a hotel that wished to expand would need to buy room permits from one that would shrink or change use, say from hotel to studio apartment rentals. In the Los Angeles basin, limits were set for various air pollutants. Companies, such as refineries, which wanted to expand, buy permits from companies that are moving out or willing to install inexpensive pollution controls. The result is stability at minimum costs. However, global efforts at Cap & Trade have not been successful. Paying some kleptocrat in South-East Asia not to harvest trees, so that you can fly your private jet without guilt hasn't protected the forests, or stabilized air pollution. (Take note again, Al Gore.)

Some of the difficulties of implementing the property rights solution include measuring the scientific and economic effects of the activity to identify the ideal quantities, the political problem of assigning rights, and the legal problem of enforcing and transferring rights. And one of the most important insights of behavioral economists is the importance of endowment effects. (We value what we have more, once we have it than before we acquire it.) Applying this idea to the **Coase Theorem**, we would expect that once the property right has been decided (often by a court), the property right holder may not be willing to accept as low a compensation for trading it, as he would have before. In other words, the endowment effect makes reaching an agreement to trade less likely.

Despite all that we have learned about externalities and the environment, some ill-conceived policies still dog us. In my home town, Santa Barbara, we have one of the largest Air Pollution Control Boards in California. There are 26 Monitoring Stations in the country which only has three regions of urban density. The prevailing winds blow dust and pollen into the air, where it concentrates as it rises in the mountains. Most of our pollution comes from this natural process, or from natural oil seeps in the nearby ocean channel. Some pollution comes from passing ships and other mobile sources, such as autos and trucks. Only 2% of our air pollution comes from fixed sources. Whenever we achieve a pollution goal, the standard is tightened by the authorities, the bureaucracy grows, and the rules and fees proliferate. Progress is slow and expensive, because the rules impact only minor sources. Scientific progress is ignored, as the bureaucracy defends its turf.

Years ago, there was a major political struggle over the issue of **acid rain**. The belief was that the coal fired electric plants in the Ohio River Valley were putting soot in the air that was carried by the winds to New England and Maritime Canada, where rain precipitated the ash into lakes and rivers, increasing acidity, and harming fish and forests. Years later, scientists concluded that the true cause of the acidification was reforestation. The forests had been cleared by farmers for two centuries (1620-1820). But as agriculture moved to richer regions in the West, and as the farms of New England and Eastern Canada were abandoned, the forests reclaimed their ancient territories. The falling leaves from these forests were the source of the acidity. (But we are getting ahead of ourselves.)

The costs of cleaning up the ash from the power plants was estimated from lowest, switching to lignite coal or natural gas ($250-$800/ton removed) to highest, installing stack scrubbers ($1000/ton) which would catch the ash, as it left the smoke stacks. The Clean Air Act of 1977 required the most expensive technology, the scrubbers. Why ? A coalition of self-interested groups, (coal-miners, environmentalists, industrial and political interest groups), pushed the alternative that would suit their goals, regardless of cost to industry, or consumers.

We can conclude that, because individuals make choices in which they consider benefits as well as costs, incentives matter. Public policy makers should consider benefits and costs, too. Some of the important costs are monitoring, compliance, and administration. Results matter. Sound familiar ?

Some questions for review and examination:
Define **Public Goods** and give several examples.
Why will markets fail to provide the optimal level of Public Goods?
Compare and contrast 1) public provision (government), 2) private provision (clubs), and 3) the private for profit (business) provision as methods of producing, paying, and distributing public goods.
Define **Externalities** and give examples of both positive and negative externalities.
Why will the market fail to provide the correct quantities of goods with externalities?
How are **market failures** related to **private property rights** ? {Discuss the Coase Theorem.}
Identify and Evaluate 1) command & control, 2) tax & subsidy, and 3) marketable property rights, as methods of resolving the inefficiencies of externalities

Some Sources for Global Warming & other Environmental Issues:
Fred Singer & Dennis Avery *Unstoppable Global Warming*, Rowman & Littlefield, 2008
Roy Spencer, *Climate Confusion*, Encounter Books, 2008
Bjorn Lomborg, *Cool It*, Vintage 2008
Bjorn Lomborg *The Skeptical Environmentalist* Cambridge University Press 2001
Petr Beckmann *Eco-hysterics & the Technophobes,* Golam Press 1973
John Maddox *The Doomsday Syndrome,* McGrawHill 1972
humorous:
P.J.O'Rourke *All the Troubles of the World,* Atlantic Monthly Press 1975

Elephant at a Waterhole, Etosha National Park, Namibia

Lesson #2.7 Market Structures and Efficiency

Continuing our investigation of market failures, we will consider various competitive environments. Recall that we mean by market failures are outcomes for which marginal social benefit does not equal marginal social cost. Accordingly, the quantities produced and consumed are not efficient.

We must first define an **industry**. Our inclination is to identify products that appear similar, or have similar uses, as in the same industry, but this subjective judgment is risky. Better to use the evidence of consumer behavior. **Cross-price elasticity** compares *the percentage change in the price of one product to the percentage change in sales of another product*. If this calculation generates an elasticity estimate greater than zero, there is evidence that consumers treat the products as substitutes, and the larger the cross-price elasticity the stronger the substitutability. Identical products should have a cross-price elasticity approaching infinity. This approach will answer the awkward questions:

Is a Subaru a substitute for a Mercedes ? Is Perrier a substitute for Coca-Cola ?

We think of competition on a scale from one extreme in which there are many substitutes, no producer alone influences price, and all goods in the group sell at the same price (**perfect competition**) to a situation in which there is only one producer and there are no substitutes (**monopoly**). There are intermediate cases of **imperfect competition** which shares many of characteristics of perfect competition, such as ease of entry and exit, but the products are not identical (They are "differentiated"), and **oligopoly**, a situation of a few producers who have similar products and large shares of the market. We have investigated competition. Let's consider monopoly, here.

Why would a market be characterized by only one producer ? Sometimes, the market is small in relationship to the best level of production. The relationship between market size and efficient scale of production will determine how many producers can survive in a market. For example, automobile assembly plant requires large capacity. To bring average costs to a minimum, large volume (in the order of 100,000-200,000 autos, per year) is needed to spread high fixed costs and give the chance to recoup large sunk costs. A small market like South Korea would not support several automobile companies, if they could only sell domestically. One company would increase production, lower average costs, cut prices, and drive the others out of business. We call this situation, **natural monopoly**. Many utilities fall into this situation. Would installing several water lines, electrical lines, or sewer lines, for every building make any sense ? The duplication of resources would be hugely expensive, and the revenues from splitting the market into small pieces would be meager. Better to have one provider and minimize costs.

Often, monopoly results from government policies. We have already mentioned patents and copyrights, as temporary monopolies that provide incentives for innovation. There are also exclusive charters, such as the British East India Company, or The Hudson Bay Company. These were common among the European colonial powers, but also in authoritarian and crony-capitalist regimes of more recent times (Nazi Germany, white ruled South Africa, and today's Russia).

Sometimes, monopoly results from the ownership, or control, of a critical resource, such as beryllium, or diamonds. And sometimes, monopoly results from clever management strategies, such as using profits from one activity to subsidize another until the competition drops out, or building excess capacity, as a creditable deterrent to new entry by potential competitors. Similarly, I might establish a competitor within my corporate group to give the appearance of competition to both customers and potential entrants. We did that when we published a couple of travel magazines in the "distressed travel" niche. Both magazines were vehicles for selling our products, but readers and other travel providers believed that they were independent entities of journalistic integrity. Finally, a strategy that I have used is **limit pricing** for which I don't charge as much as I could, because I don't want to incite competition. As we say, "pigs get fat, hogs get slaughtered." I'm happy to be successful pig.

To understand why we don't like monopolies, a comparison of incentives, choices, and outcomes with perfect competition is in order. Recall that the perfectly competitive firms take the market price as given. Often from experience, and with the help of their trade association, or their government, they estimate the price at which they can sell their product, and produce as long as their marginal cost is less than or equal to that price. Then, they check to see whether their total revenue exceeds total costs for that quantity of sales. The essential condition of competition is that the choice of the quantity to produce by the individual producer does not move the price. Hence, we can say, for the competitive firm, the unchanging price is also marginal revenue. Sell another unit; I get the same price; I get the same addition to revenue. We say that the condition for making the most profit is: Produce as long as marginal cost is less than marginal revenue and check that for that quantity, total revenue exceeds total costs.

The monopolist faces a more complex problem. As the only seller in the market, the quantity which he chooses to offer for sale can only be absorbed, if he adjusts his price. (Remember the Law of Demand ?) If he is already meeting Demand at the current price, additional sales will require a lower price. Thus, in a sense, the monopolist runs the danger of spoiling his own market. Consider the local and sole pizza restaurant in a small town. He sells three dozen pizzas a day at a price of $10 each. His total revenue is $360. He knows that there are more customers out there and estimates that he can sell another dozen pizzas if he lowers his price to $9 each. If he does so, then he must lower his price for everyone. The extra 12 pizzas don't increase his revenue by 12 x $9 = $108, but by something less. Total sales will be four dozen at $9, or $432, a gain of $72, not $108. His marginal revenue is $6 per additional sale. And he shouldn't lower his price and increase his production, unless he can produce at a marginal cost less than $6 per pizza.

What is going on ? The additional sales add to his revenue (12 x $9 = $108), but the price cut for his existing customers from $10 to $9 reduces his revenue by $36. His marginal revenue is $108 - $36 = $72. Notice that the maximum profit strategy remains the same --- expand production as long as you can add more to your revenue than you add to your costs (marginal revenue > marginal costs). What has changed is that the price no longer equals marginal revenue, the new price must be greater than marginal revenue to compensate for the erosion of prior price. This means that the monopolist will not expand until price equals marginal cost. He restrains production to maintain price. And this is the cause of the distortions and inefficiencies of monopoly.

Let's review and set out the principles for measuring these distortions.

1) Monopolies will produce less than competitive firms. As a result, they will charge a higher price. Consumers pay more for the product that they are able to buy. We call this a transfer of **consumer surplus**, the difference between what a consumer pays and what the good is worth to him, a measure of his gain from the exchange.

We can measure this transfer from consumers to the monopoly by the difference between the monopoly price (higher) and the competitive price (lower) times the monopoly quantity sold. Some economists would argue that the consumers' loss equals the producers' gains, so we shouldn't consider this a loss to society. Personally, I have no trouble making the normative judgment that price should equal marginal cost, and a price above marginal cost is unjust.

2) Monopolies are able to charge a higher price, because they produce less. The monopoly can't simply charge a higher price, much less "charge whatever he wants." This is a crazy idea. The consumer can always choose not to buy. However, the reduced quantity available must be rationed. That is why the price rises. The valuc of thc loss from producing too little is the difference between the quantity produced under competition (the larger) and the quantity produced by the monopolist (the smaller) times the competitive price.

3) There is also a loss of consumer surplus for the lost sales. This would be the triangle between the demand curve and the competitive price line and represents a loss of consumer surplus which is not transferred to producers. We can measure it by the change in price times the change in quantity divided by two.

4) Because monopolies produce less, they hire fewer resources. Many economists would contend that this is a saving to the economy, because those resources will find alternative employment at the same rate of pay and marginal product. I am uncomfortable with those assumptions. In a competitive world, they would be employed in this industry, and they would be producing more value. (Otherwise, the employer couldn't bid them away from those other activities.) So, I consider this a distortion, although estimating the cost to society in terms of net loss vs net gain in alternative employment may be impossible. Anyway, the resources, which are no longer employed because of reduced production, would be paid the area under the supply curve between the competitive quantity and the monopoly quantity.

So, without the naïve view that consumers should always pay less or the producers should always receive more, we can see that monopoly creates three problems, all because monopoly will not expand production that lowers its net revenue.

Do monopolies always earn profits ? We might guess that the increase in price assures profit. We would be wrong. We always need to compare total revenue to total cost. Even though we produce as long as marginal revenue exceeds marginal costs, this does not assure that the difference exceeds fixed costs. Consider public transportation, such as buses. Even charging $2 a ride, they can lose money. Their fixed costs are large and their revenue barely exceeds variable (operating) costs. Monopolies can lose money.

This raises another problem. If an important good or service cannot be produced profitably, or least at break-even, it won't be produced. What can we do ? We could consider the social value of the service. We would measure that as the area under the demand curve. (Yes, economists can estimate a Demand Function and measure that area.) We can measure total costs, both fixed and variable. We can even add a return on sunk costs. If total benefit exceeds total cost, then we should consider a subsidy to cover operating losses. If we charge the customers the correct price (= marginal cost), then the required subsidy may be large. The beneficiaries should pay the subsidy with an access fee, but usually we charge the community through general taxes as a crude approximation of social benefit.

What should we do about monopolies ? And what do we do ? The first step is to define the industry and the market. We know how to define the industry --- all products that are strong substitutes, as measured by cross-price elasticity. We define the market geographically --- how far will the consumers go in the search for the best value ? This could be three miles for groceries or fast food, or fifty miles for specialty items such as new autos. Then, what are the concentration ratios for that industry in that market ? The Herfindahl-Hirshman Index squares the market shares of the four largest firms, and adds the result. If the four largest had shares of

30%, 25%, 20%, and 15%, then index would be 900+525+400+225= 2050. You can see that a monopoly would have an HH index of 10,000 and a perfectly competitive industry would approach 100 or less. The Federal Trade commission has considered an HHI of 1,800 to be evidence of concentration. Fortunately, size and concentration are not enough. The legal criterion for monopoly is *both the existence and the use of market power*. How would we identify use (or abuse) of market power ? By the difference between the monopoly price and the competitive price --- the price in the market vs. marginal cost.

When we see monopoly existing and being abused, what can we do ? If the market is large enough to support competition, we could **break up the monopoly**. We would require the firm to sell off assets. This was the approach to Standard Oil in 1911. Unfortunately, the creation of a number of regional Standard Oils, such as Mobil, Chevron, and Exxon left some residual, regional market power, but let's not quibble.

Natural monopolies present a different problem. The market is too small to support competition, usually because of large sunk and fixed costs. The former deter entry and latter weigh on current production. We don't want a lot of small inefficient firms wasting resources and raising prices to cover their high costs. We want to take advantage of economies of scale, but we want to avoid the limited production and high prices of monopoly.

Another solution is **government ownership**, often called "nationalization" even when local governments own and manages the industry. Common examples are public utilities, such as San Diego Power & Light which has been well managed. However, too often the government owned and managed monopoly becomes captive to customers leading to low prices, under investment, and poor service, or to politicians, managers and employees, leading to high prices and wasteful operations, such as Pemex, the Mexican petroleum monopoly.

Another alternative is private ownership with **government regulation**. Private companies are granted monopolies by government charter, but limited in the price that they can charge for service. The advantage of one fixed price is that it resolves the price greater than marginal revenue problem. If everyone is charged the same price, then price doesn't change with increased sales, and the regulated monopoly will expand until price equals marginal cost, just like the competitive firm.

For years, the agencies charged with regulating local monopolies established the maximum price according to an **average cost principle**. In other words, average costs would be calculated by dividing total costs by quantity. Included in total costs would be a reasonable return on investment. So, if the utility has an investment of $100 million and a reasonable return is 10%, then $10 million would be added to the accounting costs before the division. Unfortunately, this approach invites inefficiency, especially excessive capital investment. Companies with high costs will be able to raise their price to recover the costs. Companies with huge capital investments will be permitted to increase their price. Companies regulated according to this principle (average costs plus ROI) became characterized grand facilities and excess capacity.

In the 1970s, the regulators changed their calculation. By observing prices and costs in competitive markets, the regulator could argue that marginal costs should be X and therefore, the correct price would be X. This would lead to the competitive solution. Problems occur when this correct price leads to excessive profits, or losses. Windfall profits associated with a protected monopoly cannot be justified, and no one will choose to operate a regulated price which does not allow them a reasonable profit. So, the second step is to auction the right to a temporary monopoly. Bidders will calculate the potential for profit, and bid as much as they must, to gain it.

The government will capture some of the monopoly profits which can be returned to the consumers, or used for other public purposes (you can guess which is more likely). An example is the five year contract for local garbage service which our county auctions for each service area. In the case of a money losing monopoly, consumers can be charged a periodic access fee, separate from the user charge, to raise the needed revenues. An example would be the monthly charge from your water and sewer company to which is added a price per unit of service.

Spurred by the increased concentration of American industry during the period of rapid industrialization between the Civil War (1861-1865) and the First World War (1914-1918), Congress enacted a series of Anti-Trust Laws. They include the **Sherman Anti-Trust Act 1890** which addressed existing abuses. It prohibits conspiracy to restrain trade, such as price fixing, and attempts to monopolize, such as exclusive dealing arrangements. In applying the law, the courts recognized that some arrangements may benefit consumers. For example, assigning an exclusive territory to a distributor may increase his ability to provide access to the product. Here, in Santa Barbara, Pacific Beverage is the sole distributor of Budweiser, and Lagomarsino has the exclusive rights for Miller beer. The courts held that if the behavior benefits consumers, the behavior is permissible. They called this, **the rule of reason**. Another important law is the **Clayton Anti-Trust Act of 1914**. It addressed the issue of potential for monopoly by limiting mergers. Clayton also restrains non-competitive practices, such as price discrimination, tied sales, acquisition of competitors' stock, and interlocking directorates. The **Federal Trade Commission (1914)** was authorized as the agency which would administer the discretionary power of government under these laws. The **Wheeler-Lea** Act of 1938 gave the FTC the power to regulate deceptive practices. And The **Cellar-Kefauver** Act of 1950 expanded the FTC authority to prohibit the acquisition of competitors' assets, if the result would be restraint trade. When large companies seek approval to merger, it is Cellar-Kefauver that gives the Federal Trade Commission authority to review, approve, or reject their plan.

In addition to these laws and agencies, the Anti-Trust Division of the Dept. of Justice can bring suit, and firms injured by non-competitive practices can initiate civil litigation with the potential for triple damages.

There is one more, very important solution to the monopoly problem --- international competition. International trade can open the local monopoly to competition, but this only works for **tradeable goods**, those that can or do compete internationally. If transactions costs are high, no trade will occur. So, competition from foreign beer companies can break the Kenya National Breweries monopoly, but there is no similar international competition among taxis or hotels.

Do abuses still occur ? Temptations can be large. A few years ago, the European Competition Commission sued some chemical companies for price fixing on animal feed additives, a $300 million market. A friend who had retired from the chemical industry asked an associate, "Have you been fixing prices in the US, too ?" The response was "Not anymore !" And our laws seem to be selectively applied, under the doctrine of **prosecutorial discretion** --- prosecutors may decide not to bring cases to court that they don't believe they can win. The result is that friends may escape prosecution, and enemies may find themselves in expensive court battles. To become an enemy could be as simple as supporting the wrong political party. Some industries may receive favored treatment, as baseball did in a famous case of the Federal Baseball Club vs. National League, in a decision written by Oliver Wendell Holmes in 1922. Baseball was held to be exempt from Sherman Anti-Trust, because its games were local. This protected the reserve clause and the ten day notice of termination, until they were challenged by Curt Flood in 1970.

The Clayton Act prohibits price discrimination, yet we see it every day. **Price discrimination** is charging different prices to different customers for the same product or service. Businesses understand the principles of Demand. They would love to capture consumer surplus. As I used to say to my employees, "Who am I to deprive my customers of their right to pay the maximum that they are willing to pay ?" However, to make price discrimination work, I must be able to determine what each customer, or class of customers, is willing to pay, and then prevent resale from those who paid less to those who are being asked to pay more. For our resort in Antigua, we had three rates: garden room $100, beachfront room $125, and deluxe beachfront room $150/day. All the rooms were identical, and all were on the beach. If a week was filling fast, I would direct my staff that only deluxe beachfront rooms were available. If a week had light bookings, all new sales became beachfront rooms at the garden room rate. That was how we could achieve 90%+ occupancy at maximum room rates. Notice that this form of discrimination does not consider consumer income, just preferences for dates vs. vacancies.

In less developed countries, where the opportunity costs of small merchants are low, they will happily haggle, as method of price discrimination, as well as an entertaining social convention. In developed nations, price discrimination is more likely for high ticket items and where customers are ignorant of usual prices. But these are not the only examples. Airline passengers may pay very different prices for the same service, depending on when they bought their tickets. This is common when there are high fixed costs and a perishable product. Hotel rooms are another example. Movie-goers will encounter separate prices for children, adults, and seniors. Why is this tolerated ? It is **the rule of reason**, again. Vendors have argued successfully that they can offer more rooms, more flights, and more shows, if they can price discriminate. And if everyone is able to gain the price advantage by appropriate behavior, then no one is harmed. After all, we're all children and seniors at one time in our lives. And anyone could have booked that flight at the most advantageous time.

However, a particularly troubling form of price discrimination occurs in American higher education, and relates educational activities. A "Sticker Price" is quoted and becomes an anchor for thinking about price. For colleges, it is "tuition, room, and board." Then, the applicant is asked to submit information about his family's assets and income, including tax returns. The institution decides whether he is a desirable candidate and then offers a discount, called a scholarship. None of this has anything to do with marginal costs, but everything to do with ability to pay. Is there any other industry in which the producer can require proof of income and assets, before deciding how much to charge for its product ? And of course, every offer is unique and non-transferable. Is it any surprise that the costs of education rise rapidly, or that there is no pressure to increase efficiency, or control costs ? And the availability of subsidized students only exacerbates the problem by increasing the ability of the applicants to pay. Students feel that they are getting a bargain, because their minds are anchored in the original tuition number.

As an example, recently, I heard from my alma mater, Williams College, that the costs of serving each student average $100,000 per year (only 210 days in their year). They noted that their endowment earns more than $50,000 per student every year, and so, the most that they charge is $50,000, and everyone is getting a subsidy. The college administrators fail to recognize that their marginal costs are close to zero (one more student in the classroom adds no costs).

Consider the following budget estimates: 210 days of school at $50 per day for room and board equals $10,500. If faculty compensation averages $200,000 per teacher per year, the ratio of faculty to students is 1:10. That adds $20,000 per student. Finally, double the $30,500 to cover administrative costs, facilities, insurance, taxes etc. How is it possible that a properly managed college can have average costs exceeding $61,000 per student per year ? Using the endowment income, Williams could operate profitably (oops, a surplus) while charging he students $12,000 per year, if the college managed its costs at all reasonably. Clearly, our colleges and universities are charging more, not because they must, but because they can, --- just like any other business.

I remember returning from my military duty to university after four years, assuming that I would retain my full scholarship, as promised. At orientation, I was told that I would be required to pay tuition of several thousand dollars. I objected and was told the following day that I would receive a free ride for four years. (In fact, I had two or three scholarships going at once, and lived very well, thank-you.)

Recognizing that scholarships are price discrimination, Pres. George H.W. Bush had the Dept. of Justice sue an elite group of eastern colleges that were meeting every May to compare applications and cooperate on admission and scholarship offers. (How do you spell "collusion" ?) I learned about this abuse of power, when the president of my alma mater wrote to explain what they had been doing and complain about their treatment by the Dept. of Justice. I wrote back, saying thanks for the information, but don't let this mailing fall into the wrong hands, as it is an admission of guilt. The Federal court agreed, but was reversed on appeal with the charming decision to the effect that: "While, technically this behavior is a violation of anti-trust law, it serves a higher social purpose." I wonder what other crimes are permitted, because they serve a higher purpose ?

Earlier, I mentioned cases intermediate between perfect competition and monopoly. The first of these is **Imperfect Competition**. Profs. Eddie Chamberlin at Harvard and Joan Robinson at Cambridge presented similar analysis of this common form of competition in 1933. Chamberlin called this form, "Monopolistic Competition" and Robinson called it "Imperfect Competition." I prefer her term and will use it, although Chamberlin choice reflects his view that it combines characteristics of competition and monopoly, hence, the name.

Imperfect Competition has all the qualities of perfect competition, except one. There may be many producers, there are few costs associated with entry and exit, and there are many substitutes. However, the products are not identical. We might say that they are "near substitutes" or "imperfect substitutes." Common examples would be restaurants, fashion retailers, hairdressers, and household goods. Customers perceive differences between products. Those that have more of the qualities which customers prefer will command higher prices. Customers with attributes of less appeal will command lower prices. The variety of products expands opportunities for consumers to express their tastes. Consumer may become loyal to one product line or brand, and be willing to pay more. Because tastes vary, some consumers will be willing to pay more for some products, and others for others. However, the premium which we pay for our preferred product, or service, is not infinite. At some price difference between Coke and Pepsi, we would switch.

I usually asked my students what they pay for haircuts. I ask those who pay $50, $100, or more, why they won't go to the hairdresser who charges $30 ? They always answer that they like the cut that they get from their hairdresser and they trust her.

All of this means that producers who have designed a product or service that is different from their competition have created some market power. They can charge prices different from their competition. How different, depends on the preferences and loyalty of their customers. Producers resent competition. Selling a product at the same price as everyone else doesn't reward us for special quality. So, producers will invest in differentiating their product. Grading, such as Prime, Grade A, and Good for beef, or Brown, White, Large, Extra-large, Free Range, and Organic for eggs, are ways of signaling a difference which creates an opportunity for a price premium. Cars have different designs, engines, interiors, warrantees, etc. to justify different prices.

We might think of the effort to differentiate our product by including characteristics that our target customers associate with quality, as tilting the Demand curve. If successful, the happy customers will be willing to pay more, but some customers don't value the features and will only be willing to buy if they can pay less. So, instead of taking the price as given, as the perfectly competitive producer must, the imperfect competitor must accept that to encourage sale beyond his loyal following, he must lower his price, like a monopolist. And like any producer, he will expand production as long as marginal revenue exceeds marginal costs, and check for profit by comparing total revenue to total costs.

However, there may be no way to prevent entry. Unusual profits may attract new firms that copy our product. This increases total Supply and leads to declining prices. And soon, the excess profits disappear. So, continued high profits require constant vigilance to stay ahead competitors in designing products that meet customer needs better than the imitators. And so, fashions are modified; new models and menu items appear. Where atmosphere matters, periodic remodels are required.

When I moved to Santa Barbara, there were over 200 restaurants in town, but only one Thai restaurant, which was very profitable and always full. Soon, there were seven Thai restaurants, (three on the same street), and mostly started by former employees of the first. The restaurants were half full, and prices declined. A few years later, there were only five left (including only the original in its neighborhood).

Chamberlin and Robinson concluded that the ease of entry and exit would erode the excess profits, but leave the remaining firms with excess capacity --- the restaurant with empty tables, or the barbershop with empty chairs. They considered this wasteful. Years later, economists wondered whether we were defining the product accurately. What if one of the qualities, which we value, is convenience, and another is choice. Then, perhaps the variety of restaurants and barbershops doesn't represent waste, but a resource cost which we are willing to pay for those two valued qualities ? This is my point of view. Imperfect Competition leads to more variety and more convenience, if we are willing to pay for is. And remember, any unusual profits are quickly eroded by the entry of imitators. So, selling prices can vary, if products vary, and marketing expense to create valued difference and loyalty may be justified. These ideas are important to understanding market research, production development, and promotion.

Oligopoly is competition among the few. The usual reasons for a few companies dominating an industry are economies of scale, or industry maturity. An industry is mature, when growth slows and the market becomes saturated. Most families have refrigerators and washing machines, so sales' growth depends on new family formation and replacement. The best companies can only grow faster by increasing their market share, at the expense of less well-managed competitors. As the years go by, the industry becomes concentrated. Having only a few competitors, the remaining firms can, and must, consider the strategy of their opponents. They will monitor new product development and even pursue industrial espionage.

A friend went to work as a designer for American Motors. One day, he met an attractive young lady at the Country Club. She invited him to her house on Sunday for a swim. My friend was impressed by her lovely mansion with beautiful gardens and a private pool. Soon, her dad joined them. My friend and her father started talking cars. On Monday morning, my friend was called into his president's office and asked why he had been talking about new models with the head of design for General Motors. Oops ….

Of course, an oligopoly would rather be a monopoly. And where there are only a few competitors collusion is easier. We call a shared monopoly, a **cartel**. One of the most famous was the **Seven Sisters** which dominated the international petroleum business from 1928 to 1973. The agreements to carve up and stabilize the world oil market depended on sharing Iraqi oil production under the **Red Line Agreements** facilitated by Calouste Gulbenkian, (Mr.5%).

To sustain a cartel, the members must cooperate. When I met with the Chief Economist of OPEC in Vienna in 1976, I asked him how OPEC worked. He invited me to guess and responded to the following description with a smile. "Yes, that's how we do it !" he said.

So, the first step is to estimate Total Demand. The next is to estimate Marginal Revenue from the demand function. For OPEC, that means the total demand for energy, less the supply of alternatives (hydro, coal, nuclear, etc.) and then, subtracting non-member production (Russia, Mexico, USA, and North Sea). Next, they calculated the slope of this "Net Demand for OPEC Oil" Function.

Looking at the production functions of the members, the OPEC staff calculates marginal cost. They locate the quantity for which marginal cost equals marginal revenue and designate that quantity for total group production. For OPEC, the costs of production in the Persian Gulf are so low, that OPEC can produce, until Marginal Revenue equals zero.

Now, the tough part. The members must agree to divide the total into quotas for each producer. For OPEC, this is the work of the Council of Ministers that meets in Vienna, twice a year. Low cost producers will argue for large quotas, and so will large, powerful, and populous nations.

Once the quotas are agreed, each member limits its production to its quota and charges whatever price the market will bear (price depends on rationing). For OPEC, light, clean crude that is close to markets, such as Libyan, will fetch a higher price than heavy, dirty, distant crude, such as Arab Heavy.

Cartels usually erode over time. Their high prices encourage consumers to conserve and develop substitutes. Those same high prices attract the entry of new producers, such as Alaskan, off-shore Mexican, and North Sea Oil in the 1970s, and natural gas extracted by fracking more recently. And as long as price exceeds marginal costs, the members are sorely tempted to expand production. When many do, supply increases, and price declines. OPEC is the most successful cartel that I have known. Central to its success are the political risks in its producing areas, and the discipline imposed by Saudi Arabia through its large excess capacity. The message is, "Don't cheat, or we will flood the market, and you will suffer most."

A final problem for cartels is that more and more nations have shifted policy from encouraging collusion to outlawing it. The European Union is a good example of this change.

Questions for review and examination:
How does the profit maximizing strategy of a monopolist differ from that of competitive firms ?
How can we measure the distortions of a specific monopoly ?
Compare and contrast three policies used to correct the inefficiencies of monopolies .
Which laws and agencies authorize and enforce these policies ?
What is price discrimination ? What conditions are necessary for price discrimination ?
What problems must be solved by a cartel to be formed and to operate successfully ?
Why is it difficult to sustain a cartel ?

Lesson #2.8 Resource Markets: Labor

Now that we understand how product markets work and what the outcomes are likely to be under different conditions of information, competition, and for different product characteristics (private, public, and externalities), we can investigate resource markets. The essential concepts to understand are that *the demand for resources depends on the demand for the products that require those resources for their production.* And we must pay for those resources, if they are scarce, because we compete for the right to use them. Wages are shockingly low in poor countries, because little is produced, labor productivity is low, and there are few alternative opportunities for the numerous workers. Let's reason carefully, following the logic of markets to useful conclusions.

Production requires resources and technology. We group resources into different categories, where their behavior and employment are similar, and we apply different names for the resources and the payments that their owners receive, depending on their classification. There are workers. We may refer to them as **labor**, meaning employees, or those who organize production, whom we call **entrepreneurs**. We pay laborers a wage and entrepreneurs are rewarded by profit. Non-human resources are described as **capital** with a common distinction between **natural resources** that exist in a state of nature without creation by man, and **physical capital** which represents those products which are transformations of natural resources into goods whose purpose is to facilitate production of other goods and services. The forest is a natural resource, and the lumber is a processed resource that contributes to the construction of a house, apartment, office, or factory --- examples of capital. We pay the owners of capital a **rent**, and the owners of natural resources, a **royalty**. All of these are just names and labels. What is important to understand is that resources are needed for production, and the owners will be compensated for their use. **Technology** specifies the relationship between the product and the resources required for its production. Hence, our intent to produce a specific quantity of goods and our choice of technology will determine our demand for resources.

So, the quantity of a resource which producers would like to use, or employ, depends on the value of their product (the expected selling price), the chosen method of production (technology, a physical relationship of resources in and product out), and the cost of the resource (rent, royalty, wage, or profit).

In this lesson, we are interested in the **Demand for Labor**. The producer will consider the opportunity for profit. This will depend on the expected price of the product or service, the resources required for his planned level of production and sales, and what he must pay for those resources. With respect to labor, his costs depend on labor productivity, how much valuable product can the worker contribute, and what he must pay the worker. Economists call the contribution to production of one more labor hour, **The Marginal Physical Product of Labor**. For example, if I ask my worker to stay for one more hour to help produce more pizzas, how many more pizzas can we sell ? And what would be the difference in revenue and other costs ? If she can produce five more pizzas which we sell for $5, (less $1 of ingredients), her marginal contribution is 5 x 4 = $20. If her wage is less than $20, I would want her to stay. So, we say that the upper limit on our willingness to pay a wage to hire labor is **The Value of the Marginal Physical Product** *(Marginal Revenue x Marginal Physical Product)*. As we demonstrated in lesson #2.3, we should pursue every opportunity to add more to our revenue than we add to our costs. Hence, we hire until the **Marginal Revenue Product** = the **Wage**. What will the employer actually pay the worker ? What she is worth (the value of that incremental product) ? No; the employer will pay what he must --- the worker's opportunity cost --- just enough to get the worker to come to him rather than choose another activity. And the employer will expand hiring, as long as what he must pay (the worker's opportunity cost) is less than what the worker can contribute to revenue.

I remember reading about complaints from Brazilian employers that American companies were paying too much and making hiring difficult. I laughed. That's competition. We should celebrate it. Does this also explain why in retirement communities, "environmentalists" lobby against the entry of new employers, even clean industries ? Maybe, they don't want the workers that they currently employ --- the maids, gardeners, waiters, and public servants --- to have better opportunities that would make them more expensive.

Years ago, we were selling package travel to Tahiti from Los Angeles. We sold our package for $589 and our marginal costs were $484, so every sale netted $105 dollars, gross profit. (For details, see lesson #1.5.) We needed to decide whether to be open on Sundays to accept reservations. We paid our operators $10 per hour. If we hired two operators for nine hours (from 11am-8pm), how many tickets would we need to sell to justify staying open ? If the wage went to $15, how many would we need to sell ? Might we choose to cut back hours based on telephone traffic and sales experience ?

Now, let's turn to the **Supply of Labor**. You can imagine that demographics and qualifications will be important. The characteristics of the population will limit the supply of potential workers. Communities with a large population will have a large potential labor force. Communities with a large proportion of adults in comparison to dependents (children, elderly, and disabled) will have a large potential labor force in comparison to other communities of the same size, but with more dependents. And cultural preferences for work and definitions of appropriate employment will matter. Then, there is the important criteria of eligibility --- how many people are qualified ? So, I will not be hired to play power forward for the Los Angeles Sparks. Why ? I am not a woman, so I am not eligible, and I can't play basketball, so I wouldn't be productive.

Given these limits, the supply of labor for any specific employment will depend on the number of candidates who are eligible and their choices of employment, including self-employment, or non-market activities, such as homemaking, or attending school. So, each of us chooses how to use our time from those opportunities that are available to us. It's another limited, or "constrained", choice set.

Obviously, when we are deciding what to do, we consider all the opportunities available. We value income and benefits, but we also value opportunities for growth and advancement, responsibility and recognition, our interest in doing the work, and potential for a sense of achievement. We value peer group relations. So, just as we compare the constellation of characteristics of products when we shop, we also compare the constellation of characteristics of the alternative sources of employment.

To achieve a deeper understanding of the labor supply choice, let's consider a simple choice between accepting paid employment and using our time in some other way. We shall call the choices, working for a wage vs. leisure, even though we know that non-paid activity, such as homemaking involves work. So, how much time should we offer the employer in return for the wage ? And how much time should we keep for ourselves ?

We use the same concepts that proved useful in analyzing consumer behavior. The wage and the time available define a constraint on our opportunities. If I am offered $50/hr, my limits would be: no income with 24 hours a day for my own use, and $1200 a day with no time for myself. Of course, working 24 hours a day is unrealistic. We might think that at the limit, I could work sixteen hours for $800 and have eight hours for rest and recreation. What will we do ? Once again, preferences (and opportunity costs) matter. I will work as long as another personal hour is worth less than $50. Different people may make different choices, given their preferences for time and income.

What would happen if the worker receives a windfall, such as winning the lottery, or receiving an inheritance ? Do you think they would work as much ? Do you remember the principle of **diminishing marginal utility** ? Think about the circumstance in which you have no job. You have a lot of personal time and no income. You might be willing to give up a lot of time for some income. Now, consider a situation in which you are working forty-five hours a week at $50/hr. (earning $112,500 a year). You are given a raise to $60/hr. You have the potential to earn 20% more ($135,000) without changing your behavior. You might choose to work more, thinking that you should take advantage of the extra $10/hr. After all, any activity other than working for your boss now costs $60/hr. If you choose to work more when your wage increases, we say that the **substitution effect** dominated your choice. You substituted more work for what is now more expensive --- not working.

However, you might make a different decision. You might decide that another $22,500 in income is not as important to you as more time for other activities. You do a quick calculation: I could work 1875 hours a year at $60/hr., instead of 2,250 hours at $50/hr., and I would have the same income of $112,500. I could work 7.5 hours a day, instead of 9 hours a day. If you made this decision, we would say that the **income effect** dominated your choice. The wage increase gave you the opportunity to earn more income, and you chose to take that income in the form of more time off.

As you would expect, when there is a wage change, some people choose to work more (substitution effect), and some choose to work less (income effect). I ask my students for examples from their own experience about the choices that they made, when their wage changed. As expected, some worked more and some worked less. It's all about preference and opportunities.

Now, let's return to the worker who wins the lottery, or receives the inheritance. He's going to have more income. Do you think he will work more, less, or the same amount ? We would expect that having more income, he would want more of everything that money can buy, including leisure. We are not surprised that people with a lot of non-labor income work less, unless their job has offsetting benefits, such as status, personal satisfaction, or social opportunities. Lottery winners often say that they will continue to work, because they enjoy their job. Following up in a few months, we discover that few do continue. Ah, the income effect.

Over the last 65 years (1950-2014), male labor force participation has declined from 86% to 72% and female participation has increased from 34% to 62%. How would you explain that ? Economists consider three contributing explanations:

1) Women's labor force participation was discouraged sixty years ago by social norms that considered homemaking the best employment for women and many jobs off-limits, as too dangerous or inappropriate.
2) Educational opportunities were also restricted by prejudices. And lacking qualifications, women were not offered attractive jobs.
3) Marriages were more common and more stable. Husbands were expected to bring in income, and wives would be homemakers. More income from outside employment of women may not be as important to the family unit as contributing to home production.

All three of these changed over the last two or three generations. Women are encouraged to pursue a variety of career and educational opportunities that increase their eligibility and exert a "pull" into the labor force. Less stable families contribute to the motivation for women to be more financial independent through work experience. And laws and customs reinforce the changes in expectations and opportunities. You might say that for women, these new, superior opportunities raise their market value and for women the substitution effect dominates. Those attractive new jobs make the choice to stay home more expensive.

What about the men ? They are working less --- shorter work weeks, more vacation, and earlier retirement. How do we explain that ? Traditionally, the American adult male is expected to work. How do you feel about men, age 30-60, who don't work ? Over the last sixty years real wages have increased, and our wives have gone to work. Perhaps, the income and wealth effects are influencing the choices of American men. With the wife pursuing her career and contributing to the family income, the family may need some home production contribution from the man more than additional income. (We don't find much evidence that the man is doing more around the house {an increase of 2.5 hours/day has been estimated}, but maybe he contributes in other ways. I remember when my wife had two jobs, and I could play golf on Saturdays. Now, that was the good life.) But even if the wife isn't working, if my wage rises from good to great, I might logically choose to work less and enjoy life. I have enough income; I'd like to buy more time for myself. And I suspect that social attitudes have changed, too. I don't think we admire the executive who lives for his work and neglects his family, as much as prior generations may have.

Some people are upset by wage and income differences. Some even believe that women earn 70% of what men earn. Fortunately, this hasn't been true for more than twenty years. An important cause of differences in wages is compensation for other differences in jobs. For example, jobs have that attractive characteristics, such as location, working conditions, security, benefits, flexible hours and available overtime, will attract a lot of applicants. Other jobs that are deficient in these areas will need to pay more to off-set their disadvantages. And productivity matters, too. (The Lakers owners, the Buss family, were criticized for the huge contract which they gave Kobe Bryant in 2013 {$48.5 million for the next two years}. The family pointed out that Bryant brings in more than $60 million a year in revenue for the team.)

If we compare American men and women, adjusting for age (older workers earn more), education (years and type), and years of experience, American men earn 8% more than American women (2005 data). Among young adults who have never had children, women's earnings approach 98 percent of men's. (source: Congressional Budget Office).

In macroeconomics, we are concerned about our success throughout the entire economy in using our resources wisely. We'd like everyone who is looking for paid employment to find a suitable job. They will gain income, experience, and contribute to our material welfare. Unemployment is costly for the individuals and families involved and for the rest of us. Unemployment is wasteful. On the other hand, let's remember that many unpaid activities are important to individuals, families, and society. So, should we criticize those who choose non-market activities, such as raising a family, or volunteering for charitable work ? Our criteria should be: Are we able to provide opportunities for those who would like to work ? And this will require not only the demand for workers, but eligibility (skills) and information which matches the right workers to the right jobs.

In lesson #2.5, we addressed some of the problems of imperfect information in product markets. I believe that imperfect information in labor markets may be even more important. How do we find the best employees ? How do they find us ? It's a search process. The employer reviews his business plan to identify the tasks that must be performed. He builds **job descriptions** and estimates the numbers of workers needed for each job. He carefully considers what skills and experience are required to be successful in those jobs. These are posted as **job specifications**, so applicants can determine whether they are eligible. The employer reviews his staff (his human resource inventory), identifies gaps between his needs and his resources, and then he recruits. (You may remember these steps from lesson #1.7.) Employment services and temporary help agencies can help in the search.

   The difficulties and risks of making a hiring decision are high for both the employer and the applicant. We can review the resume for relevant experience and education. We can check references, hoping for candor. But how do we measure motivation ? Integrity ? Ability to work with others ? Because we don't know the true value of the applicant, we offer a lower wage than we would if we knew. And the applicant doesn't really know what he's getting into. Have you ever been hired after a very seductive recruitment, only to discover that the job is much less interesting and rewarding than you had been told ? I was once hired at a salary of $36,000 and 3,000 shares of stock options, only to be told after I'd moved my family and bought a house that my salary would be $27,000. And I never saw the options. (Lesson: Get a written contract before your start, while the employer is anxious to hire you.)

   What else do we do ? Many jobs include a period of probation, perhaps ninety days. This allows the employer to assess the employee and the employee to assess the job, the company, and his prospects. After probation, titles, salaries, benefits, and responsibilities will be adjusted. If one party or the other is disappointed, separation occurs without ill-feelings.

   As applicants, we signal our worth in many ways. (It sounds like the car salesman, and it is.) An advanced degree in a challenging field of study, such as mathematics, physics, or economics, a variety of experiences in leadership and team-work, such as athletics, a demonstration of inter-personal skills, such as appearance and conduct during interviews, all signal that I have what it takes to be successful. B.A. holders earn 37% more than those with some college, even if the degree has little practical relevance to the job that we do. That degree signals that we have the tenacity and integrity to finish a long and difficult program.

   Any discussion of labor markets would be incomplete without address **labor unions**. Prior to the industrial revolution, competition and the decentralization of production may have precluded the need for worker's unions. (Andrew Carnegie's father employed five men producing linen at their hand looms.) But industrialization and urbanization, under the capitalist system, in which the provider of capital (the owner) directs all activity, created a severe imbalance of power. The workers leaving the land needed jobs more than employers needed workers, and the descriptions of working hours and conditions in the formative years (1865-1905) here, and abroad, are appalling. Almost immediately, workers tried to organize to balance the power of the bosses, but in the USA, the early unions made a fatal error in trying to organize the entire social life of the worker. And the power of government was often used by the capitalists to restrain and disrupt the workers efforts to organize. **Samuel Gompers** is considered the father of the successful organization of American workers. He combined a number of craft unions into the **American Federation of Labor** in 1886. (Craft union members share a profession, such as electrician, or airline pilot. One company may have several unions representing different groups of employees.) Gompers' insight was that the workers would join a union which addressed their shared issues of wages and working conditions. These issues united them. Gompers realized that on other issues, such as politics, religion, and social activities, the workers were very diverse. The union should stay away from those issues which might divide them. In fact, American unions did not become captive of the Democratic Party, until the 1960s. A split in the AFL occurred in 1935, when some member left to form The Congress of Industrial Organizations, using an alternative model of industry based unions that include workers within the industry despite their differing skills and tasks. Examples would be the United Auto Workers, the United Mine Workers, etc. In 1955, the two organizations merged to form the AFL-CIO. The balance of power shifted during the Great Depression with the passing of the Wagner Act in 1935. It gave workers the right to organize under the supervision of the National Labor Relations Board, which was intended to assure fairness and integrity in the relations between unions, employers, and workers.

Since 1954, union membership has declined from 34% of workers to 11%, today. Many explanations have been offered. A hundred years ago, the one industry town was common, and personal transportation was inconvenient. As a skilled worker, my opportunities within range of my residence may have been few. My employer could take advantage of that, as described below. Today, we are an urban nation, to which we can add the mobility of the automobile. There are many more opportunities within range of my preferred domicile. And so, if my employer chooses to exploit me, I will find alternative employment. I don't have the same need for the union to protect my rights; I can quit. There is more competition in labor force, and that benefits both employers and employees.

Other changes are the increased importance of service and knowledge industries. When the manager can't easily replace his skilled worker (think IT technician), doesn't know how he does his job, and has difficulty measuring his productivity, the worker has a lot of power and his boss needs to treat him well. For these reasons, workers may not need the protection of a union. In addition, abuse of power, and even corruption, may have contributed to the decline of unions. Some unions extract large dues and fail to do much for the workers that they represent. However, a bigger problem may be that *the government in the form of the modern welfare state has pre-empted many of the historic roles of unions*. Labor laws, employment laws, pension laws, safety laws --- these apply to industries and workers whether they are organized, and dues paying, or not. Why would I pay several thousand dollars to my union, if the government offers me most of the same protections anyway ?

Economists have used their tools of supply and demand to analyze the economic effects of labor unions. Some focus on competitive labor markets. Not surprisingly, in competitive markets, we expect a price (wage) to emerge that balances demand (jobs and hours offered) with supply (the numbers of people seeking work and the hours that they offer). And any effort to dictate a higher wage leads to more workers looking and less employers offering. The predicted result would be unemployment. Where competition for workers is robust, this is useful analysis. Raising the wage too high will reduce employment.

I remember discussing a garbage strike with the man shining my shoes at a subway stop in New York City. The man supported unions. He was a member of the carpenters' union and was proud of the $12 hourly wage that they had negotiated. I asked him why he was shining shoes. His answer was that he couldn't find a job as a carpenter.

Consider monopoly markets. If we are working for a monopolist, he restricts production (P>MR=MC; see lesson #2.4). By limiting production, the product price rises above marginal costs, and the monopolist gains profits at the expense of consumers. The labor union may be able to tap into these profits, by demanding a share, in the form of higher wages. Of course, if the high prices lead to changes in consumer behavior, or the emergence of competition, the declining monopolist may be stuck with high labor costs that hasten his demise, and the union's.

But let's return to the situation a century ago, when companies were scattered across America, product competition may have been fierce, but competition in the local labor market was one-sided. There were plenty of workers looking for those industrial jobs, in preference to farm or service work, but few local employers. The model that economists use is **monopsony**, one buyer. Even today, I see this in my home town, Santa Barbara. If you are a doctor or a nurse, there is one hospital, and one associated clinic. The alternative to employment at these two locations is nursing at rehabilitation clinics and retirement homes.

Think about the hospital. They are paying their nurses \$30/hr. and their doctors \$100/hr. They already employ everyone who is happy at that wage. Expansion would require hiring more doctors and nurses. Wages would need to increase to attract these workers. But raising the wage for the new workers would require raising wages for existing workers. (Does this sound similar to the monopoly decision problem ?) So, the new doctor or nurse may not just cost me \$110/hr. or \$35/hr., but by raising wages for everyone, may cost \$1000/hr or \$200/hr ! So, the **monopsonist** who worries about spoiling his market advantage by offering too many jobs, will hire fewer workers. He will only hire to the point where his **marginal revenue product** (what that last worker can do for him) equals the inclusive **marginal factor cost** (all the cost increases associated with hiring that new worker {his wage plus the increase for everyone else}). The source of the problem is that the wage that the monopsonist pays his workers must increase in order to hire more workers. (This is similar to the problem of the monopolist seller who must lower his price for all customers in order to generate more sales to new and continuing customers.)

Now, in this case, by fixing the wage for all workers in similar jobs under a union contract, the monopsonist problem is removed. He can hire more people without giving anyone a raise, until he runs out of people willing to work at the contract wage. The exciting result is that the union, by fixing the wage contract, *may increase employment*, as long as the union doesn't become too greedy and enforce a contract above the wage that would exist under competition. Of course, as noted above, the problem of the local monopsonist, the only local employer for a certain set of skills, is not as severe as it was when communities were more isolated. And there must be a supply of workers willing to be employed at the union contract wage.

We can conclude that there can be valuable contributions to economic efficiency and market fairness by labor unions, but those gains will depend on market conditions and the behavior of workers, employers, and union leaders.

Questions for review an examination:
Explain what determines the **Demand for Labor** (3).
What factors determine the **Supply for Labor** in the market (3) ?
Explain how an increase in the wages offered by employers influences the Supply of labor (2).
Use an example of labor choice *from your own experience* to demonstrate the income and substitution effects of higher wages (2).

Lesson #2.9 Capital and Income

By now, we understand that the demand for resources is derived from the demand for the goods and services whose production requires those resources. As with other purchases, the buyer asks, "How useful will this resource be for me ? And what must I sacrifice to obtain it ?" Production requires resources and the methods of organizing and transforming them. We call these methods, technologies. There is nothing conceptually magical about **technology**, although we can and do become excited about methods which allow us to produce more valuable products with less valuable resources. Terms such as "high tech" or "low tech" or "advanced tech" are clichés that confuse. There is only "the best tech" and other less desirable methods. The best technology is the method that produces acceptable quality products at lowest cost (sacrifice).

And so, we consider the value of the product (it's expected selling price), the various methods by which we can produce it (technologies), and the costs of the resources required by each technology. We select the lowest cost method, and we expand production, as long as we can add more to our revenue than we add to our costs. In the jargon of economics, the rules are:

1) Expand production until **Marginal Costs = Marginal Revenue**
{= selling price in perfectly competitive markets }

& 2) Hire until   **Marginal Resource Cost = Marginal Revenue Product**
{MRP = marginal revenue times marginal physical product}

So, the demand for capital is similar to the demand for any other resource. It depends on how much additional production the added capital can contribute, and what does that additional product add to our revenue, in comparison to what we must pay to hire that added capital. The upper limit on our willingness to rent capital is **The Value of the Marginal Physical Product.** The rule becomes: *Hire until the rental rate equals marginal revenue product.*

Why must we pay for resources ? We pay when the resources are scarce and useful, and someone has the ownership (property right) and thus the right to decide on their use. To obtain the use of the scarce resource, we must match, or exceed, the next best offer (the opportunity cost). Does this help to explain why some bidders wish to exclude some opportunities for resource owners ? If women aren't judged suitable to be doctors, an abundant supply of nurses may be the outcome. If some groups are excluded from the professions, the wages of service workers may be depressed.

What determines the availability (supply) of capital ? The production of capital takes time, and the services of capital may be available for many years, until worn-out, or obsolete. Investment in maintenance and renovation can extend the useful life of capital for decades, or longer. So, *the existing stock of capital is the result of history.* Changes in the capital stock take time. Depreciation and amortization reduce the capital stock. Investment in new facilities, equipment, and inventory add to the capital stock.

By investment, we mean the use of resources to create products or services *whose purpose is to maintain or increase production of other goods and services in the future.* **Investment** is a form of spending that purchases resources, not for current enjoyment, but rather for future contributions to production. Investment in physical capital occurs when there are gains in future net profits that exceed the costs of investment by a sufficient reward which we call the yield, or *the return on investment*. We compare the change in expected future net cash-flows from the investment to the initial investment required.

Because these payments and receipts occur at different times, we must reconcile them to the same time. The interest rate provides the bridge. **Interest rates** are remarkable inventions. Saver/lenders are rewarded for their sacrifice by receiving interest payments. Deficit spenders are enabled to take advantage of present opportunities by borrowing, and will share their gains with the lenders by paying interest. So, *the payment of interest allows us to separate the time as which we earn income from the time at which we spend it*. And this movement of purchasing power alters our activities, employments, and income. Interest rates also permit us to compare value over time, as we will see in a moment. Finally, the interest rate enables us to compare a flow of payments to a one-time ("capital") value.

The market process determines the employment of capital, and its changes, in four steps. First, the existing capital is rationed. Remember that the existing stock of capital is the result of history --- the decisions to invest in maintenance, renovation, and production of new capital, vs. the depreciation and obsolescence of old capital. As you look around town, you see the existing capital stock. It is rationed among competing users by fluctuations in rent, --- what we pay for the temporary use of capital. We rent apartments, offices, factories, machines, and vehicles. If capital is scarce in comparison to its demand, rents will be high, and if capital is abundant, rents will be low. (Are you surprised that landlords oppose new construction, often under the guise of protecting the environment ?)

The users of capital have the choice of renting it from the current owners, or buying something similar. **Rent** is a flow of payments for continued use; **purchase** allows use, until some future sale. We compare the costs of the alternative ways of obtaining use. For example, we might rent an apartment for $1,500/month ($18,000/year), or we might purchase the apartment for $120,000. In the first case, we have a regular series of monthly payments defined by our lease, no potential for capital gain if the apartment appreciates, no tax advantages, but also no maintenance, insurance, or property tax obligations. In real estate, we crudely estimate these last three expenses to be one-third of our rents. So, ownership nets the landlord $12,000 per year, per apartment. If we compare the alternatives, ownership saves us $12,000 per year, but requires an initial outlay of $120,000. Hence, the yield on our ownership investment would be 10%. **($12,000/ $120,000 =10%)**

This simple example elucidates a fundamental principle. The price that we are willing to pay for the ownership of capital depends on the expected rents to be received, and the yield which we require on our investment (the funds that we commit to purchase).

Cash-flow/ Capital Value = Yield,

or equivalently, **Capital Value = Cash-flow / Yield**

We can summarize the Demand for ownership, as the result of the rationing of the existing inventory of similar capital which determines the rent, and the capitalization of those rents, as prospective users compare the costs of renting to the cost of ownership. The result is what I call, **The Demand Price for Capital.**

Consider housing prices in your community. There is an existing inventory of homes. You may rent one, or you may buy one. If the demand for housing grows faster than the supply, rents will increase. As rents increase, home ownership becomes more attractive. Prospects offer more for the existing homes. How much more ? That will depend on their tastes and income, but also on interest rates, the opportunity costs of money.

In our prior example, what would happen to the price which buyers are willing to offer for an existing, or new, apartment if rents rose to $2,000/mon ($24,000/yr.) ? Wouldn't ownership be worth $160,000 ? Now consider both cases in a world in which my mortgage costs (and my expected yield on alternative investments is 6%). If the rental rate is $1,500 mon., then ownership saves me a net of $12,000/yr. If $12,000 represents a yield of 6% on my investment, I could offer up to $200,000 to buy. If the rent is $2,000/mon, the savings is $16,000/year, and I could offer $266,667 to buy. So, the Demand Price for existing capital depends on expected rents and market interest rates. When rents increase or interest rates fall, existing capital increases in value. When rents fall or interest rates rise, asset prices will decline. (Does this explain stock market movements ? How do current and prospective earnings and market yields influence share prices ?)

To summarize, existing capital is allocated to meet demand for its use, which depends on its productivity and the value of that product. This process of rationing determines the **Rental Rate of Capital.** The rental rate less expenses determines the **Expected Cash-flows** to the prospective owners. These estimates of Cash-flow are *Capitalized* at market yields. This capitalized value becomes the price for the purchase of existing Capital, *and the price expected by the producers of new capital.* The producers of new capital will choose a level of production, in the same manner as any other, producing only if the expected selling price exceeds the marginal costs of production.

Returning to the example of the apartment, consider construction of a new building. Rents are $1,500/month. For a building with fifty units, net income is expected to be (50x12x1500x 2/3) = $600,000 per year. Ignoring the potential for capital gains and losses, and other complicating factors, assume that owners would require a 10% return on their investment. They would be willing to pay $6,000,000 to own such a building. Developers will search for opportunities to acquire the land, design the building, draw permits, and build for sale, if all costs of production are less than $6 million. New construction adds to the supply of capital and a new round of rationing begins. (Again, is it any surprise that existing property owners are prone to be opposed to new construction ?)

If we are comfortable with our understanding of the Demand and Supply of capital, let's apply the same analysis to the market for **Natural Resources**. Why do we want natural resources ? Because they are useful. (Enjoying the experience of unspoiled wilderness is a use.) Why must we pay to use them ? Because they are scarce, and the owners will decide their use.

The Demand for Natural Resources is like any other resource demand. It will depend on the value of the product that uses the resources, the technologies chosen that determine the relationship between the quantity of resources used and the quantity of valuable product obtained, and the payment to the resource owners (the price of the resource, a cost to the user.) The upper limit on our willingness to purchase the natural resources is **The Value of the Marginal Physical Product of the Resource.** We call the payment to the resource owner a **Royalty**. Perhaps, this term derives from a time when all natural resources belonged to the King who could decide their use.

Our understanding of the **Supply of Natural Resources** is complicated by the idea that natural resources simply exist as a result of natural processes, and so should be available to everyone. However, recall the central premise of economics analysis --- scarce resources must be rationed, and should be allocated to their most important use. In addition, there are costs associated with locating the natural resources (exploration), preparing the natural resource for production (development), and production of the resource (harvesting, extraction, and shipping). All of this occurs, before we actually use the resource to produce valuable products.

The investments in exploration and development are sunk costs. Production requires operating costs (fixed and variable). We will undertake the investment in exploration and development, if the present value equivalent of future royalties exceeds those initial investment costs (once done, they are sunk, but not before). The royalty is a pure rent. It is the payment to the owner and the last payment made from revenue. Consider the following example.

We expect to sell petroleum at $90/bbl. The costs of production and delivery are $40/bbl. The operating profit available to split between royalty to the owner and profit to the operator is $50/bbl. What happens if the selling price declines to $60/bbl. ? The capital and labor required to produce the petroleum must be paid their $40/bbl. If not, they will go elsewhere. They are mobile, and they have opportunity costs. What about the operator ? He has profit requirements to justify his efforts. Perhaps, these have been and remain $10/bbl. So, the residual left for royalties which was $40 (=$90 - 50) is now $10 ($60- $50). The royalty is a residual, because it represents a **pure rent** accruing to the owner, only because his resource is valuable after all other expenses are met, and he owns the property.

Why is the owner of the mineral rights paid at all for the petroleum that lies under his land, and for which he made no contribution ? Simply, because he has the property right. On the other hand, he cannot demand more than the net proceeds of the sale after all other expenses, because the other resources needed to harvest his resources will not participate, unless they receive their opportunity cost. When will the owner refuse to permit production of his natural resource ? He will choose an alternative use of his resource, when the value of that opportunity exceeds the royalty offered. Does that explain why some environmental groups keep driving up the costs of producing natural resources through law suits and excessive regulation ? Such actions reduce the royalties available, the value of ownership, the costs of purchasing the property from existing owners, and the attraction of initial investments in development.

Let's consider the farmer whose land produces crops worth $1,000/acre after all operating expenses. His land may be worth $10,000 for sale or $1,000/acre in rent (royalty). Now, local authorities impose restrictions on his production methods, such as air quality or fertilizer use, and protections for sensitive species. He can only use 50% of his land, and his net yield per acre drops to $600 (his royalty). The value of ownership drops to $6,000/acre for some parcels and zero for others.

Depletable Natural Resources present an important problem. We would like to assure that those resources which can only be used once, and then are gone, resources that might become exhausted, be conserved for use when they are most valuable. How do markets address the problem of depletable resources ? Are they likely to be wasted ? Could that lead to a resource so severe that it triggers economic crisis ?

Let us consider the production decision from the point of view of the owner of the depletable resource. We can distinguish non-renewable from renewable resources, such as oil vs. forests. Essential to this analysis is the *Time Value of a Resource.* This is another form of investment decision, and interest rates become important, once again. As remarked above, interest rates are a bridge over time, a bridge between present and future. As the owner of an oil field, I can choose, within some broad parameters based on geologic characteristics, to produce more now, or more later. I will consider the price today vs. the price which I expect in the future. For example, I might be able to gain $20/bbl in today's market (price $90 less costs $70), but I expect the price next year to be $100 and my operating costs to be $75, for a net of $25. So, my choice is to profit $20 today or $25 next year. If I wait until next year, I gain $5 or 25%. So, the expectation of a much increased profit in the future leads me to conserve today. By the way, if this is a general expectation and a general strategy, the reduced supply today increases current prices, leading consumers to alter their behavior, and the increased production in the future reduces those future prices. The ability to shift production to the future leads to conservation today, and less likelihood of scarcity tomorrow. Higher prices today encourage conservation and also the development of alternative resources and technologies. The market will tend to settle at a relationship between current (spot) and future prices that reflects the opportunity cost of funds (interest rates). **Present Value (1+ interest rate) = Future Value.** If we were to compare present value to future values in twenty years, the formula would be **PV (1+i)^{20} = FV** Think of the money that I forego today by holding the oil in the ground, compounding at rate "i" for twenty years. If today's net income is $20, then at 10% for 20 years, I would need a net income of $134.54 when I sell in twenty years to justify my restraint.

Another way to look at it, is to consider the wisdom of investing large sums to find oil that we won't produce for twenty years. Consider a large multinational oil company that has proven reserves of 4 billion/barrels at current prices and costs, and produces 200 million barrels a year. So, it could produce for twenty years, before running out. Its engineers suggest a wildcatting plan that would cost $250 million dollars and expects to find 100 million barrels of new reserves. We expect to start selling that oil in 20 years at a net income of $25/bbl. Production would be at a rate of 10 million/bbls for ten years. The present value of those 100 million bbls, spread over ten years, beginning in twenty years is:

Present Value of an Annuity of ten years at 10% equal 6.145 x 10,000,000 x $25 = $1,536.25 million. Now, we discount that sum for twenty years using the present value interest factor for a single dollar at 10%: 0.149 x {$1,536.25 million} = $228,901,250. This project would justify a current investment in exploration of $228,901,250, but it is expected to cost $250 million. Should we do it ? No. Even though we stand to gain $250 million in profits for ten years, those profits are so far away that our money can be better used on another project. Does this explain why international oil companies rarely report reserves in excess of 18x their annual production ? When they do, it is usually because of unexpectedly huge discoveries, or increases in prices that make greater recovery from existing fields possible. And every prediction of peak oil, or exhausting our resources (They recur every decade, as new analysts appear and tout their new insight.) has been, and will continue to be wrong.

If we shift our attention to **renewables**, we can generate some interesting results. Consider the forest. Trees grow, so the longer we wait, the more timber we have to harvest and sell. As a result, when we compare the opportunities to sell today, or wait to a future date, we must adjust the quantity, and well as the price assumptions. We add a growth increment and then compare values. The formula would be: **Present Value = Future Value {(1+g) / (1 +r)}**

Consider a forest that grows at 6% per year. Then, I can sell one board/foot today or 1.06 board feet next year. If expect the price to be unchanged, then holding off gains me 6%. If I also expect the price to rise, I have an even greater gain. Consider the current price of $1.25 vs an expected price of $1.30 and a growth increment of 6%. If my cost of funds is 10%, then my comparison is: **Present Value**   **Present Value Equivalent of next years' sale**
        $1.25   **($1.30 x1.06) / 1.10 = $1.2527**

Looks like the market is doing a good job. The prices are appropriate, and the rewards for selling now, or next year, are similar.

We can conclude that markets for natural resources and for capital can efficiently allocate resources. To be sure that natural resources are used appropriately --- conserved when scarce and used when abundant --- security of property rights, and access to financial markets, are essential. Financial Markets permit the shifting of cash-flows from present to future, and vice versa, through borrowing and lending. Financial markets allow us to borrow against future income, or save current income for future use. They allow us to separate the timing of production and sales from the time at which we spend. If a resource is expected to be scarce in the future, we want it conserved. We want current production reduced. Inventory practices can reconcile current and future prices. Thus, well-developed financial markets can assure highest value use. However, for the owner to conserve, he must be confident in his ability to maintain his property and realize his gains in the future. When property rights are insecure, the current property owner (or appropriator) will sell it now, and take the money and run. Then, resources are likely to be wasted. We see this often in the **common pool** problem.

With our understanding of product and resource markets, we can address the issues of income and the **distribution of income**. For most of human history, and in many parts of the world today, income is determined by the ownership of assets which are often seized violently and defended by intimidation. Any surplus is appropriated by the rulers who claim all assets and distribute them to their supporters in accordance with their loyalty. Most people have little and gain little from their exertions. As a result, they have no loyalty, and many resentments.

I observed this in Rajasthan, where the rulers resided in forts on hill-tops, defended by guards. The Amber Palace, the former residence of the Maharajah of Jaipur, sat above cliffs. It had rooms of inlaid silver, jewels, and mirrors. The Rajah reclined on a platform with is twenty-three wives in front and three thousand concubines behind him. Of course, he needed an army to defend him. He had three thousand women, and so, three thousand of his subjects had none. This form of rule has been described by Acemoglu & Robinson[1] as extractive. The opposite is inclusive. Extractive regimes may provide great wealth for the rulers, but misery for the many. The rulers have no inclination to change the system which supports them, but the nation remains poor and easily subverted. (Wellington conquered more territory in India than Napoleon in Europe.) Inclusive societies permit the participation of the many, and thus, provide incentives for work, investment, innovation, and progress. We will focus on the modern, inclusive form of organization.

Each of us has resources --- our talents, abilities, skills, and motivation, and any capital which we own, such as land, buildings, and equipment. We can use these for ourselves to generate goods and services which give us satisfaction. The resources and how we use them determine what we get and the comfort and pleasure that we derive from them. This is the purest definition of income. On the other hand, we could contract the use of our resources to others in exchange for cash, or payments in kind. And we would then exchange the cash for the goods which we desire. We do this to enjoy all the advantages of specialization which were enumerated in lesson #2.1.

Taking this broader view, we can conclude that the comfort and pleasure that we enjoy (our income) depends on the resources which we own, their value in use, our choice of employments, the payments received, and the goods and services which we purchase and use. In this sequence from resource ownership to material goods enjoyed, prices enter twice. First, there are the offers which we receive for the employment of our resources, such as wages, salaries, profits and rents. Then, having chosen how to use our resources, we receive payment and go shopping. At this second stage, the prices of products matter. So, if our services are highly valued and we choose to work, we receive large payments. Then, if the prices of those goods which we desire are low, we enjoy the ability to purchase large amounts. On the other hand, if our wages are low and prices of products are high, we don't obtain much --- we have low income.

I have friends who are neurologists. One continues to practice and enjoys a salary of over $200,000. The other decided to teach junior high school, after several years of practicing medicine. At first, she had trouble finding a job. She was "over-qualified." (What does that say about our school system ?) Now, she has taught for many years and earns less than $100,000 a year. Notice that with her resources, she could be earning $200,000 practicing medicine, but she chooses to teach. Then, there is the issue of paying taxing and receiving transfers to determine spending power.

I visited New York and stopped by a major investment bank. Everyone there asked, if they could switch jobs with me. I was earning $100,000 a year and living in Santa Barbara. We calculated what they would need to earn in New York City to enjoy a similar life-style. It was $600,000.

If we think of nations or communities, similar analysis will help. We ask what are the resources available and who owns them ? How are they valued in the market ? How are they actually employed ? How are the payments received by the resource owners spent ? On what goods and at what prices ? You would not be surprised to learn that middle class families in poor countries enjoy a luxurious life-style, because the prices of the services which they consume are low.

And this analysis suggests that if we want to improve our material situation, we should 1) increase the resources owned by the people (education, health, and vocational skills are important), 2) the value of those resources (strong demand for products and high productivity through investments in capital and technology will help), 3) equality of opportunity (access and competition will even incomes), and 4) low prices for the products which we purchase complete the loop.

You might ask, "How are we doing ?" Consider education, health, opportunity, investment, and low prices. Do we have quality educational opportunities for everyone, especially the poor ? Do we have access to health care and broadly available training in home economics that can help us make better decisions for our families ? Are we encouraging public and private investments, or neglecting them ? Do we encourage low prices, or through wasteful legal and regulatory obstacles, raise prices ? I have seen estimates that one-third of the cost of housing in California is the result of permitting processes and government imposed fees. When we slow the growth of jobs, or construction of housing, the privileged pay more, but they still get the best opportunities. It's the least among us who don't get jobs or housing, and are left further and further behind. There may be plans for affordable housing, but it rarely appears. Consider building market rate housing. Each family that moves up to a better home, vacates their current domicile which becomes available to another family. Each worker who moves up to a better job vacates his current job which will be filled by someone else, moving up. Economic growth creates opportunities, because it creates needs for more resources. Economic growth raises incomes. Do you think that the inequality of income in the poorest nations is an accident, or the result of decades of slow economic growth ?

In addition to considering the income of individuals and families, we like to compare incomes across an entire society. When we do, we usually ignore the uses of the income that we receive, that is the psychological dimension of material enjoyment. Consider the family that has a Mercedes auto that cost them $40,000 and the family that has a Hyundai that cost them $20,000. Is the first family twice as well off ? We know that they value the MBZ twice as much, because they bought it. But would the other family ? Then, there is the confusion of income and wealth. In this incomplete analysis, income is the payments that we receive (ignoring what we can buy with it). Wealth is the value of what we own, to be realized in one payment, if we sell our assets. So, I can rent my home to someone for income of $24,000/yr. or I can sell it for $240,000. We'd say that my income is $24,000 and my wealth is $240,000. What about the landlord who enjoys income of $300,000 and whose buildings are worth $3,000,000, in comparison to the physician who earns $300,000, but owns no property. We'd say that they have the same income, but very different wealth. Is that true ? Finally, the income that we earn varies a great deal over our life-time, rising from twenty to fifty-five years of age, then declining rapidly from sixty-five to death. All of these issues should be considered, as we try to evaluate income distribution.

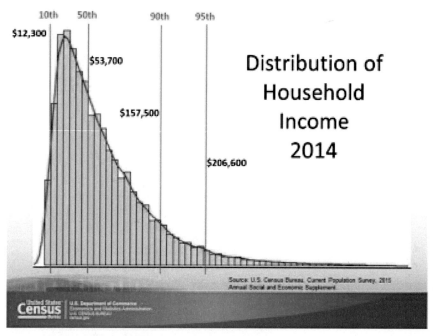

Explaining the *Chi Squared* Distribution
1) Age matters; why ?
2) The interaction of normally distributed, independent
characteristics, such as intelligence, dexterity, luck, and social skills

Typically, the income distribution of a society has the shape of a Chi-squared distribution. This is a skewed shape, rather than a normal, bell-shaped, distribution. From the axis on the left toward the right, the numbers increase for a while, then they tail off, so that only a few enjoy very high measured income. Why ? First, we should correct for age. We expect young people who are beginning their work lives and old people who are retiring, and living off declining assets, to have low income. So, the old and young will fall in the early segments, and the middle aged will appear in the middle to high range. Now, consider what skills and abilities can contribute to earning income. Would you say that intelligence, social skills, dexterity, beauty, and even luck, matter ? What if each of these are normally and independently distributed? Then, we would expect most people to be blessed in some ways and deficient in others. They would fall in the middle of the income distribution. A few would be blessed in many ways and would land in the highest income zone, and a few would be cursed with multiple deficiencies, and therefore, be exceptionally poor. In other words, under reasonable assumptions, we would expect the distribution to be skewed --- no evil or exploitation required, although some sympathy from the winners for the losers may be appropriate.

Recent work by Mary Daly of the Federal Reserve Bank of San Francisco indicates a great deal of mobility within the middle three quintiles of the income distribution. She compared the income of children to the income of their parents at the same age, and found that the likelihood of the children landing in the same or different quintiles was about even. However, she found that the children of the top 20% are likely stay in the top 20%, and the children of the bottom 20% are likely to stay in the bottom 20%. (About half move up or down, but about half remain.) Before we leave this topic, we will ask, what can be done to increase absolute material well-being and also income mobility. And when we look at the last decade, we find that the distribution had remained stable, except for the top 1%, and that change is dominated by increased in income in the financial services industry and senior executives of large multinational corporations, not business in general.

Occasionally, we hear that incomes in the United States are less equal than other developed nations. There are several reasons. First, the USA is large geographically, and diverse demographically, unlike many nations in Europe (although immigration in the EU is changing the latter, and leading to greater inequality.) Second, the revolution in civil rights, especially women's rights, both of which are desirable and were long over-due, may have a perverse effect on income distribution. Because we tend to live, work, and go to school with people of similar backgrounds, highly educated men marry highly educated women. Together, the family income will be very high. Consider two traditional families with one earner. Family A has income of $60,000 and family B has income of $100,000. The difference is $40,000. The wives are similar in education and background to their husbands. The wives go to work. Wife A earns $50,000 and family A's income rises to $110,000. Wife B goes to work and being similar to her husband earns $90,000. Family B's income is now $190,000. The distribution of family incomes has become more unequal. Surely, we would not wish to hold back family B, or blame them for the situation of family A, which by the way is an improvement for them, too.

Let's shift our attention to the poor. First, let's acknowledge the problems of measurement and definition. As a senior citizen with a comfortable home, no mortgage, and a comfortable endowment of consumer durables, my expenses are low, until my age and health start to bring new costs. We also tend to compare pre-tax income, when we should compare disposable income --- that is income available after taxes and transfers. Surely my eligibility for Social Security and Medicare raises my income above that reported on my IRS forms. Many people receive transfers in-kind, such as food stamps, housing subsidies, scholarships, etc., not to mention those miscreants mentioned in lesson #2.4 who enjoy rent controlled apartments and own a home on Long Island, as well. Ideally, we could compare life-time income and consider the value of assets owned (wealth), and even the satisfaction that the goods available bring, as well as the pain of deprivation. However, "the perfect is the enemy of the good." So, let's do the best we can.

First, what is **poverty** ? We might agree that inadequate income, the inability to purchase the goods and services that humans need to live in comfort and dignity, is a good definition. However, that abstract concept is difficult to realize. Is poverty absolute deprivation which could be measured in specific quantities of consumption, such as food, housing, health care, clothing, education, etc. ? Or is poverty a relative standard in which we compare the ability to consume of the family to the average, or median, family ? We estimate that 20% of families have less than 50% of median income, ignoring differences in consumption patterns or regional costs of living. Are they poor ? Our practical standard is an absolute one which has little relevance today. The measure of poverty that we use is income less than three times an adequate food budget. By this measure 9-15% of the population are poor, less after accounting for transfers in kind, such as food stamps and housing subsidies.

When we study the poor, we find common characteristics of **behavioral dependency**. Deficiencies in education are common. Less than 2% of adults with high school degrees are poor. Family status is important. 28% of female headed households are poor. Families with two adults resident are unlikely to be poor. Employment is important. Few who work full-time are poor. And the poor are more likely to be victims and perpetrators of crime.

We have many programs to help the poor, but they are badly targeted. While a majority of the elderly were poor sixty years ago. The poverty rate of seniors is now similar to the general population. Social Security and Medicare are major reasons for these gains, but most of their benefits go to the better off seniors. Other government programs include unemployment insurance, job retraining, counseling, and placement to ease the costs of unemployment and increase job mobility. There are also income maintenance programs and in-kind transfers, as mentioned above. The number enrolled in welfare declined dramatically under legislation passed by the Republican Congress and Democratic President in the 1990s. Instead of open-ended support, a contract for an array of needed short-term support was connected to an employment development plan such as education. Unfortunately, these incentives were removed by President Obama, and dependency has returned to former levels.

There is a fundamental dilemma in income support programs, which have three inter-dependent dimensions. We would like to be generous in benefits, especially for those families with no income. So, we must define eligibility and set a minimum benefit. Then, we must phase out the benefit as income increases, but those reductions are similar to a tax, reducing the gains from earning income, and thus the incentive to become independent. Finally, the combination of the benefit and the reduction rate determine when the family no longer receives any subsidy. Together, all three dimensions determine the over-all cost of the program.

For example, if we set a minimum benefit of $12,000 per year for a family of four, we are only meeting 50% of the poverty level of income. If we reduce the benefit by 33% for every dollar earned, we will still be subsidizing the family until they earn $36,000, but working to earn the $36,000 will only raise their net income by $24,000. Finally, if we fail to integrate our various subsidy programs, we may have some families receiving a combination of income and subsidies in excess of $40,000, while others receive only $12,000 or less. My daughter worked for the state of Massachusetts to integrate their welfare data base to track combined benefits and assure that families get what they need but with equal benefits for those in similar circumstances (Remember the idea of horizontal equity from lesson #2.5 ?). She encountered fierce resistance from the welfare case workers who see themselves as advocates for their clients who always need more.

What may we conclude ? If we are concerned about income, especially for the poor who lack what we think they need, however we define that, then *we should emphasize equipping them with skills, including health, education, and job experience.* We should insure that they live in safe and healthy neighborhoods, that they are aware of opportunities for improvement, and that they are able to keep most of the rewards which they have earned. We don't need to tear down the successful, although we shouldn't ignore dishonest profits or income.

We are reminded yet again that economics is the study of the allocation of scarce resources. Individuals make choices. They consider benefits and costs. Therefore, incentives matter. Public policy makers should compare benefits to costs, too. Some of the important costs are monitoring, compliance, and administration. Results (effectiveness) matter. Coercion is often ineffective.

Questions for review and examination:

Contrast *physical* capital and *financial* capital.

Explain the relationship between **the *Rental Rate* of physical capital** and **the *Demand Price* of physical Capital**.

What determines the **production of new Capital** ? *{hint: there are four steps}*

What determines the **development of Natural Resources** ?)

What determines the **Distribution of Income** in a market economy ?

Explain the dilemma of welfare design in terms of benefits, incentives, and total program cost.

Bibliography for Markets:
[1]Daren Acemoglu & James Robinson, Why Nations Fail, Crown 2012
Daniel Ariely, Predictably Irrational, Harper Collins 2008
Angus Deaton, The Great Escape, Princeton University Press 2013
Fred Hirsch, Social Limits to Growth, Harvard 1976
Daniel Kahnemann, Thinking Fast and Slow, Farrar, Straus, and Giroux, 2011
George Katona, Psychological Economics Elsevier 1977
David Landes, The Wealth and Poverty of Nations, Norton 1999
Bjorn Lomborg, The Skeptical Environmentalist, Cambridge 1998
Tibor Scitovsky, The Joyless Economy, Oxford 1976
Thomas Sowell, Wealth, Poverty, and Politics, Basic Books 2015
Richard Thaler, MisBehaving, Norton 2015

Three forms of capital for transportation: Smart car in Rome, Tuktuk in Bangkok, and ox cart in Cochin, India

Part Three
Banking and Financial Management

"We want the facts to fit the preconceptions. When they don't, it is easier to ignore the facts than to change the preconceptions."
--- Jessamyn West (1902-1984)

The Roman Forum, today

Lesson #3.1 Money, Banking, and Financial Markets

As we learned in Part Two, Microeconomics, prices ration and signal. Typically, we exchange goods or services for money, followed by a subsequent exchanges of money for goods and services. Money serves as a means of payment, facilitating exchange transactions, and also as a method of comparing value, and one of many tools for saving. In addition, the regulation of the overall supply of money in the economy is one of the main methods of public policy for influencing the level and rate of change in economic activity.

So, what is **Money** ? It is *whatever serves the functions of money*. We look at what people use as a **unit of account**. How do they state and compare prices, and account for revenue, expenses, assets and debts ? We ask, what is the commonly accepted method of payment ? And what are the most liquid savings instruments ? By **liquidity,** a desirable quality for an asset, we mean the extent to which an asset has the characteristic of being easily converted into the means of payment --- quickly, inexpensively, and with assured value. Obviously, what we identify as money itself is the most liquid asset of all.

Most societies have money, because it is so useful. Money facilitates exchange. Money avoids the problem of *double coincidence of wants* --- the inefficiency of searching for the partner who has what you want and seeks what you have to sell. Money provides one standard of comparison of value. Money provides a savings vehicle with low resource costs. (Think of how marvelous is the efficiency of providing a useful service, such as saving, with a simple piece of paper, or a bookkeeping entry, rather than tying up scarce and valuable resources, such as gold or silver.)

The oldest forms of money are commodities, often taking the form of coins, but these are bulky, indivisible, and heavy. So today in many nations, we use paper currency and bank deposits, payable on demand. But the exchange value of money must be stable to assure acceptability. Thus, in countries experiencing chronic inflation of their own currency, other forms of money are adopted. When we were in Argentina in 2012, all expensive transactions (such as real estate, jewelry, and fine arts) were quoted and payable in US dollars. Pesos were accepted for common transactions, such as meals and taxi rides.

Why is Money valuable ? Like every other resource, *money is valuable, because it is useful, and it is scarce.* When it becomes less useful, perhaps because its value is unstable, or when it becomes less scarce, perhaps because the government, with the cooperation of the central bank, borrows and spends excessively, the value of the money falls. We call a sustained decline in the value of money, **inflation**. Hence, regulating the supply of money to be large enough to support full employment spending, but not so large that it causes inflation, is an important responsibility of the central bank, in our case the Federal Reserve System.

Let's review. We can identify three forms of the **Demand for Money**: 1) **Transactions Demand** --- the money balances that we want to hold to manage our cash-flows, given the irregular size and timing of our receipts and payments, 2) **Precautionary Demand** the money balances that we hold to make payments for unexpected expenses (a contingency fund), and 3) **Speculative Demand** --- the money balances that we hold to take advantage of unexpected opportunities, such as falling asset prices, when interest rates rise or recession occurs. Obviously, institutions and habits, payment methods, availability of short-term credit, economic stability and instability, price and interest rate risks, etc. influence the Demand for Money for these purposes. (We owe these distinctions to John Maynard Keynes.)

As a result, we expect the **Demand for Money** to be proportional to economic activity, measured as nominal Gross Domestic Product, and to change only slowly, over time. We call the relationship between Money Supply and economic activity (nominal Gross Domestic Product) **velocity**. It is just a ratio. Do not read too much into the name. Think of the amount of money with which you are comfortable given your cash-flows, uncertainties, and likely opportunities. Perhaps, your income is $60,000 per year ($5,000/month) and you keep $10,000 in your checking and savings accounts. Then, your velocity is $60,000/$10,000 = 6. For the American economy, this ratio varies 1.5-1.9 over the business cycle.

Another important service provided by money is *the stimulation of saving and investment* by separating the act of earning income from the act of spending. Borrowing and lending of money moves purchasing power from the hoards of savers to the borrowers who have opportunities to spend. This process redistributes spending and resources, changing the mix of production, increasing economic activity and employment, and improving income distribution.

Recognizing money as general resource ration coupons can help you to understand this. Every dollar in your pocket, or your bank account, represents your entitlement to some of society's resources. You can use it yourself, or make available to someone else by lending. If you spend it, you gain some good or service, and others are motivated to employ resources and produce that good or service for you. If you lend the money to someone else, you don't use it. They do. And others will organize resources to produce goods and services for them. So, if your used your money to buy strawberries, your neighbor might be employed growing and harvesting berries. But when you lend your money to a contractor, he buys equipment and hires workers to construct housing, and your neighbor becomes a construction worker. The movement of money also moves resources, changing the size and composition of our economy.

In this process, financial institutions perform important roles. Banks mobilize and allocate purchasing power through offering savings and credit instruments. Banks are also the main source of money supply and payments services. On a broader scale, **financial markets** provide for the creation and exchange of financial instruments (securities) in order to bridge the needs of savers and borrowers. In addition, markets in which existing securities can be traded (exchanged), enhance the liquidity of those *primary* securities and make them more attractive to more savers, reducing costs for the borrowers.

What is a **security** ? When I lend you my money, I am helping you to take advantage of an opportunity today. I am foregoing the opportunities which I might have, while you have my money. Naturally, I expect, and require, that you share a portion of your gain, in the form of interest, profits, or dividends. And you are happy to do so, because without my loan, you couldn't seize your opportunity. Once you have my money, you will decide when to repay me. So, I would like to document your promise to make specific payments to me. This document becomes my security that you will repay me. It specifies my rights, and your obligations, *while you have my money*. Hence, the name for a promise future payment of series of payments is a **security**.

As we borrow and lend, either directly through agreements between the savers and borrowers, or indirectly through financial institutions which borrow from savers and then lend to borrowers separately, acting as intermediaries, the cost of borrowing and the reward for lending is often expressed as **the interest rate**. An interest rate is a signal of the sacrifice that borrowers will make through an increase in future payments, and the gain to the lender through the increase in his future receipts. You can think of the interest rate as the *rental rate* of loanable funds. As such, it is a price. And the interest rate will rise, or fall, as needed to ration the flow of funds between borrowers who demand credit and savers who supply it. As with any other market, competition is required to assure efficient allocation of savings, and markets must be accessible to all potential savers and borrowers. Deficiencies of financial markets are a major source of slow economic growth and chronic mal-distribution of income. But when financial markets are well-developed, the outcome is economic growth (production), more equal income distribution (borrowers and savers sharing gains), price stability (again, more product supply), innovation (borrowers can undertake new ventures), and better job creation (workers move to more productive activities). Ironically, these gains were not well-understood by economists, until the 1970s, when Ron McKinnon and others began to highlight them.

In our nation, common financial institutions include commercial banks, savings banks, saving & loan associations, credit unions, insurance companies (life and property-casualty), pension funds, investment banks, securities brokerages, and investment companies, such as mutual funds. Why aren't all financial transactions directly between buyers and sellers, borrowers and lenders ? In other words, why do financial institutions exist ? Specialist institutions can acquire and use information to manage risks. They can enjoy a large volume of similar transactions which reduces their average costs and diversifies their risks. Participating in markets continuously, gaining information about other participants, prices, and risks, reduces the problem of asymmetric information (when the securities issuer has better information than the investor) that plagues individual and intermittent investors. As a result, the financial institutions can charge higher interest rates and fees, and reduce costs, creating an opportunity for profit.

The basic principle is to offer the source of funds, the saver, a security with the characteristics which he prefers (perhaps liquidity and safety through a checking account), so he will lend the bank money at a low cost in interest and services. Then, taking that money, the bank creates a loan for the borrower tailored to his cash-flow needs, so he is willing to pay more. The bank lives on the difference, or **net interest margin**, (also called "the spread").

A good example of this process is the **bank loan**. Each loan is unique, catering to the specific cash-flow needs of the borrower. Because each is unique, these loans are not liquid and are not traded, or traded only between closely associated "correspondent" banks. In recent years, some of these loans have been sold to savers, and others have been consolidated into large packages which have been sold under new names. After all, a security is just a promise of future cash-flows. It can be as simple as an IOU, or as complex as a share of the receipts from a thousand mortgages. These innovative packages derive their value from the underlying securities which have been included. Hence, we call the new securities, **derivatives**. As you imagine, establishing the value of a complex cluster of securities is very difficult, and the abuses of this process have caused many failures, losses, and even the disruption of the financial system, as occurred in the USA in 2008. (Both my brother-in-law and my sister-in-law, at different times, made comfortable livings valuing these securities for the financial institutions that owned them but had no idea what they were worth.)

Because banks borrow heavily from depositors, they have little tolerance for losses. Typically, 8% of liabilities are equity, which means 92% are debt. A small decline in value of their assets can wipe out a bank. So, commercial banks are reluctant to accept risk. As a result, they have developed a process for qualifying borrowers that they call **the Five 'C's**. These are useful concepts for anyone considering making a loan, including businesses extending credit to their customers.

Character is the first and the most important. *Will this borrowers honor the loan agreements, even when to do so is very difficult ?* There is no substitute for character. We assess character by looking at past performance, such as credit reports and references. But there are other indicators, such as stability --- time on the job and in the profession, time in business, roots in the community such as home ownership, and even psychological characteristics. Who do you think would be more reliable: teachers and engineers, or actors and lawyers ? The first group lives by the rules, and the second group think they can make their own rules.

When I was a community banker, I remember a father and two sons who borrowed to build four condominiums and were caught in a recession. They couldn't sell the finished condos and fell further and further behind on their payments, until the loan was due, and they couldn't pay. One of them came by my office every Friday to tell me what they were doing, until they sold the condos to an investor for the outstanding balance of the loan. They lost eighteen months work and all their cash investment. When the market turned, they came to ask for a loan for a new project, I was happy to oblige.

Another borrower promised to pay a loan on February first. I saw the money for the pay-off come into his account in early January and go out again, soon thereafter. On February first, he came to ask for an extension. I asked him whether he has received the money to pay me off (knowing that he had), and he admitted that he had but he'd used the money to make another investment. If he had paid as agreed, I would have happily made a new loan, but he ignored his promise to the bank, so I demanded payment and asked him to find another bank. These two different customers showed their characters.

With businesses, I would often visit their facilities to observe staff morale and the way the boss treated his team. At dinner, I would observe how he treated his wife. These observations would tell me about his character. He might charm me when he needed a loan, but would he be equally considerate when it was time to pay ? I would often say, "I will lend money to a borrower who will pay me before he feeds his children, because I will have confidence lending him the money to feed his children. But I don't lend money to borrowers who have excuses for failing to honor their commitments."

If character is reliable, then we are concerned about the ability to repay. "You can't get blood from a stone." So, we analyze the borrower's **capacity** by measuring his **cash-flow**. Ideally, the activity promoted by the loan provides the income to repay it. But there can be cash-flow from other activities that will repay the loan. I like "defense in depth" --- three sources of repayment: the activity itself, another activity in case the first fails, and the sale of a liquid asset, if the second fails, as well.

I like to know that the borrower has considered the events over which he has no control and that might disrupt his ability to pay. We call these **conditions**. He should know his business better than I, and should be able to anticipate these problems. I want him to identify them for me, and inform me of his contingency plans. This gives me confidence in his abilities.

If these conditions are met, the lender should require a substantial commitment of the borrower's own cash, **capital**. For example, I will lend 75% of the cost of the Christmas inventory, or the construction of a new restaurant. Because he has a stake, the owner will struggle to overcome obstacles to protect his own investment, and by doing so, he protects me. The borrower who wants 100% financing can walk away from the business and the debt too easily.

Now, we are close to an agreement. We can talk terms and conditions. For the safe loan (1% may default for truly unanticipated reasons), I can offer generous terms. I may also ask for the pledge of assets as **collateral** to secure the loan. A lender doesn't want to own your home, your factory, or your inventory, but if he has your pledge in the form of a deed or UCC1 equipment filing, he will have your attention when time is tough. Collateral doesn't make a bad loan into a good loan, it just gives the lender some priority, legally and practically.

You can see that the art of lending required knowledge, skill, and experience. What do you think of "crowd funding ?"

We could do similar analysis of other financial institutions. For example, what does an insurance company do ? An insurance company offers a contract. In return for a series of small regular payment (the premiums), the insurer promises one large payment in the event of any specific covered losses. The insurance company invests the premiums until they must pay out, and this helps to offset their costs and provide their profit. The customer has substituted a small, predictable series of expenses, for unlikely but potentially disastrous losses. The insurance company can provide this service by studying loss probabilities and offering many contracts to many customers to diversity its risk, converting the insurer's losses into regular expenses.

Financial markets are arrangements that facilitate the exchange of securities. They may require face-to-face meetings of the principal parties, such as a banker and his loan applicant, or the meetings of agents for the principals, such as brokers and dealers. (A broker is the agent for the buyer or the seller; a dealer is a market maker, holding inventory and willing to both buy and sell for his own account.) Over the last few generations, more markets have developed that have no physical location, but constitute secured communications systems, (first telegraph, then telephone, then telex, and now computer networks). Access to any market must be restricted to approved participants to assure security and the honoring of commitments. We distinguish **primary markets** in which the securities are originated and sold for the first time, from **secondary markets** in which existing securities are transferred. The proceeds of the initial primary transaction will flow to the issuer, but subsequent transactions may not involve the issuer at all.

We also distinguish financial markets by the characteristics of the securities traded. So, **money markets** are the markets in which securities maturing in less than one year are bought and sold. Examples would be bank deposits, bankers' acceptances, treasury bills, trade credit, commercial paper, and bank loans. These are tools for liquidity management, as needed for irregular cash-flows. For example, a business with large cash balances would seek safe and liquid investments for some extra income, and would purchase one or more of the securities mentioned above. When the firm's cash position deteriorates, they will sell the securities, or issue their own to raise cash. **Capital markets** are markets for long-term funds. Common instruments would be shares of ownership (stocks), bonds, and mortgages. Investment bankers advise companies and organizations, which wish to raise money, of the types of securities that are suitable, prepare the documents for review approval by the regulators (usually, the Securities and Exchange Commission), and sell the securities, remitting the proceeds, less fees and commissions, to the issuers. Stockbrokerage firms and authorized bonds dealers act as agents for investors in the purchase and sale of existing securities.

Recall that a security is simply a promise to make one or more payments and to honor specific responsibilities while the issuer has the investor's money. Consider this situation: You lend me a sum of money, say $10,000. I have the money and go ahead with my plans. Who determines when I repay you ? Correct answer: I do. I have your money. I'll pay you when I'm ready. How do you increase the probability that I will pay as agreed ? First, we do the credit worthiness analysis described above (the 5 "C"s.) Second, before you give me the money, you insist on a document which states clearly your rights and my obligations, while I have your money. That document is a **security**. It doesn't guarantee that you will receive your money when its due, but it helps. If the promise can be transferred, we call it a **marketable security**.

Securities are used by the financial manager to assure that his organization has the resources needed to operate and achieve its goals. So, we talk about the three responsibilities of the financial manager ("the three 'A's"). First, the financial manager organizes the accounting reports to present the financial data in forms which facilitate evaluation. Then, he performs financial analysis and planning by evaluating the needs for increased resources (production capacity). From the business plan, he identifies the expectations for revenue, expense and cash-flow. (These would be sales, costs, and the timing of receipts and payments.) From these, he identifies the size and type of assets that will be needed, such as inventory, plant, and equipment. This allows him to determine the dollars required. We call this the function of **assessment of needs.**

Next, the financial manager must **acquire** the funds needed to obtain the assets. He selects the appropriate mix of sources of funds -- -which sources, in what amounts, and on what terms. Short-term borrowings in the form of suppler credit and bank loans may be appropriate for financing inventory and accounts receivable (customer credit); bonded indebtedness and share of ownership would be suitable for investments in plant and equipment. Associated with each source of funds are costs, risks, and restrictions on management. The priority should be: 1) Will the funds be available when I need them ? 2) What are the burdens of the terms imposed by the funds provider ?, and 3) What is the cost of borrowing ?

The funds (liabilities) are now **allocated.** The financial manager makes the investment decisions, selecting projects and programs, and finally commits dollars to specific activities and assets, and monitors their use. So, the financial manager has a critical role in operation of the organization. Sometimes, we distinguish areas of financial responsibility, such as the **Treasurer** who manages external relationships with bankers and investors as well as conducting the financial planning, and the **Controller** who is responsible for internal financial management, such as accounting and performance evaluation. All managers (production, personnel, marketing, accounting, and planning) are well-advised to master the skills of finance.

What should be the goals of the financial manager ? Profit (measured by earnings per share) is not enough. The value of a company depends on earnings and risk, both in quantity and quality. When we say that we want to maximize shareholder value, we accept the notion that owners require a sustainable yield at an acceptable level of risk (liquidity, solvency, and political risks). The timing of earnings matters. Earlier is better than later. Cash-flow matters, because cash pays bills. And risks matter. Liquidity is the ability to meet obligations, to handle disruptions to cash-flow without embarrassment, and to seize unanticipated opportunities. Solvency means that the value of assets exceeds that of debts. You might say that "more is better" for all three criteria, but there are often trade-offs. More equity or liquidity hurts profitability, for example.

How much risk are the owners willing to accept ? From the point of view of the saver selecting securities to hold as store of value and gain, higher risk requires an expectation of higher reward (yield, "return on investment"). To increase, or even sustain, the value of the company, the financial manager must assure that his owners and bondholders receive the reward that they require. They will compare his securities to other similar opportunities in terms of default risk, liquidity, exposure to inflation, and tax treatment.

Risk is *the possibility of an outcome other than what we expect*. So, risk can be positive (better outcome), or worse (disappointing outcome). We can measure the recent risk experience

174

by the variability of the return (yield) in the past few years. **Holding Period Yield** considers income and change in value (capital gain or loss), average investment, and time period. The formula would be:

$$\text{Yield (or ``rate of return'')} \quad = \quad \frac{\{\text{Income} + \text{Capital Gain}\} / \text{Time}}{\text{Average Investment}}$$

So, our definition of risk would be the variation in average return, measured by the standard deviation of the holding period yield. When we analyze the sources of these variations, we find that general factors and company related factors are almost equally important. **General risks** are the variations caused by influences that effect all kinds of securities, such as inflation, taxes and regulations, and natural disasters. **Specific risks** are those that effect the company and its immediate competitors. We analyze specific (or "company") risk by considering the situation of our customers (if they are doing well, that helps us), our suppliers (will we have any surprises in the availability, or price of our materials ?), and our competitors (do they constitute a threat, or can we sustain our advantages ?). Then, we assess the quality of management. We do this by comparing the financial statements to the business plans of the company. We analyze financial ratios, which measure profitability, liquidity, asset efficiency, leverage and coverage, to see whether performance matches expectations, at acceptable levels of risk.

The influence of **general risk** requires three steps. First, we must identify the events that bring risk. Then, we must estimate the probability of each event. Finally, we must ask, how would this event effect our company ? Over the years, a statistic which measures the susceptibility of our company to general risk has been developed. A regression of the holding period yield of our company against the holding period yield of some general index, such as the Standard & Poor 500 index, gives us a slope coefficient which we call **Beta**. It compares the instability of our yield to that of the market. A *Beta* equal to "1" suggests that they move equally in response to the general risk; a *Beta* of "2" would suggest that our company's yield is twice as volatile, as the market in general. If we anticipate a lot of negative, general risks, high *Beta*s might be considered undesirable. If we don't expect much general risk, or all general risks are positive, we might not worry about a high Beta, and may even consider it attractive. However, it is only one criterion, and it has been abused by securities brokers to encourage sales.

In comparing securities (and companies), we should consider their risk profiles. Among them we might compare companies with similar *Beta*s. After all, risky securities should sell at lower prices and higher yields. So, comparing a company with low risk exposure to one accepting high risk would be a mistake. However, even within a group of companies with similar Betas, there will be some differences in yield, and we call the variation from the average, *Alpha.* Obviously, we like companies with positive Alphas, that is higher returns than their peers. Again, we should be cautious in using these tools, as there will be a tendency of *regression to the mean.* General Electric outperformed its peers for years, during the leadership of Jack Welsh, but has underperformed since.

All of these tools and issues are important to the financial manager, as he designs his management strategy to maintain and increase the value of his company.

Let us complete this lesson by considering value, historically and even currently, a great source of confusion. **Value** is what we are willing to pay to receive the benefits of ownership. Value is a one-time payment for a flow of benefits. Value looks to the future. *If I buy this, what benefits will I enjoy, while I own it and when I sell it ?* The past doesn't determine value and neither do the costs of production. I don't care what you paid for that painting, or that car. I care about the enjoyment that I will gain while I own it, and the profit, or loss, that will occur when I sell it. The costs of production are important, only when we consider the profit and thus the desirability of new production. So, the method of valuation is always the same. There are three steps:

1) Identify the benefits by dollars and time of receipt
2) Discount each benefit to determine the present value equivalent
3) Add up all the Present Discounted Values to get the total Value today

For example, if I expect a company to pay a dividend of $1 each year, and no other gain, I will ask what yield would satisfy me ? If my required yield is 5%, my value would be $20.

Why ? $20 x 5% = $1   How did I get that ?   Value times Yield equals recurring benefit.

$$\textbf{Value x 5\%} = \textbf{\$1} \rightarrow \textbf{Value} = \textbf{\$1/(5\%)} = \textbf{\$1 x (20/1)}$$

We call this calculation **capitalization**, converting a cash-flow (one dollar each year) into a one-time value, a capital sum.

Conclusion: What have we done in this introduction to finance ? We introduced money, banking, financial market, financial management, and valuation. There were a lot of new ideas. Don't worry, you'll see them again, many times, until they become familiar and you become comfortable with them.

Questions for review and tests:

What is the Economic function of finance ?

What is money ? Why is it valuable ?

What do the following financial institutions do: commercial banks, insurance companies, investment banks, securities brokerages ?

Why is a well-developed financial system important to a healthy economy and society ?

What is risk ?

What are the sources of risk ?

How do we assess risk ?

And how do we adjust for risk ?

The Plaza of Commerce in Lisbon, where the Finance Ministry is located and the treasure fleets arrived.

Lesson #3.2 Central Banking and Money

During the industrial revolution, national governments and money center banks began to recognize the need for central banks. The Bank of England (est.1694) provided the model, and the classic exposition of the responsibilities of the central bank was written by Walter Bagehot (Lombard Street).

Central Banks began as banks to their government, providing means of payment, floating bonds, and managing the currency. Duties expanded to banking the commercial banks, first providing expanded payment services, such as settling clearings between banks and delivering and picking up currency.

Bagehot emphasized the importance of functioning as a **Lender of Last Resort**. Commercial banks hold small amounts of cash, but large deposits at other banks for clearings, and much larger securities portfolios, as well as loans of little liquidity. Investment banks and brokerages hold many securities and borrow heavily to support them. The cash may constitute immediate (or "primary") liquidity, and the securities are a secondary source of liquidity, to be sold, when loan demand surges, or deposits run off. In the event of a general scramble for liquidity, many banks would be selling securities at the same time, and securities prices (not just for bonds, but for loans, as well) could decline dramatically. These declines in securities prices could render the banks technically insolvent, because banks operate with high leverage (often 12:1, or more). The value of assets sold under these conditions would be less than the banks' liabilities to depositors and other creditors. In fact, the banks would prefer not to sell these earning assets at the knock-down prices, but the appearance of insolvency could cause a panic of creditors, including both depositors, and other banks. The banks could be ruined, and their customers could lose much of their deposits, as well as their access to the banks as traditional sources of credit. Business would contract, and economic depression would follow.

To avoid these dire consequences, the central bank should be willing to lend the cash needed against the banks' holdings of securities and loans as collateral. The money advanced would be a portion of the value of the collateral, encouraging and assuring repayment. The difference between the market value of the security and the loan amount is called, the **discount**, and the difference between the loan and the repayment, **the discount rate**. At our central bank, the **Federal Reserve System**, the discount rate and the list of eligible collateral are posted every week. If the rate is 4% and the loan of $10,000,000 is requested for three months, then the FRS will require a pledge of collateral valued in excess of $10,100,000. A failure to repay would lead to sale of the collateral. Borrowing from the Central Bank is not always easy, as central bankers, like parents, will review the request with skepticism. (No loans to expand your holdings of commercial loans or securities paying higher rates. How did your liquidity management practices fail you ?) In a general panic, the central bank will be more generous. In 1987, when the US stock market crashed, the Federal Reserve announced willingness to lend against virtually any security including home mortgages.

Another responsibility, perhaps growing out of the Lender of Last Resort experience, is the supervision of the banking system. The central bank will dispatch auditors (bank examiners) to review the policies and the performance of their members. The handy acronym **CAMEL** (capital, assets, management, earnings, and liquidity) describes the issues. 1) Does the bank have adequate **capital** (net worth and long term debt) to protect its creditors in the event of liquidation ? Prior to 1980, Savings and Loan associations often operated with 3%, or less, capital, under the faulty assumption that their concentration in mortgage lending gave them more stability and less risk. Today, a common view is capital equal to, or exceeding, 8% of total assets is desirable. (Of course, many bankers would dissent.) 2) **Asset quality** is judged by auditing a sample of various classes of assets for their payment history, liquidity, and correct documentation. (You may be shocked to learn that many loans are made without due diligence, perfection of collateral, and even without signed notes.) In particular, loans will be classified as conforming (to terms and policies), non-conforming, classified (non-performing), and loss. 3) The assessment of **management** requires a review of the bank's policies (liquidity, investment, lending, fraud prevention, and asset/liability management). The policies must be suitable, sensible, and most importantly, consistently applied. 4) The criterion of **earnings** refers to profit and quality. A consistently profitable bank, whose profit derives from standard banking services, has the strength to correct its problems from earnings. A bank without profit, or whose profit comes from risky ventures, may have difficulty recovering from other problems when they occur. 5) Finally, **liquidity** refers to the ability of the bank to meet its short-term obligations. This requires the careful management of cash-flows and deliberate strategy with regard to the match, or mismatch, of the duration of assets and liabilities. For example, the matching of a three year loan with a three year deposit poses no liquidity risk (there may be default risk), but the funding of that loan with demand deposits would be risky, unless we are confident that the deposits will roll over for the entire period. Typically, demand deposits whose purpose is to manage the depositor's cash-flows (payments and receipts) are stable, but savings deposits, which may come and go, seeking small gains in interest rates, or accumulating for a specific purpose, and then being spent, are less reliable. The bank must be capable of paying the market rate to borrow deposits, as necessary to support its investments.

The Federal Reserve will have auditors (bank examiners) in major money center banks continuously, moving from area to area. In the case of small country banks, the examiners may visit every three years, and complete their work in six weeks. They would visit more often if a bank had substantial exceptions in its last review. The examiners will confer with bank officers, as they conduct their review, to assure accurate understanding, and they will report to management for a discussion of results, before filing their final assessment. And because our central bank is owned by its members, who elect six of the nine directors of each of the twelve regional Reserve banks, there is some potential for giving the member bank (the one being examined) the benefit of the doubt.

The United States has a varied history of banking and bank regulation. Alexander Hamilton encouraged the creation of a central bank, fashioned after the Bank of England. The First Bank of the United States was chartered for twenty years, commencing in 1791. The new government owned 20% of the stock. It was banker to the new government, and to the commercial banks of the time, but it also competed with those other banks by offering deposits and loans. It would also occasionally embarrass those banks by presenting their bank notes for immediate exchange, threatening their liquidity and creating great resentment. (A bank note was originally simply a non-interest bearing receipt for gold, silver, coins, or other bank notes. They circulated, because of the convenience of paper means of payment, as long as the issuing bank was trusted.)When the 1st Bank of the US' charter expired, it was sold to Steven Girard. However, the inflation associated with the War of 1812-1815, led to a new central bank, the Second Bank of the United States with similar organization and responsibilities. Its charter was allowed to lapse in 1836, and there was no central bank in the United States until 1914. Banks were chartered and regulated by the states, and by the Comptroller of Currency, in the Dept. of the U.S. Treasury. The crisis of 1907 raised again the issue of central banking. Sen. Nelson Aldrich led Congress to create the Federal Reserve System, and President Wilson signed it into law on Dec.23, 1913.

Unlike other countries, our Federal Reserve System consists of **twelve regional banks**, owned by its members who are assessed a small fraction of their capital for the purchase of shares. There are nine directors of each bank: three selected by the large banks (city banks), three selected by the small banks (country banks), and three selected by the Board of Governors in Washington, DC. The seven governors, who constitute **The Board of Governors**, are nominated by the President and confirmed by the Senate for staggered 14 year terms, so that they will have some independence from political pressures. Nevertheless, resignations provide opportunities for the President to appoint more than four governors in eight years, and Washington is a small town, and congressional hearings and political pressures can be heavy.

Policy is formulated by the **Federal Open Market Committee** which includes all twelve bank presidents and seven governors. This committee (FOMC) meets every six weeks. Depending on the style of the chairman, staff presents reports on financial and economic conditions, the regional presidents report their local conditions and views, and the chairman either builds a consensus (Bernanke), or announces his policy preferences (Greenspan). Five of the twelve Presidents vote (New York, plus four others in rotation) and all seven Governors vote. This is the official vote which is recorded, but there is likely a broader consensus for the policy.

The Federal Reserve System has five important functions. 1) It serves as banker to the US Government, underwriting securities, taking government deposits, and honoring government payments. This avoid the conflicts of interest that exist in most states where commercial and investment banks compete for the favor of the local government to keep cheap deposits and enjoy large underwriting fees("pay to play"). 2) The FRS performs the payments clearing function for its member banks. Banks have always had a need to bundle the checks (orders from customers to transfer funds) and exchange them with the banks of origin. For this purpose, they organize **clearing houses** or contract with **correspondent banks**. The Federal Reserve improved this system by routing payments through its regional banks. The micro-encoding on the bottom of your checks is the routing instructions for the "proof" machines and total, balance, and package the checks for presentation to their origin. Today, the checks are filmed and the transfers communicated by secure computer network, but the principles remain the same. A reliable system for transferring funds is very important for facilitating commerce, especially across a large nation, and internationally. 3) The Federal Reserve regulates its members in accordance with the CAMEL principles that were described above. Banks are tempted to compromise liquidity and solvency in the pursuit of profit. If they fail, communities not only risk losing their savings, but also their access to credit. So, the integrity of the banking system is important to the health of the economy. The recession of 2008 amply demonstrates these risks. 4) The Federal Reserve also lends to its members, using their securities as collateral. There have been outright purchases of securities, such as the TARP program recently, but the more traditional practice is to *discount paper*, meaning lend a portion of the value of an approved list of securities. Also, the FRS will purchase securities with an agreement that the seller repurchase them at a higher price which constitutes a small gain similar to an interest charge. These are called **repurchase agreements** or "Repos." The purpose of this service is to provide immediate liquidity to a member, or to the entire system, during a crisis. Banks hold securities as a way of earning some income from their deposits, while waiting for good lending opportunities, and as a back-up to their primary liquidity --- cash in the vault and deposits at other banks. If they need more liquidity to manage their cash-flows of deposits and loans, they will sell some securities. In a general liquidity crisis, many financial institutions may try to sell at the same time, depressing securities prices, creating real or paper losses and so, imperiling the solvency of the banks. (Think Bear-Sterns, AIG, Indy-Mac, Country-wide, Merrill-Lynch, and Lehman Bros. in the crisis of 2008.) By borrowing from the FRS, the banks don't dump their securities at the same time, and prices need not collapse. This function was well-executed in the crisis of 1987, and arguably again in 2008. 5) Everyday, we hear about the Federal Reserve's conduct of domestic and international **monetary policy**. The idea is to regulate money supply and interest rates to achieve the optimal balance of supply and demand in the national economy, giving us full employment, economic growth, price stability, and a sustainable international balance of payments.

Money supply is important, because of its relationship to spending. A balanced economy has the right amount of spending to encourage the full-employment of resources, stable prices, and a sustainable international balance of payments. A substantial portion of money supply is provided by the central bank, and is often called, **money base**. In the United States, money base has usually been about one-eighth of money supply, but currently (2016), it's more than one-quarter. The rest of the money supply is provided by commercial banks, when they make loans.

Our Federal Reserve System uses three policy instruments to influence money supply and interest rates by changing money base. They are 1) Reserve Requirements, 2) Discount Loans and 3) Open Market Operations. **Reserve Requirements** specify a sum of cash in the vault and deposits at the central bank that must be held in proportion to the bank's deposit liabilities. Banks list their various liabilities daily, average them for the week, and apply a percentage rate to each (the reserve requirement for that class of deposits). The calculations and the required balances are reported weekly. I have seen rates as high as 10% for demand deposits (checking accounts) and 3% for savings accounts, but today, many rates are zero, or close to it. The idea is to limit the ability of the banks to expand their loans and investments by tying up deposits in required reserves (effectively non-interest bearing loans to the FRS, until recently when the FRS started paying interest on deposits). Many people incorrectly believe that reserve requirements somehow protect depositors. If the reserves are required, they are not available to protect anyone. Reserve requirements simply limit banks, and, by tying up deposits, raise the costs of funds for them. Changes in required reserves (increases reduce bank liquidity, and decreases raise liquidity) are a blunt instrument changing the banking system's excess reserves and thus their ability to make loans and alter money supply. Hence, our FRS relies less and less upon them.

More important are the **discount loans** which we described above. Members apply for loans offering a list of eligible collateral. Their regional Fed evaluates the proposal, and if agreed, then advances something less than the face value of the collateral. In normal times, these amounts are small, several hundred million dollars out of several trillion dollars of FRS obligations. The discount rate is the charge for borrowing. And the purpose of the service is to prevent the dumping of securities in a weak market. Recall that Bagehot called this "the Lender of Last Resort Function."

The most important method of influencing money supply and spending, by changing Federal Reserve assets and liabilities, the source of **money base**, is called **Open Market Operations**, meaning the buying or selling Treasury securities, (or other assets, including foreign currency deposits, "foreign exchange"). This is the most flexible method for changing money base, and operations are undertaken daily, when financial markets are open.

In the morning of every business day, at approximately 9:30 EST, the chairman of the Federal Reserve System, the President of the New York Federal Reserve Bank, and the Head Trader (also at the New York Fed) participate in a conference call. They share information on current market conditions and the activities of our own Treasury (receiving revenue and making payments) and foreign central banks (swapping dollar deposits with their own to regulate their own currencies' values). The three leaders then formulate a plan to neutralize the activities of these other players and add their own adjustments to achieve the overall goals of the FOMC for the period between meetings. The head trader returns to the floor, directs his staff to the appropriate actions. They solicit bids from registered government securities dealers, and complete the purchases and sales by late morning.

By buying or selling government securities, the dealers, and the banks and other customers that they represent, change their own holdings of securities and deposits at the Federal Reserve System. The rippling of subsequent transactions changes holdings of currency and deposits throughout the financial system. The purchases of securities by the Fed will raise their prices and depress their yields. The sellers will make decisions to hold currency or bank deposits, and the changes in bank deposits will change bank reserves. Accordingly, the banks will wish to alter their investments, including loans.

The sequence of changes in spending may begin with the creation of money base by the central bank whenever it chooses to purchase any asset. (It pays by creating a new FRS liability, either a deposit or currency.) This is money base which equals currency plus bank reserves. Then, the banks take their new deposits and other borrowed funds and invest in some combination of securities and loans. The purchase of securities doesn't increase their supply, but will increase their prices and depress interest rates. However, the issuance of new loans will increase the banks' assets (the loans) and liabilities (the deposits granted in exchange for the loan obligation). The deposits associated with the loans are new money. This money exists, until extinguished by repayment of the loan. Because the borrowers' purpose in borrowing is to spend, the increase in money supply increases spending.

To review the mechanics of changes in money supply:
step 1: Fed increases Money Base through purchases of Assets.
step 2: Public chooses Currency Vs. Demand Deposits.
step 3: Banks respond to change in Reserves.
step 4: New Loans increase Money Supply.
step 5: Borrowers spend their new Money, stimulating sales, production, and asset prices.

We call the relationship between money base, which the Federal Reserve System controls, and money supply which includes money base and the money created by bank lending, the **Money Multiplier**. If this relationship is stable, or at least predictable, then adjustments to money base can change money supply, and with the addition of one more ratio, the **velocity of money**, the level of total spending. This is the foundation of Monetary Policy.

The table below shows the relationships

	12/2007	12/2009	12/2011	12/2013
Money Base =	$ 856 billion	$ 1,797	$ 2,539	$ 3,272
Money Supply (M2) =	$ 7,606 billion	$ 8,385	$ 9,221	$ 10,686
money multiplier ratio =	8.9	4.7	3.6	3.3

As you can see from the table, a relationship which had been so stable, varying cyclically from 7-9, has been unreliable during the recent recession and weak recovery. In fact, of the increase in money supply over the six years (+$3,080 billion), five-sixths was provided by the Federal Reserve (+$2,416 billion). The banking system has only added $856 billion.

What determines this **money multiplier** ? The financial institutions, and their customers in the public who sell the securities, decide to hold a mix of currency and deposits. The banks that receive the new deposits choose to hold a combination of cash and deposits at other banks, securities, and new loans. In an uncertain environment, the banks and the public may choose to increase their liquidity (holding more cash and near cash assets, and reducing debts). And in a weak economy, the quality and volume of new loan requests may be poor and low. Finally, if banks are paying more attention to cleaning up problems: collecting loans, selling weak assets, and responding to regulatory criticism, they will not expand their loan portfolios and thus money supply does not grow as anticipated by the central bank.

So, the Federal Reserve typically responds to recession and falling inflation by increasing the growth rate of money base and anticipating a proportionate increase in money supply and spending. Interest Rates will decline. (They may be already declining, because of weak loan demand in a weak economy.) Ideally, spending revives under the influence of lower interest rates and increased system-wide liquidity. However, this link is not guaranteed.

Savers may not alter their behavior. Lower interest rates discourage saving and encourage spending (the substitution effect). Why save, if there is little reward ? Why not enjoy more consumption, now ? But low rates also encourage saving, because our wealth goals will be harder to achieve (the income effect). Golly, my savings are growing more slowly, so I'll need to save more to get to my goals....

And businesses will not borrow for investment, unless they need additional capacity to achieve their sales and profit goals. In a weak economy, businesses typically suffer from excess capacity. Until that capacity deteriorates through depreciation and obsolescence, and/or prospects for additional sales improve, businesses will not borrow to add to capacity. When they are ready to expand, the low interest rates will help, but until then, the low rates merely inflate asset prices. (a thrill for Wall St., but not too important to the rest of us. By the way, the much maligned J.M. Keynes pointed all of this out in The General Theory. Too bad, no one reads it, anymore.)

Complicating an already frustrating problem of regulating the economy through monetary policy is choosing the appropriate indicators. *Our goal is full-employment with a sustainable international balance of payments.* Unfortunately, measurements of GDP and employment are slow in arriving, and subject to errors and revisions. We generally don't know how the economy performed, until six months later. So, we are tempted to use easily and rapidly available indicators. Money supply data is received and aggregated every week. If it were perfectly correlated with spending, this would be helpful. The oldest relationship in economics is called the **Quantity of Money Equation**:

Money x velocity = Price Level x Real Gross Domestic Product
where "velocity" is a constant

Unfortunately, **velocity** is not a constant, as we will see in Part Five: Macroeconomics.

Even worse, is reliance on "the interest rate." Interest rates are just prices, the rental rates of money. They change in response to the supply of saving and the demand for credit. When an interest rate goes up, it signals an imbalance (Demand for short-term funds exceeds the Supply), but does not tell us whether demand increased more than supply, or supply decreased more than demand. When Jimmie Carter was President, the Federal Reserve responded to rising interest rates by increasing money base at 15% per annum. Why were they surprised that spending increased by 15% and prices by 13% ? If they had looked a money supply which was growing rapidly, they would have realized that the problem was rapid growth of money demand responding to negative real interest rates (interest rates below the rate of inflation).

Worst of all is a target for the international value of our money, the **foreign exchange rate**. During the Great Depression, our Federal Reserve focused on maintaining the international value of the dollar ($20/oz. gold), while money supply fell 27% from 12/28 to 4/33 and 12,500 banks failed.[1] Spending fell proportionately, and prices by 27% as well.[2] We will learn more about the conduct of monetary policy in Part Five: Macroeconomics. For now, let's conclude by observing that stabilizing the economy through monetary policy is not easy, and it isn't the only important function of our central bank.

Another important responsibility of the central bank is the regulation of the banking system. **Investment banks** help organizations to raise funds from savers. Investment banks facilitate the creation of a variety of new securities, and then undertake to sell these new securities to savers. They may, or may not choose, to hold some securities for their own account, (merchant banking), or for trading. These securities may be of any maturity: money market issues, intermediate term securities such as loans, but usually we associate investment banks with capital instruments such as shares and bonds. **Private banks** are owned by individuals, or partners, and make investments with money provided by those few and well-qualified owners. They are not incorporated. In the USA, **merchant banks** provide capital to businesses through equity investments. The distinguishing feature of **commercial banks** is that that they both take deposits and make loans. Today, a further distinction of commercial banks is that their deposits are insured by the Federal Deposit Insurance Corp. Because of the short maturities of their obligations to depositors, commercial banks prefer working capital loans. They may wander into term loans and consumer credit to the extent that their deposit base is stable. Thus, we should think of commercial banks as money market institutions and investment, private, and merchant banks as largely, but not exclusively, capital market institutions.

Because the provision of reliable means of payments, secure forms of saving, and the ready availability of credit, are so important to economic health and progress, and because the inclination to vary from prudent management principles in the pursuit of incremental profits, as well as the temptations of theft and embezzlement, banks are heavily regulated. After all, banks are the repositories of the savings of the public; banks create money through loans; banks purchase large volumes of securities; banks extend the credit which is vital to economic health; and banks assist governments in collecting taxes and by underwriting loans to governments. However, this necessary purpose of protecting the public, including other financial institutions, burdens banks by raising costs and reducing management flexibility.

If you doubt that regulation is necessary, consider that one-third of all banks in the US failed during the Great Depression and money supply declined by 27%, as mentioned above. During the high inflation of the 1970s, many Savings & Loans were losing deposits, or paying more for them than they earned on their portfolio of mortgage loans. Most would have been insolvent, if they had been required to mark their assets to market. And our history has many instances of outrageous fraud, most recently Bernie Madoff, and rogue traders such as Nick Leeson who brought down Barings Bank, and Jerome Kerviel of Societe General. Locally (San Diego, but with Santa Barbara connections), we have the J. David Dominelli scandal, a Ponzi scheme based on bogus Foreign Exchange trading.

And there are many predecessors, such as Charles Keating of Lincoln Savings & Loan who enlisted five senators (Cranston, DeConcini, Glenn, McCain, and Reigle) to defend him from "regulatory harassment." Initial convictions were over-turned (faulty instructions), but new convictions were obtained for bankruptcy and wire fraud. Lincoln S&L went bankrupt in 1989; the taxpayer bailout of Lincoln S&L cost $3 billion.

In 1972, Michael Sindona purchased control of Franklin National Bank from Lawrence Tisch and used it as a vehicle for money laundering. In 1974, Franklin National Bank (20th largest bank in the country at the time) failed. In 1984, the seventh largest bank in the country, Continental Illinois Bank, failed, largely because of bad loans purchased from the Penn Square Bank of Oklahoma. In 2008, Washington Mutual and Country-Wide banks failed because of large positions in "sub-prime" mortgage lending. For a while, Country-Wide originated 20% of all mortgages in the USA. And its founder/chairman/CEO, Angelo Mozilo, influenced Congress and key regulators through his "friends of Anthony" favored lending practices.

In my own experience, I recall being under intense pressure to make loans, as a new officer of a community bank in 1981, when the prime rate was 21% and we were lending at prime plus 3%. At those rates, there were only two kinds of borrowers making loan requests --- those who couldn't pay and those who had no intention of paying. (I focused on collecting existing loans and working with sound businesses that had been caught in this high rate squeeze.)

At about the same time, a manager, whom we all trusted more than any other, was discovered to have booked fictitious loans, embezzled the money, and advanced the loan due dates each month to hide the theft. Later, a customer that I had expelled from the bank for daily over-drafts for several months, successfully obtained a $300,000 loan, because the president of our bank was persuaded that the customer and I "had a personality conflict." (The bank took the full loss, because the court held that the bank should have known the customer was a bad risk.) Another time, I was criticized for sending back checks written on the overdrawn account of the CEO's son. When we discovered that he had a cocaine problem and was losing his father's business (and his mother's home {she had guaranteed a loan}), I never heard an apology. Do you agree that regulation is needed ?

In the United States, we have a dual banking system and a variety of regulatory agencies. Banks may be state, or federally, chartered. They are regulated by the banking commission of the state that charters them or by the Comptroller of Currency, an agency of the US Treasury. In addition, banks that chose to be members of the Federal Reserve System are regulated by it. And banks that are insured by the Federal Deposit Insurance Corporation (FDIC; virtually required to attract deposits) are also regulated by it. So, in addition to the banks own auditors, there will be visits from the state or the Comptroller's office, from the Federal Reserve, and from the FDIC.

The purpose of **Deposit Insurance** is to prevent bank runs (panics), which were common prior to the creation of the Federal Reserve System in 1914. When weakness was suspected, prudence led depositors to try to recover their funds, before the bank failed. However, the very process of withdrawals, when the bank held illiquid assets such as loans and securities, could cause a solvency crisis. Deposit insurance reassures customers that they will recover most of their deposits when their bank fails. Unfortunately, the availability of deposit insurance also creates **moral hazard**. There is no market discipline for the risk-taking banks, and no reward for the prudent banks. Their cost of funds will be similar, based on their status as an insured bank, rather than their financial strength.

Risk-Based Capital Requirements are an effort to compensate for this problem. They, assign weights to different asset classes, and then determine a suitable total capital requirement. For example, Cash & Treasuries 0%; municipal bonds 20%; mortgages 50%; loans 100%. So, if we believe that 10% capital is desirable, and the bank holds cash & treasuries 10, munis 10, mortgages 20, loans 60, then the capital requirement would be: $0 + 0.4 + 1.0 + 6 = 7.4$ even though the total assets are 100. A bank holding only cash and government securities might be required to hold only 2% equity, while a bank heavy with loans and mortgages would approach 8%. Risk-based deposit insurance premiums also discourage risky investments.

When a bank gets into trouble, insolvency can be addressed through discount lending from the Federal Reserve System. But bankruptcy will require liquidation, "purchase & assumption," the method by which the regulator mediates a sale to a healthy bank which purchases the assets and assumes the liabilities. Because the later exceed the former, the regulator often must buy some of the least attractive assets, or extend favorable loans to the buyer.

Regulators have developed a system whose elements are captured in the acronym **CAMEL**. They will audit for Capital adequacy, Asset Quality, Management Policies, Earnings and Liquidity. The bank will be rated from 1-5. These are often described as strong, satisfactory, fair, marginal, and unsatisfactory. The loan portfolio is particularly important. Loans are classified as Conforming, Non-conforming (to policy or regulation), and Scheduled (meaning dangerous concentrations with a customer or industry). Adversely classified loans are adjusted for exposure to risk with portions to be charged off right away, though efforts to collect will be continued. Substandard loans (because of a weakness of cash-flow or collateral) 20% charge-off; Doubtful (a strong probability of loss) 50% charge-off; and Loss (judged uncollectable) 100% charge-off. This is necessary, because banks will tend to carry loans on their books and even accrue interest (shown as income), even though the scheduled payments are not being made. This is misleading and can be fatal, as unrecognized losses "snow ball."

Finally, there are a number **Social Activism Laws** imposed by Congress in response to pressures from constituencies. Some serve the purpose of assisting unsophisticated bank customers, such as **Truth in Lending Disclosure**, which helps borrowers to understand the true costs of the loan. Others cater to groups that feel unfairly excluded from access to credit, such as the **Equal Credit Opportunity Act**, as if banks would ignore profitable lending opportunities. A source of losses, and more recently a contributor to the financial crisis of 2008, is the **Community Reinvestment Act** which requires proportionate lending in the markets which the bank serves.

Other government agencies can also skew the management strategies of the banks by favoring, or even requiring, lending that would otherwise be considered imprudent. The **Federal National Mortgage Association** ("Fannie Mae") purchases mortgages from banks with money raised by issuing its own bonds. From 2000 to 2008, FNMA increased the portion of mortgages which must be made to less creditworthy borrowers as a condition of continued purchases. Banks were required to make imprudent loans and did so in anticipation of rapid resale to Fannie Mae. (As Charles Prince, Chairman/CEO of Citigroup, said in July 2007, "As long as the music is playing, you've got to get up and dance. We're still dancing.") When the crisis hit, the banks and agencies were stuck with bad mortgages in their portfolio pipelines. The result of this easy credit was initially housing price inflation, and then massive defaults and foreclosures. Extending credit to those who cannot pay is not doing them any favor.

Many of these regulators were created during the Great Depression, when banks and brokerages were failing, and many families and businesses suffered heavy losses and were starved for credit. One of the most important was **The US Banking Act of 1933**, popularly known by its sponsors, Senator Carter Glass and Congressman Henry Steagall, as **The Glass-Steagall Act**. Its four provisions limited the securities activities of commercial banks (defined as institutions that take deposits (soon to be insured by the FDIC) and make loans). Members of the

Federal Reserve System were prevented from 1) dealing in non-government securities for customers, 2) investing in non-investment grade securities for customers, 3) underwriting or distributing non-government securities, and 4) affiliating with companies involved in such activities. Banks had to choose to be commercial banks, or investment banks which would be free to own and underwrite all kinds of securities, but would not take deposits and would not benefit from deposit insurance. For many years thereafter, many of the most important investment banks were partnerships which used the partners' capital, heavily leveraged with bank borrowings, to carry out their activities. This "own money at risk" was important in assuring prudent management. Repeal of Glass-Steagall was completed by the Financial Service Modernization Act of 1999 (the Gramm-Leach-Bliley Act), only a few years after many major investment banks had converted from partnerships to joint-stock corporations. And the wild times began ....

Along the way, Congress passed **The Financial Institutions Reform, Recovery, and Enforcement Act of 1989** (FIRREA) as the final phase in resolving the Savings & Loans crisis that had been caused by the volatile inflation and rising interest rates of the 1970s. Economic recovery from 1982-1989 brought inflation and interest rates down, enabling Congress to clean up the mess without huge expenses to the Treasury. The **Resolution Trust Corp**. was established to close insolvent S&Ls and pay off their insured depositors. A new **Office of Thrift Supervision** assumed the regulatory authority that had been so badly bungled by the **Federal Home Loan Bank Board** (a FRS clone for S&Ls). The FDIC assumed the responsibility for deposit insurance and the FSLIC, like the FHLBB was abolished. A new Federal Housing Finance Board took over the duty of supervising the twelve Federal Home Loan Banks. Crucially, *FIRREA gave Freddie Mac and Fannie Mae new responsibilities to support mortgages for low income families*. This had nothing to do with the clean-up and was the origin of the pressure on banks to make imprudent loans to "sub-prime borrowers", a decade later.

Gramm-Leach-Bliley removed the barriers to commercial banks, investment banks, and insurance company affiliation. Sandy Weil's Citibank group combined Citibank, Travelers' Insurance, Primerica, and Smith-Barney. The idea of one-stop shopping for financial services (the financial "supermarket") was fashionable. (It hasn't worked out, and in 2015, the trend is toward divestment and renewed focus by financial institutions.) Rep. John Dingell had argued that the result of permitting such combinations would be banks that would be "too big to fail," taking excessive risk, and requiring tax-payer financed bail-outs. But the pressure of the numerous and well-financed Wall Street lobbyists was irresistible, and academic economists were often supporters because of their excessive confidence in new concepts of financial engineering and risk management. Unfortunately, Dingell was right.

The trends in banking regulation had been toward relaxation throughout the post-WWII period, but the financial crisis of 2008 quickly changed the mood. Congress's response was the Dodd-Frank, **The Wall Street Reform and Consumer Protection Act of 2010**. Ironically, Sen. Dodd and Rep. Frank had been obstacles to financial reform during the prior decade, publicly humiliating regulators such as Brooksley Born (Chairman CFTC) and Sheila Bair (Chairman of the FDIC) who warned of the impending crisis. (Dodd and Frank did not salvage their careers and were encouraged to retire by the voters.) The purpose of Dodd-Frank was to promote financial stability by improving accountability and transparency, to end "too big to fail," to protect the taxpayer from further "bail-outs," and to protect consumers of financial services. All major financial regulatory agencies were effected --- FDIC, SEC, SIPC, the Comptroller of Currency (US Treasury), and the Federal Reserve System. Three new agencies were created, The

Financial Stability Oversight Council, The Office of Financial Research, and The Bureau of Consumer Financial Protection. The Office of Thrift Supervision was eliminated and its powers transfer to the FDIC, the Federal Reserve System, and the Comptroller of Currency.

Thus far, we have focused on the regulation of commercial banks. And you may rightly conclude that bank regulation is complex and onerous. Is it effective ? Recurrent financial crises suggest that the industry is susceptible. Regulators are subject to political pressure, and politicians are too unsophisticated to be reliable. Still, the alternative is to return to the rampant manipulation and fraud of the nineteenth and early twentieth century, and the more recent excesses of greed and incompetence in the S&L and commercial banking business.

Questions for review and tests:
How is the Federal Reserve System organized and what are its responsibilities ?
How large should Money Supply be ?
Explain why too much money causes inflation and too little money causes recession.
How does the Federal Reserve System influence Money Supply ?

[1] Milton Friedman and Anna Schwartz, A Monetary History of the United States, Princeton U. Press 1963 pages 351 and 712-714

[2] Bureau of Labor Statistics, Consumer Price Index, historic tables.

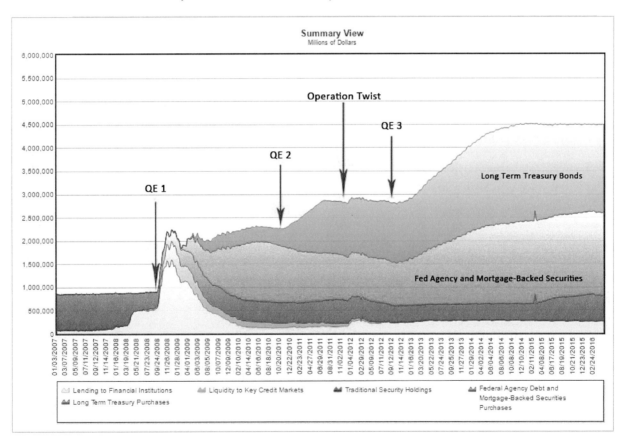

A chart of Federal Reserve System holdings of Securities. Source: Federal Reserve Bank of Cleveland

Lesson #3.3 Interest Rates and the Time Value of Money

Money represents a claim on society's resources. Useful for transactions, precaution, and speculation, money can also be considered ration coupons. If you have in your wallet $40, then you can claim $40 of society's resources. And in order to claim resources that you do not already own, you will need to exchange something of value. In most cases, that "something of value" is money, precisely because money is so useful in acquiring other resources. In order to accumulate the resources that we desire for current enjoyment, or future production, we need money. Indeed, often our ability to take advantage of opportunities is limited by our income and liquid wealth. Access to additional money gives us access to expanded opportunities and can help us to manage risks.

Those who enjoy income, or wealth, compare their own opportunities for spending now with their plans for the future. They may save by hoarding commodities, or other real assets, but they may be enticed to lend money to borrowers, if they are offered an attractive reward. (Remember that by **saving**, we mean abstinence.) **Investment** is a form of spending whose intent is to maintain or increase our ability to produce in the future. Thus, by saving, we sacrifice the use of the money now and accept some risk of loss. Yet, we may wish to save for those future opportunities or expenses, in which case, we must look for methods of "storing value," until we need it. If the savers lend, then the borrowers are able to take advantage of more and bigger opportunities now. So, the saver/lenders deserve a reward for their sacrifice, and the borrowers are willing to share their gain with the lenders who make their gain possible. We can see that the ability to borrow and lend allows us to separate the earning of income from the act of spending, and the interest rate plays a vital role in facilitating this transfer of purchasing power. Consider the business that could earn a 20% return on investment, if they could borrow the money needed for assets and operations. That business would be happy to pay 10% interest, or dividends, to their creditors. This willingness of borrowers to pay interest means that the use of money today has an opportunity cost, the rate of interest that could be earned or must be paid.

But these observations only describe one of many important roles of **interest rates**. The interest rate is not only *the reward for lending and the cost of borrowing*, but also a *bridge between present and future value*. If we wish to compare cash positions at different times, we must use the interest rate. We are all familiar with compound interest which calculates the growth of principal over time. The formula is:

Present Value   times   (1 + interest rate) $^{Time\ in\ years}$ *equals   Future Value*

So, one dollar saved today at 10% for twenty years would be   **$1 (1.10) ^{20} = $ 6.73**
This is the glory of compound interest --- each year the principal grows and in the next year, interest is earned on the new, larger amount. We might say that, in a world of certainty, a dollar today is worth $6.73 in twenty years, if the interest rate is 10% for the whole twenty years. What is less obvious is that a certain promise of $6.73 in twenty years is equivalent to $1 today. Why ? Because, if we had $1 today, we could save it, and have the same $6.73 in twenty years. In other words, we can go forward by multiplying (compounding), or backwards by dividing (discounting). In the latter case, the formula would be:

188

Present Value   equals   Future Value divided by (1 + interest rate),   once for each year

This ability to compare cash at different times by using the opportunity cost is essential for the evaluation of opportunities that generate varied payments and receipts over time. By compounding or discounting, we can render the cash-flows comparable. The following table demonstrates the use of these principles in the evaluation of two alternatives for the development of property which I undertook years ago in California:

Montecito Valley Ranch Sales & Profits Estimates   8/30/1991

Site	Land Area	Land Value	House Area	House Value	Totals
1	2.06	550	4800	960	1510
2	1.52	600	5800	1160	1760
3	1.78	550	5300	1060	1610
4	2.51	1050	6100	1220	2270
5	2.8	1000	5800	1160	2160
6	1.13	650	4900	980	1630
7	1.14	650	4800	960	1610
8	1.44	700	5300	1060	1760
9	3.06	950	6200	1240	2190
10	1.42	800	6300	1260	2060
11	1.89	700	3334	300	1000
12	3.18	950	6500	1300	2250
13	1.22	650	5000	1000	1650
14	1.18	650	4500	900	1550
15	1.77	650	5500	1100	1750
16	4.64	1100	5700	1140	2240
17	12.59	1350	6500	1300	2650
18	5.49	1400	5800	1160	2560
totals:	50.82	14,950	98,134	19,260	34,210

total estimated sales value of land & residences:
THIRTY-FOUR MILLION TWO HUNDRED TEN THOUSAND DOLLARS

Assumptions:
1) lot areas per Penfield & Smith Tract Map 14,038 (revised 8/28/90)
2) improvement values at $200 per square foot
3) only residential improvements on lot #11 are measured at cost.
   Hobby Horse stable is not valued.
4) construction costs are estimated at $140 per square foot.
5) marketing costs are assumed to be 5% of gross sales revenue

Profit Estimates:

First Alternative {no appreciation & no discounting in $'000}

Sales	less	construction costs	less	marketing costs	**profit**

34,210	2700 + 13,600	1710	**16,200**

Second Formulation { appreciation at 5% per year; discount at 12% }

	Year 1	Year 2	Year 3	Year 4	Year 5	Year 6	Year 7	Year 8
Sales	0	1	3	3	3	3	3	2
Value	0	1900	5700	5700	5700	5700	5700	3800
Costs								
Construction	2770	1500	2200	2200	2300	2300	2300	800
Commissions	0	100	300	300	300	300	300	10
Profit								
	-2700	300	3200	3200	3100	3100	3100	2900
with appreciation:								
	-2700	315	3530	3700	3770	3960	4150	3890
with appreciation & discounted:								
	-2411	251	2513	2351	2139	2006	1877	1760
cumulative discounted value of appreciated profits:								
	{-2411}	{-2160}	353	2704	4843	6849	8726	**10486**

Estimated profit for fully built & sold project, expressed in present value: $10,486,000

Third Formulation for Pure Lot Sales:						totals:
lot sales 1	3	3	3	4	4	17
Gross Sales						
830	2490	2490	2490	3320	3320	14,940
Costs						
2742	125	125	125	166	166	3,449
Cash-flow						
{-1912}	2365	2365	2365	3154	3154	13,403
With 5% appreciation:						
{-19112}	2483	2607	2738	3834	4025	15,687
discounted at 12%:						
{-1707}	1979	1856	1740	2176	2039	**8,083**

Present discounted value of pure lot sales: $8,083,000

You can see that the procedure requires estimating the cash-flows, both payments and receipts, for all periods, selecting a discount rate (I used my cost of capital and also an expected inflation rate), and applying those interest rates to all the cash-flows. In this case, I discounted to obtain an estimate of what I would need to save today to generate these expected future cash-flows. The initial expense (investment) to acquire the property, plan, and obtain approvals was $3,600,000. Thus, the gain from lots sales would be $4,483,000, and from full build out $6,886,000. We chose the lot sales, as less risky and sufficiently rewarding. The actual outcome was better than expected.

This exercise hints at another important role for **interest rates** ---- *a bridge between income and capital value*. We might ask what would be we willing to pay to own a building whose net rents are $1,000,000 per year ? Ignoring for the moment the potential for capital gain or loss, the **capital value** would depend on our required rate of return, an interest rate. For example, if we require a yield (notice the synonyms) of 10%, then $1 million is 10% of what ? The answer is $10,000,000. Similarly, if we see a building for sale at ten million dollars, and its annual net income is one million dollars, we would say that the buyer expects a yield of 10% on his purchase price.

So, the common formula is	**Value times Yield equals Income**
But it is equally true that	**Income divided by Yield equals Value**
Or	**Income divided by Value equals Yield**

Not so obvious, but very importantly, the use of interest rates to reward savers who transfer their funds to borrowers, and the use of the interest rate to compare the cash-flows of various projected opportunities, and the use of interest rates to compare cash-flows to one-time prices, *all improve economic growth, reduce inflation, and enhance the equality of incomes.* Remember the functions of **finance**. If we move money, we move purchasing power, we move the pattern of spending, and thus, we move the distribution of resources. Those with the best opportunities can claim them by offering interest to those with the money. Production increases, and with more supply come lower prices, and the gains are shared by workers who have moved to these profitable activities, and with the entrepreneurs who borrow, and the savers who lend.

Now, let us turn our attention to calculating Interest Rates. **Simple interest** multiplies the interest rate by the number of years and applies the result to the initial principal. There is no compounding. This would have been used years ago, when calculations were difficult to complete. Raising the simple interest rate charged could compensate for the lack of compounding. The formula:

Principal x interest rate x time in years = interest earned

Compound interest is common today, in part because our calculators make the computation easy, and we like the idea. We multiply the principal times (one plus the interest rate), once for each year until maturity, as shown in the formulas on the first page of this lesson. The use of the exponent for the number of years is just short-hand for:

Principal x (1+ i) x (1+ i) x (1+ i) x (1+ i) x (1+ i) x (1+ i) x (1+ i) …..

For daily compounding, multiply by (one plus the interest rate/365), once for every day until maturity.

Often, we use the expressions rate of return, or yield, as equivalent to the interest rate. They are expressed as percentage gains or losses, at an annual equivalent. The difference is that the interest rate is often a contracted rate contained in the promise of a security. The rate of return, or yield, is often an estimate of expected, or actual, gain or loss, of which the interest may be only a portion. Some common yields are:

Current Yield = the annual interest received   divided by market price paid

For example, a bond with a par value of $1000, a coupon rate of 6%, and ten years to maturity, is trading at $1090. Hence, the annual interest would be $60 divided by a price of $1090, gives a current yield of 5.5%. This can be useful to judge whether the current income is attractive, but it ignores the potential for capital gains, or losses, as the price changes. Similarly, current yield ignores the principal payment at maturity. Considering the same bond, if we buy it for $1090 and hold it to maturity, we will lose $90. This depresses our result. Hence, we have another concept which includes both income and capital gain or loss. We can call it, **Holding Period Yield**, or **Yield to Maturity**, depending on our intention and expectation. To capture the compound interest effect, we use a weighted average of our initial purchase price and our final selling or maturity value. Consider the same example:

$$\textbf{Yield to maturity} = \frac{\textbf{Annual Coupon Interest} + [\{\textbf{Par - Price Paid}\}/\textbf{Time held}]}{\textbf{0.6 Price Paid} + \textbf{0.4 Par Value at maturity}}$$

Substituting our numbers:

$$\frac{\$60 + [\$1000-\$1090]/10}{654 + 400} = \$51/1054 = 4.84\%$$

You can see how that final loss, even after ten years, depresses the yield. Of course, we might conclude that the current yield of 5.5% and the yield to maturity of 4.84% are adequate given considerations of risk, liquidity, taxability, and comparison with other similar opportunities.

There is not just one interest rate; there are many interest rates. The variety of characteristics of the many securities available suggests that they will be exchanged at different prices and yields, depending on their supply and demand. The Supply of securities depends on the history of issues by those who wish to raise funds (we might call them borrowers), while the Demand for securities depends on the preferences of savers. Investment banks study carefully the inventory of existing securities, and the flow of new ones, to determine the patterns of supply and demand, and the preferences of issuers and savers. We might think of the interest rates and securities prices, as fluctuating to compensate for the characteristics of the security, and its attractiveness to savers. (Recall that, when the price of a specific security changes, while the promised payments do not, the yield changes in the opposite direction. For example, if I pay $20 and you pay $16 a few days later, for security that pays a $1 dividend, I will earn 5% and you will earn 6 ¼ %.)

Simply put, we can say that interest rates fluctuate, because of shifts in the supply of savings and the demand for credit. Rents, like prices, adjust to balance supply and demand. *The interest rate is just the rental rate of money.* This is why we must look at all sources of the supply of saving, and the demand for credit, to understand the movement of interest rates. For example, you will rarely see an increase in long-term interest rates without a strong demand for new residential mortgages, although government and corporate borrowing matter, too.

We often observe that interest rates rise during an economic boom, when borrowers compete for loanable funds, and decline during recession, when the demand for credit falls. In addition, expectations for future inflation matter. Savers will require a "real" reward for their abstinence. If the rate of inflation is 2%, then a yield of 6% may be acceptable. But when inflation is 8%, the same 6% would mean a loss of purchasing power. Savers would reasonably require a contract, or "nominal" rate, of 12%. Failing that, the saver will spend now, or hoard real assets which will maintain their inflation adjusted value. Borrowers may be willing to pay the higher 12%, if they have confidence that they can raise their income by more and in an inflationary environment, the borrower who purchases now, pays the current price and sells at the inflated price.

Other important determinants of yields are default risks and liquidity. **Default** occurs when any element of the contract is violated. **Liquidity** is the ability to sell the security quickly, at low transaction cost, and with assured value. Default risk and lack of liquidity are undesirable. Hence, securities with these unattractive qualities must offer higher yields to attract savers. We often compare the yields of US Treasury debt of various maturities, which we consider default risk free and highly liquid, to other securities. For example, we track the difference between Treasury bond yields and corporate bond yields. When the difference is small, we think that savers are optimistic and willing to pay more for corporate bonds, because risks are considered small. When the difference (the spread) widens, we suspect that savers are buying Treasuries and avoiding Corporates which they perceive as riskier. Thus, the spread becomes an indicator of saver confidence. We can also look at the differences in yields for corporate bonds based on their ratings by investor services. As a rule of thumb, "A" quality bonds are making payments as agreed and can be expected to do so even in difficult times, and "B" quality bonds are making their payments but may have difficulty in troubled times. A large spread suggests saver fear, and a small spread suggests a lack of anxiety. Please, remember that only a fool goes in search of risk, assuming that with risk comes high yields. No, no, no. Instead, we ask if the offered price is low enough, and thus yield high enough, to compensate for the risks associate with this security. It's the risk that depresses the price and thus raises the yield required.

Differences in **tax status** can lead to different prices and yields. Savers compare opportunities, and adjust for differences. In the same way, that they can be enticed away from their preferred maturities, and risk and liquidity characteristics, by higher yields, differences in tax treatment can enhance or discourage purchases. For example, interest payments made on the debt state and local governments are not taxed by the Federal government, and interest paid on Treasury debt is not taxed by state and local governments. We call the state and locals debt **municipal bonds**, or "Munis." Consider the alternatives of buying Treasury, Municipal, and Corporate Bonds:

The corporate bond is taxed both federally and locally. If the respective tax rates are 24% and 9%, then a corporate bond that pays 7%, yields net after tax 4.69%. The Treasury Bond that pays 6% but is subject to Federal Tax, with no local tax, yields net after tax of 4.56%. And the Municipal bond that pays 5%, with no Federal Tax, yields net after tax 4.56%, possibly the full 5% if "double tax exempt", meaning exempt from state as well as Federal Income Tax.
We can also "gross up" the expected yield to maturity to a Taxable equivalent yield:

Municipal yield 5% divided by {1 - the tax rate} = taxable equivalent yield

Thus, the double tax exempt bond offering 5% would be equivalent to Treasury offering 6.58% or a corporate bond offering 7.46%. We are asking, "What would I need to earn, if the security were taxable?" We should not be surprised to see that pre-tax Treasury and Muni yields are predictably below corporate yields.

Another important influence on interest rates is **maturity**. Savers have preferred maturities based on their plans for income and expenses. For example, a young couple planning for retirement may have a thirty year goal. For their daughter's education, the target may be fifteen years in the future. And they may be saving for a down payment on a home which they hope to purchase in five years. Businesses may be borrowing short-term to manage cash-flow, medium term for equipment, and long-term for factories. The interest rates for securities of different maturities will vary depending on the preference of savers and borrowers. When we compare the interest rates at different maturities, we call it, **The Term Structure of Interest Rates**. When we plot the different rates, we call the result, **The Yield Curve**.

To draw an accurate and useful yield curve, we need to compare bonds that are identical in every respect except maturity. For that reason, we use US Treasury zero-coupon bonds. They have the same default risk, very similar liquidity, and no coupon effect. (Bonds with different coupons will sell at different prices and yields, based on the timing of the cash-flows. For example, a high coupon bond, say 7%, will be less volatile than a low coupon bond, say 4%, because more of the total payments come earlier for the first {the 7% bond}. And of course, the high coupon bond will always sell for a higher price, because its payments are larger.)

We anticipate that longer maturity bonds will sell at lower prices and higher yields than shorter maturity bonds, because the long bonds are less liquid and riskier, not in the sense of default risk (we're comparing US Treasuries), but with respect to price and reinvestment risk. **Price risk** occurs when the price changes as a result of general conditions, such as changes in the rate of inflation, or market interest rates. When interest rates change, all securities will be reevaluated and their prices will move accordingly. In the spring of 1987, when market interest rates rose by 1%, long-term bond prices fell by 15% in order to match the available yields. **Reinvestment risk** occurs when we have a target for wealth which requires reinvesting the income received from our securities. Every time we receive an interest payment, we must reinvest the money to achieve our goal through compound interest. If rates fall during our holding period, we must reinvest at the new lower rates, depressing the growth of our wealth. So, in general we like to find securities that match our holding period, or some variation thereof (We'll discuss the concept of **duration** in lesson #3.4 and in Part Six of this book.) Of course, we might be enticed out of our comfort zone, to shorter or longer, maturities, if the rewards are attractive. Here is a normal yield curve, taken from an article posted on Wikipedia. Notice that the difference between Money Market rates (maturity less than one year) and capital markets rates (maturity more than ten years) is about 2% (or in Wall St. jargon: "200 basis points").

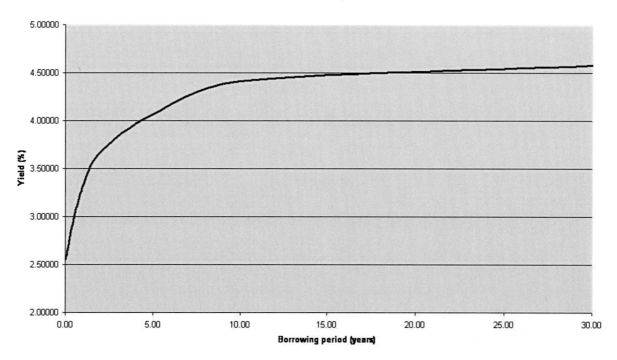

Yield curve as at 9th February 2005 for USD

Many savers prefer near matches of maturities and holding periods. This suggests that there are market segments, such as the money market for managing liquidity, intermediate market for property & casualty insurance companies and equipment financing, and capital market for life insurance, mortgages, and corporate bonds. Each market has a flow of funds and resulting interest pattern, but they are separated, because the participants do not perceive the securities as substitutes.

Another contributor to the shape of the Yield curve is **liquidity preference**. This is the idea that for considerations of risk, savers prefer shorter maturities, and borrowers prefer longer maturities. Hence, savers who prefer more liquidity to less, will require a reward for investing in securities involving less liquidity. And borrowers will be willing to pay that "premium."

However, there are savers who are willing to move out of their comfort zone (their preferred market segment), if the reward is great enough. The markets and their interest rates will be loosely connected. Consider the yield shown above (Feb.9, 2005). If I were willing to take the risks (price and reinvestment) associated with longer maturities, I could earn and extra 2% per year. Will I ? Consider my possibilities. The final calculation of my holding period yield will be the outcome of my principal growing at the contracted interest rates. For example, I might have a planning period of fifteen years. I could purchase a bond with a fifteen year maturity, and in the case above, I would earn 4.5% each year. If I could reinvest my interest receipts at 4.5%, my compound yield would be 4.5%. However, each year, I am closer to maturity, my reinvestment period is shorter, and my likely yield on the reinvested income lower. Another choice, would be to purchase a longer term bond, such as thirty year maturity, and earn slightly more. I still have reinvestment risk, but I also have price risk, because I plan to sell in fifteen years and I don't know what price the remaining payments of the bond will fetch at that time. Finally, I could choose a short-term bond, say five years, and reinvest the entire principal plus interest in something else for the remaining period. In fact, there are a variety of possibilities (a sequence of 15 one-year bonds, or 5 three year bonds … You get the idea.) What would I do ? I would choose the strategy that will give me the best combined yield.

To review, we are considering three strategies. 1) Buy short term and roll over as these securities mature, 2) Buy long-term and sell when I am ready to cash-out and use the money for my planned purpose, and 3) Match maturity to my holding period, accepting the reinvestment risk. (There is a fourth strategy, using **duration** that will be discussed in Part Six: Investing.) To decide which strategy to use, I must consider my expectations for future interest rates. For example, if I expect interest rates to rise, I might be smart to buy a short-term bond, or even hold cash. I would sacrifice some yield now (look above, 4% for five years vs. 4.5% for fifteen years), but my bond would mature and I could purchase a new bond in five years at the new higher rate. And I would avoid the decline in value of any long-term bond as interest rates rise. On the other hand, if I think that rates will fall. I might choose to purchase a long-term bond, taking advantage of today's high rates and enjoying a nice capital gain, when I sell. If I am uncertain of the trend of interest rates, I might choose to match the maturity of my bond to my holding period.

The implication of this, **expectations theory** of the yield curve, is that when savers expect interest rates to rise, they will shorten the maturities of their holding, buying near term maturities (whose prices will rise and yields fall) and selling long-term bonds (depressing their prices and therefore raising their yields). The yield curve will become steeper.

On the other hand, when savers feel that interest rates are likely to fall, they will sell short-term securities in order to buy long-term bonds, locking in today's high rates and anticipating nice capital gains, when interest rates do fall. The Yield curve will become flat, or even inverted. That is short-term maturities will fall in price (rising in yield) and long-term bonds will respond to rising demand by increasing in price (and falling in yield).

You might logically ask, why would anyone purchase a long-term bond whose price has risen above par and which yields only 4% if purchased now, when they can earn 6% on a two or three year note ? The answer is that the yield curve only captures yield to maturity and does not reflect potential capital gains or losses. If we normally require an extra 1-2% on thirty year bonds over 2-3 notes, then, the condition described suggests that savers expect a capital gain of 4% to get their required 8% vs. the 6% offered on those 2-3 year notes.

So, we can use the **Yield Curve** to interpret the expectations of savers, remembering that those expectations are often wrong. When we see a normal yield curve (rising 1-2%), savers appear to expect a stable pattern of rates. The required increase is the "normal forwardation," a typical reward for sacrificing liquidity. When we see steep yield curve (rising 3% or more), we can conclude that savers expect interest rates to increase and are avoiding long-term bonds and their anticipated declines in values. When we see a flat or inverted yield curve (in the 1980-1982 recession, short-term rates were 3.5% higher than long-term rates.), savers are buying long-term bonds in anticipation of large capital gains when rates decline. (In that 1980-1982 period, bond rates declined by 5% and many existing bonds increased in value by 20%, or more.)

We can even use the yield curve to predict future interest rates, with the strong caveats: *expectations are often wrong.* (Don't bet the bank.) Take the simple case of the yield curve on January 2, 2004, the first working day of the year. The five year T-bond yield was 3.45% and the 10 year T-bond 4.45%. I could consider a five year bond followed by another five year bond, or the one ten year bond, if I thought that the combination would earn more. Savers will purchase the combination that they believe will give them the highest yield. As they buy and sell, prices and yields adjust. There is no more incentive to change allocations when the combinations will generate the same results. So, if I am indifferent to the buy the short-term and roll-over to another or buy the long-term, then we can interpolate the expected five-year rate:

$$\text{Principal } (1.0345)^5 \quad (1+X)^5 \quad = \quad \text{Principal } (1.0445)^{10} \quad -> \quad X = 5.23\%$$

Remembering that the yield curve reflects the decisions of many thousands of sophisticated market participants, as well as millions of savers staying within their preferred maturities, and these securities traders are actually buying and selling ("putting their money where their mouth is"), we can have confidence that the yield curve reflect a consensus of expectations. However, if we recall that the "normal fowardation," or shape to the yield curve, our estimate may exaggerate expectations of future rates.

In November of 1981, while vice president of a bank with asset-liability management as a collateral responsibility, I plotted a yield curve for treasury bills, weekly for one year (these money market rates are important to commercial banks). The yield curve rose for six months and then took a sharp drop. It inverted. I suggested to my directors that the participants in the money market were telling us that rate would drop sharply in the spring. I even interpolated the expected rates, week by week. I recommended a conservative strategy in case the expectations were realized. I recommended fixing loan rates and floating deposit rates. Where deposits rates were to be fixed, I recommended shortening maturities by offering better yields for shorter Certificates of Deposit. In that instance, the yield curve proved very accurate. Interest rates dropped in June, and continued to fall for several years.

Consider that large inversion of the bond yields in the same period (3.5% in 1981). If the five year rate was 14.5% and ten year rate was 14%, what was the yield curve suggesting five year rate will be in 1986 ? Solution 13.64%. If my bond portfolio has a duration of 20 years, then I could expect a capital gain of (0.36 X 20) = 7.2%, more than compensating for giving up ½% for five years.

CHART 1
Yield curve shapes

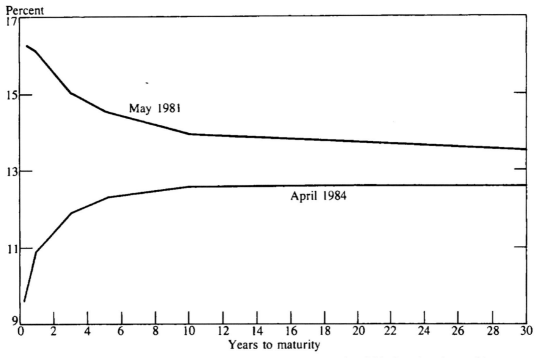

Source: Alan Garner, "The Yield Curve and Inflationary Expectations" Federal Reserve Bank of Kansas City Review September/October 1987

Permit me one final observation before we leave interest rates, for now. We often read about the Federal Reserve controlling interest rates. This is as silly as the idea of controlling prices. The Federal Reserve will monitor various interest rates, for example, the **Federal Funds Rate** at which banks lend deposits to each other as a measure of money market liquidity, and the thirty year US Treasury bond rate, as a proxy of capital market conditions. In combination with changes in volumes of deposits and securities outstanding, the movement of the relevant interest rate is suggestive. For example, rising rates and volumes suggest the demand for credit at that maturity is growing more rapidly than the supply of savings offered. Falling rates and volumes suggest falling demand with little change in supply. Rising rates and falling volumes suggest falling supply with little change in demand, and falling rates with rising volumes suggest supply growing faster than demand.

The only way in which the Federal Reserve can fix an interest rate is to fill the gap between Supply of Saving and Demand for Credit for that type of security, *at its target interest rate*. When the supply of bonds exceeds the demand, a Federal Reserve interest rate strategy would require large purchases of T-Bills, T-Notes, or T-Bonds, (depending on the interest rate to be manipulated). In the absence of such intervention, bond prices would decline and associated interest rates would rise. Similarly, when the demand for securities by savers is strong, their prices will tend to increase, and interest rates will fall. This occurred globally from 2000-2008, when extraordinary saving by the prosperous in emerging nations sought safe havens. The central banks could have kept interest rates up, only by providing more bonds. Even our large federal deficits of the period were not enough.

What happened during the unprecedented government deficits of President Obama's first term ? The Federal Reserve bought trillions of dollars of bonds, and so, prevented interest rates from rising. Accordingly, our conclusion should be that the interest rates are determined by the Supply of Saving and the Demand for Credit, from all sources. The Federal Reserve is only one player, although a major one. And its focus on fixing an interest rate requires the purchase or sale of securities to balance total demand and total supply of those securities at the target rates.

Questions for review and tests:
Define interest rates and what economic functions do they serve ?
Distinguish nominal interest rates from real interest rates.
What is the relationship between interest rates and asset prices ?
What is risk and how do we measure risk ?
Explain the Term Structure of Interest Rates. {Define and analyze}
How can it be used to anticipate interest rate movements ?

The king's palace and the adjacent financial center of Fes, Morocco. The Moroccan King welcomed and protected the refugees from Spain.

In contrast, the Hapsburg Kings of Spain who implemented the inquisition, were bankrupt five times during the 16th century, "the Golden Age," a period of conquest and unparalleled riches from their new empires.

Lesson #3.4 Commercial Banks

Traditionally, a bank would take deposits of bullion or coin, and issue a receipt (a bank note). The **bank notes** would be acceptable in exchange within the neighboring market area. Hence, the bank notes became money. This form of money was more convenient than carrying gold, or silver, which were heavy, indivisible, and subject to loss or theft. As banking evolved, these complementary services of taking deposits for safe-keeping, easy access, and the provision of convenient means of payment evolved. The issuance and redemption of bank notes was succeeded by the processing of orders to pay against the customer's account (checks), and the provision of **official checks** (money orders, travelers' checks, cashier's checks). Still later, banks introduced electronic funds transfer (by secure telephone, telex, credit and debit cards, and international clearing networks {such as SWIFT}). The stability of deposit totals, despite the ebb and flow of deposits and withdrawals by individual depositors, led banks to extending loans to businesses, governments, and later, to consumers. So, we typically identify three functions of commercial banks: providing 1) means of payment, 2) methods for saving, and 3) loans (credit). By the 1970s, banks recognized that these activities are all methods of providing customer services that manage their liquidity --- accepting deposits when their customers have surpluses, making loans when the customers have deficits, and clearing and receiving payments. They saw new opportunities for services that reduce the risks of illiquidity and hedge other financial risks, as well. In the United States, the legal definition of a bank is "a member of the Federal Deposit Insurance Corporation." Other regulatory definitions include, "an institution that accepts insured deposits and makes loans." In other words, a financial institution that does one, but not the other, is not a commercial bank.

A bank leverages its equity by issuing long-term debt and taking deposits. The degree of leverage is high (90% debt is considered conservative.). The funds available are held as cash in the vault or deposits at other banks for clearing purposes (5-10%), used to purchase securities (10-50%), and lent to borrowers (40-85%). The income from the loans and securities needs to cover the costs of operations, the interest expense of the bank's own debts (including payments to depositors), loan and securities losses, and a modest profit for the owners. Management's challenge is to achieve profitability at an acceptable level of risks, of which there are three. **Liquidity risk** is a problem of cash-flows. Deposits ebb and flow, securities are purchased and sold, loans are issued and repaid, interest is received on securities and loans, and interest is paid to depositors and other creditors. In addition, there is income from related services, such as safe-deposit or credit card fees, and there are expenses for wages and occupancy. Particularly troubling is the mobility of deposits and loans. Bank customers expect most of their deposits to be available on demand (some classes of Time Certificates are not), and borrowers may repay loans early, late, or not at all. So, the bank must carefully manage its cash-flows. Second, there is **Credit risk** which goes to the quality of assets. Will loans and securities be paid, as agreed ? This issue includes the credit risk associated with having deposits at other financial institutions. Heavy losses caused by the default of loans, or securities, can wipe out the bank's equity. Third, there is **Interest Rate risk** which takes two forms. First, there is the risk associated with managing the spread, or **Net Interest Margin**. The bank must assure that the average interest income on its assets exceeds its average cost of funds by a difference large enough to cover operating costs, provision for losses, and a small profit. Community banks have often targeted a spread (NIM) of five percent, of which 3% is for operations, 1% for loss provision, and 1% for profit. The second form of interest rate risk is its contribution to **insolvency** which can occur whenever the value of the bank's assets falls below its liabilities to others. This can occur, because of defaults (credit risk), or as a result of increases in market interest rates which depress the value of fixed income securities and loans, while at the same time, increasing the competitive cost of retaining deposits. Rising interest rates can depress the value of assets which reduces net worth, while also squeezing the NIM and thus the profitability which might bail the bank out.

Consider the balance sheet of a typical bank. The bank uses is own equity and funds borrowed from others. Its sources of funds are liabilities. Industrywide the average mix of liabilities would be approximately: Demand Deposits 13%, Savings & Time deposits 57%, other borrowed funds 19%, and Equity 11%. The banks uses of funds for the acquisition of assets, and the mix is roughly, of total assets: cash 9%, securities 19%, loans 53%, and all others, including premises and equipment, trading assets, and intangibles 19% .

Sources of income are the interest earned on loans and securities, plus fees for services, trading profits, and securities inventory gains. The expenses include interest paid on deposits and other debts, as well as salaries, occupancy, purchased services, and taxes. Because banks are so highly leveraged with 11% equity and 89% debt, or Assets/Equity = 10/1, and Return on Average Assets of 1 ¼ % will generate a return on Equity of 12.5%, and this is the typical objective of the bank. ROA = 1.25% and ROE 12.5% is considered good. Of course, this does not account for all banks.

The pursuit of profit will tempt banks to compromise on liquidity and solvency. Because loans can be tailored to the specific needs of borrowers, they usually carry higher interest rates than securities. However, the loans are not easily called or sold, if the need to raise cash arises. And because long-term securities (and loans) also carry higher interest rates, banks are tempted to *play the yield curve* by taking in short-term, low interest deposits, and using them to purchase longer-term securities and loans. However, if rates rise and the retention of deposits becomes expensive, while the earnings on those securities and loans are fixed, the squeeze is on. The classic event to illustrate the point was the collapse of the Savings & Loan industry in the 1980s. In the floating foreign exchange rate and inflationary environment of 1971-1981, interest rates on deposits rose from 3 ¾% to 5 ½%, and then higher. Deposits ran off from regulated banks to money market funds that could pay rates close the rate of inflation. Meanwhile the S&Ls had used their deposits to make fixed rate real estate loans. When the pattern was deposits at 3%, loans at 6%, and onto the golf course by 3 p.m., the life of an S&L executive was sweet. But, when deposit rates climbed above 5% and most of their assets were earning 6%, the spread disappeared. And selling existing 6% loans in a 9% world would have led to substantial losses. So, some S&Ls slowly bled to death, and others simply collapsed. The mess wasn't resolved until 1990, when a combination of low inflation, low interest rates, and regulatory reform restructured the industry. Thus, to succeed in banking we must balance the tension between the goals of liquidity, and solvency, and profitability.

That banks need liquidity (sources of cash) to meet customer withdrawals is obvious. As important are the needs to meet customer requests for credit and to pay off borrowings. Banks have a high portion of liabilities subject to immediate payment, many of which are highly sensitive to changes in market interest rates. In addition, banks generally have longer maturities on their assets than their liabilities, which discourage hasty liquidation of assets. And the maintenance of public confidence is very important, particularly for the uninsured liabilities. Hence, careful planning and management of liquidity is essential.

Fortunately, contemporary data processing technology allows banks to monitor their expected cash-flows and aggregate them. On the asset side, we have the flows of income and principal payments from existing contracts and on the liability side, the interest payments and anticipated withdrawals. To these, we add funding requirements for anticipated lending and securities purchases, and targets of liability retention and acquisition. Typically, bank departments report weekly their status and their expectations to an Asset/Liability Committee that reviews the reports and reconciles liability goals to funding needs. Integral to this strategy is the maintenance of cash, marketable securities, borrowing facilities with correspondent banks and with the Federal Reserve System, in order to manage unexpected changes in liabilities, or opportunities to acquire worthy assets.

Banks solicit **demand deposits** by offering payment services. We think of these as checking accounts, but banks call them DDA, because they are payable on demand, i.e. upon the presentation of a check, which is an order for the bank to pay on behalf of the customer. Banks like demand deposits, because they are not interest rate sensitive and are reasonably stable, despite the individual flows in and out. A larger portion of liabilities today are various **savings deposits** which have lower costs for banks because fewer services are required, but are more likely to migrate for small differences in interest rates. Among these are passbook savings, and time deposits (specific maturity contracts) of two kinds: retail CDs that are non-negotiable (not transferable) and Large TCDS which are negotiable (meaning transferable).

Among non-deposit sources of bank funds are borrowings from other banks via exchange of deposits at the Federal Reserve (called "Fed Funds"), repurchase agreements, and commercial paper. Banks keep deposits at their Federal Reserve, or with correspondent banks in order to meet reserve requirements. Any excess can be lent to other banks over-night, or longer. When I was at Bankers' Trust, which was large at the time ($11 billion), it borrowed 20% of its total liabilities in Fed Funds every day, a profitable habit, but one routinely criticized by the regulators. Banks may also borrowing from their district Federal Reserve Bank. Traditionally, these were short-term, often less than two weeks, but during crises **Term Discount Loan facilities** have been available. These loans require that the Federal Reserve System control the eligible collateral, a list of which is published weekly. The Fed considers such borrowing to be a privilege that should not exceed 2% of the bank's total domestic deposits, but this too may be waived in a crisis. The Fed will criticize and even deny loans to banks which appear to be borrowing, while increasing their earning assets (a clever bit of interest arbitrage).

Commercial Paper is a short-term note (< 271 days), sold at discount, and carrying a bank guarantee. One of the oldest forms of borrowing, commercial paper has become more important with the expansion of the money market mutual fund industry. These MMMFs are often hungry for risk free investments of very short maturities. As an alternative to a conventional bank loan, banks can lose loan business, but gain some income in fees for their guarantees. Banks have also learned to use commercial paper by having affiliates, such as bank holding companies, issue the paper and then, purchase loans from the bank itself.

Repurchase Agreements involve the sale of a liquid asset, such as a Treasury Bill, with a matching agreement to repurchase it, at a future date and slightly higher price. They provide a secure saving instrument for the lender, and an inexpensive source of funds for the borrower. Agreements may be over-night or longer. A *Reverse Repo* is a purchase with a commitment to sell later. This would be a very short-term savings tool.

Capital Notes and **Debentures** are conventional forms of term debt. Because these are relatively expensive, they are lightly used.

Banks choose a mix of non-deposit sources of funds, depending on the costs, reliability, volatility, and maturity of each source.

On the **asset** side of the bank balance sheet, **cash and deposits** at other banks ("due froms") will be held, as needed, to handle the inflow of some deposits and the outflow of others, and as required reserves. The **securities** portfolio is a secondary source of liquidity --- a place to park surplus deposits for some income, until attractive loan opportunities arise, or until deposits are allowed to run off to avoid unnecessary costs. Liquidity and Investment policies should dictate which correspondent banks are worthy to hold our bank's deposits, and which securities are suitable for the bank to hold. Regrettably, banks can be careless in their exposure in the form of deposits at weak banks and by the purchase of poor quality, or illiquid, securities. (There are parallels in sloppy lending practices.) All bank assets may be traded for additional income. The exchange of deposits at international banks is the foundation of the **Foreign Exchange market**, and the trading of bonds among financial institutions enhances the bonds' liquidity, and thus suitability as a source of secondary liquidity for the owners.

Loans are a central source of income for banks, and a fundamental service for the economy. Loan policy specifies the types of loans considered suitable by management, the market service area, and the limits and proportions for each class of loan in the bank's portfolio. The policy will also specify the operating procedures by which loans will be approved, funded, monitored, and collected. Loan officers and committees will have the limits of their authority approved by the Board of Directors. Guidelines for pricing and terms, schedules, fees, and rates are specified, and work out procedures for problem loans stated.

Loan officers will solicit business by reviewing the financial plans of their customers, assessing their needs, and recommending a financing plan. I would often recommend a combination of loans, including bonds, mortgages, term-loans, and working capital loans, even recommending competitors, or government agencies, for some of the business, when that would be advantageous to my client. This would enhance that customer's confidence in me, and often leave me with the most profitable piece of the action.

The **loan request** includes the purpose and amount of the loan, the sources of repayment, and financial exhibits, such as audited financial statements and tax returns. The loan officer, or loan team, performs their **credit analysis**, and makes a recommendation to those with the necessary approval authority. The loan is documented and recorded (booked), the funds are advanced, and the lender implements a system to monitor the loan and collect the promised payments.

Because banks are so highly leveraged, they cannot afford losses. Although aggressive banks may take calculated risk, accepting the probability that 5% of their loans may become problems requiring "work-outs," a loss ratio of 0.7% is considered the maximum acceptable. So, careful evaluation prior to advancing funds is essential. After all, once your customer has your money, he decides when and whether to repay you, promises and collateral notwithstanding.

Analysis begins with the audited financial statements of the company, and in the case of closely held companies, the tax returns. Credit reports from independent agencies, and references from suppliers and customers are required. A visit to the place of business to observe the conditions of facilities and inventory, and the morale of the staff, is recommended. The financial statements are analyzed for liquidity, debt coverage, asset to sales efficiency, and profitability. The results are compared to industry standards (Troy, Dunn & Bradstreet, and Robert Morris Associates publish sources for comparison). Collateral is appraised.

The banker is looking for evidence that the money that will be available to the borrower (his, ours, and other) will be adequate for the activity, that there are multiple and reliable sources of repayment, and that management demonstrates evidence of competence. You will recall an earlier discussion of the "Five C's" of credit --- character, capacity (cash-flow), capital, collateral, and conditions in lesson #3.1.

The loan is structured to meet the borrower's needs for funds on a low risk repayment schedule, and for the protection of the bank, including recovery in the event of default. Proper documentation requires 1) a Note, specifying the amount of the loan, the borrower, the creditor, and the schedule of payments, 2) a Loan Agreement, including covenants, stating the rights of the creditor and obligations of the debtor while the loan is outstanding, 3) a Security Agreement specifying the relationship of the loan to any collateral that is pledged to its repayment, and 4) any guarantees or warrantees.

Consumer loans rely heavily on the borrower's character and purpose of the loan. Credit history is suggestive, but stability of employment, local residence, and career are indicative. I always required a minimum of two years employment and local residence, with home ownership preferred. Income validated by tax returns can help verify ability to pay. Mortgage payments in excess of 35% of income are considered high. Relationships to the bank in the form of deposits, loans, and history of responsible account management, are all helpful.

I recall one customer, a minister, who requested a small loan "for the wedding ring and honeymoon that he couldn't afford when he married." I had reviewed the file and found that he had made the same request a year earlier (and received the loan). I denied the request and was threatened that he would tell his flock never to do business with my bank. On the other hand, I recall a recent divorcee worried about requesting a small loan, because she had no credit history. (This is often true of young people too.) I pointed out that she was a stable member of the community with no history any problems. I made the loan, and had no regrets about either decision.

Real Estate loans are large and their maturities are long. Hence, a bank is unwise to carry mortgages. Therefore, real estate loans need to conform to industry underwriting standards, so that they can be sold. **Appraisals** are important. I always asked my appraiser to be candid --- what would I realize, if I had to sell the property within six months ? Other considerations include assessing 1) the ability to "perfect" title --- lien priority, property description, and lender liability for hazards, 2) the borrower's history of property management, and 3) local real estate market conditions. 4) **Title reports**, including boundaries, easements, natural hazards (such as earthquake faults), and prior liens, are essential. And 5) Title insurance will be required.

Loans should be monitored regularly. Conditions change. Problems are best addressed early. So, the payment record is checked, the collateral condition and value are reviewed, reminders of dates for title renewal are logged, and borrower's financial statements are requested and reviewed regularly (less so for home mortgages than commercial loans). Troubled loans (not technically delinquent but non-conforming in some way) are monitored more closely.

Some of the "Red Flags" for credit departments are 1) delays in payments or submission of financial reports, 2) sudden changes in accounting methods, 3) company restructuring debt or eliminating dividends, 4) declines in the market value of the company's stock, 5) deterioration of financial ratios (see lesson #3.6), 6) deviations from budget projections, and 7) changes in deposit account behavior.

When the borrower can't meet his obligations, the bank is obliged to "work-out" the loans. The bank's goal is to maximize the recovery of funds. If the bank has been performing its loan monitoring duties, then, the trouble may be identified early and adjustments made before the borrower becomes desperate and uncooperative. A workout team separate from the lending team can avoid conflict of interest. The loan originators may be too close to the borrowers and have their own egos invested in the customer and the loan. Nevertheless, their knowledge of the customer and the industry is important. (And requiring that the lending officers participate in the cleanup can be sobering.)The workout team must investigate what other problems the borrower may have, such as taxes or litigation. Collateral must be checked and documents reviewed for condition and completeness. Then, negotiations are held with the borrower to speed repayment and add additional collateral. The key principle for the bank is that any adjustment must reduce the bank's risk.

When a delinquent loan customer is candid and cooperative, adjustments can be made. Few banks wish to seize collateral, or shut down a business. Such action often leads to losses, and always are bad for bad public relations. However, when the customer is obstreperous, prompt seizure of collateral is best. I recall sending a collection team ("Repo men" --- for repossession) to Newport Beach to seize a Mercedes from a customer who had been slow in paying for all five years of his auto loan. The car was up on blocks with no wheels, parked in his driveway. My team had brought wheels. The customer laughed when he called the next day, and he paid the balance of his loan plus my costs. Another collection involved a motorcycle (who lends for a motorcycle ?). The Repo team rolled it off the porch and down the driveway, and roared off to the sound of shots from the borrower. Other cases were sad, as when we foreclosed on a good business that lost its best customer, and its largest account receivable debtor declared bankruptcy in the same month. Fortunately, that customer stayed with the bank was soon "back on his feet" with our help.

Let us consider measuring a bank's performance. There are the financial flows that change the balance sheet. In addition to deposit flows, new loan funding and old loan repayments, as well as securities purchases and sales, financial inflows include loan income, securities income, cash and deposit income, fees for services, and trading profits. The financial outflows include deposit interest expense, interest paid on non-deposit borrowings, wages and salaries, occupancy expense, provisions for loan losses, and miscellaneous expenses. Interest income is typically 70%, and non-interest income 30%, of total income. Interest expense is typically 54%, and non-interest expense 46%, of total expenses. The flow of funds includes changes in assets, changes in liabilities, net income less charges, and changes in equity. The critical financial ratios for measuring performance are:

ROE= return on equity = net income/ net worth   *measures return on owners' investment.*

ROA= return on assets= net income/average total assets   *measures management efficiency.*

NIM= net interest margin =   (interest income – interest expense)/assets   *"the spread."*

Non-interest margin =   (non-interest income – non-interest expense) / assets

Net Bank Operating Margin

= {Total Operating Revenue less Total Operating Expense}/ Average Total Assets

Net Returns prior to special transactions

= net income after tax, but before securities and other extraordinary gains and losses.

Earnings Spread

= {interest income / average earning assets} less {interest expense/ interest bearing liabilities}

Earnings Base Efficiency   =   Earning Assets / Total Assets

Assets per employee.

We also use a variation of the **Dupont ratios** for banks. A bank's Return on Equity (ROE) depends on the interaction of the operating margin, asset efficiency, and financial leverage. A well-managed bank might resemble this combination of ratios:

$$\frac{\text{Net Income}}{\text{Operating Revenue}} \quad \frac{\text{Operating Revenue}}{\text{Ave. Total Assets}} \quad \frac{\text{Ave. Total Assets}}{\text{Equity}} \quad = \quad \text{ROE}$$

$$\frac{12 \text{ million}}{130 \text{ million}} \quad \frac{130 \text{ million}}{1{,}000 \text{ million}} \quad \frac{1{,}000 \text{ million}}{100 \text{ million}} \quad = \quad 12\%$$

These numbers assess the contributions of revenue and cost management, asset mix strategy, and financial leverage. Imagine a bank whose ratios are 6%, 6%, and 33x; its ROE would be 11.88%, slightly lower than our example, but with poor efficiency and very high leverage (3% equity vs. 10%). You can see how the Savings & Loan industry courted disaster in the 1970s.

In addition to decomposing profit, we can use financial ratios to assess bank risks. For example, crude measures of **credit risk** are: 1) the ratio of non-performing assets to total loans, and 2) the ratio of charge-offs to total loans. Crude measures of liquidity risk are: 1) purchased funds (deposits from other banks for which interest is paid) versus total liabilities, 2) net loans to total assets, and 3) cash assets and money market instruments owned to total assets. More purchased funds ("hot money") means more risk of rising costs to prevent run offs; more loans to assets means less liquidity, as loans may be difficult to sell, or to collect, early. On the other hand, more cash and MMIs are more liquidity, as long as they are obligations of sound institutions.

Investors' assessments of the bank's **risk of insolvency** include the price: earnings ratio of its shares, and the spread between the yield on the bank's debt and Treasury bonds of similar maturity. These can be indicators of general attitudes toward the industry, but deviations from industry averages are clear signals. Recently, regulators have imposed formulas for **risk based capital requirements**, applying a formula to the bank's holdings of various assets and liabilities. And simulations of extraordinary market conditions with assumptions of asset and liability behavior (*stress tests*) have resulted in new assessments of bank exposure. None of these are entirely satisfactory, as the statistical relationships which appear to be consistent in normal times, may be unstable in times of general distress.

Important tools of **Asset/Liability Management** are Rate Sensitivity GAP and Duration GAP analysis. These are methods of measuring exposure to the market risks of interest rate and asset price changes.

Rate Sensitivity GAP is identified using a spread sheet which assigns each asset and liability to a window showing when it can, or must, be re-priced. For example, all floating rate assets (mostly loans tied to the prime rate) and floating rate liabilities (checking and savings deposits payable on demand) would be in the 0-30 day box. Fixed rate securities, loans, borrowing, and deposits (such as TCDs) would be placed in the month of their maturity. Equity which never matures goes in the last box.

Example:

	0-30 days	30-60 days	60-90 days	90-180 days	180-365 days	1-2 years	>2 years longer
Assets:	100	100	100	300	300	50	50
Liabilities:	200	200	300	50	50	100	100
GAP	-100	-100	-200	+250	+250	-50	-50

205

In this case, the bank is exposed to the risk of rising interest rates during the three months in which liabilities would need to be re-priced before asset earnings could be adjusted. This would squeeze the NIM. However, the bank is well-positioned for a falling interest rate environment. To reduce its Rate Sensitivity risk, this bank could lower the maturities of its loans and securities holdings, or float their interest rates. It could also extend the maturities of its fixed rate deposits by sweetening the rates that it offers on the longer maturities. Oddly, most demand deposits are placed in the last box, the no maturity box, because they are held to manage cash-flow liquidity and are not interest rate sensitive, even though legally the DDAs are payable *on demand* and have immediate maturity. This would not be true for over-night deposits such as Federal Funds borrowed. They would be highly sensitive and must be "marked to market," daily.

The Duration GAP is calculated by spreading all the expected cash-flows, of interest and principal, for both assets and liabilities. Duration is a number which estimates the average time until the cash is received or paid, where each payment is weighted by its share of the total of all payments based on their present values. (Now, there's a mouth full !)

Let's take the example of a bond with these characteristics (Par $1000, coupon 6%, maturity five years) in a general interest environment of 5%. We can identify the cash-flow

	Today	One Year	Two Years	Three Years	Four Years	Five Years
If current market rates are 5%, then		$60	$60	$60	$60	$1,060
the Present Values are:		57.12	54.42	51.84	49.38	831.04

The Present Value of the bond is the sum of all present values = $1,043.80
And each payments share of the total is:

		5.47%	5.21%	4.97%	4.73%	79.62%

The average time until we receive a dollar of cash-flow is the time to each payment, weighed by its importance: 4.48 years = .0547 x 1 + .0521 x 2 + .0497 x 3 + .0473 x 4 + .7962 x 5
Duration has the nifty property that it provides a useful estimate of interest sensitivity.

Duration times the interest rate change = (-1) times the percent change in asset value
So, in the case of the bond above, an increase in bond rates for similar bonds of 1% would lead to a change in the market value of our bond of -4.48%, wiping out most of one year's income.

If we were to perform this exercise for all bank assets and all liabilities separately (thank goodness for computers), we can estimate the **Duration of our Assets** and the **Duration of our Liabilities**. For example, the Duration of the Bank's assets might be 1.5 years and that of its liabilities 0.80 of a year. This mismatch exposes the bank to a change in net worth as market interest rates change. For example, an increase in market rates of 1% would depress asset values by 1.5% and liabilities by 0.8%. Equity would be squeezed by 0.7% of Assets. A bank with 10% equity would have 9.3% equity, if all assets and liabilities were "marked to market."

You can see why financial institutions like falling interest rates which inflate the value of their existing assets, and why they fear rising interest rates. Banks which fail to plan for these possibilities are planning to fail, (to borrow a phrase from Peter Drucker). Many S&Ls failed to adapt to the volatile interest rate environment that followed the collapse of the fixed exchange rate system in 1970. They were taking saving deposits at 3 ¼% and making home loans at 6%. When inflation rose to 9%, higher interest rates followed. To keep deposits, the S&Ls were allowed to increase their deposit rates to 5 ¾%, but that was not enough. And of course, a mortgage paying 6% was unattractive to investors in world of 9% inflation. With durations of 6 years, the mortgages declined in market value by 12% or more. So, the S&Ls could sell their mortgages at a huge loss, or slowly bleed to death paying in interest for deposits almost as much as they were earning (or more) with no room for operating expenses or loan losses. The debacle was not resolved until late in the 1980s when interest rates declined and S&L regulation was reformed.

Prudent banks have management policies specifying acceptable rate sensitivity and duration GAPs, and discuss this at Asset/Liability Committee meetings, along with estimates of interest rate trends. (We used the term structure of interest rates for that purpose.) When interest rates were expected to fall, we would accept larger GAPs, and when interest rates were expected to rise, we change our pricing to reduce the GAPs.

Final topics which are often overlooked in banking texts are the **principal/agent** and **fraud/embezzlement** problems. Often, there is pressure from senior management to generate loans, and trading profits. The loan officers may cut corners, or completely ignore, loan policy and lending regulations, correctly assuming that the loans will not sour for many months, by which time the loan originator has moved on. So, he gets credit for generating loans, and loan fees, but escapes responsibility. In addition, some customers will falsify their exhibits. If they perform as agreed, no one will be the wiser, and entrepreneurs always expect their plans to be successful --- "if only those bankers were more creative." Some businesses are prone to money laundering. For example, occupancy and rental income for real estate and hospitality (hotels) can be inflated to create "legitimate" income. (Meyer Lansky founded a major Caribbean tourism company to wash money for the mob.) Traditional banks will begin a trainee's assignment with collections, in order to caution him against arrogance in lending.

With respect to trading, bank customers often have a relationship of confidence and trust, which leads them to contact the bank whenever they need to buy or sell securities, or buy or sell or participate in loans. They don't "shop around." They assume that their bank will offer them a fair deal. Unfortunately, again under pressure to generate earnings and earnings growth, the bank's traders may charge large spreads, based on the mathematical quirk that a small difference in yield can lead to a large difference in price. (For example, a 0.20% {20 basis points} difference can be a 3% difference in price for a long-term bond. Whereas, a 20 basis point spread may sound reasonable, a 3% bid-asked price difference would be shocking.)

I recall commencing work at a community bank and observing that the bank's CFO would call his correspondent for a Fed Funds quote and then promise to call back in an hour. This is a violation of the code of traders --- you either hit the quote, negotiate a quote, or pass. When you call back, there will be new quote based on market conditions. Only the Federal Reserve itself is given the courtesy of a quote from government securities dealers which will be honored an hour later. So, I informed the CFO and the President that if I were the trader at the correspondent bank, I would be shaving ¼% off every deal that I gave our bank. A week later, when our president asked his opposite number about my comments, he was told that they'd been shaving ¼% for a year, but they wouldn't do it anymore.

When traders and lenders get greedy, they risk alienating their customers. Again, one trader, or account executive, might get away with taking advantage of a customer for a while, earning a big bonus and promotion for the profitable business. However, like the neighborhood shopper, the customer notices sooner, or later, that he isn't getting a fair deal and abandons the relationship. Soon, the bank gets a reputation for taking advantage of its customers, and then its days are numbered. Bankers' Trust learned this, after years of "go-go" growth, driven by derivatives sold to customers as risk hedges. The bank imploded after law suits from customers who successfully claimed that they had been misled by bank officers. Bankers' Trust was acquired by Deutsche Bank in 1998.

Lenders may also violate their approved lending limits, by-passing the bank's approval processes. Worse, traders can build positions in excess of their authority, exposing their bank to huge losses. You may have read of the collapse of Baring Bank in 1995, as a result of unauthorized positions of trade Nick Leeson. In 2008, Jerome Kerviel made losses of 4.8 billion Euros for Societe Generale. Famous bank failures caused by careless lending include Charles Keating's Lincoln Savings & Loan. His bank survived scrutiny with the support of key senators known as "The Keating Five" (Alan Cranston {D-CA}, Dennis DeConcini {D-AZ}, John Glenn {D-OH}, John McCain {R-AZ} and Donald W. Riegle {D-MI}).

Bankers are also subject to employee theft. For that reason, they insist on **dual control**. Significant transactions require two signatures; safe-keeping requires two keys. But some people are lazy, careless, or trusting, and others are thieves. You will recall my story reported in lesson #2.1 of the bank officer who created several small loans to fictitious customers, advanced the funds to herself, and then advanced the payment due date each month on the computer. Of all the bank's employees had been asked who was least likely to steal, we would have named her. Never assume that your judgment is better than the evidence.

The same could be said for regulators. When Charles Prince of Citibank testified that his bank was too big for senior managers to control, our bank regulators should have reached the obvious conclusion --- too big to manage is too big to exist. In the run up to the financial crisis of 2008, leading government regulators (Larry Summers, Alan Greenspan, Tim Geithner, Robert Rubin) refused to heed the warnings of Brooksley Born (Chairman, CFTC), Sheila Bair (Pres. FDIC), June O'Neil (Dir., CBO), and others. Arrogance often leads to failure; corruption can delay the inevitable.

Questions for review and tests:
Explain the profitability, solvency, and liquidity issues for commercial banks.
What techniques do banks use to manage these problems ? {Be specific.}
Explain the five C's of credit. {You may wish to revisit lesson #21.}
What are some of the difficulties of regulating financial institutions ?
Explain the purposes, advantages, and disadvantages of deposit insurance.

Even the Vatican Bank has been the victim of corruption and incompetence.

Lesson #3.5 Financial Ratios for Business

In lesson #1.4 (management and value), we introduced the three basic financial statements: the statement of condition (balance sheet), the income statement, and the cash-flow statement. They are important in understanding where we are, and how we got there. Too many businesses have their accountants prepare financial statements which are duly forwarded to their banks and other creditors, but otherwise ignored. Many officers and directors don't know how to use them as management tools. If we take the time to analyze the statements, looking behind the numbers for the tale that they tell, we can learn a lot about our strengths and weaknesses, and where to give our attention to improve performance and to manage risks. In this lesson, we will develop a number of ratios that can be compared to our peers and also tracked over time to discern trends. We will learn to torture the numbers until they confess.

I like to start by analyzing **profitability,** the difference between revenue and costs. As you recall, we group costs into four classes: Cost of Goods Sold (largely inventory), General Administration and Sales (overhead, including marketing), Interest Expense (depends on our sources of financing), and Income Taxes. We have measure profit for each. **Gross profit** is the difference between Revenue and Cost of Goods Sold. It tells us whether we are selling at good prices (the responsibility of our sales department) and sourcing our inventory at low prices (the responsibility of our purchasing department). We can express Gross Profit as a percent of sales, using the formula:

Gross Profit Margin = {Sales - Cost of Goods Sold } / Sales

This measures the burden of variable costs, and the contribution of additional sales to profit. Hence, the **GPM** is also called the ***Contribution Margin*** --- How much gross profit will be added for another dollar of sales. This is very useful in negotiating selling prices and credit terms. If we subtract General Administration and Sales Expense (overhead), we get a second measure which we call operating profit. We have considered all operating costs. We have not yet considered financing or tax expenses. And we can express operating profit as a percentage of sales. So, we call this measure:

Operating Profit Margin =   {Sales - COGS - GA&S} / Sales

This measure is independent of the financial strategy of the firm (the reliance on debt and equity). And it tells us whether we are controlling our fixed costs, or letting them run wild. Consider that just as your sale force can be lazy, offering large discounts and sacrificing revenue, and your purchasing team may order from the book of existing suppliers, rather than seeking the best suppliers and negotiating the lowest costs, administration tends to add overhead, padding their staff and facilities, and launching poorly considered R&D and promotional programs. Our goal is for every dollar to work equally hard to generate sales and profit. The Operating Profit Margin (**OPM**) tells about all three.

We should not be the hated "bean counters" who challenge every expense and demand unrealistic performance. However, we can ask why our prices are lower than our peers, our costs of inventory higher, and our overhead larger. We should not starve our company for resources, but we should require justification, as the first step in an improvement plan.

We can also calculate **Net Before Taxes (NBT)** which subtracts interest expense from operating profit, and **Net Income (or Net Profit)** which subtracts the final cost, taxes. **NBT** depends on debt management, both the size of our borrowing and its average interest rate. **NI** depends on tax planning. Whereas, Operating profit depends on operational management, NBT and NI depend on the Finance Department.

We like to see that our products sell at strong prices and that we control our costs. We also ask, how well do we use our investments in assets to generate sales and profits ? You will remember that business is organized to make a profit (the difference between revenue and costs). In order to operate the business, we must have assets, such as plant, equipment, and inventory, and also cash, accounts receivable, and intangibles. We want the assets that we need, but no excesses, because we must borrow money from owners (equity) or creditors (debt), to support the assets. Hence, a measure of how well we select those assets is a comparison of profit to the average total assets available during the period under review. In a sense, ownership is saying, "We took our money (equity), and borrowed some more (debt), in order to provide you with assets. Now, how did you do with those assets ?"

Return on Investment, *also called "Return on Assets," =   Net Income / Average Total Assets* This ratio indicates how effective management is in selecting investments to make profits. We can also compare the ROA (or ROI, same thing) to our **cost of capital**. For example, our capital (long-term financing) might be 50% debt and 50% equity. If the debt costs us 6% after tax and the owners expect a return of 12%, then, our average Cost of Capital is 9%. If the managers cannot generate a Return on Assets greater than 9%, then we are wasted our time and money.

Our final measure of profit compares our Net Income to the owner's equity:

Return on Equity = Net Income / Net Worth

ROE measures how effective management is 1) in generating sales and pricing products, 2) in controlling costs and profit margins, 3) in selecting profit generating assets, and 4) in leveraging the owners' investment.

Let's consider that last idea. Management takes the owners' equity which could support a firm of limited size, sales, and profit. When management leverages this equity by borrowing from creditors, the company can acquire more assets and undertake more production, sales and profit. If the additional revenues are greater than the added costs, then the owners' earnings are boosted by the borrowing. They are *leveraged*. There are risks associated with leverage, which will be addressed below, but for now, from these five profitability ratios, we can deduce how the company is generating its profit (or loss).

Businesses also need **liquidity**, the ability to meet their current obligations as they come due, to seize new opportunities, and to manage emergencies that require cash. For these reasons, businesses hold cash and marketable securities, and arrange stand-by lines of credit. They also hold assets of varying liquidity, such as Accounts Receivable and Inventory. In assessing liquidity, we consider two sources, cash-flows and balance sheet measures. The most cautious structure of financing would be to support long-term assets, including *permanent* current assets (the minimum current assets that must be maintain to conduct the business) with long-term debt and equity (financial capital), and the temporary increases in current assets with current liabilities. We call this the **principal of suitability** --- matching the maturity of assets to the maturity of liabilities. Thus, the assets are converting to cash as the debt become due, and risks of insolvency are low. If we support long-term, illiquid assets, such as minimum inventory and accounts receivable, or worse, plant and equipment, with current borrowings, such as accounts payable and notes payable, we will need to roll over our borrowings to pay off current debts. The assets financed will not be converting to cash and will still be needed to operate the business.

Among the most traditional measures of liquidity is **Net Working Capital** is measured by the difference between current assets and current liabilities.

Net Working Capital = Current Assets minus Current Liabilities

Assets and liabilities are current, if they will be collected as cash within a year, or must be paid in cash within a year. Thus, some current assets are supported by borrowing in the form of current liabilities, but the rest must be supported by long-term funds (financial capital). Hence, the difference between current assets and current liabilities is called *net working capital*. In theory, the conversion of current assets is a source of the cash to meet the current liabilities. Unfortunately, in the normal course of operations, some current assets are collected, but others are being generated by the purchase of new inventory, and pre-paid assets (such as rent and insurance), and by the booking of sales under credit agreements as new accounts receivable. So, the assumption that current assets, other than cash, will be a source of liquidity is misleading. Perhaps, it's better to think that when current assets exceed current liabilities, there is a cushion in case some of those assets prove unconvertible, because they become damaged, lost, obsolete, or uncollectable.

Net Working Capital is a number, not a ratio. We like to use both numbers and ratios, because size matters, and so does proportion. NWC of $100 million would be a lot for a company of $1 billion in assets and sales, but trivial for a company of $10 billion in assets and sales. So, we could compare Net Working Capital to Annual Sales to estimate its adequacy. More often, we use the current and quick ratios.

Current Ratio = *Current Assets / Current Liabilities*

The Current Ratio gives an indicator of the ability of our liquid assets to cover our current obligations (CL). For small businesses, we like a ratio of 1.5, or more. Large businesses with very stable and diverse cash-flows can operate with a current ratio of 1:1. Some, businesses are so strong (Walmart, Proctor & Gamble) that they can operate with Current Ratio of 1:0.9. What does that mean ? These companies are financing all of their current assets with short-term credit, because it is cheap. And their suppliers, bankers, and commercial paper lenders are happy to lend, because they have so much confidence in the borrower.

The Quick Ratio (also called, "the Acid Test") subtracts inventory from current assets, in order to compare only the most liquid of assets to current liabilities.

Quick Ratio = {Current Assets - Inventory} / Current Liabilities

A Quick Ratio greater than one, is usually considered adequate.

As mentioned above, balance sheet liquidity can be misleading, because the liquidation of assets to meet liabilities would disrupt operations. More reliable is the liquidity provided by cash-flows.

Operating Cash-flow considers the company's income statement, and changes in current assets and current liabilities. What happens in the process of operating the business ? We purchase and process inventory, we sell the goods and collect payment immediately in cash, or extend credit as accounts receivable, and collect later. In this process, we borrow from suppliers in the form of accounts payable, and from banks and other creditors in the form of notes payable, and from employees and suppliers in the form of accrued expenses. So, we generate revenue, incur costs, and earn profits, while our current assets and liabilities ebb and flow. To calculate operating cash-flow, we track all of these changes. From the income statement, profit should provide cash (when we get paid), and some expenses recorded when we calculate profit are not paid immediately, such as depreciation and amortization.

Next, we acknowledge the effects of changes in our balance sheet. Increases in non-cash current assets use cash; decreases free up cash; increases in current liabilities means more borrowing, sources of cash; and decreases in current liabilities means using cash to pay debts.

So, we begin with our initial cash position. Then,

Step One: *Add profit and "non-cash expenses," such as depreciation and amortization*
Step Two: *Subtract increases in Accounts Receivable and Inventory (they tie up cash)*
Step Three: *Add increases in Accounts Payable, Notes Payable, and Accrued Expenses*
                (new borrowings supply cash)

The power of **Operating Cash-flow** is the knowledge that the continuing conduct of our business either provides us with liquidity, or absorbs it. For businesses that use more cash than they generate, we talk about the rate at which we are *burning cash*. In that case, we better have enough balance sheet liquidity to meet our needs for cash, until operating cash-flow turns positive. On the other hand, a business with strong operating cash-flow has money to invest in expansion (more assets), or to reduce its obligations, repaying debt, buying back shares, or paying dividends. Don't you like it, when you end the month with more cash than when you started ? Don't you worry when you have less ?

We can use operating cash-flow as a number, or compare it to current liabilities, or to sales to get of feeling of whether it is adequate.

Operating Cash-flow / Current Liabilities

or   **Operating Cash-flow / Sales**

I favor operating cash-flow to current liabilities, and love it when a company has such nice operating cash-flow that it could pay off all its current liabilities in three years or less.

Even better is the measure that we call **Free Cash-flow**. We calculate operating cash-flow, and then subtract our commitments to acquiring new long-term assets (investing) and to paying off debt, buying back stock, or paying dividends (financing). This gives us a measure of the cash-flow that is uncommitted and truly available (free) for discretionary use. Some businesses are acquired for their propensity to generate free cash-flow, when the company's other businesses are sound, and expanding, but absorbing cash. In that case, profitability of the free cash-flow generator may be a secondary consideration.

The final sources of liquidity to be assessed are the **Stand-by Credit Facilities**, measured by the unused credit lines from suppliers and banks. These should be established and maintained through clear and confident relations with creditors, an important duty of the Treasurer. Creditors must understand your company's condition, strategy, and sources of repayment. Bank credit lines can be cancelled, so overreliance on stand-by credit is dangerous.

Conclusion. An accurate assessment of liquidity can only be achieved by looking at *all six measures*. Companies with excellent operating and free cash-flow may compromise on their balance sheet liquidity. Companies with poor cash-flows must build and maintain strong current and quick ratios, and substantial net working capital on their balance sheets. Adequate liquidity is critical to the organization's reputation, survival, and ability to seize opportunities.

Another important set of ratios help us to evaluate management's ability to implement strategy effectively, neither wasting resources by excessive investments in assets nor starving operations with insufficient assets. We call these the **Efficiency Ratios**. We must acquire assets to support operations. We must choose the right assets and borrow the money to acquire them. We can borrow from creditors (debt), or from owners (equity), but either way involves expenses, (interest to creditors, or dividends and opportunity costs for owners). Because the purpose of the asset investments is to support operations, we compare the specific assets to the sales activity. If assets don't contribute to sales and profit, then they are wasted investments. Nevertheless, management will often pad the assets that they control to assure results, and even simply to enjoy the perquisites of power. Financial officers often have the unpleasant task of trimming these

212

wasteful assets without the deep understanding of operations that would assure the right cuts and the best investments. This creates tension between "the bean counters" and the other managers.

Our **Asset Efficiency** ratios help us to estimate the average speed with which various assets are converted into sales and cash. **Inventory Turnover** compares the Cost of Goods Sold to the Average Inventory. By using COGS, we are close to comparing "likes to likes" --- COGS includes Inventory sold rather than Sales which include Profit. We can also convert the Inventory turnover to an average time in inventory:

Average *Age* of Inventory   =   365 days / {Cost of Goods Sold / Average Inventory}
So, if our inventory turnover is 6:1, then our average age is 61 days from purchase to sale.

Just as production and sales require inventory, sales often requires the extension of credit to our customers. When we deliver the goods and the customer accepts them, (that is the customer acknowledges that we have fulfilled our responsibilities under the contract), we can book our revenue and expense on the income statement, and add a new asset, an increase in Accounts Receivable. When we are paid, we deduct the account receivable and add an equal amount to Cash. Because the extension of credit requires us to wait to be paid, and that increases our borrowing costs, we want to know how effective this credit program is in creating new profitable sales. We compare average Accounts Receivable to Sales for the **Accounts Receivable Turnover** ratio. Once again, we can multiply this ratio by 365 to get an Average Collection Period.

Average Collection Period =   365 x {Average Accounts Receivable / Sales}
A refinement, which I prefer, is to compare only credit sales to average Accounts Receivable, for the obvious reason that we offer credit to generate sales, and thus the sales to customers that use the credit are important.

In the liability side, we are interested in the use of supplier credit. Suppliers will often offer terms that are less expensive and less restrictive than those offered by outside lenders, because the supplier has calculated the effect on his gross profit margin and is willing to accept the risks. We compare our average Accounts Payable to our annual purchases of inventory, the total of cost of goods sold and the change in inventory over the period. If we multiply by 365 days, we get the

Average Payment Period =   365 x   {Accounts Payable / Annual Purchases of Inventory}
We interpret this as the average amount of time needed to pay our accounts payable, or the average time for which the supplier is carrying the financing of our inventory. As with other ratios, this is a general assessment. Supplier terms may vary and we are implicitly averaging the timing of payments for costs of goods sold.

Having assessed the contributions of inventory, accounts receivable, and accounts payable, we look at the long term investments in fixed assets, such as plant and equipment. In this case, we compare average fixed assets to sales.

Fixed Asset Turnover   =   Sales / Average Fixed Assets
Finally, we can summarize the overall effectiveness of our Asset investments as:

Total Asset Turnover   =   Sales / Average Total Assets
By this time, you are probably wondering why we compare a flow such as sales or purchases to an average of assets. From a management point of view, *the average total for an asset category represents a crude idea of the assets were available during the time period in which we were operating.* To compare end of period assets to sales would be unfair, if the assets were acquired toward the end of the time period, and thus not available earlier. Similarly, if we disposed of assets near the end, and we used final assets for comparison, we would be exaggerating the

efficiency of management over the whole time period. Remember that one of our important tasks, as financial managers, is to assure that the resources needed are available in a timely manner, and also, that there are no wasted assets.

We have considered some measures of liquidity and exposure to liquidity risks. Now, we need to consider the prudent use of debt. The purpose of debt is to expand the company's operations without diluting ownership. What we commonly call, **financial leverage**. Success raises the return on equity for the owners. Hence, we must assess not only the level of debt, but the exposure to the risk of default on the obligations to our creditor, and also the contribution to increased return on equity for the owners. The three elements must be considered together. We are asking: 1) To what extent are we relying on debt ? 2) Can we handle it ? 3) Is the debt improving our profitability enough to justify the strategy ?

Financial leverage is the use of fixed cost financing to *magnify* returns; it also magnifies *risk*. Consider two homeowners who both purchase their homes for $100,000 and sell them a year later for $200,000. They both have a profit of $100,000. If the first homeowner pays all cash, then his profit is 100%. If the second homeowners put $50,000 cash down payment and borrows the other $50,000 for the purchase, he will have some financing costs that reduce his profit (say by $10,000), but his rate of return is higher $90,000 / $50,000 = 180%. If instead, the homes are sold at a loss (say purchase at $100,000 and sale at $75,000), the all cash buyer has lost 25% of his investment, but the leveraged buyer has lost ($25,000 + $10,000 financing) /$50,000 cash = 70% of his investment. So, leverage cuts both ways. We can see how useful leverage can be, but also how important prudence is to the use of leverage. The first step in evaluating the organization's leverage is to calculate the extent to which it is relying on leverage to support our assets. I like a simple formula:

Debt Ratio = {Total Liabilities - Net Worth} / Total Assets

(Notice that I am using the balance sheet, Total Assets equal Total Liabilities = Debt plus Equity. One of the common sources of confusion is the use of the same term, *Total Liabilities*, when we mean all Liabilities including Net Worth, but at other times when we only mean Total Debt. When you encounter the expression, *Total Liabilities*, check to be sure which way the term is being used.)

Equivalent ratios are **Equity/ Total Assets** or **Debt/ Equity**. Obviously, the portion that is debt is the just one minus the portion that is equity. Big deal. Whereas, the debt/ equity ratio needs a little more thought. We can convert it. If Debt/Equity = 2/1, then debt 2/3 and equity 1/3. Because of the extra step in interpretation, I use the others. Anyway, the higher the ratio, the more assets are funded by borrowing, the more *financial leverage*. There is nothing inherently good, or bad, about this ratio. It simply states a fact. We use this proportion of debt and this proportion of equity. That is our strategy.

Next we ask, can we handle this amount of debt ? Because of its importance to risk, we use four measures. First, we compare our operating profit (synonyms Operating Income, and Net before Interest and Taxes) to our interest expense. This gives us a feeling for the "room" between the income that could be used to meet these obligations and the payments that are promised. Sometimes this coverage ratio is called *"Times Interest Earned."* Same thing. Don't worry about the jargon.

Interest Coverage Ratio =   Operating Income / Interest Expense

The acceptable ratio should be decided by the Directors. Often, we consider 5:1 desirable in normal times, decreasing to 3:1 an acceptable minimum in difficult times. As the economy or our industry declines 5:1 can quickly become 3:1. Below that, we worry that further deterioration of operating profit may imperil our ability to meet those interest payments. What about a Coverage: Ratio of 25:1 ? Our directors may reasonably ask whether we should use more leverage to boost ROE. Does this explain why strong, cash rich companies, such as Microsoft or Apple, would issue long-term debt to buy back stock, or pay extraordinary dividends ?

Many companies use **leases**, as a way of acquiring assets without the large outlays of cash involved in outright purchases. In that case, the companies have the fixed payments of the lease obligations, as well as interest payments on debt. Fixed payments are interest, principal, leases, and preferred dividends. Hence, we should use a broader measure of exposure. Remembering that we deducted lease payments in calculating operating profit, we must add them back, before calculating coverage.

Fixed Payments Coverage = Operating Income plus lease payments / all fixed payments

When I analyze *coverage*, I like to ask: What is the ratio between operating income and the interest expense that I can impute at going rates ? In other words, the income statement may understate the fixed payment exposure, if the debts or leases were acquired toward the end of the period, or on unusually favorable terms. The true burden may become higher in the near future. So, I will estimate that burden based on the company's long-term debt at market rates.

By now, you know that cash pays bills. So, we also use **Cash-flow Coverage** by which we compare **Operating Cash-flow / Interest Expense** and **Cash-flow to Fixed Payments** This last takes the form: **(Operating Cash-flow + Leases Payments) / All Fixed Payments** However, we must remember that principal payments and dividends are paid with *after tax dollars*. Hence, the income requirements must be *grossed up* to get the required pre-tax income: For example, the Operating Income to Fixed Payments Coverage ratio would use the formula:

$$\frac{\text{Operating income plus (adding back) lease payment expenses}}{\text{Interest expense plus the same lease payments plus \{(principal payments \& pref. dividends)/(1-our tax rate)\}}}$$

Once again, your Directors will select coverage ratios with which they are comfortable, as limits on your ability to use financial leverage to boost ROE. This takes us to the final ratio that must be considered in assessing leverage strategy, the **Return on Equity**. You remember this from our exposition of profitability measures above. Consider the financial organization of the company. The owners make some money available to management. We call this equity or net worth. The owners could use this money to acquire assets and operate the business. However, if management chooses to use the equity as a foundation upon which to borrow more money (debt), the company can acquire more assets and generate more activity, sales and profit. With the debt comes risk. So, the final question which we wish to ask is: "How's this strategy working out ?" Are we boosting return on equity (ROE) enough to justify the size and risk ?

Many years ago, a junior executive at DuPont realized that result which we seek**, Return on Equity**, the reward for the owners can be decomposed into three contributors:
1) The **Net Profit Margin**, (Net Income / Sales)   which depends on our abilities to generate sales at handsome prices and to control costs.
2) Our **Asset Efficiency**, (Sales / Ave. Total Assets)   which depends on our ability to select the right investments in assets, the ones that contribute to sales.
3) **Financial Leverage**, (Ave. Total Assets / Equity)   which is our choice of financial leverage.

Putting them all together, we can understand how we achieved our **Return on Equity**.

A few years ago, I compared Phillips Petroleum to Exxon. Looking only at ROE, we'd say Phillips is better managed.

	Return on Equity	=	Net Profit Margin	x Asset Efficiency	x Financial Leverage
	Net Income/Equity	=	Net Income/Sales	x Sales/ Ave.Assets	x Ave.Assets / Equity
Phillips	19.8%	=	3%	1.1	6/1
Exxon	16.25%	=	5%	1.3	2.5/1

Having checking the DuPont ratios, which do you think is the better company ? Phillips relied on a lot of leverage to achieve its ROE; Exxon uses its resources better to achieve its results.

About the same time, I had my students take a look at DuPont, itself. The recession was hammering bulk chemical demand and prices. We wanted to know, how are they doing and do they have a sound strategy ? So, we asked: **What's wrong at DuPont ?**

	1989	1990	1991	conclusion
Profitability Trends				
ROE	15.6%	14.1%	8.4%	poor
ROA	8.5%	6.1%	3.9%	poor
NPM	6.9%	5.7%	3.6%	poor
Liquidity Trends				
Current Ratio	1.21	1.22	1.45	better
Net Working Capital	1996	2210	3381	good
Operating Cash-flow	4867	5146	5461	very good
Financial Leverage				
Equity: Assets	0.539	0.430	0.463	good
EBIT Coverage	8.4	6.4	5.3	weakening but still good
Return on Equity	15.6%	14.1%	8.4%	poor
Asset Efficiency				
Receivables	51.9 days	51.8	54.3	under control
Inventory	48.2	44.1	43.0	improved
Total Asset Turn	1.2	1.07	1.06	burden of fixed assets

DuPont Ratios:

	Profit Margin	Asset Turn	Financial Leverage		ROE
1989	6.9%	1.20	/ 0.539	=	15.6%
1990	5.7%	1.07	/ 0.431	=	14.1%
1991	3.6%	1.06	/0.463	=	8.4%

What can we conclude from this analysis ? The profit margins and asset efficiencies were poor and deteriorating, as we would expect in a deteriorating economy, especially when your core business is commodities which face a lot of competition. Financial leverage was contributing to profitability, but should not be increased. During this time of troubles, DuPont was building liquidity and maintaining coverage to protect itself from the risks that it faces. Meanwhile, DuPont needed to give attention to disposing of poorly performing assets, and improving profit margins. In fact, DuPont considered reducing its reliance on highly competitive products, such as bulk chemicals, and expanding into less price sensitive areas, such bioengineered products.

I hope you can see the usefulness of financial ratio analysis.

Questions for review and tests:
Explain the measures of *liquidity* and *leverage*.
(hint: You must explain at least 4 measures of liquidity and 3 measures of leverage).
Why is balance-sheet liquidity not enough ?

What else must be measured to assess the contribution to profit and risk of a leverage strategy ?

Explain the measures of *profitability* and *efficiency* ?

(Hint: You must explain at least 5 measures of profit and 4 measures of efficiency.)

How do the DuPont ratios help us to understand the forces that determine our **Return On Equity** (ROE) ?

Exercise:

Choose a major company (Fortune 500).

Using any of the internet financial services (such as Yahoo Finance), or a major brokerage (such as Schwab), download the financial statements of your company, and calculate the four sets of financial ratios that we have studied.

What do they tell you about the management of the company ?

An Elephant behind a tree as we changed a tire in Tsavo Park, Kenya.
Is there an elephant hiding in your business that you don't see, because you aren't looking ?
Analyze your financial statements.

Lesson #3.6 Working Capital Management

In our last lesson, we developed an understanding of the usefulness of financial statement analysis in assessing our situation. You might say that the financial statements report the results of our past decisions, policy executions, and external conditions. Now, we are ready to use the financial statements to plan new initiatives and modify existing activities.

Important tools are the **Pro Forma statements.** We construct estimates of what we expect the financial statements to be in the future, if we take appropriate actions. There are several steps required, of which the first is to adjust the most recent financial statements to what they would be, if we were operating efficiently. We calculate our financial ratios, as described in lesson #3.5, and compare those ratios to industry averages, and to our best performing peers. (Some would call this *bench-marking*.) Next, we adjust each line item to what it would be, if we were operating as efficiently as can reasonably be achieved. (I like to project a three year adjustment period to move from existing ratios to the efficient ones.) At this stage, we are not assuming any change in sales, just an improvement in the organization of existing activities.

Next, we prepare our sales projections. Use your strategic plan and be realistic by product group. Now, you are ready to prepare the *pro forma* statements, which are estimates of future financial statements, and which serve as the basis for performance evaluation.

To prepare the **Pro Forma Income Statement**, we identify and distinguish fixed and variable Costs for *each expense line.* We adjust each expense line item to be consistent with our sale projections. Remember that we are projecting our numbers at our intended efficiency ratios. Cost of Goods Sold (mostly variable) should change at the same percentage as sales, but General Admin & Sales (mostly fixed) must be estimated based on program needs (our planned changes in overhead). Interest Expense will depend on our reliance on interest bearing debt as part of our financing plan (moving toward our optimal capital structure). Finally, we apply our tax rate to Net Income Before Tax. (Observe the magnification effects of *leverage* on NIAT.) I repeat this process for three or more years, to track our intended march toward the goals of our strategic plan.

To prepare the **Pro Forma Balance Sheet**, first remember to adjust our most recent Balance Sheet to our target *efficiency ratios*. Then, consider the asset and liability changes that result from sales growth, cash-flows, net income (profit), and investment requirements. For example, inventory and accounts receivable can be expected to grow proportionately to sales, unless our policies change. Similarly, accounts payable will grow proportionately. We can apply the same percentage growth to these that we assume for sales growth. We call the natural increase in accounts payable, a *spontaneous source of financing*. By allocating expected profits to dividends or retained earnings, we can assess the needs for external funds. And we can choose the mix of current liabilities, long-term debt, and equity that supports our total asset requirements, while balancing our needs for balance sheet liquidity, debt service coverage, and financial leverage.

The major advantages of pro forma statements are the assessment of the changing needs for assets to support our sales goals, the acknowledgment of the trade-offs between sources of financing, the resulting integrated plan for acquiring the needed financing, and finally, the subsequent use of the pro forms to evaluate performance.

We could use the following exhibit as a guide to creating our pro forma statements:

Income Statement

Revenue	% change in sales
less **Cost of Goods Sold**	% sales change
equals **Gross Profit**	% sales change
less **Gen'l Admin. & Sales Expense**	fixed costs estimate change, not simply a %
Equals **Operating Profit**	*(change magnified by operating leverage)*
less **Interest Paid**	change if debt or interest rates paid change
less **Taxes**	change with income
equals **Net Income**	*(change magnified by financial leverage)*

Balance Sheet

Current Assets

Cash & Cash Equivalents	% sales
Accounts Receivable	% sales
Inventory	% sales
Pre-paid Expenses	% sales

Long-term Assets

Plant & Equipment	depends on needed capacity
less Depreciation	changes based on % of Plant and Equipment
Investments	
$ in non-liquid assets	discretionary
Intangibles: Goodwill & Patents	discretionary

Current Liabilities

Accounts Payable	% change in inventory
Notes Payable	change to achieve current ratio and net working capital objectives
Accrued Expenses	% change in sales

Long-term Liabilities (Capital)

Long-term Debt	change to achieve optimal capital structure, including acceptable coverage ratio, as directed by our Board
Net Worth	change to achieve optimal capital structure including return on equity as directed by our Board

(Don't omit changes due to profit or loss, and dividend commitments)

Statement of Cash-flows   a reconciliation of beginning and ending cash positions

Beginning Cash plus

Net Income

current profits are the first addition; then, add back non-cash expenses

Adjustments for Operations

changes in current assets and current liabilities

Adjustments for Changes in Long-term Assets (Investing)

purchase or sale of long-term assets

Adjustments for Changes in Capital (financing)

debt, equity, and dividends paid

Result is **Ending Cash**

In each case, add changes which are sources of cash and subtract changes that use cash. These can be identified from the pro-forma income and balance sheet statements, as well as discretionary investment, assets sales, and payment decisions.

This exercise of building pro forma financial statements is very useful. We can anticipate problems and opportunities, discipline our management, and track performance. I built pro forma statements for each month of the first year, and for each quarter of the first five years of our Antigua resort venture. We completed the first year within $3,000 of each line item for each month. Although our financing plans changed, when OPIC offered us very favorable terms for financing expansion, the development strategy remained the same, and we sold the property within three years for a profit, well in excess of our projections. The guidelines provided by the pro forma statements were essential in generating the consistent performance that added value to the property.

Armed with our recent financial statements and projected "pro formas," we can analyze our current assets and current liabilities. Let's consider each, one at a time. The first task would be to estimate our **Cash** requirements. To do so, we must analyze our **cash cycle** and build a **cash budget**.

For many companies, the most vital activity of financial management is the support of day-to-day operations. In the **Operating Cycle**, we purchase inventory, produce our product or service, book the sale, and collect the account receivable. We start with cash and end with cash. The time required depends on our production techniques and sales methods. We can measure the operating cycle as the total of the average age of inventory and the average collection period. For example, when we looked at Dupont in Lesson #3.5, we noted the 1991 average age on inventory was 43 days and average collection of accounts receivable was 54.3 days. So, Dupont's operating cycle was 97.3 days. **The Cash Conversion Cycle** measures the time in which the company's *own* cash is tied up. We subtract from the operating cycle, *the average payment period on accounts payable and other cost of goods sold (COGS) accruals.* We didn't estimate that for Dupont, but if Dupont pays its suppliers every 60 days, then Dupont is using its own money for only 37.3 days.

Ideally, the cash conversion cycle is **negative**. That is receipts (inflows) would *precede* payments (outflows). This is the case for companies that receive large cash deposits against future sales. For example, airlines, cruise lines, and resorts receive deposits before services are rendered. There are also retailers which extend little credit to customers, but received generous terms from suppliers, such as jewelers. Costco operated on this principle by requiring cash or credit card payments (all receipts within three days), while using supplier credit for 30-90 days. However, typically, a business has **positive** cash conversion cycle, meaning that more money is tied up in inventory, accounts receivable, and pre-paid expenses than is being borrowed in accounts payable, and accrued expenses. This raises the business's requirement for working capital.

On the other hand, the cash cycle can be managed by reducing the average inventory through Just in Time (JIT) and Enterprise Resource Planning (ERP) systems that coordinate production with suppliers, by shortening our own production cycle, and by moving out finished goods more quickly. In addition, we can speed the conversion of accounts receivable by revising our credit terms and collection practices, including using direct deposit and electronic transfer of funds. Finally, we can delay payments, without damaging credit or incurring charges, by using a *tickler system* to assure prompt payment, while using available credit. All of these methods are greatly eased by the use of computer networks to track production, delivery, and orders, as well as receipts, payments, and due dates.

In the old days, an acknowledgment from our customer accepting our goods would be filed in a box containing partitions for each day of the next few months. Similarly, as we received a bill, we would decide to pay within ten days, accepting the discount, or pay on the last day of the credit period. The invoice would be placed in a box, in the appropriate slot, and checks would be cut, signed, and mailed when that day had moved to the front. (Customers and suppliers with whom we had a dispute would receive special attention.) Now, our computer system performs these tasks and alerts us to payments due.

Strong bank relationships are important for cash management, including fast processing, available credit, and modest investment income on savings. All banking services and fees are negotiable, based on the overall relationship. Often, we need to remind our bankers of the various relationships that we maintain --- deposit balances, credit facilities, and payment processing, so that they can calculate the associated costs and benefits to the bank and adjust charges accordingly. You should strive for a balanced relationship with your banks. One that is mutually profitable and confident.

Now, we can tackle one of the most important tasks of management --- assuring that the irregularities of cash-flows (both receipts and payments) do not disrupt or embarrass the organization. **Liquidity** is needed not only to assure the timely completion of transactions, but also to handle disruptions caused by emergencies and to be prepared to seize opportunities. These motives were described by J. M. Keynes as *transactions, precaution, and speculation*. The financial manager should review the organization's cash position every morning for receipts, payments, pending receipts and payments, and current balances. (You may wish to do this for your household as well.)

We compare our position to our **cash budget**, prepared from our marketing department's sales forecast. Consider external factors, such as economic conditions and forecasts (how are our customers doing ?), and internal prognostications (staff estimates based on products, competition, and consultations with customers). Ask tough questions ("drill down") to assure that estimates are realistic. From those projections, we can estimate revenue and operating costs, spreading them over the near future. (I like the next twelve months.)

Next, we convert the accruals of revenue and expense into cash-flow estimates by adjusting to the time at which they will be received or paid. With respect to income, we log cash sales as they can be expected to occur, and spread credit sales over the period in which we expect to collect them. These conversions are based on our past experience, as conversion percentages of sales for each period.

For example, consider the business which has 50% cash sales, 30% receivables collected within a month, and the final 20% collected within two months. Then, their cash receipts would be estimated:

	Jan	Feb	Mar	Apr	May	Jun	Jul	Aug	Sep	Oct	Nov	Dec
Sales	100	90	120	100	80	80	80	60	---	---	70	100
Cash	50	45	60	50	40	40	40	30	---	---	35	50
One month	30	30	27	36	30	24	24	24	18	---	---	21
Two month	14	20	20	18	24	20	16	16	16	12	---	---
Receipts:	94	95	107	100	94	84	80	80	34	12	35	71

For expenses, we log cash payments for the time at which they are incurred, and credit payments for the dates at which they will be paid. These are based on our accounts payable strategy. Important elements of our payment projections include rent and lease payments, wages and salaries, tax payments, fixed asset outlays, interest payments, principal payments, dividend payments, and stock repurchase commitments. Non-cash revenues and expenses should not be included in our cash budget.

Next, we can estimate Net Cash-flow for each period as cash receipts *minus* cash expenses. And finally, we add our Net Cash-flow to Beginning Cash to obtain our expected Ending Cash balances for each period.

Now, we can consider the support of operations with current assets by a combination of inexpensive current liabilities and expensive, but stable, long-term financial capital. *Current Assets* are often called working Assets. *Current liabilities* are sources of short-term finance, but they have short maturities and must be paid when due. Hence, though cheap and easily available, they are not entirely reliable and thus carry risks for the borrower. **Net Working Capital** is portion of the Current Assets supported by long-term financing (hence the expression which combines "working" and "capital"). So, we calculate:

Net Working Capital = Current Assets minus Current Liabilities

Using expensive borrowings in the form of long-term debt and equity (owners expect high returns) to support current assets, which carry low returns on assets, increases our stability, but reduces our profitability. Fortunately, the more predictable are our cash-flows, the less working capital is needed. In fact, some large companies operate with negative net working capital, meaning that their current liabilities exceed their current assets. They are supporting the highly profitable long-term assets with cheap current liabilities. However, those same long-term assets are illiquid and the current liabilities must be paid or "rolled over" on favorable terms. Most companies cannot take the associated risks. In fact, the **Risk of Insolvency** is often measured by net working capital.

To summarize,
1) Current Assets are usually less profitable than Fixed Assets.
2) Therefore, increasing Current Assets may reduce profitability.
3) Current Liabilities are often the *least expensive* source of finance.
4) Decreasing reliance on Current Liabilities requires increased reliance on more costly sources, and thus leads to less profitability.

Conclusion: Increased Current Assets and/or Reduced Current Liabilities will reduce insolvency risk, but at the expense of reduced profitability. Thus, we should plan carefully for the optimal financing mix.

From our cash budget and pro forma cash-flow projections, we can identify the organization's permanent financing needs for current assets, as well as its maximum financing requirements. Having projected long-term assets in our pro forma balance sheet, in a manner consistent with our operational plan, as shown in our pro forma income statement, We add the lowest total of non-cash current assets. These are our minimum financing requirements, and prudence suggests that they be supported by capital (long-term debt and equity). The temporary fluctuations in current assets can be met by adjustments in current liabilities. Creditors providing current liabilities will see that their loans are "self-liquidating" and so, our creditors will be accommodating, offering favorable terms and conditions.

Let's consider our needs for current assets. **Cash & Marketable Securities** balances are our most liquid assets. We use Money Market Instruments such as Treasury Bills, high quality Commercial Paper, Bankers' Acceptances, and Certificates of Deposit. They share important characteristics of liquidity --- no default risk, assured value, and fast sale on small margins and commissions. We hold cash and near-cash (marketable securities) balances for making and receiving payments as they become due (transactions), unexpected needs (precaution), and unexpected opportunities (speculation). Our cash-flow budget helps us to anticipate the periods of large cash inflows which will require the selection of marketable securities investments as temporary stashes of surplus liquidity, and the periods of cash drains which will require an increase in current liabilities. The variability of cash-flows in both totals and timing, as well as estimates of probabilities of extraordinary cash requirements, will suggest the size of a safety reserve. Finally, don't ignore ability to borrow short-term, when estimating your liquidity needs (a reminder of the importance of bank relationships). Consider the following example.

When operating several travel related businesses, including hotels, and packaged tours, we were also building a resort in the West Indies, on a very short schedule. We negotiated the purchase in June, took ownership in July, renovated and expanded the facilities, and opened on December 16th. Our investors were assessed $100,000 payable in four equal installments of $25,000. At the time, we had $600,000 in our checking account, and my boss asked me to move the deposit to an interest bearing account. I demurred with the observation that the bank would value the $600,000 where it was, but would not feel any special relationship, if they were paying us interest (deposit interest rates were 6% at the time). I wanted some special attention, if our cash-flow was disrupted. In September, we needed a loan of $250,000 to bridge a deficit. The loan was approved and funded that day, even though its purpose, construction in the Caribbean, violated bank policy. The recognition of the bank's needs and motives saved us from embarrassment.

Next, let's consider each of the current assets and liabilities, one by one.

Accounts Receivable represent the extension of credit to our customers, in order to encourage more purchases. They are often as much as 3/4 of current assets and 1/3 of total assets. You will remember from lesson #3.5 that the ratio of accounts receivable to sales is a measure of their effectiveness. Now, we consider the design and analysis of our credit program.

The first step is to decide of who will be eligible for credit sales. We call this **Credit Selection** and use the *five C's of Credit* to assess credit worthiness. (You will remember these as: *Character:* indicated by credit history and legal status, *Capacity:* the ability to pay indicated by cash-flow, *Capital:* evaluated by financial leverage & profitability, *Collateral:* the unencumbered assets available to be pledged as security, and *Conditions:* plans for addressing the risks associated with the economic and business climate.)

We obtain **Credit Information** from our credit application, credit reports, references, and financial statements (audited are best). References are often cautious about revealing private or negative information. So, asking questions siting specific information obviously provided by the applicant, and requiring only Yes or No responses will elicit the most useful answers. For example, "The company indicates that you have extended credit of mid five figures ($35,000-65,000) for up to six months. Is this accurate ?" or "Has the company always paid as agreed ?" We are interested in the terms offered by other creditors and the average payment periods. We will also analyze the financial ratios, including trends over the last three years and last four quarters, with emphasis on cash-flow and coverage. We can then classify the applicant A-B-C and design our terms accordingly. We will consider the costs of investigation and monitoring, and the risk of losses.

For example, we may require cash sales initially during a probationary period, and then offer increasing amounts of credit as the relationship matures. A rule of thumb is to limit total credit outstanding to one customer to **10%** of their financial strength, measured as their average net worth plus free cash-flow.

We must establish **Credit Standards** and **Credit Terms.** Key variables will be 1) The effect on *Sales Volume* (tighter standards will reduce sales; relaxed standards may increase sales)   2) The associated *investment in accounts receivable* (carrying costs are the interest paid or foregone, on average cost of goods sold, for credit sales only) and 3) *bad debt expenses* (including administration costs and charge-offs).

Credit Terms include the **Cash Discount** and the **Credit Period.** Terms will vary from industry to industry, but consider the classic 2/10/90. These terms mean that the customer can take the discount of 2%, if he pays within ten days. Otherwise, he pays the full price within ninety days. Notice that the Credit Period is actually eighty days (90 minus 10). Increases in cash discount should increase the portion of cash sales, and may reduce bad debt losses and collection expenses. However, total sales may fall, and gross profit margin is reduced. A longer credit period should increase sales, and will increase the portion of credit sales, carrying costs, collection costs, and charge-offs.

To design our credit terms, we start by estimating the anticipated change in credit sales from a change in credit policy. For example, more generous terms will lead to an increase in total sales and an increase in the portion of existing sales taking advantage of credit instead of paying cash (taking the discount). The anticipated growth of accounts receivable will depend on the new credit sales volume and the change in the average collection period. We can measure the gain in **Gross Profit** by applying our gross profit margin to the increase in sales. Then, we need to calculate the new financing costs and the increase in expected charge-offs and collection costs.

Carrying Costs depend on Cost of Goods Sold. So, we apply our COGS: Sales ratio to the new level of sales, and divide by the *new* accounts receivable turnover rate to get *new* amount to be financed. By applying our effective accounts payable interest rate cost, we can calculate our *new financing costs.* By comparing these *new* financing costs to our current financing costs, we get the change in financing costs for the new program (called *marginal financing costs*).

Then, we estimate the added collection costs and charge-offs to get the change in accounts receivable program costs. If the increase in gross profit exceeds the increased administrative, financing, and charge-offs, the program change makes sense.

Example:

	Sales	Credit Sales	A/R Turn	A/R	COGS/Sales	Carry Costs at 8% & charge offs & collection expense
Current						
	$1,000,000	80%	4x	200,000	70% $140,000	$11,200 & 20,000 & $20,000 Current costs $51,200
Expected						
	$1,200,000	85%	3.5X	291,429	204,000	$16,320 & $36,000 & $24,000

New Program costs = $76,230 Marginal Program Costs = $25,030

So, for the plan envisioned, we expect an increase in gross profit of $60,000 (Can you see how I got that number ? $200,000 x 30%), and an increase in financing costs of $25,030. Looks like we should try the new program for a net gain of almost $35,000.

So, the **Credit Standards Decision** is based on the answer to the question: *Does the contribution to Gross Profit exceed the additional costs ?* You may wish to segregate customers into groups with similar risks and expenses, evaluate each group, and extend appropriate terms. You have already noticed that large gross profit margins make credit programs attractive. Is that why we see generous terms from jewelers? And small gross profit margins make the extension of credit difficult. Is that why supermarkets and discount department stores prefer cash, or credit card, payments ?

The credit program must be managed. Total credit outstanding for each customer must be tracked, as well as the time that the debt has been outstanding. We call this process the **aging of receivables**. A matrix is created with a line for each customer. Columns name the customer on the left, the amounts outstanding for each month is in the middle, and the total exposure (the sum of the monthlies) on the right. We compare the total to our credit guideline for the customer, and the monthlies for conformance to credit terms, and for changes in the pattern of payments. Large exposure and/or a slowdown in payments are warnings to step up our collection efforts.

Lest you think that the careful monitoring of exposure is too burdensome, consider the alternative. One of my best customers at the bank, a true professional at his craft, defaulted on his loan, and lost his house and the house that he had bought for his parents, when 1) his most important customer, accounting for 50% of his billings, chose to move their work "in house," and another account which was 25% of my customer's Accounts Receivable declared bankruptcy. So, diversify your customer base, limit your exposure to any one customer, and monitor all credits regularly.

When collecting, maintain a cordial relationship with your customer's payables clerks. They aren't the ones establishing policy. They have been directed what to pay and when. Debtors are often ashamed and will avoid informing us of problems. They often feel bad about violating terms. Stress integrity (keeping commitments), candor, and encourage early consultation, if delays in payments are expected. Letters should be polite reminders. Threats are more likely to alienate the debtor than to prompt payment. Similarly, telephone calls, or emails, should be polite inquiries. "Gee, I notice that invoice #12345 hasn't been paid. Did I make a mistake ? Is there a problem ?" Their accounts payable clerk will often volunteer information, sometimes, even unloading a tale of woe. Be sympathetic. You want to be the first one paid, not the last. Personal visits to their business may be necessary. They can't be ignored, and you get to observe operations, and the embarrassment often gets results. Stay calm, but be persistent. Collection agencies are expensive, and may bring more costs than results. However, they do signal your tenacity. The last resort is legal action. It's expensive and timing consuming. Bankruptcy can stall proceeding and recovery may be unlikely, even if a judgment is obtained.

Another important commitment of working capital is **inventory.** Our objective is to assure uninterrupted operations with minimum losses from damage or obsolescence, and minimum storage and financing costs. The management team will have different points of view. As financial managers, we are eager to minimize costs; the production managers usually want more inventory to maintain production continuity; the marketing managers want finished goods inventory to assure prompt delivery; and the purchasing managers want to buy in bulk to receive discounts. We can reconcile these views by advocating the consideration the *opportunity costs* of resources in planning.

The management of inventory has improved by the application of computer networked systems that integrate the old scheduling techniques. The concept is *just in time*. That is receiving inventory on station exactly as needed, thus saving on storage, breakage, and obsolescence costs. However, many small orders can mean higher prices, and transportation and administrative costs. The networking solutions are various named Materials Resource Planning (MRP), Management Resource Planning (MRP2), Enterprise Resource Planning (ERP), and Economic Resource Planning (ERP2). The concept is to link all stages of production into an integrated system of scheduling. The first step is **systems analysis** which identifies each stage of production, the resources and time required for each, and the critical path. Quality standards for each stage are negotiated between customers and suppliers. Then, as orders are received, the system can check for available finished goods, goods in process, and parts. In the ERP systems, the availability of production stations and operators is also assessed. Orders for parts and materials are transmitted. For ERPs, work orders for stations and personnel are also generated. As a result, parts and materials, sub-assemblies, and finished products are coordinated, and inventories minimized. There may be many deliveries of small batches of parts and materials every day. Such a system requires close co-ordination and trust between operational groups and contractors, and low cost logistics. Fortunately, delivery services such as Federal Express (FedEx) and United Parcel Services (UPS), as well as transport companies, have adapted.

The final category of current assets is **pre-paid expenses.** Examples are rent and insurance which must be paid in advance. Management of pre-paids is limited to careful assessment of needs for the assets and negotiation of terms. As relations with suppliers mature, terms may be renegotiated from payment in advance to cash, or even credit.

Let's now turn our attention to **current liabilities**. If we reduce our needs for current assets, we reduce our need for supporting liabilities. As we consider our sources of funding (liabilities), our priorities must be 1) reliability (will the credit be available when we need it ?),   2) terms (are the terms {payment dates and amounts, loan and security agreements} reasonable, or burdensome ?), and   3) associated costs (interest and fees).

Our **accounts payable** are the result of our choice to use **trade credit.** They are the other side of accounts receivable. We are using trade credit, rather than offering it. As before there are three elements: the cash discount, the discount period, and the credit period. The **Cash Discount** offered is the percent reduction in purchase price, if payment made within a specific period. The number of days that the discount is available, is typically 5-20 days. We call that the **Cash Discount Period. The Credit Period** is the difference between the cash discount period and the days until the full payment is due. This is often 30-120 days. The starting date for calculating the discount and credit period is specified in the sale contract. It may be date of invoice, or the end of that month. Competition between sellers usually leads to similar trade credit terms.

To decide whether to pay cash or use the credit terms, we must analyze the associated costs. Taking the credit terms means foregoing the cash discount. Losing the discount is an implicit interest charge. *The true purchase price is the discounted price.* For example, consider credit terms: **2 /10 net 30 EOM**   (A 2% discount is offered, if the invoice is paid in full within ten days of the end of the month {EOM}).   If we don't take the discount, we get

20 days credit; for this we pay 2%. The cost is **{2 / 98}   x { 365/ 20 } = 37% APR** Expensive !

Consider another example: 2 /15 net 60 EOM. If we don't take the discount, we get 45 days credit for which we pay 2%. Our cost is **2 / 98 x 365 / 45 = 16.6% APR**   Better !

Final example: 2/10 net 120 EOM   Cost is **2 /98 X 365/110 = 6.8%**   Attractive ! We can even put a dollar value on the credit terms. In other words, credit terms can be integrated into price comparisons, when evaluating alternative suppliers. Continuing the last example: Borrowing at 6.8% for 110 days, when your next best rate offered is 10% is worth

The rate difference   annually   equals the percentage price difference

(10%-6.8%)   x   (110/365)   =   0.96% of the price

If we stretch our accounts payable, we may extend the availability of borrowed funds and reduce effective cost of financing. However, we may damage credit terms, or cause retaliation (goods denied, or prices marked up). So, the best strategy is to choose cash or credit and then "tickle" the payment for the last day of the chosen period. And we should be consistent in our payment practices. Remember that relationships of trust are essential to managing our business risks.

Before we tackle money market borrowing and factoring, consider **accrued expenses.** These are the opposites of pre-paid expenses. In this case, we are using the services before paying. One large source of accrued expenses is the lag in payments to employees that occurs, because we pay employees after they complete the work, whether it's weekly, monthly, or longer. Thus, we owe the wages and salaries and have use of the funds, until we make the payment. Another important accrued expense is taxes. We make quarterly tax payments, but have use of the money, until we pay. The temptation to delay payment may be substantial, but the risks are huge. Employees who worry about being paid on time will be looking to find other jobs. The tax authorities can shut you down, before any notice or adjudication is made. So, maintain sufficient liquidity to make those payments as due.

I remember being stunned by my boss who announced that because of our investment commitments, we wouldn't be able to pay our employees their December wages and salaries. I was amazed that he would consider this ! I stopped him and worked out a strategy that allowed us to meet all obligations on time. It was a close call.

What about bank loans ? Banks prefer short-term, self-liquidating loans. Remember how highly leveraged and illiquid banks are. A mismatch between the maturities of their deposit liabilities and their loans exposes their Net Interest Margin to risk. And **Revolving Credit Agreements** are commitments by the bank to a line of credit of specific size and period of time. We may find revolving credit attractive, with the idea that we pay a modest fee for the bank's commitment, and then only pay interest on the funds used. However, banks often find these commitments unappealing. Customers use them only when in need, and many customers may encounter liquidity problems at the same time. Banks must set aside funds, or tap their own ability to borrow, to support the lines of credit, for which the commitment fees are not adequate. So, banks prefer a specific loan for a clearly identified purpose, with several sources of repayment, and a payment schedule that is reasonable but firm.

There are several costs associated with borrowing from banks. We begin with the interest costs. **Loan Interest Rates** may be fixed for the term of the loan, or variable (*floating*) based on some reference rate. This reference rate is chosen to maintain a spread between costs and interest income. For example, if the bank's marginal cost of funds is 3%

and its overhead is 4% (including loan loss provision), then the reference rate might be 8%. However, competition is also important. Banks cannot maintain a reference rate that is substantially above their competitors. Years ago, this reference rate was universally called, **the Prime Rate**, and was represented as the rate of interest charged to the most important customers for short-term (90 day), low risk loans. Other customers were quoted rates that rose with risk and maturity, such as "prime plus 2.5%." When lawsuits established that some customers were receiving rates "below prime", such as "prime minus 0.5%," customers who thought they were receiving the best rate were offended. In response to the legal and public relations issues, the terms base rate, or reference rate, were adopted. At my community bank, we commonly offered *prime plus 2%* to our best customers, because they were small businesses, borrowing for six months, or more.

Borrowers may prefer fixed rate loans in order to fix their costs, but banks prefer floating rate loans, because of their recurring need to bid for deposits in a changing interest environment. Of course, if banks expect market interest rates to fall, they will encourage fixed rates for loans.

There may be substantial other costs associated with bank borrowing. For example, **Compensating Balances Requirements** are average deposits to be held at the bank during the loan. After all, every borrower maintains bank balances, somewhere. For your lender, these deposits are his raw material inventory. Why not keep them with him ? Compensating balances are only a problem, if the borrower wouldn't keep them anyway. (That is: a problem only if the required balance exceeds clearing balance needs.) The good news is that float counts, because it's money that the bank has, until they must pay your checks. **Annual clean ups** are a period of time during which a line of credit is not used. The ability to pay-off the credit for a time (usually a month) demonstrates that the company has adequate liquidity and is not using the line of credit as a substitute for permanent working capital. The **Term Loan Agreement** specifies operating restrictions, while the loan is outstanding. It may include collateral, financial ratio maintenance, even insurance for the lives of key officers (with the bank as beneficiary in the amount of the loan). These terms can impose limits on management actions, as well as added expenses.

To calculate the costs of borrowing, we must consider 1) all costs (interest, fees, and compensating balances, 2) the net amount available for use, and 3) the annual equivalent rate.

$$\frac{\text{All Costs associated with the financing}}{\text{the Net Amount Available for Use}} \quad x \quad \frac{365}{\text{Loan Days}} \quad = \quad \% \text{ APR}$$

For example, consider a loan amount of $500,000 with maturity of 90 days, a loan origination fee of $300, an interest rate of 7%, and a compensating balance requirement of 10%. Then, the calculation would be:

$$\frac{\{\$300 + [\$35,000 / 4]\}}{\$450,000} \quad x \quad \frac{365}{90} \quad = \quad 8.04 \%$$

For large, well-established firms, **Commercial Paper** may be an alternative to bank borrowing. Commercial paper is the *short-term, unsecured promissory note* of a financially strong firm. It is sold by direct placement, or dealer placement. A *Fee* is paid to a bank for guaranteeing payment (1% per annum is typical). These notes are sold *at discount* to par. The gain in value is the return. Buyers include all sorts of organizations and enterprises looking for marketable securities, as sources of modest income for temporary surplus funds. The following example of *270 day Commercial Paper* demonstrates the cost to issuer (borrower)

```
PAR                           =  $1,000,000
less fee ¾ %                  =       7,500
less discount at  4 % per annum =     30,000
funds available to borrower   =     962,500
```
$$\textbf{APR} = \{ 37{,}500 \ / \ 962{,}500 \} \ \textbf{x} \ \ 4/3 = \textbf{5.195\%}$$

Banks may, or may not, require **collateral** to secure their loan. For loans that do require collateral as protection for the creditor (lender), there will be a **Security Agreement** which specifies the terms of the loan, identifies specifically the collateral pledged, and assigns the rights to the creditor. A *Public Filing* allows other creditors to be aware of the debt and the assignment of assets. Collateral doesn't reduce the risk of default, but it does increase the creditor's options and helps keep the debtor's attention on the obligation. The bank doesn't want to seize and sell the asset. That would be bad public relations and often results in a loss, anyway. Creditors prefer collateral which has a useful life similar or longer than the term of the loan. And of course, liquid assets are preferred. The **Ratio of Loan Amount to Collateral Value** is a consideration which can increase the likelihood of repayment and reduce the probability of loss, if the collateral must be seized and liquidated. Interest rates are typically higher, because of the administrative expense of perfecting title to the collateral and monitoring its status. There are also **Commercial Finance Companies**, called "asset based lenders" or "hard money lenders," that look to the collateral for repayment. They are the last resort for desperate borrowers.

Support for working capital loans usually takes the form of liens against accounts receivable, or inventory. In the case of pledging accounts receivable, the lender will evaluate the accounts receivable, considering the agings, concentrations, and financial strength of obligators. The lender will classify the accounts receivable and offer a *maximum percentage of face value* which he will advance, considering the credit worthiness of the borrower and the obligators. Loan documents, including security agreements, will be executed, and title to the receivables perfected and control of collection of the accounts receivable will pass to the lender. The borrower's customers may never know that their obligations have been assigned to the bank, receiving only a notice to remit payment to a P.O. Box controlled by the bank. Receipts are credited first against the loan balance, and then to the borrower's deposit account, often in the percentage split of the loan-to-value advance.

An alternative to borrowing against accounts receivable from a bank is **factoring**. A factor is a specialized financial institution that collects receivables from customers and should understand its industry very well. Factors are common in the garment industry, where designers take orders from retailers and contract with manufacturers to make and ship the goods. In order to pay the manufacturers, cash is needed long before the retailers pay the designers.

Factoring involves the *Sale of Receivables* to the factor, with or without recourse. The factor evaluates the quality of the receivables and identifies the receivables that it will purchase. The terms negotiated include discounts from the face value of the receivables, and fees. The payments to the originator may be take the form of 1) Advances prior to the collection of the accounts, or 2) Credits as payments are received. Factors will pay interest on credit balances. Aside from converting credit to cash, factoring will save the originator collection costs. However, the vendor should be careful to evaluate their customers to assure that the accounts receivable generated will be attractive to their factor.

Inventory financing may also require liens. The inventories of raw materials and finished goods are preferred, because they have market resale value (liquidity). Perishable items, goods in process, and specialty items are undesirable, because of storage and liquidity problems. Inventory must be tracked by checking regularly, including logging inventory received and inventory sold. Banks will charge the borrower for these added costs.

Inventory loans may take any of three forms. **Floating Inventory Liens** are general liens on inventory; as items are sold, they are removed and the loan is reduced, or new inventory is acquired, valued, and substituted. Because of difficulties in tracking and controlling these inventories, advances will be small portions of value (30-50%). **Trust Receipt Inventory Loans** are used for high value items, identified by serial numbers. Lenders may advance 80-90% of value. Liens are recorded against specific serial numbers. "Flooring" of car inventories for dealers would be an example. **Warehouse Receipt Loans** occur when an independent warehouse company controls and arranges storage and release of inventory in a secure section of its facility. A *Terminal* Warehouse handles inventory for many customers at a central facility. A *Field* Warehouse is in a secured area of the borrower's facilities. All the costs of administration are borne by the borrower. These expenses remind us of the appeal of supplier credit, if it is available.

Questions for review and tests:

Explain the steps in preparing a cash-flow budget and pro-forma financial statements, as planning tools.

Explain the percent sales method and its use in estimating a company's external financing needs. (Be careful to enumerate all steps in applying the % sales method. Hint: there are at least six steps.)

Explain the principle of suitability and the hazards of ignoring suitability.

What other factors are considered in selecting the sources of external financing ?

Explain the three motives for holding cash and marketable securities.

Compare and contrast the operating cycle and the cash conversion cycle.

Explain the three elements of accounts receivable management.

How would you evaluate the profitability of a specific request for credit ?

Compare and contrast: factoring, supplier credit, bank loans, and commercial paper, as sources of short-term, external financing.

Moving inventory in New Delhi, India

Lesson #3.7 Financial Capital Instruments & Leases

You are familiar with the important economic functions of financial markets --- providing reliable means of payments, originating securities that broaden the opportunities for saving and for borrowing, and other instruments, such as swaps and insurance, that help clients to manage their financial risks. Recall that **securities** are given to the provider of funds (the saver, lender) by the user (the borrower, spender). They *secure* the transaction by stating clearly the rights of the lender and the obligations of the borrower, while the credit is outstanding. They help us to avoid misunderstandings, and they enhance the probability that commitments will be honored. In evaluating securities, we must identify the promise, assess the likelihood that the promise will be honored, and then determine the value of the promise. Think of any security primarily as a promise of a cash-flow --- one or more payments over the life of the obligation.

Financial Capital Instruments are long-term securities. They permit the issuer to acquire funds that will be available for many years, allowing the issuer to undertake long-term investments in activities without worrying about untimely repayment obligations. In this lesson, we review the characteristics of a variety of capital instruments. In the broadest classes, we can distinguish debt, equity, and hybrid securities. In lessons #6.5 and #6.6, we will elaborate in detail on the methods of valuing bonds, shares, and preferred stocks.

We begin with the **Bond Contract**. This is a form of debt. Bonds have four important characteristics. **Par Value** ("face value") is the sum that is promised to be paid at maturity. It is also the basis for the calculation of interest payments. In the US, typically par value is $1,000, and bonds are traded in round lots of ten bonds. However, there are issues with pars of $10,000 and even $25,000. The **Coupon Rate** is the interest rate to be applied to the par value to determine the total annual payments to the bond holder. Usually, these payments are made semi-annually. So, a bond with a par of $1,000 and a coupon of 6% will pay interest of $30, twice a year. There are special cases, such as floating rate bonds, whose interest payments are adjusted according to some reference rate, and zero-coupon bonds which are sold at discount and pay no interest. The third element is the **Maturity Date**, the date on which the final interest coupon and the par value are paid to the bond holder. Finally, there is an **Indenture Agreement** which specifies the terms of the contract, including the rights of bondholders (creditors) and the obligations of issuer (debtor). There will be a **Trustee**, a bank that will manage the bond records and payments. The trustee will also sue on behalf of the bondholders, if the debtor violates the agreements (defaults).

Bonds are created in a variety of forms to meet the needs of borrowers and lenders. The closer the investment bank can meet the needs of the borrowers, the more they will be willing to pay in interest, and the closer the design meets lender preferences, the less expensive will be the program for the borrower. Ideally, the design of the issue reassures lenders without burdening borrowers, and the transfer of funds can be achieved at low cost.

Some of the variants are:

Fixed Maturity bonds are very straight forward. Interest is paid semi-annually, and principal (par) is paid at maturity. **Serial Bonds** are issued in *series*, a group of bonds carrying different maturities and rates under the same offering. For example, a billion dollar issue may include ten sets of bonds, each totaling $100 million, with one set maturing each year starting in year eleven and ending in year twenty. The proceeds are used for the same purpose, such as the purchase of six commercial aircraft. The appeal to the bond buyers is that they can choose a preferred maturity, and if they choose one of the longest, they know that the retirement of earlier maturities protects the value of their loan by reducing the total debt outstanding, even though the collateral value (the planes) depreciates. For the borrower, the serial bonds can offer lower rates on the shorter maturities and thus save on total interest expense. **Sinking Fund Bonds** commit to the retirement of a portion of the debt annually, after a specific date, until all bonds are paid. This will reduce the debt, as the collateral depreciates. In this case, the issuer (debtor) can purchase the required par value of bonds in the open market, or call them from bondholder randomly, in order to meet the retirement obligation. If the bonds are selling at a discount, then the issuer will buy the bonds in the market. If the bonds are selling at a premium, the required number of bonds will be called. This latter possibility is unattractive to bondholders. **Consols** are bonds which carry no maturity. Their market value will gyrate with market conditions. (The British government borrows in this way.)

Bonds may also carry provisions that give options to the debtor, or to the bondholder. When we use the term a **Call Provision**, we mean that the holder of the options may "call the security to him," if he pays the designated price. **Callable Bonds** give the debtor the option of refinancing, if he is willing to pay the **Call Price**. Of course, the debtor will want to refinance, if market conditions offer him the opportunity to do so at new lower rates than he is paying on the existing debt. Perhaps, his coupon is 6%, but he has been advised that he could issue new bonds at 5%, or sell shares at a very high price. On a large issue, saving 1% each year could be a lot of money. Naturally, the call provision is unattractive to the bondholder. He's quite happy that he has a 6% bond in a 5% world. He can hold it and enjoy the extra income, or sell the bond to other savers, at a premium. To offset the disadvantage to the lender, the indenture may include **Call Protection**, a period of time before the debtor may call the bond and a call premium (above par value) that will be paid, if the bond is called. For example, the call provision on a bond issued in 2015 with a twenty year maturity, may state that the debtor may call the bond at $103 per $100 after Jan.1, 2020.In this way, the bondholder is assured his yield for the first five years and a small gain if the bond is called thereafter. A less common feature is a **Put Provision**, which gives the bondholder the right to require that his bond be repurchased by issuer. When we use the expression "put," we mean that the holder has the option to "put the security" to the other party and must be paid the agreed price. Put features on bonds may protect the bondholder from deteriorating financial conditions of the debtor, and may serve to protect the debtor from hostile take-overs, a form of *poison pill* defense. A put feature may be valuable in a rising interest rate environment, or when actions of debtor increase risk and reduce value of the security. Why would a borrower give this privilege to his creditor? He does it to attract investors and sell the debt at low cost.

We can also distinguish bonds by the type of security offered in the form of collateral. Many bonds are unsecured, meaning no specific assets are pledged to the repayment of the debt. This are often listed as **debentures** --- unsecured, general obligations of the debtor. However, popular forms of secured bonds are **Mortgage Bonds** which are secured by real estate; and **Equipment Trust Certificates** which include liens on specific, high value equipment, such as aircraft, ships, or railroad box cars.

There are also **Income Bonds** for which interest is paid, only out of income. These are more common in Europe than America, where they are usually issued in the restructuring plans of troubled companies.

Bonds are often rated by specialized agencies to help potential investors judge their suitability. Some of the rating services are Moody's, Standard & Poor, Fitch's (for banks), and Best (for insurance). Examples follow:

Ratings:	Standard & Poor	Moody's
investment grade	AAA+ to AA-	Aaa1 to Aa3
medium	A+ to BBB-	A1 to Baa3
speculative	BB+ to B-	Ba1 to B3
junk	CCC to D	Caa1 to C

The ratings are based 50% on company analysis: cash-flow, leverage & coverage, profit, and asset efficiency, and 50% on general risk analysis: industry group & pricing power. Crudely stated, 1) investment grade means all obligations are being met and the rater is confident that they will continue to be met even in tough times, 2) medium means that obligations are being met, but the company could have difficulty in tough times, 3) speculative means that obligations are being met but unconventionally, such as out of the sale of assets, 4) junk, these issues have no visible means of support.

Share of owners are commonly called "stocks" here in America. (In Britain, "stock" is a synonym for inventory.) I will use shares, stocks, and equity interchangeably, as terms for **Equity Capital.** The shareholders are fractional owners. They have the right to elect Directors who hire the officers and establish policies. Shareholders have the right to vote directly on material matters, such as mergers and acquisitions. (Debt holders only gain voting rights, if covenants have been violated, i.e. in the event of default.) Shareholders have claims on income and assets, but those claims are subordinate to the claims of creditors. (Shareholders are the last paid.) And dividends can be paid to shareholders, only after interest on debts and preferred dividends are paid. If the company is liquidated, the company's assets are sold and proceeds paid first to employees and customers, then second to government, third to secured creditors, fourth to unsecured creditors, and finally to equity holders, the shareholders. Naturally, the owners expect substantial dividends and capital gains (increase in the value of their shares) to justify the risks that they take as residual claimants.

Equity is permanent financing. It does not mature. Accordingly, the liquidity of shares is an issue, and access to secondary markets is important and will effect value and stability of share prices.

Dividends paid by the company are not a tax deductible expense; interest payments to creditors are. And dividends received by the shareholders are taxed as ordinary income. These are other reasons why equity is an expensive source of financial capital.

Preferred Stock has some of the characteristics of common stock shares and some of the characteristics of debt. Preferred stock has a par value (often, $50 or $100) and pays a dividend based on a percentage of its par value (or a fixed dollar amount, if the preferred (pf) stock has no par value). Shares of preferred stock are senior to the rights of common stock holders with respect to dividends and par value in liquidation, but those preferred shares are subordinate to the other obligations listed above (employees, customers, etc.). Preferred issues are commonly used by utilities, banks, and insurance companies, and may be part of a merger or restructuring plan. Preferred stock can increase financial leverage for the common shareholders, without compromising the company's credit rating or its coverage ratios for senior debt.

Preferred stock has tax advantages for corporations. Under US law, inter-corporate dividends are 70% tax excludable for the recipient. And preferred stockholders are not normally given voting rights. Hence, the company that wishes to support a supplier, or commercial customer, may do so by purchasing a preferred stock offering. The investing company has priority over the common shareholders and gains some income at a low tax rate, and the issuer gets some permanent financing without diluting ownership, or incurring a heavy interest burden.

In difficult times, the preferred dividend may be omitted, while interest on debt may not. If the preferred dividend is omitted ("passed"), payment of common dividend is prohibited. In liquidation, preferred shareholders receive par value, if funds are available after satisfying employees, customers, government, and creditors.

The fundamental features of preferred stock are the par value, the dividend (expressed as a percentage of the par), and the dividend dates. There may be restrictive covenants which specify the rights of the preferred shareholders and obligations of the issuing company. Examples are rules for the continuity and payment of dividends, for "passing" (omitting the dividend), for the sale of senior securities, recourse in the event of mergers or sale of assets, rules for net working capital maintenance, payment of common dividends, and common stock repurchase actions. Most preferred stock has a cumulation provision which requires that dividends that have been "passed" ("omitted" or "in arrears") must be paid, before a common dividend is paid. Some preferred issues may have participation provisions which allow for participation in the increased dividends of the common stock in accordance with some formula. Preferred stock may have Call or Put features. Finally, there may be conversion features which allow preferred shareholders to exchange their shares for shares of common stock, again in accordance with a stated formula based on the preferred share's par value and a conversion price for the common stock. For example, preferred shares with par value of $100 may be exercised at a conversion Price of $25. Therefore, one share of preferred stock exchanges for four shares of common.

From the issuer's point of view, preferred stock has the advantage of increasing financial leverage with the flexibility that comes with the ability to pass the dividend if necessary. However, the preferred share's seniority to common shareholder claims, the high cost (the dividend is not a tax deductible expense), and the lack of liquidity of preferred shares, are disadvantages. The cost is generally higher than debt financing.

As indicated earlier, **Common Stock** represents ownership. The company may be **privately** owned by individual, **closely held** by small group, such as family, or **publicly** owned by a large number of unrelated investors. The common stock's par value is not important. Often, it is low to minimize property tax in some states, and to minimize the liability of the owner in the event of bankruptcy. However, when there are several classes of common stock, the par may relate to voting power of the several issues. (For example, Par $50 may have two votes, whereas Par $25 might only get one vote.) This convention leads to the peculiar entries under **equity** of Paid-in at Par, Paid-in in Excess of Par, and Retained Earnings. Consider the firm that issues a million shares with Par of $1. The proceeds of the issue are $20 million. The balance sheet entry would be $1 million paid in at par and $19 million paid in excess of par.

We can think of three numbers for shares: authorized, issued, and outstanding. The first are the number of shares authorized by the Directors under the corporate charter; the second are the number of shares issued by sale to investors; the third, shares outstanding, may be less than shares issued, if some shares have been repurchased by the company. Those repurchased shares will be held as treasury stock (no voting, dividend, or liquidation rights), and can be resold without further regulatory approvals.

The shareholders have voting rights in the election of directors and approval of major issues (usually, one vote per share owned). However, there may be special classes, such as non-voting "Class A." In 1958, Ford gave the family special class B shares by which the family could retain control of 40% of the voting rights. Another variant is super-voting, by which long-term owners get more votes. (This has been called "The Smucker's defense". Shares held 4 years or more were given 10 votes by Smucker's, as deterrence to corporate raiders.) Also, higher classes may get dividend and liquidation preferences, while lower classes get voting preferences. Voting may be done at the annual meetings or by proxy, a provision for absentee voting. Proxy statements are disclosures which are regulated by SEC. In the case of electing directors, there may be majority voting, one vote per director or issue, per share. Or there may be **cumulative voting** which allocates to each shareholder one vote per share times the number of directors' positions. This total may be allocated as the shareholder wishes. The purpose of cumulative voting is to create more opportunity of minority views to be represented on the Board. (I like the idea, but my friends who have been CEOs or Chairmen hate it. They don't like the troublesome insurgents.)

     Dividends are paid at the discretion of Board of Directors, usually quarterly. They may be payable in cash, stock, or merchandise. Similarly, the Board may authorize **Stock Repurchases**, using the company's cash to increase its financial leverage, boosting ROE, book value, and the share price, as the equity base shrinks. Share repurchases give existing shareholders the choice to sell for cash, or to enjoy capital gains, as the shares appreciate. The payment of dividends reduces retained earnings (a "spontaneous" source of financing) and therefore, increases the firm's need for external funds. However, dividends may be valued by shareholders, and thus contribute to a higher and more stable share price.

     The Board of Directors decides on whether, when, and how much, to pay in dividends. There are four dividend dates: the date on which the Board of Directors announces a dividend (the date the dividend is "declared"), the day on which the shareholders are identified (the shareholders "of record" date), the first day on which you could purchase the shares without being eligible for the dividend (the "ex-dividend" date) which is four days before the "of record" date, and the date on which the dividend is paid.

     Many companies will offer dividend reinvestment plans. Shareholders sign up, and dividends are used to purchase new shares. These are taxable transactions, but have little or no transaction costs. To honor these plans, the company may buy outstanding shares, or issue new shares.

     Some companies may pay dividends only after the equity needs of the company have been met. However, the company must consider the preferences of its shareholders. Are dividends valued by your investors ? Or would they prefer that retained earnings be plowed into new assets for growth ? Is the payment of dividends a factor in determining share value ? I suggest that *consistency* in the payment of dividends may be the key. Investors choose firms *whose existing dividend policy* meets their preferences. Shareholders consider the opportunity costs of retained earnings vs. dividends paid (taxed and then reinvested).

     Several factors effect **Dividend Policy**. Capital impairment restrictions (under the law) may prevent the company from paying dividends which would reduce book value below par value, or the restriction may prevent payments of dividends from paid-in capital. Dividends may not be allowed when company is in default on liabilities, insolvent, or bankrupt. Restrictive Covenants in loan agreements, or indentures, may limit, or prohibit, dividends if specific financial conditions are violated.

     Naturally, company policies matter. Rapid growth requires capital for investment in assets. Retained earnings provide funds directly and reduce the cost of new debt issues by lowering risk.

     There are several types of dividend policies. A **Constant Pay-out Ratio** policy will specify a percentage of earnings per share. However, if earnings per share vary, then so will the dividend. And a variable dividend may contribute to unstable share value. A **Regular Dividend** policy will be stable, perhaps a pay-out ratio is based on average EPS over the business cycle (a few years). The stability of the dividend can help stabilize the share price of a cyclic company in a cyclic industry, such as steel or autos. A third policy pairs a **Low Regular Dividend with an occasional Extra-ordinary Dividend** policy. This strategy requires very clearly statements of intention by the Board of Directors in order to be understood and valued by owners.

Stock Dividends have no real value; the dilution of EPS and book value will cause equal and opposite declines in share value. The company "pays" for new stock by shifting retained earnings to capital paid-in at par and paid in excess of par lines on their balance sheet. Similarly, **Stock Splits** will lower share price and may broaden market, and **Reverse Splits** will raise share price with no change in the value of the owners' positions.

Stock repurchase involves the company reducing its cash, or increasing its debt to reduce the shares outstanding. This will alter the capital structure and/or liquidity of the company, and with it, the liquidity, leverage, and coverage ratios. The share price should increase, because there is less dilution of ownership. The shares that are repurchased become treasury stock and may be reissued at any time. The effect on shareholders is the same an option to receive a cash dividend or reinvest it.

Stock rights grant existing shareholders the right to purchase additional shares. They are often granted for closely held and illiquid issues, in conjunction with new offerings. Existing shareholders know and presumably like the company. If they choose to exercise their rights, fewer shares need to be sold by the underwriter to other investors. **Preemptive rights** to purchase additional shares can protect shareholders from dilution of their ownership. For **rights offerings**, the Board of Directors sets a "date of record" and the stock trades "ex rights" four days earlier. Holders of record may exercise, or sell their rights, or let the rights expire. The Rights are exercised at **subscription price**, and their value depends on the number of rights required, time to expiration, and the difference between market price and the subscription price. Management must decide the subscription price (below market) and the number of rights needed to purchase a share (shares to be sold vs. number of shares already outstanding). Common stock has the advantages of 1) no maturity, hence no repayment, 2) increased equity which increases the company's ability to borrow, and 3) minimum constraints on owners and managers (no indentures). However, issuing common shares dilutes earnings and control, and is costly, because shareholders have high expectations for yield.

I need to note that there are many **international common stocks**. They may be listed on foreign stock exchanges. And they may be listed on American exchanges, if approved by the SEC and the particular exchange. A common practice is the sale of **American Depository Receipts**. A bank purchases a large block of shares of an international company. The bank registers the holdings with the Securities Exchange Commission which requires the usual disclosures, including financial disclosures according to SEC standards. The bank creates ADRs that represent shares of the holdings of the bank, and the ADRs are listed on an exchange and sold to the public. (You might say ADRs are derivative securities.)

An important alternative to raising financial capital, or using term loans, to acquire assets is **leasing**. Leases are contracts for the use of an asset. Payments are tax deductible expenses. The **lessor** is the owner who receives payments, as well as any investment tax credit and depreciation deductions. The basic types of leases are 1) **operating leases** which are contracts which may be canceled. Payments under operating leases are less than initial cost of the asset, and the life of the asset exceeds the term of lease, (although it may become obsolete). Finally, the asset is returned to the owner at end of lease term, although the lessee may have right to purchase the asset at that time.

2) a **financial lease** (or "capital lease") has a longer term and may not be canceled. Total payments exceed acquisition costs of lessor. These are often used to acquire the use of buildings, land, or large equipment, without tying up large amounts of financial capital. The FASB requirements for a capital lease are 1) ownership transfers at end of lease, or 2) the purchase option is below fair market value, or 3) the term of the lease is 75%, or more, of useful life of the asset, or 4) the initial present value of the lease contract is greater than 90% of the fair market value of the asset.

There are several variations of leasing arrangements. A **direct lease** occurs, when the lessor owns the asset to be leased. A **sale-leaseback** occurs when the lessee sells asset for cash, and then leases back the same asset from the new owners, making fixed periodic payments. A **leveraged lease** has the lessor acting as an equity partner, with a lender supplying the balance of the acquisition cost.

The terms of the lease contract include 1) a description of asset, 2) the duration of the contract, 3) the lease payments and due dates, 4) the maintenance, tax, and insurance responsibilities, 5) the renewal and purchase options, and 5) the consequences of violations.

Leasing can be an attractive source of finance. We compare the costs of a lease to the costs of a purchase. We find the after-tax cash outflows under the lease. These are the tax adjusted annual lease payments plus the cost of exercising any final year options. And we find after-tax cash outflows under a purchase, including loan payments and maintenance costs, and tax adjustments, such as investment tax credits and depreciation. Finally, we calculate the present value of the two streams of cash outflows. (We use our after-tax cost of debt as the discount rate. See lesson #3.8.) We choose the alternative with the lower present value of outflows.

We account for our leases differently depending on their classification. The **capitalized lease** is recorded with the present value of the lease payments shown as asset and as a liability on our balance sheet. On the other hand, the features of an **operating lease** are disclosed in footnotes to financial statements.

The advantages of leasing begin with the lease payments being tax-deductible expenses. Notice that lease payments may include payments of principal and interest, and so, our tax deduction is larger than a simple deduction of interest alone. On the other hand, we don't get the depreciation deduction. (The owner/lessor enjoys that.)

Leasing can provide 100% financing and effective depreciation of land. If we were to purchase a building, we could depreciate furniture, fixtures, and equipment at one rate, and the building at another, but we couldn't depreciate the land. However, with a lease, all payments are deductible, and our payment likely includes the owner's total cost. And the attractiveness of being an owner/lessor to capture the depreciation tax deduction leads to competition that passes some of that benefit along to us in the form of lower lease payments.

Consider purchasing a building for $2,000,000 of which improvements are $1.5 million and the land $0.5. I sell the building and lease it back under a twenty-five year capital lease. I make lease payments of $150,000 per year and a residual purchase price of $500,000. I don't have any money tied up in the building, and all of my payments are tax deductible. If I purchase and hold the building, I get depreciation and any mortgage interest deduction, but no tax credit for my principal reductions.

And we obtain the services of the asset without showing deteriorated financial ratios. (You will remember that when we calculate financial ratios, we should adjust our coverage ratios to include all fixed payments.) A major appeal of the use of sale-leaseback is the improvement of a company's liquidity. Other advantages include avoiding the costs associated with the obsolescence of the equipment, and the restrictive covenants associated with bonds and loans.

However, there are **disadvantages to leasing**. There is no stated interest cost. (You can impute the effective interest rate from the comparison of present values.) So, costs may be quite high. (In my example above, the rate is slightly above 6%. For the lessor with large taxable income, the depreciation capture may be more valuable.) Second, the contracted payments must be made, even if the asset becomes unusable or obsolete. Third, the lease may prohibit the lessee from making alternations or improvements that would enhance its usefulness. And finally, any salvage value will be realized by the lessor, as owner.

I hope this brief summary of the variety of capital instruments permits you to recognize a few of the important characteristics.

Questions for review and tests:
Compare and contrast bonds, common stock, and preferred stock.
Compare and contrast capital leases and financial leases.
What are the advantages and disadvantage of leasing ?
How would you compare the costs of purchasing to the cost of leasing ?
What are the considerations in selecting a dividend policy ?
A Note has a Par Value of $1,000, a Coupon Rate of 7% and a maturity of exactly four years. If Notes of similar maturity and risk are offering a yield of 6%.
What should the market price of the Note be ? (Show all calculations, and explain each step.)

Rice fields in Cochin, India

Lesson #3.8 Capital Structure and the Cost of Capital

The **Cost of Capital** is a calculation of the weighted average cost long-term financing. Firms should progress toward the lowest cost, or **optimal capital** structure. The actual cost of capital, and particularly the incremental cost, (the cost of raising additional capital), is the magic number in determining whether a project will increase the value of a company. The cost of capital is the **rate of return** which the firm must obtain to maintain the market value of its shares. To calculate the cost of capital, the cost of each element of long-term financing must be calculated and then averaged.

The firm's **capital structure** is the mix of long-term debt and equity. Capital structure influences the firm's market value (its share price times shares outstanding) by its effects on *risk and return* (yield) for the owners. So, management must understand the relationship between *risk, returns, and share prices.*

Let's start with the concept of **leverage**, *the use of fixed costs to magnify the effect of a change in sales onto the return on equity.* Leverage is achieved by fixing a portion of costs, so that changes in sales magnify changes in profit. We can distinguish two types of leverage, which is achieved by substituting fixed costs for variable costs. An example may help. Consider two companies with similar operating profits but different structures.
Company "A" out sources many functions. Company "B" carries out those tasks internally.

Sales	100	+20% =120		100	+20% = 120	
COGS	70	+20% = 84		40	+20% = 48	
Gross Profit	30		36	60		72
GA&S	10	no change	10	40	no change	40
Operating Profit	20		26 (+30%)	20		32 (+ 60%)

Assume that sales increase by 20% and that fixed costs do not change. You can see that the "fixed costs" imply a magnification effect. Of course, a decline in sales is also magnified. We call this **Operating Leverage**, which can be calculated by the ratio:

Gross Profit / Operating Profit

In the example, Company "A" has operating leverage of 30/20 = 1.5, and operating profit increases by 1.5x the change in sales (20% x 1.5 = 30%). For company "B" the operating leverage is 3x the change in sales (60/20 = 3) and 20% x 3 = 60%.

Financial Leverage is achieved by using debt with its fixed payments as a substitute for equity. It's about the financial structure of the company, and the magnification of changes in operating profit on net income and thus, earnings per share.

Let's expand the example to consider financing:
Both companies require 100 in assets to support its activities, and both companies have 40% current liabilities, so they need 60 in capital. Company "A" is conservative its 80% equity and 20% debt, while Company "B" relies heavily on debt 20% equity and 80% debt. Company "A" pays 6% on its debt and company "B" (being more risky) pays 7%. So, the income statements are:

	Company A			Company B		
Operating profit	20	+20%	24	20	+20%	24
Interest Expense	1		1	4		4
Net Income Before Tax	19		23 (+21%)	16		20 (+25%)

When operating profit increases by 20%, the percentage increase in NBT is larger, as shown.

We can calculate the **financial** leverage by the ratio **Operating Profit / Net Income before Tax**
For company "A"   20/19 = 1.05   for company "B"   20/16 = 1.25
The 20% increase of operating profit becomes 21% in NBIT for "A" and a 25% increase for "B."

If the company's tax rate is constant and the number of shares outstanding is also unchanged, then there will be no further magnification, as we move from Net Before Tax to Net After Tax, and earnings per share. Therefore, we can compare the percentage change in EPS to the percentage change in Operating Profit, or the simple ratio of **Operating Profit/Net Income after Tax** to measure financial leverage.

Businesses choose a strategy for operations and operating costs, and also a strategy for financing, their combination of debt and equity. They also consider the trend of sales (up or down) and the volatility of sales (the variability). Considering the acceptable changes in Net Before Tax, they choose a strategy which combines both forms of leverage. **Combined Leverage** is:

Operating leverage times Financial Leverage

Measured by **Gross Profit/ Operating profit** multiplied by **Operating profit/ Net Before Tax**
Simplifying by cancellation, we get the measure of Combined Leverage:

Gross Profit / Net Income before Tax

In our example Company "A" has combined leverage of 1.5 x 1.05 = 1.575, and a 20% increase in sales is estimated to contribute to a 31.5% increase in NBT.
Company "B" has combined leverage of 3.0 x 1.25 = 3.75, and the same 20% increase in sales would lead to an increase of NBT of 75% !

Let's check the number to see if our estimates are accurate. We need to include the changes in operating profit:
Company "A"   sales increase to 120 and operating profit to 26, subtract interest expense of 1. To get NBIT of 25, an increase from 19 to 25 is an increase of 31.6% !
Company "B"'s operating profit increases to 32; subtract its interest expense of 4 to get NBIT 28. The increase from 16 to 28 is 75%.

Of course, a decline in sales is also magnified. Can you calculate the effect on Net Income Before tax of a 20% declines in Sales ? (I get Company "A" NBT = 13; and Company "B" NBT = 4   How do feel the Directors and shareholders will feel about this ?) To review,

1) Fixed Operating Costs *magnify* the effects of changes in sales on the firm's
   operating earnings (and they magnify risk).
We can measure the *degree of operating leverage* as we did:
   Gross Profit / Operating Profit
or in three other ways that are equivalent:
   % change in EBIT   /   % change in Sales
   or   **{Gross Profit / Sales }   / { Operating Profit / Sales }**
   or   **Gross Profit Margin / Operating Profit Margin**
Can you prove that they are all the same ? Remember your definitions.

2) Firms can choose fixed or variable costs techniques for accomplishing operating functions, as a matter of strategy. For example, producing "in-house" vs. outsourcing. These strategic decisions alter operating leverage. Leverage raises **business risk**, the ability to meet obligations, e.g. operating costs. Operating leverage raises **breakeven sales** requirements. So, calculating breakeven levels can be useful in evaluating the risk. We will consider financial break-evens here. (You have seen break-even quantity calculation before, in Lesson #1.5.)

Gross profit measures the gain in revenue from each additional sale. Hence, we often call the gross profit margin, the *contribution margin.* If my price per donut is $0.75 and my COGS (additional costs of making and selling a donut) is $0.05, then each additional sales yield gross profit of $0.70 which can be used to cover overhead, interest expenses, and taxes. To determine the sales required to cover our over-head, (GA& S), we can gross up the overhead as follows:

General Admin. & Sales divided by Gross Profit Margin = Operating Break-even Sales
We can apply the same principle to calculate the break-even sales requirement including fixed financing expenses:

[GA&S plus financing costs] divided by gross profit margin = pre-tax breakeven sales
In the examples below, the breakeven sales requirements are:

	Walmart	**Phillip Morris**
Operating break-even	$15 billion / 20% = $75 billion	$16 billion / 40% = $40 billion
Adding financing	$16 billion / 20 % = $80 billion	$17.2 billion / 40% = $43 billion

Operating leverage raises fixed costs, so we need to be confident that we can exceed the break-even sales at the new level of fixed costs. Does this explain why new companies outsource many activities, but bring them inside, as sales grow and become more stable and predictable ?

3) Let's review **Financial leverage.** Fixed financing cost magnify the effects of changes in operating income on net income. (And they magnify the risk of default.) Examples of fixed financing costs are the interest on debt, lease payments, and the dividends on preferred stock. We measured financial leverage as **Operating Profit / Net Income Before Tax** but we could use:

% change in NBT   /   % change in Operating Profit
Remember that one measure of financial risk is the coverage ratio, comparing operating profit to fixed financing expenses, such as interest expense, lease payments, and dividends. We can also use cash-flow coverage in a similar way. Let's add financial breakeven points to help us to evaluate and compare different financing plans.

When operating income equals fixed financing expenses, we are breaking even. How far can sales fall, before we hit that point ? As we increase our reliance on debt and incur these additional costs, we gain financial leverage, but also raise our breakeven point. This suggests that we need to co-ordinate our combined leverage (**total leverage**), the effect of fixing some operating and some financing costs. We measured combined leverage above by:

Operating Leverage   times   Financial Leverage   =   Total Leverage
But we could just as well use   **% change in NBT / % change in Sales**

Thus, our total risk is a combination of combined effect of operating and financial leverage. Does this explain why companies with *high* operating leverage choose *low* financial leverage ? Does this explain why companies with *low* operating leverage choose *high* financial leverage ? Does this explain why *cyclical firms* choose to minimize operating and financial leverage ?

The following offers a comparison of two large corporations. While the example is a few years old, the ideas are still relevant. We'll compare:

	Walmart '96	**Phillip Morris '95**
Sales	93,627	66,071
COGS	74,564	39,617

Gross Profit	19,063	26,454
{GPM}	**20.36%**	**40.04%**

GA&S	14,951	15,928

Operat. Profit	4,112	10,526	
{OPM}	**4.39%**		**15.93%**

Operating Leverage:	**4.64**	**2.51**	GPM/OPM
interest on debt	888	1,179	

EBT	3,224	9,347	
{NPM (before tax)}	**3.44%**		**14.15%**

Financial Leverage

{OPM/NPM}	**1.28**	**1.13**

Combined Leverage

Op Lev X Fin Lev	**5.91**	**2.83**

Contribution Margin Breakeven Sales:
Fixed Costs / Gross Profit Margin

15,839/20.36%	17,107/40.04%

Break-even sales	**$ 79,195**	**$ 42,767**

Why would WalMart want more leverage than Phillip Morris ?
Consider the DuPont Ratios for each:

NPM	Sales/ Assets	Assets/Equity	Return on Equity
Walmart			
2740/ 93,627	93,627/35,180	35,180/ 13,741	
2.93% x	**2.661** x	**2.56**	= **20.0%**
Phillip Morris			
5,450/66,071	66,071/53,180	53,180/13,385	
8.25% x	**1.24** x	**3.93**	= **40.2%**

Operating Leverage is high for Walmart, because their GPM is low. They need leverage to generate a good ROE. Phillip Morris has a large Operating Profit Margin, so leverage is not needed to generate a strong ROE.

Consider now to our **capital structure**, the combination of long-term debt and equity that forms the foundation of our balance sheet, and enables us to conduct our business. Recall from the first few lessons of this book that we organize a business to make profit, which requires sales and the control of costs. In addition, we need assets to support the activities that generate sales and to assure consistent payment of our obligations. To support those assets, we borrow money. The money that our owners make available with no set obligation to repay, or to pay interest or dividends (although they may be expected at some future time) is called **equity** (also called Net Worth). All other forms of borrowing are called **debt**. Debt imposes obligations on the borrower which are specified in the term loan agreement or indenture. And debt endows the lender (creditor) with specific rights, while the debt is outstanding.

Two famous Economists, Franco Modigliani and Merton Miller[1] argued that under certain assumptions, capital structure doesn't matter. Unfortunately, when the assumptions, such as *no bankruptcy costs*, don't hold, the combination of debt and equity are important.

Let's look at the elements of capital structure. **Debt** confers tax benefits to the borrower, because interest payments are a tax deductible expense. Thus, for a profitable company which can borrow at 6% and faces a 33% tax rate, its effective cost of funds is 4%. On the other hand, debt imposes contractual obligations to make payments are promised, and any failure (even a delay) is a default which can trigger sanctions, including bankruptcy proceedings. Lenders will consider "The Five C's" of which cash-flow, operating profit stability, and coverage ratios are most important. Lenders will require higher interest rates to compensate for differences in risk and liquidity, if they are willing to lend at all. Term loan agreements and loan covenants will specify rights and obligations in the hope of reducing risk and assuring recovery in the event of default. **Equity** dilutes ownership and earnings per share. Dividends are not tax deductible to the payer, or the recipient (an important exception is preferred stock dividends paid to other corporations), and owners expect high yields to compensate for their position, as residuals recipients of income and capital gains.

We can expect the after tax cost of debt to be low, but it will rise as the debt ratio increases, because coverage ratios deteriorate. Accordingly, variations in operating profit and operating cash-flow are more likely to interfere with promised payments. The cost of equity is high, and it increases as debt ratios increase, because the owners, like the creditors, are exposed to more risk of loss and even bankruptcy. Capital structure is the weighted average of debt and equity. As a result of the considerations above, **the Cost of Capital** will decline initially as the debt: assets ratio increases from zero and returns on equity are magnified by financial leverage, but later the cost of capital increases because coverage ratios deteriorate.

Consider the following example: Assume that 1) our Debt Coupon is 6%   2) with a tax rate of 33%, our after tax cost is 4%, and 3) our Equity investors' expectation is 12%. Then, if we rely 100% on equity, our cost of capital is 12%, but if we rely on each equally (50% debt, 50% equity), and our coverage ratios are reasonable (5:1 or more), then our Cost of Capital will be   (4% + 12%)/ 2 = 6%. However, if we continue to expand our reliance on debt to, say 75% debt and 25% equity, then our coverage ratio will deteriorate (from 5 to 3.3), and creditors may require 9% and owners require 16% to accept the risks. Now our Cost of Capital will be 8.5% ({9% x 2/3} x 0.75 + 16% x 0.25). So, there is likely to be a capital structure which minimizes our cost of capital. In fact, there is a range within which cost of capital is minimized. It is defined by *the financial leverage that achieves a minimum required return on equity for the owners, and minimum fixed payment coverage ratios* (operating income and operating cash-flow) for the creditors. This will be the range of **optimal capital structure**.

Over the business cycle, we may vary our mix of long-term financing (capital structure). During the boom, when earnings and share prices are high, but so are interest rates, we will retain earnings and issue new shares, increasing equity, as a portion of our capital structure. This will improve coverage ratios, but depress the return on equity. During the recession, when share prices and interest rates are low, we will substitute debt for equity, increasing our ROE, but reducing our coverage ratios. So, we move back and forth within the range defined by our Board of Directors by the limits of the minimum acceptable returns on equity and the minimum acceptable coverage ratios.

Now that we understand the concepts, let's refine out techniques, as we must as financial managers. The calculation of the *cost of long-term debt* (Bonds) requires three steps:
First, we identify the **net proceeds of the debt issue**. That is, the dollars available after floatation costs (the discounts, fees, and commissions). So, a $100,000,000 bond issue may yield

net proceeds of $97,000,000. Second, we calculate the **before tax costs**. That will be the combination of coupon interest and amortized discount.

For example, if the issue's coupon is 6% and maturity twenty years, then:

Pre-tax cost $= \dfrac{[\text{Interest plus amortized discount}]}{[\{\text{Price} \times 0.6\} + \{\text{Par} \times 0.4\}]} = \dfrac{6 + \{3/20\}}{\{97 \times 0.6\} + \{100 \times 0.4\}} = \dfrac{6.15}{98.2} = \mathbf{6.26\%}$

Step three is calculation of **after tax costs** by applying our tax rate (state and federal):

Before Tax Rate x [1 - your tax rate] = 6.26% times (1 – 40%) = **3.76%**

You can see the appeal of relying on debt in high tax jurisdictions, if we can maintain good financial ratios.

The Cost of Preferred Stock is easy to calculate: *Preferred Dividends / Net Proceeds* So, the preferred issue of $50 million with a dividend of 4% of Par (= $100) and net proceeds of $49 million is simply $2/49 = **4.08%**

The Cost of Common Stock is trickier. We must impute from the price that investors are willing to pay to hold our shares, and our dividend and earning performance, what investors expect of us. We can use **The Gordon Model:**

Value = Dividend / {required rate of return minus the dividend growth rate}

As I discussed in lesson #1.4, and as will be demonstrated in more detail in lesson #6.5, fundamental value depends on benefits (earnings or dividends) capitalized at our required rate of return and adjusted for expected growth of the benefit. Accordingly, we can rearrange terms and deduce that:

Market Required Rate =   **Dividend / Price + Growth Rate of Dividend**

The Gordon model suggests the conclusion that the market participants value shares for two elements, the growth rate and the current dividend yield. And if we have been paying a dividend of 4% and growing at 5% per year, then we can reasonably conclude that our shareholders are content with a yield of 9%. If they are not, our share price would fall, until the combination of current dividend yield and growth achieved a satisfactory yield.

Contemporary investors appear to value earnings per share and growth of EPS in a similar manner. In some cases, dividends are almost irrelevant, if EPS are growing. In this case, we modify the Gordon Model by substituting EPS for Dividends:

Value = EPS / (required rate of return – EPS growth rate)

or   **Required Rate of return = EPS/ Price   + Expected EPS Growth**

To obtain our cost of new equity, we need to "gross up" our shareholders' required rate by the ratio of net proceeds to total issuing costs. For example, if shareholders have demonstrated an expected yield of 12% and we are paying 4% for the underwriting, then our costs will be (12% / 96%) = 12.5%.

An alternative, and complementary method, of estimating shareholders requirements is the **Capital Asset Pricing Model.** We look at the yield for companies that share our ***Beta***, an estimate of susceptibility to general risk (see lesson #6.3). This will be a risk free rate (usually taken to be the higher of the Treasury bill rate, or the inflation rate) plus a risk premium which has historically averaged 6% for "blue chip" stocks and 8-10% for small and medium sized companies. Analysts ("Quants") can provide you with the current CAP plot. So, if you know your company's **Beta**, you can estimate the market yield required by investors.

You will note that companies whose growth is slowing need to boost earnings per share, and, as that becomes more difficult, will need to increase their dividend in order to attract dividend oriented investors and thus, stabilize their share price.

Now, armed with our estimates of after tax cost of debt, cost of preferred shares, and cost of equity, we can calculate our **weighted cost of capital**, based on the portions of our total capital provided by each.

A few years ago, I calculated cost of capital for DuPont. Long-term Debt was $5,677 million, and represented 40% of DuPont's capital. The average interest rate on DuPont's debt was 6.8%, and its tax rate was 31%. Equity was $8,436 million, representing 60% of DuPont's capital. DuPont's Price: Earnings per Share ratio was $65/ $5.61 = 11.5. Applying our analysis:

6.8%   times   (1 – 0.31) = 4.69%   average after tax **cost of debt**

Using the Gordon Model for valuing stocks: yield = (dividend/ price) + growth rate.

The dividend was 2.5% of the price and the growth rate was 6.5%.

Thus, the estimated rate of return for investors was **9%**.

For a second opinion, we check the P/E ratio:

Earnings per share / Price = 1/11.5 = **8.7%.**

This confirms the idea that investors require a 9% return. Hence, the weighted average cost of capital for DuPont at that time was:

Debt: 4.7 % times 40% share plus equity: 9.0% times 60% share = 1.80% + 5.40% = **7.20%**

The combined cost of capital for DuPont was 7.20%

One of the reasons for managing our cost of capital to keep it in the range of **optimal capital structure** is the effect on the value of our firm. Recall that the optimal capital structure is not a precise number, but a range, whose limits are 1) enough financial leverage to achieve a satisfactory return on equity and 2) enough equity to assure prudent debt service coverage ratios.

A traditional approach to valuing our firm is based on the concept that the firm is worth some multiple of its operating profit. Net income will then depend on capital structure and taxes. Accordingly, if we *minimize* the cost of capital, we will *maximize share value.* In the following formula, the *market value* of the company is the *capitalized value* of its earnings.

Value =   EBIT {1 - tax rate }
Cost of Capital

The EBIT-EPS Approach to Optimal Capital Structure (optimal financial leverage)

To help us evaluate various financing plans, we could use graphic representations, placing Earnings per Share on the "Y" axis and associated operating profit (EBIT) on the "X" axis.

Recall that   **Operating Profit (EBIT) less interest and taxes = Net Income**

And   **Net Income / Shares outstanding   = Earnings Per Share**

We can plot **Earnings Per Share** as **EBIT** increases. We repeat for different capital structures, such as no debt, 10% debt, 20% debt, etc. The Degree of financial leverage is reflected in the slopes of the plots. Notice that a constant tax rate and constant number of shares outstanding implies that changes in Net Income before Tax, Net Income after Tax, and Earnings per Share will be proportionate.

({NBIT – interest expense} times {1- tax rate}) divided by shares outstanding =   earn per share

Another measure of risk is reflected in the EBIT intercepts --- the level of operating profit which would result in no net income. This is the financial breakeven point, where earnings per share equal zero. To repeat, it will be the intercept of our EPS/EBIT line with the "X" axis. The intercept on the "Y" axis will be the EPS loss when there is no EBIT but interest must be paid. Indifference between different financing plans will occur when the Earnings per Share for *several plans are equal,* and will be identified by the intersection of two or more financing plan lines. The financial risk associated with each plan can be estimated the financial breakeven intercepts and the coverage ratios. In these ways, the plots help us to evaluate and compare different financing plans. We would ask: "For the likely range of EBIT, which is the best structure to generate an acceptable range of EPS ?" (Note: While helpful, this last form of analysis has the weakness of ignoring the financial market's assessment of risk, as it influences the rate of return required by investors.)

As an example, consider a company with total capital of $1 billion, but using various amounts of debt. Vary operating profit $50 million, $75 million, and $100 million. We'll keep book value constant (@$10 per share), so less equity means less shares outstanding.

Example #1 no debt and no interest expense; operating profits vary from $50 -75-100 million
On our plot, the "X" axis and the "Y" axis intercepts are at "zero", the origin.

EBIT	EBIT less interest expense	after tax		per share		
50	**$ 50,000,000**	**x (1-30%)**	**/ 100,000,000 shares**	**==**	**$0.35**	**EPS**
75	$ 75,000,000	x (1-30%)	/ 100,000,000 shares	==	$0.525	EPS
100	$100,000,000	x (1-30%)	/ 100,000,000 shares	==	$0.70	EPS

Example #2 Using 20% debt. This creates financial leverage, but imposes interest expense, say 7%, ($14 million for $200 million in debt). Equity would be $800 million. On our plot, the "x' axis intercept is at EBIT = $14 million, and the "y" axis intercept is at -$0.123 EPS, a loss of 12.25 cents per share, (assuming that we recover of some our loss through tax loss carry forward).

EBIT	EBIT less interest expense	after tax		per share		
50	$ 36,000,000	x (1-30%)	/ 80,000,000 shares	==	$0.315	EPS
75	**$ 61,000,000**	**x (1-30%)**	**/ 80,000,000 shares**	**==**	**$0.534**	**EPS**
100	$ 86,000,000	x (1-30%)	/ 80,000,000 shares	==	$0.753	EPS

Example #3 Using 30% debt. This creates financial leverage, but imposes interest expense, say 7%, ($21 million for $300 million in debt). Equity would be $700 million. On our plot the "x' axis intercept is at EBIT = $21 million. And the "y" axis intercept is at EPS = -$0.21, a loss of 21 cents per share, (assuming that we recover of some our loss through tax loss carry forward).

EBIT	EBIT less interest expense	after tax		per share		
50	$ 29,000,000	x (1-30%)	/ 70,000,000 shares	==	$0.29	EPS
75	**$ 54,000,000**	**x (1-30%)**	**/ 70,000,000 shares**	**==**	**$0.54**	**EPS**
100	**$ 79,000,000**	**x (1-30%)**	**/ 70,000,000 shares**	**==**	**$0.79**	**EPS**

In this example, if EBIT is $50 million, then the "no debt" strategy is preferable. At EBIT of $75 million, there is little difference between structures. At EBIT of $100 million, the 30/70 ratio yields the highest EPS. Of course, each strategy alters our operating income to debt service coverage ratio.

	Example #1 coverage	Example #2 coverage	Example #3 coverage
EBIT $ 50 million	**infinite**	50/14 = 3.57	50/21 = 2.38
EBIT $ 75 million	infinite	**75/14 = 5.35**	75/21 = 3.57
EBIT $100 million	infinite	100/14 = 7.14	**100/ 21 = 4.76**

Concern about coverage may lead us to sacrifice some EPS for less risk, choosing "no debt" for EBIT = $50 million, 20% debt for EBIT =$75 million, and 30% debt for EBIT =$100 million.

Questions for review and tests:

Explain the calculation of a company's cost of debt.

Explain the calculation of a company's cost of equity.

{Be sure to clarify calculations of the costs to the firm of raising capital in each way.}

Explain the calculation of a company's combined cost of capital.

Compare and contrast operating leverage and financial leverage.

How would you calculate: financial leverage, operating leverage, and combined leverage ?

How would you identify the Optimal Capital Structure for your firm ?

[1] *Modigliani, F. and Miller, M. "The Cost of Capital, Corporation Finance and the Theory of Investment" (1958) American Economic Review **48** (3): 261–297*

A Mahout with his elephant, Cochin, India

Lesson #3.9 Capital Budgeting and the Acquisition of Financial Capital

The financial planning process begins with **the strategic plan.** You will recall the steps of strategic planning from lesson #1.8. Remember Peter Drucker's mantra, "Those who fail to plan are planning to fail." In brief, the steps are 1) the *Mission:* defines the firm, its purpose, and its values 2) the *Objectives:* financial measures of success, 3) the *Situation analysis:* condition, products, customers, and resources, 4) *SWOT analysis:* strengths, weaknesses, opportunities, and threats: both internal and external, 5) the *Goals & Timetables:* short-run and long-run, and 6) *Budgets:* the commitment of resources and development of measures of achievement (including efficiency) for accountability.

The strategic plan defines the types of long-term investments that would be suitable and the criteria for comparison. **The Capital Budgeting Process** is the systematic program for evaluating and selecting long-term investments. Examples of capital expenditure are the expansion of operations, the replacement of equipment (when maintenance costs are increasing), and the renewal of equipment, such as overhauling, or retrofitting. Other purposes are marketing programs, research and development projects, and institutional reorganization.

Where do we begin ? First, we must generate a number of proposals. Encourage employees, talk to customers, and consult suppliers. Next, review the ideas for fit with our plan, consistency with our mission, and for comparison of risks and rewards. Then, refer the likely proposals to the appropriate group for analysis. Identify the level at which analysis should occur. All groups, which will be effected by the decision to accept and implement or reject the proposal, should participate. Delegation may be done by size of dollar outlay, or by importance to the organization. Critical projects will need to be analyzed at higher levels of management. When a decision to implement a program has been made, resources must be allocated, and responsibility, matched with authority, assigned.

As we develop ideas, we can identify *independent projects* whose cash-flows are unrelated to other projects, *mutually exclusive projects* which, if chosen will eliminate some other projects, and *interdependent projects* whose costs or benefits will be altered by the implementation of other, related projects. Our ability to implement projects will be limited by the availability of resources, including funds for needed assets, and staff and management time and talents. Hence, projects must be compared and ranked by their likely contribution to the success of the organization.

The first step in choosing to accept, or reject, a project must be whether it meets our policy guidelines, as expressed in the mission and objectives of our strategic plan. Then, the entire steam of costs and benefits associated with the project over its expected lifetime must be identified and compared. Then, the projects can be ranked for priority by their contribution to the success (and therefore value) of the firm. We adopt the projects with the greatest value, until we have exhausted our resources. Lower value projects are shelved, and sometimes suggested to partners.

Having determined that a proposal is consistent with our mission and our situation, (few mistakes are more costly than losing focus by undertaking activities that distract us from our core identity), cash-flows must be estimated. Conventional cash-flows involve payments before receipts. For example, we install equipment, purchase inventory, process and ship goods, before receiving payments from customers. However, there are unconventional cash-flows for which the inflows precede the outflows. For example, we pay for travel or insurance in advance. There are annuities which are a series of equal payments, and there are the more typical *mixed streams* of uneven cash-flows, varying in amount and timing. The relevant cash-flows for planning purposes are the *incremental after-tax outflows* and *subsequent after-tax inflows*, associated with the project.

The major cash-flow components are 1) the initial investment, 2) the operating cash-flows, and 3) the discrete cash-flows associated with expansion, replacement, or termination of the activity. Replacement must consider the liquidation costs associated with termination of existing activities, as well as new cash-flows in comparison to the cash-flows of continuing existing activities without replacement. For many managers, this is emotionally difficult to do.

My friend, Brooks Firestone, reported to the Board of Directors of Firestone Tire and Rubber that Michelin was introducing a superior, radial tire and urged Firestone to do the same. However, the directors delayed, in order to depreciate recently installed conventional equipment. The company never recovered.

In replacing the obsolete VW Beetle, Volkswagen had choice between the recently acquired Audi sedan and their own VW Type 3 and Type 4 models. They chose their own in order to justify the large sunk costs of their development. Their decision almost sank the company. The Audi model was introduced later, as the "Fox," "Rabbit," or "Golf" in different markets, and saved the company, but five years were wasted.

Similar stories can be told about IBM's delay in introducing a PC with the Intel 386 chip which created an opportunity for Compaq to grab market share. So, the lesson is: *If replacement yields a positive present discounted value, considering all costs, you'd better do it, or your competitors will.*

To find the **initial investment,** consider 1) the cost of the new investment (net), 2) the installation costs (which can be capitalized and depreciated), 3) the proceeds from sale of the old asset, and 4) any tax implications (tax credits on investment, and tax obligations from sale of asset in excess of book value). To find the **operating cash-flows**, compare the *after-tax* cash-flows. Begin with anticipated revenue, expenses, depreciation, and taxes. Assuming no radical differences between accrual and cash basis, because we're looking at annual estimates, operating cash-flow will be net profit after taxes plus depreciation. If we are considering replacing or altering an existing project, then we must estimate the change in cash-flow, (*incremental cash-flow*) by comparing the cash-flows from existing activities *in each time period* to cash-flows from new projects under consideration. Armed with our estimates of **initial investment** *and* **incremental operating cash-flows, we can ask:**

1) Can we handle the financial requirements of this project ?
2) What is the value of this project, and how does it compare to other opportunities ?

Although some methods of evaluation are superior, you will often be asked to calculate as many as five different values for ranking projects. The two unsophisticated capital budgeting techniques don't consider time value of money; the three more sophisticated do, but in different ways. **Average Rate of Return** is calculated by dividing average profit by average investment. It uses accounting profits rather than cash-flows, (If profit is tied up in non-cash assets then, cash is not available.), and it ignores the time factor in value of money. (Earlier cash flows should be preferred to later.) **Payback Period** is the time, until the initial investment is recovered. Subtract from your initial investment the cash-flows for each year, until you reach zero. Now, the project is relying on its own cash for future operations. So, this method considers some cash-flows; there is some implicit consideration of time; and it may be a crude, unsophisticated measure of risk. However, the choice of acceptable payback period is arbitrary, and most importantly, payback period ignores *post-payback* cash-flows. So, a project that dies a few years after payback may be chosen over a project that takes longer to payback, but lasts for many years thereafter, and may even have enormous profits after payback, too. Nevertheless, many unsophisticated directors will want to know this number (demonstrating a bias dear to behavioral economists --- that we view our own initial investment as different from subsequent dollars, like the gambler who treats early winnings as "playing with house money" rather than his own).

The better and more sophisticated capital budgeting techniques apply the **present value** concept in order to compare cash-flows and establish value. We introduced this concept in lesson #2.9 and expanded it in detail in lesson #3.3. Because capital projects generate a stream of revenue and expenditure over time, and waiting for dollars has an opportunity cost (explicit when we must pay to borrow, implicit when we use our own money and therefore sacrifice the reward of other investments, saving, or lending), we need to account for the differences in timing. So, for each project, 1) we identify the amount and timing of each payment, --- cash receipts and cash payments, as we described above. 2) Then, we discount each payment *(that is, we determine the present value of each)* using our **cost of capital** as our discount rate, because it is the opportunity cost of our long-term financing. 3) We total the present values of all receipts and payments. 4) We subtract the initial investment from the present value of all those future cash-flows. The ***Net Present Discounted Value of a project*** is the discounted value of *all* the associated cash-flows, including the initial investment. Our decision rule becomes: _accept the projects with the highest NPDV_. Rank from highest NPDV to lowest, and cut off when investment funds and management resources are exhausted.

Intuitively, this means that we accept the projects that add the most value to our company. NPDV tells us that, if we implement the project and cash-flows work out as estimated, we will have increased the value of the company by that amount. If the initial investment is $10 million, and the NPDV is $8 million. We could say that to generate the same stream of net revenue, we should have invested $18 million, but we only had to invest $10 million. That's a good deal. The following table is one that I used to determine the value of a real estate project that we undertook in the wealthy community of Montecito, California. My estimates of value and costs were based on appraisals, and consultations with architects, contractors, and realtors. The first set is an estimate for building out the homes, and the second is for lot sales.

Do you remember the example of the Montecito Valley Ranch from lesson #3.3 ? (If not, take a look.) Do you remember whether we decided to build out the houses over eight years, or just sell lots ? The former would generate over $34 million in gross revenue and $10.4 million in NPDV. The latter would generate $8 million in NPDV. (Answer: we chose to sell lots and take the $8 million at low risk, rather working so hard with so many risks for an extra $2.4 million. Remember, "Pigs get fat, but hogs get slaughtered.")

Some directors like another method, called the **profitability index** which compares the present discounted value of the cash-flows to the initial investment. Formula:

PDV of cash-flows /   initial investment

PDV of all cash-flows, except the initial investment is used. The decision rule is: _Accept projects whose Profitability Index > 1.0_   We might also rank projects by their index, larger is better. This means that the project adds value. The problem common to all ratios, as with this index, is that it ignores size. Size does matter. Bigger projects may do the most to enhance the value of the firm.

When I was a corporate financial officer, I would often be asked to calculate the **internal rate of return** (IRR) for a project. Conceptually, it is easy, but the implementation is tedious. IRR is the discount rate which equates the initial investment to the present discounted value of all subsequent cash-flows. It is taking our present value vs. future value formula and solving for the discount rate that balances the two forms of cash-flow rather than the number

PDV or FV obtained by discounting or compounding at some interest rate. We can estimate the IRR if the future cash-flows are an annuity:

a) calculate payback period.

b) for the life of project find Present Value Annuity Factor equal to the payback period.

c) the discount rate associated with that PVAF (present value annuity factor) is your IRR.

if the cash-flows are a mixed stream:

a) calculate the average annual cash-flow (ignore the initial investment).

b) divide by the initial investment to get a payback estimate.

c) estimate IRR in the same manner as an annuity.

d) iterate:

1) Use your estimate of IRR to calculate PDV; if your result is positive, adjust IRR *up*.

2) If your result is negative, adjust your IRR *down*.

3) try again.

Once, we estimated the internal rate of return, the decision rules are: *Adopt projects whose IRR is greater than your cost of capital.* Rank projects from the highest IRR to the lowest, and cut off when investment funds are exhausted, or the cost of capital reached.

Aside from the tedium of finding the IRR, there are important problems. The size of the project and its potential contribution to company value is ignored, again. The logic is shaky, because the IRR number assumes that all cash-flows generated over the life of the project can be reinvested at the same rate, when in fact, there will be reinvestment risk. Nevertheless, some directors are familiar with the concept of internal rate of return and will try to demonstrate their brilliance by asking for it, and you should be able to answer. Then, you can comment on the superiority of NPDV by pointing out that *Net Present Discounted Value* assumes that all cash-flows can be reinvested at your cost of capital. This is realistic, because you could always retire debt and equity and save that much. *Internal Rate of Return* assumes that cash-flows can be reinvested at this project's own IRR. This is not realistic, because the best projects offer exceptional returns, not available in other projects. (However, don't get too cocky. Projects rarely work out exactly as anticipated. The colleague that you humiliate today is sure to point this out, when the accounts are settled.)

Before we move on, let me offer an example in which I estimated IRR to please the owners and potential investors in our resort in the West Indies, The Pineapple Beach Club. We raised $3 million for the project and planned to return the investors' cash in the fifth year, giving them 60% ownership thereafter.

Example of IRR from Santa Barbara-Antigua Land Development
identify cash-flow for investors

	year 1	year 2	year 3	year 4	year 5	year 6
repay principal	0	240	240	1000	1520	
{other distributions					1480	5000}
Ltd. Partners shares 60%					888	3000
total distributions to LPs	*240*	*240*	*1000*	*2408*	*3000*	

average payment = 6,888/6 = 1,148 PVAF = 3,000/1,148 = 2.61

For PVAF = 2.61 at 6 years, IRR = 30%

check PDV vs. Initial investment:

142,012 + 109,240 + 350,128 + 648,544 + 621,529 = 1,871,453 too low

try 20% = 166,667 + 138,889 + 482,253 + …..

251

You can see that project evaluation is a creative process. There are eight steps. Be careful. Be as accurate as you can. (When you are overly optimistic, you only fool yourself and set up unrealistic expectations.) Most importantly, set your ego aside, and ask those with experience for some rules of thumb, and again, later for review and validation of your estimates. The steps are 1) identify problem or opportunity, 2) acquire information --- such as market conditions or technology, 3) identify and evaluate the alternatives, 4) for those that "fit," identify the cash-flows by amount and timing, 5) select a discount rate, such as *your* cost of capital, 6) calculate the present values of each alternative, 7) select and implement the choice with the highest Net Present Value, and 8) monitor progress, evaluate, and modify.

For review, I offer the following hypothetical examples, to show the differences in the three most common methods, payback, IRR, and NPDV. Notice that which is superior depends on your point of view.

Examples:
Option "A"
Initial Cost $1,000,000
Future Net Cash-flow $200,000 per year for 8 years

Option "B"
Initial Cost $1,000,000
Future Net Cash-flow $170,000 for 12 years

Option "C"
Initial Cost $1,000,000
Future Net Cash-flow $150,000 for 16 years
Present Value @ 9%

Analysis:

	Payback	Internal Rate of Return	Gross PV	Net PV
Option "A"				
	5.0 years	less than 12%	$1,107,000	$107,000
Option "B"				
	5.9 years	**greater than 13%**	$1,217,370	$217,370
Option "C"				
	6.7 years	less than 13%	$1,246,950	**$246,950**

Which Project should be chosen and why ? Option "C" adds most to net worth

Now that we know how to manage working capital (lesson #3.6), evaluate projects (this lesson), and select our capital structure (lesson #3.8), we are ready to acquire the necessary funds to fulfill our ambitions. *How do we know that we need external funds ?*

Recall the process of Strategic Planning (lesson #1.8) and planning through the development of Pro Forma Financial Statements (lesson #3.6). We can think of the process of organizing a business as connecting four elements:

#1 Profit requires **#2 Sales** & control of **Costs** which require investments in **#3 Assets**

which must be funded by borrowing **#4 Liabilities** from owners or creditors. As we build our pro forma financial statements, we start with estimates of sales revenues (depending on both prices and quantities). Then, we estimate costs, based on reasonable, efficient ratios. Next, we estimate the required investments, the assets needed to support the activities. These, too, are based on efficient ratios. But let's be clear: *Build your pro forma statements on your own experience and industry averages. Do not assume that you will outperform your past or everyone else in the industry. Strive for excellence in execution and enjoy pleasant surprises and rewards, but don't plan on them.*

Now that we have estimated the assets that we will need, (what we call the *Assessment* responsibility), we can look for the money --- the best total, and combination, of liabilities. We consider sources within the company and its operations, **retained earnings** and **depreciation** (non-cash expenses). Profits provide cash, and non-cash expenses permit us to hold onto cash for a while longer. There will be some *spontaneous* growth of liabilities, as we expand our activities, such as **accounts payable** and **accrued expenses**. And we review the burden of our **dividend policy**. Now, we have an idea of how much money must be raised externally, the difference between our requirements and the internal sources. As we consider the merits of different sources, we must consider 1) assured availability, 2) associated restrictions on our management flexibility, such as term loan agreements, covenants, and collateral requirements, and 3) costs in the form of interest and fees. Finally, we should consider how our choices among sources will influence our movement toward our optimal capital structure (lesson #3.8).

Before we continue, **dividend policies** require some attention. The payment of dividends reduces retained earnings (a spontaneous source) and therefore, increases the firm's need for external financing. However, dividends may be valued by shareholders, and thus contribute to a higher and more stable share price. The Board of Directors will decide whether to pay dividends, when and how much. Companies will often offer **Dividend Reinvestment Plans**. Shareholders will authorize the company to issue new shares in lieu of paying the cash dividend. Even though the shareholder never sees the money, technically, the company has paid a dividend and then used the proceeds to buy the new shares. Accordingly, even with dividend reinvestment, the shareholder has a tax liability, but there are no transactions costs for the reinvestment purchase. The company may buy outstanding shares or issue new shares in order to provide shares to the reinvestment clients.

There are some disagreements on the relevance of dividend policy. Some believe that dividend payments a *residual* to be paid if the company has no better use for retained earnings. In that case, dividends would be paid after the equity needs of the company have been met. On the other hand, the payment of dividends may be valued by the company's investors, and thus, a factor in determining share value. You can see that management needs to understand why its shareholders own their shares. If they want growth, management must deliver growth, and dividend policy can't interfere with financing growth. If the company is mature, growing slowly, but stable and dividend paying, shareholders who desire those features will be attracted, and management must deliver those virtues. Investors choose firms *whose existing dividend policy* meets the investors' preferences. Hence, I believe that *consistency* of dividend policy is important.

I believe that shareholders consider the opportunity costs of retained earnings (financing growth) and dividends income (which will be taxed and may be reinvested). If they want capital gains from company growth and have confidence in management's ability to generate growth, then they will prefer retained earnings (hence, a low or no dividend policy). If they need income, or do not believe management can generate growth, they will prefer receiving the dividend.

There are legal and contractual issues that effect dividend policy. Many states have **capital impairment restrictions** which prevent the companies from paying dividends which would reduce book value below par value, or permit dividends only from retained earnings (and not from paid-in capital). In addition, dividends may not be allowed when company is in default on liabilities, insolvent, or bankrupt. **Restrictive covenants** in loan agreements or indentures may also place limits on dividend payments. And lenders won't lend to the company for the purpose of paying dividends. (You want us to put our money in, so you can take your money out ?) If the payment of dividends raises the companies need to issue debt or new shares, then optimal capital structure may be violated, coverage ratios compromised, and ownership diluted. So, the important considerations are the effect of policy on share price and assuring sufficient financing for the firm.

With respect to raising funds, we have many choices. We use a combination of financial capital and money market borrowings (bank loans and commercial paper) to support our current assets. We use leases and term loans to support equipment requirements. And we use financial capital --- shares, mortgages, and bonds --- to provide a foundation for our long-term investments (plant and equipment and intangibles), as well as for a portion of other permanent assets. The issues of these securities may be private or public. Private offerings to a few qualified investors do not require registration, (except at the state level), but public offerings must be registered and approved by the Securities Exchange Commission (SEC). With these ideas in mind, we can design a combination of securities to be offered to external funding sources to fill the gap between the total assets that we require and the existing funds available and anticipated internally.

For the public offering, we prepare a **Business and Financing Plan** which describes the activities of the issuing company --- its products or services, its market, and its production processes. We add SWOT analysis, including analysis of our situation, our strengths and weaknesses, and the external environment: our competition, market opportunities, and also threats. We document management's expertise, and we provide existing financial statements (if we are already operating) and realistic pro forma statements and budgets for the planned activities. Usually, these are preceded by an executive summary.

Investment banks provide links to the financial markets that are the sources of financing. Their regular participation in financial markets should give them expertise which they use to help us design our financial plan (as described above), select the most reliable and inexpensive sources of funds, receive regulatory approval, and finally place the new securities with willing buyers. This **advisory function** is important and includes the types of securities and best features, appropriate pricing and timing of securities sales, the best choice of markets, and of course, helping our team to prepare the needed documents for the SEC and the public. Our investment bank may offer to take all the risk of selling our securities by purchasing the entire offering at a discount and then selling it to their customers. This is called a **Full Underwriting**. Otherwise, the investment bank may simply offer to make its "best efforts," reporting progress in taking orders and leaving us to decide whether to go ahead, or cancel, the offering. The investment bank may agree to serve as a **market maker** in the new issue for several months or a year, being ready to buy or sell to stabilize the market value of the securities, until conditions settle down and most of the securities have found a home.

In the days before huge investment banking corporations (prior to 1985, many of the most important investment banks were partnerships), investment banks combined to form *underwriting syndicates* which would share the responsibilities, rewards, and risks of bringing new issues to market. The managing ("lead") underwriter would negotiate with the customer, design and price the issue, and take care of the registration. The notices that we see in newspapers and magazines, called *Tombstones,* identify the syndicate for the public. The syndicate members who promote and sell the issue would be called the *selling group.* The managing underwriter would receive expenses plus 15% of fees for his work. And the selling group would share the remaining 85% evenly for their commitment and their performance. So, if I made a commitment to sell 20% of the offering and actually sold 30%, I would get 25% of the 85% (= 21.25%) of the group's total fees and commissions.

Emerging small corporations may need to rely on **venture capital**. These are specialist financial institutions that take combinations of equity, debt, or convertible securities, as a condition for advancing funds. There is often a multi-year strategy with funds and securities being issued as performance benchmarks are achieved. Companies often complain about the compensation required by venture capitalists, but they ignore the substantial liquidity and default risks accepted by the venture capitalist.

The initial issuance of securities to the public is called "Going Public," and requires corporate charter authorization, a resolution of the board of directors, and registration with the SEC (under the Securities Act of 1933). The idea is that the registration statement (prospectus) provides the information that will permit potential investors to make informed decisions about the value and suitability of the purchase. Of course, *full and fair disclosure* doesn't assure that investors will use the information available. I look for a prudent and appropriate use of the funds (buying securities from existing officers and directors is not.), for reputable principals (no convicted criminals in control), and for well-qualified officers and directors who bring experience and diverse skills related to the operation of the company (no celebrity "window-dressing").

The investment banker should become an important part of our financial management team. So, selecting a reliable investment banker is important. Do the investment banks that are offering to help us have experience in our industry, in our financial markets, and with our types of securities ? Expertise in our industry and a record of successfully raising funds is critical. Promises are more common than performance. Are these investment bankers offering full underwriting, or just best efforts ? Is that important to us ? (We may be doing a "rights" offering to existing shareholders, and full underwriting is not needed.) Are we important enough to attract competitive bidding, or are we more likely to use a negotiated contract ? Where will these securities be listed and traded ? Will this investment banker make a market in the security, and for how long ?

Often a **private placement** is more advantageous than a public offering. Public offerings provide greater liquidity (ease of resale), and also share price stability. Public offering helps to establish the value of the company, and facilitate future offerings. However, the costs are significant, the ongoing public reporting requirements are burdensome, ownership is diluted, and the company may be exposed to a hostile take-over.

Questions for review and testing:
Explain the steps in the capital budgeting process.
Compare and contrast: *internal rate of return, payback period, & present discounted value.*

Explain the four services are provided by Investment banks.
Explain the distribution process for new securities issues.

Bibliography for Finance:
Donald C. Bauder, Captain Money and the Gold Girl   Harcourt Brace 1985
Milton Friedman and Anna Schwartz, A Monetary History of the United States, Princeton U.
        Press 1963
James Grant, The Money of the Mind Farrar Straus Giroux 1992
Simon Johnson and James Kwok, 13 Bankers   Pantheon Books 2010
John Kay, Other People's Money   Public Affairs 2015
Laurence Kotlikoff, Jimmy Stewart is Dead: Ending the World's Ongoing Financial Plague…,
        Wiley 2010
Michael Lewis, The Big Short, Norton 2010
Hernando de Soto, The Mystery of Capital, Basic Books 2000

I must acknowledge a great debt to several important texts which I used for many years and which influenced my approach to teaching and to organizing this material. The most important are Lawrence Gitman and Chad Zutter, Principles of Managerial Finance, 14th edition, Pearson 2015, and Peter Rose and Sylvia Hudgins, Bank Management & Financial Services 9th edition McGraw-Hill

Appendix: Example of Project Evaluation

Montecito Valley Ranch Sales & Profits Estimates   8/30/1991

Site	Land Area	Land Value	House Area	House Value	Totals
1	2.06	550	4800	960	1510
2	1.52	600	5800	1160	1760
3	1.78	550	5300	1060	1610
4	2.51	1050	6100	1220	2270
5	2.8	1000	5800	1160	2160
6	1.13	650	4900	980	1630
7	1.14	650	4800	960	1610
8	1.44	700	5300	1060	1760
9	3.06	950	6200	1240	2190
10	1.42	800	6300	1260	2060
11	1.89	700	3334	300	1000
12	3.18	950	6500	1300	2250
13	1.22	650	5000	1000	1650
14	1.18	650	4500	900	1550
15	1.77	650	5500	1100	1750
16	4.64	1100	5700	1140	2240
17	12.59	1350	6500	1300	2650
18	5.49	1400	5800	1160	2560
totals:	50.82	14950	98134	19260	34210

total estimated sales value of land & residences:
THIRTY-FOUR MILLION TWO HUNDRED TEN THOUSAND DOLLARS

Assumptions:

1) lot areas per Penfield & Smith Tract Map 14,038 (revised 8/28/90)
2) improvement values at $200 per square foot
3) only residential improvements on lot #11 are measured at cost.
   Hobby Horse stable is not valued.
4) construction costs are estimated at $140 per square foot.
5) marketing costs are assumed to be 5% of gross sales revenue

Profit Estimates:

First Alternative {no appreciation & no discounting in $'000}

Sales	less	construction costs	less	marketing costs	**profit**
34,210		2700 + 13,600		1710	**16,200**

Second Formulation { appreciation at 5% per year; discount at 12% }

	Year 1	Year 2	Year 3	Year 4	Year 5	Year 6	Year 7	Year 8
Sales	0	1	3	3	3	3	3	2
Value	0	1900	5700	5700	5700	5700	5700	3800
Costs								
Cons	2770	1500	2200	2200	2300	2300	2300	800
Comm	0	100	300	300	300	300	300	10
Profit	-2700	300	3200	3200	3100	3100	3100	2900
with appreciation:	-2700	315	3530	3700	3770	3960	4150	3890
with appreciation & discounted:	-2411	251	2513	2351	2139	2006	1877	1760
cumulative discounted value of appreciated profits:	{-2411}	{-2160}	353	2704	4843	6849	8726	**10486**

Estimated profit for fully built & sold project: $10,486,000

Third Formulation for Pure Lot Sales:						totals:
lot sales 1	3	3	3	4	4	17
Gross Sales						
830	2490	2490	2490	3320	3320	14940
Costs						
2742	125	125	125	166	166	3449
Cash-flow						
{-1912}	2365	2365	2365	3154	3154	13403
With 5% appreciation:						
{-19112}	2483	2607	2738	3834	4025	15687
discounted at 12%:						
{-1707}	1979	1856	1740	2176	2039	**8,083**

**Present discounted value of pure lot sales:
$8,083,000**

Which plan would you choose ?
We chose to sell lots with an offer to build for the lot buyer.

Index

Bibliography

Daren Acemoglu & James Robinson, <u>Why Nations Fail</u>, Crown 2012

Martin Anderson, <u>Imposters at the Temple</u>, Simon & Schuster, 1992

Daniel Ariely, <u>Predictably Irrational</u>, Harper Collins 2008

Henry Bagish "Confessions of a Former Cultural Relativist" Santa Barbara City College 1981

Walter Bagehot, <u>Lombard Street</u>, Hyperion Press 1962

Donald C. Bauder, <u>Captain Money and the Gold Girl</u> Harcourt Brace 1985

William Bernstein, <u>A Splendid Exchange: how trade shaped the world</u> Grove/Atlantic 2008

Alan Blinder <u>After the Music</u>, Stopped Penguin, 2013

Raymond Bowman, <u>International Business Basics</u>, {self-published}, 2002, Santa Barbara

Arthur Brooks, <u>Gross National Happiness</u> , Basic Books, 2008

Robert Calderisi, <u>The Trouble with Africa</u>, Palgrave 2006

Robert Carbaugh, <u>International Economics</u>, 14th edition, South West 2012

Tim Clissold, <u>Mr. China,</u> Harper Collins, 2006

Paul Collier, <u>The Bottom Billion</u>, Oxford 2007

Angus Deaton, <u>The Great Escape: health, wealth, and the origins of inequality</u>, Princeton 2013

Edward F. Denison, <u>Accounting for United States Economics Growth</u> Brookings 1974

Dowling, Welch, & Schuler, <u>International Human Resources Management</u>, SouthWest 1999

Peter Drucker, <u>Management Tasks, Responsibilities & Practices</u>, Harper & Row 1974

                      Adventures of a Bystander, Harper Collins 1979

William Easterley, <u>The Elusive Quest for Growth</u>, MIT 2002

                  The White Man's Burden, Penguin 2006

Manuchar Farman Farmanian, <u>Blood and Oil</u>, Random House 1997

William Fleckstein, <u>Greenspan's Bubbles: the age of ignorance at the Federal Reserve,</u>

Norman Fosback,   <u>Stock Market Logic</u>, 1976 The Institute for Econometric Research

Milton Friedman & Anna Schwartz, <u>A Monetary History of the United States</u>, Princeton 1963

Robert Gates, <u>A Passion for Leadership</u> Knopf 2016

Benjamin Graham, <u>The Intelligent Investor</u>, Harper 1973

Benjamin Graham & David Dodd, <u>Security Analysis</u>, 6th edition McGraw-Hill 2009

James Grant, <u>The Money of the Mind</u>, Farrar Straus Giroux 1992

Ricky Griffin & Michael Pustay, <u>International Business,</u> 7th edition, Pearson Education 2012

Fred Hirsch, <u>Social Limits to Growth</u>, Harvard 1976

Glenn Hubbard & Anthony O'Brien, <u>Principles of Economics</u>, Custom edition, Pearson, 2003

Simon Johnson and James Kwok , <u>13 Bankers</u>, Pantheon Books 2010

Daniel Kahnemann, <u>Thinking Fast and Slow</u>, Farrar, Straus, and Giroux, 2011

George Katona, <u>Psychological Economics</u> Elsevier 1977

John Kay, <u>Culture & Prosperity: The truth about markets,</u> Harper Business , 2004

              Other People's Money, Public Affairs 2015

John M. Keynes, <u>The General Theory of Employment, Interest, and Money</u>, St. Martin's 1973

Mel Krauss & Harry Johnson, <u>General Equilibrium Analysis</u>, Allen & Unwin 1974

David Landes, <u>The Wealth and Poverty of Nations</u>, Norton 1999

Edwin Lefebvre, <u>Reminiscences of a Stock Operator</u>, Wiley 2010 {based on Jesse Livermore}

Michael Lewis, <u>The Big Short</u>, Norton 2010

     <u>Liar's Poker</u> Norton 1989

     "Beware of Greeks Bearing Bonds," *Vanity Fair*, September 2010

Arthur Lewis, <u>The Evolution of the International Economic Order</u>, Princeton U. Press 1977

Bjorn Lomborg, <u>The Skeptical Environmentalist</u>, Cambridge 1998

     <u>Cool It</u>, Vintage, 2007

Peter Lynch, <u>One Up on Wall Street</u>, Simon & Schuster 1989

Burton Malkiel, <u>A Random Walk Down Wall Street</u>, Norton 1975

Richard McGregor, <u>The Party: the secret world of China's communist rulers</u>,

     Harper-Collins 2010

Ronald I McKinnon, <u>Money & Capital in Economic Development</u>, Brookings 1973

     <u>Money In International Exchange</u>, Oxford 1979

     <u>The Order of Economic Liberalization</u>, Johns Hopkins 1991

     <u>The Rules of the Game</u>, MIT 1997

John Micklethwait & AdrianWoolridge, <u>A Future Perfect</u>, Crown, 2000

Minxin Pei, <u>China's Crony Capitalism</u>, Harvard University Press 2016

Karl Polanyi, <u>The Great Transformation</u> , Beacon 1944

Michael Porter, <u>The Competitive Advantage of Nations</u>, *Free Press. 1990*

Pietra Rivoli, <u>The Travels of a T-shirt in a Global Economy</u>, Wiley2009

Alan Rugman & Richard Hodgetts, <u>International Business</u>, McGraw-Hill 1994

Tibor Scitovsky, <u>The Joyless Economy</u>, Oxford 1976

Robert J. Shiller, <u>Irrational Exuberance</u>, 3rd edition, Princeton U Press, 2015

Adam Smith, <u>An Inquiry into the Nature and Causes of the Wealth of Nations</u>,

     edited by Edwin Cannon, Random House 1994

Thomas Sowell, <u>Wealth, Poverty, and Politics</u>, Basic Books 2015

Hernando de Soto, <u>The Mystery of Capital</u>, Basic Books, 2000

Ben Stein, <u>License to Steal: the untold story of Michael Milken</u>, Simon & Schuster 1992

     A shorter version appeared in "Barron's" Feb.19, 1990

George Stocking, <u>Middle East Oil</u>, U. of Illinois Press, 1970

John B. Taylor, <u>Principles of Economics</u>, 5th edition, Houghton-Mifflin 2006

Richard Thaler, <u>Misbehaving</u>, Norton 2015

Ludwig Von Mises, <u>Bureaucracy</u>, Yale Press 1944

Peter Wallison, <u>Hidden in Plain Sight</u>, Encounter Books, 2015

Denis Wright, <u>The English Amongst the Persians</u>, Heinemann 1977

James Q. Wilson, <u>Bureaucracy</u>, Basic Books 1989

About the author

Peter Naylor has been a Professor of Economics & Finance at Santa Barbara City College since 1987. He received his education at Williams College and Stanford University. He taught at Pitzer College, Claremont University 1977-1981. His business experience includes banking, international travel management, and real estate development. His publications include papers on macroeconomics in Namibia, tax policy, international energy markets, and financial development. His awards include a Fulbright, a Carnegie Foundation, and a Brookings Institution fellowship. He has also served on several local non-profit boards and public commissions. At SBCC, he has taught Economics, Finance, and International Business for thirty years. He was President of the Instructors' Association and chief negotiator at various times from 1992-2006.

35

Made in the USA
San Bernardino, CA
11 August 2017